YO-BSN-649

COLLEGE OF MARIN LIBRARY
COLLEGE AVENUE
KENTFIELD, CA 94904

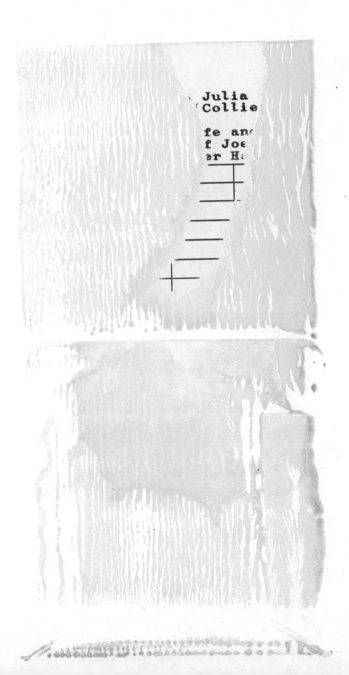

THE LIFE AND LETTERS OF
JOEL CHANDLER HARRIS

AMS PRESS

NEW YORK

Joel Chandler Harris

THE LIFE AND LETTERS OF
JOEL CHANDLER HARRIS

BY JULIA COLLIER HARRIS

WITH PORTRAITS
AND OTHER ILLUSTRATIONS

BOSTON AND NEW YORK
HOUGHTON MIFFLIN COMPANY
The Riverside Press Cambridge
1918

Library of Congress Cataloging in Publication Data

Harris, Julia Florida (Collier) 1875-
  The life and letters of Joel Chandler Harris.

  Bibliography: p.
  1. Harris, Joel Chandler, 1848-1908. I. Title.
PS1813.H3 1973   818'.4'09 [B]   72-168247
ISBN 0-404-00059-2

Reprinted by arrangement with Houghton Mifflin Company,
Boston and New York

From the edition of 1918, Boston and New York
First AMS edition published in 1973
Manufactured in the United States of America

AMS PRESS INC.
NEW YORK, N. Y.   10003

TO THE MEMORY OF
MARY HARRIS
AND TO
ESTHER LaROSE HARRIS
THIS BOOK
IS REVERENTLY AND AFFECTIONATELY
DEDICATED

CONTENTS

CONTENTS

ILLUSTRATIONS

ILLUSTRATIONS

THE LIFE AND LETTERS OF
JOEL CHANDLER HARRIS

THE LIFE AND LETTERS OF JOEL CHANDLER HARRIS

CHAPTER I

BIRTH AND PARENTAGE

At least three localities in Eatonton, Georgia, are pointed out to the inquisitive visitor as the birthplace of Joel Chandler Harris. Father himself always referred to "Putnam County" as the place of his birth. One of his earliest and most trusted friends, Mr. C. D. Leonard, of Eatonton, says: "A very old and thoroughly reliable citizen of Eatonton told me way back in the seventies that Joe was born about six miles northwest of Eatonton, in the neighborhood of Lumsden's Mill, now owned by Steve Martin. This mill is on Little River and is a popular picnic resort for Putnamites."

On the other hand, one of the oldest and most highly respected matrons of Eatonton remembers being told by an acquaintance in December, 1848, of the arrival of young Joel at a house which stood near the present site of the Baptist Church, and which was then known as "Billy Barnes's Tavern." This house has long since been torn down.

In reality, the exact spot of a man's birth is of minor importance to posterity, and I am sure father would be gently amused and somewhat astonished could he know that in his case enough importance had been attached to the exact locality to have caused it to be a matter of dispute. The man who, with perfect simplicity, made himself at home with little children, with the slaves in the cabin and the humble beasts of the field, never troubled himself about family trees and ancestral halls. He loved the rolling Bermuda meadows, the red-clay gullies, the far-stretching cotton-fields, the slow-moving, muddy streams, and the oak and hickory forests of old Putnam with an intensity that time never dulled; its people were to him the "salt of the earth"; and the belief that he was loved and cherished by these "middle Georgians" made him feel that he was a citizen of the county at large, and that all Putnamites were his near kin and neighbors. He belonged to Putnam County, and that was enough!

We know, then, that Joel Chandler Harris was born on December 9, 1848, somewhere in the vicinity of the village of Eatonton, a sleepy little town in middle Georgia, which had a court-house and town square, a tavern, several wide streets, many fine trees, and a number of old colonial homes. Many of these stately structures still rise solemnly from behind their boxwood borders, giving pleasure to the stranger as he peers at them through the screen of odorous cedars and brightly blooming crepe-myrtles and oleanders which shelter their columned piazzas from a too-penetrating gaze.

Joel's grandparents were Georgians; the maiden name of his maternal grandmother was Turman, a modification of the original name Tubman, and she was of Scotch origin. She had two daughters, and she often referred to Joel's mother as "Lady Sensible" and to the sister as "Lady Beautiful." The latter was fond of dress and "good times," and Joel's mother, Mary Harris, in later life told of ironing countless white petticoats for her pleasure-loving sister; for in those days a young lady was not considered well dressed unless she tripped lightly under the weight of two or three starched petticoats, with elaborate flounces.

The Harris family was a prominent one in middle Georgia and had well-known connections in that part of the State; so it can readily be imagined that consternation overtook the relatives of "Lady Sensible" when she conceived a fancy for a man inferior in station and education. The common mistake of vociferous opposition was made in this instance; the spark of preference was fanned into the flame of love, and Mary Harris separated herself from her family, left her home in Newton County, and accompanied the man of her choice to Putnam. The details of the days that followed are meager and confused, and Mary Harris's story, from this point until after the birth of her child and her desertion by its father, partakes of the nature of legend. We know that she and her mother were reconciled, and that the latter joined Mary and her baby in Eatonton, where they lived for a time at the end of Marion Street, and later in the old Eatonton Hotel, where the grandmother died. The latter was said by Eatontonians to have been a quiet, reserved little woman, who kept much to herself and who rarely left the house, even for church-going. Mary Harris, on the contrary, was lively, sociable, and had a keen sense of humor.

Very few of Mary Harris's contemporaries are now alive. Mrs. Frank Leverette, of Eatonton, is one of them, and her daughter, Miss Frances Lee Leverette, has been good enough to give me the following account of the friendship that existed between her family and Joel's mother in the old days: —

BIRTH AND PARENTAGE

"We first knew 'Miss Mary' through my Aunt Telitha Slack, the sister of my maternal grandmother Wyatt and the wife of Dr. Slack, a prominent physician of Newton County. The Slacks were neighbors of 'Grandma Harris' and her two daughters back in the days before 'Miss Mary' and her mother moved to Putnam County.

"We all loved 'Miss Mary' just as we loved our own grandmother, and my father, especially, was devoted to her. He liked to get into an argument with her; and she was always a match for him, so my mother tells me, when it came to discussing politics and local affairs, for she kept herself posted on all the questions of the day. My mother was an invalid for many years, about that time, and she says she has enjoyed many a night listening to my father and 'Miss Mary' carrying on a discussion while sitting before the big wood fire. 'Miss Mary' was our neighbor for many years; in fact, until she went to live with 'Uncle Remus' in Atlanta. I remember well the little gate which my father had cut through the garden so we could be even more neighborly.

"Not only during the day, but very often on long winter evenings, 'Miss Mary' would come up to knit and talk by the family fireside. Quite often the family group would be augmented by 'Miss

Jane' Conner and 'Miss Isabella' Prudden, other close neighbors.

"I am going back this far just to prove the old saying that 'little pitchers have big ears,' for as a child in the chimney corner, I heard rumors of the sad chapter in 'Miss Mary's' life, and in later years I was therefore able to understand the rejoicing of my mother and father, 'Miss Jane,' 'Miss Isabella,' and other Eatontonians when 'Miss Mary' made her preparations to bid farewell to her friends on the eve of going to live with her boy who had made good in the then wonderful city of Atlanta!

"As the 'little pitcher' heard the story, and as my mother and others have since told me, it seems that 'Miss Mary' was just one of those hundreds of good women who loved a man unworthy of her. In this instance, 'Miss Mary's' mother and sister, who were connected with the best families in their section, crossed her in her inclinations, and this only served to make her love the man of her choice the more.

"So there was a family breach, and 'Miss Mary' stood by her lover in spite of family objections. It was some years before she and her sister were reconciled, but her mother and grandmother joined her in Eatonton, and lived with her there.

[6]

BIRTH AND PARENTAGE

" 'Uncle Remus's' father was an Irishman, and from him the boy inherited his bright blue eyes and his sense of humor. The young Irishman worked near 'Miss Mary's' home as a day-laborer, and it seems certain that his humble calling and his lack of ambition were the causes of the family's objections. The boy's father knew, of course, of the bitter opposition of 'Miss Mary's' family, and that he would never be received or recognized by them; and old friends say he was not strong enough to stand up under such conditions. At any rate, he left Putnam within a short time of his child's birth and was never again seen there.

" 'Miss Mary' was a woman of rare mental qualities. My father used to say she was the smartest woman he ever knew. Her strength of character equaled her strength of intellect, and when she awakened to her mistake in casting in her lot with a man so lacking in courage and loyalty, she put aside all romantic notions, took up her burden, and staked all on her boy. She discarded his father's name and gave her family name to Joel, and no one ever heard her mention his father again.

" 'Miss Mary' was held in high esteem in Eatonton and she numbered amongst her friends the best people of the town. As an instance of these friendships: Mr. Andrew Reid, who built and owned

[7]

for years one of the finest homes in Eatonton, sympathized so heartily with her in her struggles to get on after cutting herself loose from her family and putting aside all claim on the boy's father, that he gave her a little house back of his own for a residence. He did this so that he and his family might have her for a neighbor and help her along. Later our family occupied the Andrew Reid house and in this way 'Miss Mary' became our neighbor. Private schools were expensive in those days, and Mr. Reid, who was wealthy, paid the tuition of Joel in the village school.[1] 'Miss Mary,' so her old friends say, had several good offers of marriage, but she was indifferent to them and centered her whole life on her boy. She never had cause to regret her devotion, for Joel's attentive care and affection for his mother were prominent traits from his childhood."

In one of his short stories, father thus writes of his hero's native town: "His lot was cast amongst the most democratic people the world has ever seen,

[1] Mary Harris also received friendly assistance, during the early days of her residence in Putnam County, from Dr. Henry Branham, a well-to-do practitioner of Eatonton, who had married her aunt, Verlinda Harris. It is said that Dr. Henry Branham's brother, Dr. Joel Branham, a physician noted throughout the country-side for his skill, learning, and humanity, was present as attending physician at Joel's birth.

and in a section where, to this day, the ideals of character and conduct are held in higher esteem than wealth or ancient lineage."

Did he not have the town of his own birth in mind when this was written? As a poor boy, deserted by his father and living in poverty with his hard-working mother, he had every opportunity to shiver under the chill of snobbism, if such an atmosphere had prevailed in his native village.

That this was never the case is a splendid tribute to the fine humanity of old-time Putnamites. Undoubtedly they were endowed with that priceless "intelligence of the heart," which, when combined with common sense and neighborliness, constitutes a people amongst whom it is a joy to live. And so, as if conscious of the flavor of his surroundings, the little half-orphan drew the genial air of the hospitable town into his lungs and grew and thrived with the traditional persistence of a red-haired boy.

CHAPTER II

BOYHOOD IN EATONTON

In those far-away days, life was not too hard on the child and his mother. Kind neighbors, whose homes were as generously stocked as their hearts, were full of hospitality towards the occupants of the little house, and Mary Harris tended her home and garden and took in sewing for a living. In an old scrapbook, battered and dog-eared, I have found a few odds and ends of papers that throw some light on those years. One of them is a memorandum of work done by Mary Harris for the family of J. A. Turner, of the Turnwold plantation, where Joel later served his apprenticeship as a printer. It states that J. A. Turner is indebted to Mrs. Mary Harris for the making of

1 coat	$2.50
1 pr. pants	1.50
1 vest	1.00
4 shirts	4.00
	$9.00

When the mother was not busy with her needle, her spinning-wheel, or her pots and pans, she could usually be found working amongst her flowers. She loved flowers dearly, and therefore she was successful with them. She exchanged slips and seeds with her friends, and often proffered advice as to how their garden-beds should be arranged. There was in the neighborhood one garden which gave her considerable worry. It had in it nothing but flowers that "grew flat on the ground," as she said. It seems that the man of the family had purchased the flower-seeds, so "Miss Mary" straightway offered her services in making a selection of plants from the seedsman's catalogue tall enough to vary the monotony of this ground-gripping flower-plot. Young Joel must have employed the spade and hoe often in his mother's garden and then and there acquired the love of all growing things that was one of the passions of his later life.

A great reader herself, Joel's mother spent many an hour before the wood fire in winter evenings reading to him. Long after the restless winds had scattered the ashes of those hickory logs to the far corners of old Putnam, and when the dark hair of the young mother was dark no more and her energetic carriage had lost its youthful vigor, the creator of "Uncle Remus" wrote in a literary biography for "Lippincott's Magazine": —

My desire to write — to give expression to my thoughts — grew out of hearing my mother read "The Vicar of Wakefield." I was too young to appreciate the story, but there was something in the style or something in the humor of that remarkable little book that struck my fancy, and I straightway fell to composing little tales, in which the principal character, whether hero or heroine, silenced the other characters by crying "Fudge!" at every possible opportunity. None of these little tales have been preserved, but I am convinced that since their keynote was "Fudge!" they must have been very close to human nature.

At this time Joel was a small, wiry lad, undersized and frail-looking behind his veil of freckles, but he was as sound and supple as a peach-tree switch and bursting with vitality and mischief. He loved animals and learned to manage horses when he was only a midget by the side of the smallest of them. One day his mother was horrified to see him rattling down the main street behind a team of lively coach-horses, handling the reins with all the confidence of a six-foot hostler.

Many were the pranks he played upon his associates in these days. Like "Brer Rabbit" he made up for his lack of size by his agility and shrewdness, and there was a spice of the devil in him as well. On market-day it was the custom for the farmers to bring their produce to town and gather around the court-house, when the horses would be taken out of the shafts and hitched to the rack on one side of the town square.

BOYHOOD IN EATONTON

Young Joel passed by the rack one day when every available hook held fast knotted the tie-rein of a horse. There had been a heavy shower, and pigs were wallowing in the puddle near the rack. With a vigorous and well-directed gesture the young rascal shot a rock in the midst of the porkers; they fled in a panic toward the horses, the latter took fright, broke loose, and galloped helter-skelter down the main road. The memory of this mischievous prank must have been with father when he describes, in "On the Plantation," the joke played by Joe Maxwell on the sleeping recruits. In this case the boy turns loose the tethered mules and frightens them with a sheet, the result being that they stampede and rush pell-mell through the tents, carrying everything before them and frightening the half-awakened soldier boys worse than a battery of guns.

In this connection we read of Joe Maxwell, who from all accounts might have been Joel Harris: —

It would not be fair to say that Joe was a studious lad. On the contrary he was of an adventurous turn of mind, and he was not at all fond of the books that were in his desk at Hillsborough Academy. He was full of all sorts of pranks and capers, and there were plenty of people in the little town ready to declare that he would come to some bad end if he was not more frequently dosed with what the old folks used to call hickory oil.

JOEL CHANDLER HARRIS

I am indebted to Mr. C. D. Leonard, of Eatonton, one of the boyhood friends of young Joel, for
the following account of play-days and truant-days
in the little country town during the years 1855–62:

"I first met Joe when we were six and seven
years old," writes Mr. Leonard. "His mother
told me that Joe was one year older than I. My
family had just moved to Eatonton and Joe began to come to see me and my brother Jim very
soon after our arrival there. After getting acquainted in regular boy fashion, we began to go
around together, gradually extending our tramping grounds from the streets adjacent to my home,
to the 'White Mud Gullies' and the livery stable
owned by Mr. McDade, who was a great favorite
with the boys of the community; and our acquaintance ripened more rapidly after we found the way
to 'Aunt Betsy' Cuthbert's, an old negress who frequently gave us treats of ginger-cakes, potato biscuit, and *flat chicken pies*. 'Aunt Betsy' was famous for her ginger-cakes. Like the average boys
of that time we asked nothing better than to play
with her grandchildren, and she would often call
us up and treat us to ginger-cakes and biscuits.
One call from her door and out of the 'White Mud
Gullies' we youngsters would come trooping in response to 'Aunt Betsy's' voice.

OLD "UNCLE" AND "AUNTY" AT EATONTON, GEORGIA

BOYHOOD IN EATONTON

" Close by 'Aunt Betsy's' house there was a large barley-patch belonging to Mr. Harvey Dennis, who is frequently mentioned in 'On the Plantation,' and here we boys would play hide and seek in the tall barley.

"Joe and I would hang around Mr. McDade's livery stable all day, for a chance to see the fine horses the drovers of that day would bring to Eatonton, and to get a chance to ride one of these horses, even if it was only across the street to the blacksmith shop, or to water at a near-by branch. Frequently the horse-drovers would let us exercise them with a longer ride, and Wheeler's cavalry never contained two prouder cavalry men. Another great treat for Joe and me was the privilege of going to the country with old Uncle Ben Sadler, when he went after corn and fodder for the horses. Old Uncle Ben was a very interesting character, and a typical negro of that time. He worked at the stable and took a great interest in Joe and me, and was always glad for us to be allowed to go with him. Uncle Ben in after years became a mail-rider between Eatonton and Monticello and died in the service of the Government, highly esteemed by both whites and blacks.

"About a year after we got acquainted, Joe and I started to school to Miss Kate Davidson, who taught a 'mixed school' for boys and girls. Among those I specially remember in the school were Miss Lou Prudden, Miss Sallie Prudden, and Miss Lula Grimes. Joe and I were often guilty of playing truant. We would sometimes stay out of school for a week. During this time we would hang around the livery stable, because our parents never came that way, and we felt safe on this account. In a few months Joe left Miss Davidson's school to go to the Academy, where all were male teachers. After a year or more I was sent there too. In this school Joe and I had as an almost constant companion, Hut Adams, who was about four years our senior, but who seemed to prefer to go with us rather than with the larger boys of the school. It was a strange thing to all of us that Joe, although he did not seem to study much, was always well prepared when it came to reciting his lessons, and got along as well as any of the rest of us.[1]

"Joe and Hut and I would go and come from school together. We three stayed together and played spinning tops, shooting marbles, and jump-

[1] Captain John S. Reid, of Eatonton, who was assistant in the village Academy somewhere around 1860, and whose friendship for Joel Chandler Harris extended through a lifetime, remembers him as a slender, rather delicate-looking lad of ten years, who did not take a very prominent part in outdoor sports, but who was full of life and mischief. "Never much of a student," said his old teacher, "but quick to learn."

ing poles. We had two ways of going to school and found great pleasure in varying our coming and going. One way was through the main street, and the other was through what was then known as the "Town Commons," which led the back way through town and by Mr. Edmond Reid's watermelon patch and peach orchard, where we were very often guilty of appropriating a few watermelons and peaches.

"Hut would go into the patch after the melons, then to the orchard for peaches, and Joe and I would receive them over the fence. A few times Hut was run out of the patch, and then such a race as Hut, Joe, and I had across the Commons! Mr. Reid was a very wealthy planter, and did not care so much for the melons and peaches as he did for the fun of seeing us run; because he always had plenty of fruit.

"Mr. Harvey Dennis, one of Putnam's oldest citizens and a famous fox-hunter, and, as I have already said, often mentioned in 'On the Plantation,' written by Joe, lived just above Joe's home at this time. Mr. Dennis loved the hunt and always kept eight or ten hounds for fox-hunting. On Saturdays Joe and I would go down on the branch, clap our hands, and yell to attract Mr. Dennis's dogs, in order to take them off rabbit-hunting. Mr. Dennis did not like for his dogs to hunt rabbits, and it was great fun for us boys to steal his dogs away in this fashion for an all-day hunt. We loved the music of their voices as they would come trooping down the hill to the branch, and we hurried away over the hills by 'Aunt Betsy' Cole's, a noted fortune-teller of those days, thence out to Colonel Nicholson's farm.

"Joe had a dog named 'Brutus,' which we called 'Brute' for short, and he was always along with the hounds. When Mr. Dennis would come home and find his 'dogs gone again with those boys,' he would frequently saddle his horse and hunt us up, sometimes finding us two miles or more away. When he would find us he was never rough in either his manner or speech, simply saying, 'Boys, you've got my dogs again.'

" We would, however, always pay him back during the season with rabbits when we would have good luck on one of these chases. And another way that we secured his goodwill, after stealing away his dogs, would be to carry the game on one of his hunts. Frequently he would take us into his father's peach orchard and give us all the peaches we could carry home; and in fact was good to us in every way. His kindness naturally led us to appreciate him very highly as a man.

"Joe was always remarkably polite and respectful to older men and women, and both men and boys loved him. For instance, Mr. Dennis considered him a very remarkable boy even when a little chap, and understood the spirit that prompted Joe to toll away his dogs, and instead of being angry was always amused. Joe, of course, was at this time too young to hunt the fox, so Mr. Dennis, in order to keep his dogs in trim and training, would let Joe and me drag the fox-skin over a trail, sometimes two miles long. He would give us a thirty minutes' start and it was great sport to us to hear the hounds take up the trail, and come baying and barking in rich voices of different tones, just as if they had jumped a fox and were engaged in a real chase.

"Joe's dog 'Brute' had a great habit of howling on moonlight nights, and he would very frequently get under the window of Mrs. Harris's bedroom and howl for hours. Finally Joe's mother became exasperated, and conceived the idea of filling a basin full of bricks and small rocks, which she suddenly emptied on old 'Brute' one night. Needless to state Joe's mother was never troubled again with 'Brute's' howling.

"Hut Adams was always resourceful as a playmate, and it was he who had the idea of the 'Gully

Minstrels,' often mentioned by Joe in later years, when he would visit Eatonton. Hut was 'Boss' of the minstrels, Joe was the 'funny man,' and I was the 'treasurer.' The minstrels were given in the big White Mud Gully close to 'Aunt Betsy' Cuthbert's. Our charge for admission was ten pins, and the minstrels were well patronized. I soon had a box full of pins and no use for them. Since we were 'stuck' on pins, the famous minstrels disbanded.

"Joe loved a joke and was good at playing them. He played many on Hut and me, but Hut was his favorite victim, though he would always have to fairly fly when he played one on Hut, since the latter was so much our elder he could whip either of us easily. Joe and I would go to the river to fish and swim together, and go in bathing. We loved to hunt plums, bird nests, and wild strawberries. Joe would come to my home early Saturday mornings and sit on the fence and joke, while brother Jim and I had to work in the garden and sweep the yards before we could go. He made a first-class playmate, but he would 'hedge' on Saturday work.

"The first time I ever went to Sunday School, it was with Joe. We went to the Baptist Sunday School, which was held in a room of the Female Academy. Our Sunday afternoons were spent on the small branch below Joe's house. Very often

Hut Adams would join us, though Hut's father was a very prominent church man and insisted on a strict observance of the Sabbath by his whole family and all of his servants. Hut was the only one of our famous trio that ever possessed a handkerchief in those days. So when he did go with us he would let us use his handkerchief for seining for minnows in the little washouts along the branch. I remember quite well that we would return home rather conscience-stricken and afraid to tell where we had been or what we had been doing.

"Many a time in after life (for we remained warm friends to the day of his death) Joe and I spent happy hours talking over these boyhood days."

Like other fun-loving, joke-playing little boys, rough-and-tumble on the surface, Joel had a tender, susceptible heart. He never forgot a kindness and in after years he was wont to refer to those who, in days long past, showed favors to the red-haired lad. In an editorial written toward the end of his life, the reader is allowed just one little glimpse into the sensitive, reticent depth of the boy's heart: —

"The Farmer raised the lid and peered at the nest and eggs again, so frail, so delicate, and so beautiful. How wonderful it all seemed to be! As

he stood there, more than forty — yes, well-nigh
fifty — years suddenly came out of the dark and
backward abysm into which they had disappeared,
and the Farmer, a small boy, was showing a wren's
nest to three girls near the old school house in the
little town where he was born. Their names came
sighing into his memory from far away, vague
whispers from the shores of Mystery. He remembered how beautiful they were, and how gentle and
tender and kind they had been to a lonely little lad
whose name the Farmer never will tell you. Beautiful, tender, and kind, and dead these forty-odd
years — dead and glorified before they could even
dream what life has in' store for even the most fortunate of those who drink deeply from its chalice."

CHAPTER III

FROM the vantage-ground of middle years, father
wrote: —

It was a great blessing for a young fellow in the
clutches of poverty to be raised up among such people
as those who lived in Eatonton when I was a boy, and
whose descendants still live there. I have not the
slightest difficulty in the world in referring all that I
have done or hope to do to the kindly interest which
the people of Eatonton took in my welfare when I was
too young to know anything of the difficulties of life or
the troubles that inhabit the world by right of discovery
and possession. But Eatonton was not a newspaper
office, and I had to leave there in order to stick my head
in an ink fountain. There came a time when I had to be
up and doing, as the poet says, and it so happened that
I was in the post office at Eatonton reading the Milledgeville papers when the first number of the "Countryman" was deposited on the counter where all the
newspapers were kept. I read it through, and came upon
an advertisement which announced that the editor
wanted a boy to learn the printer's trade. This was my
opportunity, and I seized it with both hands. I wrote
to the editor, whom I knew well, and the next time he
came to town he sought me out, asked if I had written
the letter with my own hand, and in three words the
bargain was concluded.[1]

[1] *On the Plantation,* p. 14.

The editor mentioned was Mr. Joseph Addison Turner, of "Turnwold," a plantation nine miles from Eatonton, and the boy who felt that he "must be up and doing" was less than fourteen years old. But "the thoughts of youth are long, long thoughts," and doubtless Joel's thoughts were of his mother and her needs. So he "put away his tops and marbles, packed his little belongings in an old-fashioned trunk, kissed his mother good-bye, and set forth on what turned out to be the most important journey of his life."

Mr. Turner himself came to town to get the boy, and while the two travel down the country road behind the editor's large gray horse, Ben Bolt, let us find out what we can about Joel's new home.

Turnwold comprised a large tract of land in Putnam County, which had passed from the Spivey family into the hands of Mr. William Turner, the father of J. A. and William Turner. The paternal homestead is still standing on an elevation at some distance to the left of the house later occupied by J. A. Turner, editor of the "Countryman." A beautiful avenue of oaks leads up to it, and though it is now dilapidated and weather-beaten, it is not lacking in dignity and a charm of desolation. Its old hand-hewn timbers are riddled with worm-holes, and have faded to a soft, silvery, rain-washed gray.

TURNWOLD

The wide hall, extending through the house, and now standing open to the mercy of the elements, is flanked on either side by high-ceiled rooms, and in one of these Mr. William Turner kept his books, the nucleus of a library which later became famous throughout several counties.[1] Outside, the air is scented with the odor of huge boxwood bushes which encircle the entrance of the house, and to the right is the old family burying-ground, enclosed by an iron fence. Here the graves are covered by a matted carpet of periwinkles whose starlike blossoms in the summer-time reflect the blue of the heavens above. Some of the old tombstones, stained and moss-covered, commemorate the dead of seventy-five and a hundred years ago. The land between the old house and the residence formerly occupied by J. A. Turner is now set out in crops, mainly cotton, but in the old days it was wooded, for the Master of Turnwold was a lover of trees, and himself planted the ground between the homes, for a space of several acres, in oaks, hickories, and other native trees. This forest became so dense

[1] This library, now scattered, contained about four thousand volumes. Amongst the writers represented were Shakespeare, Moore, Byron, Cooper, Burns, Swift, Shelley, Goldsmith, Hood, Wordsworth, Milton, Tasso, Scott, Bulwer, Holmes, Dickens, Hugo, Macaulay, Hume, Grimm, Irving, and Bryant; also volumes of encyclopædias and several works on ornithology and botany.

[25]

that it was infested with hawks, but its owner refused to thin it out.

This part of the estate was laid out under the direction of the landscape gardener who planned the grounds of the Smithsonian Institution, and on his advice Mr. Turner set out a garden of native wild flowers on the fringe of the wood. At the close of the Civil War, when the property passed into other hands, great havoc was wrought amongst the trees, and gradually most of them were chopped down. But at the time Joel arrived at Turnwold we can picture him as in the midst of beautiful rolling farmlands, flanked by valuable forests, beyond which sweet-scented Bermuda meadows stretched far away to the horizon.

After the death of the head of the family, the old homestead passed into the hands of Mr. William Turner, his father's namesake, and as a bachelor he occupied it for a number of years with his widowed sister, Mrs. Hubert. It is said he was not much of a farmer, but enjoyed his books and his "toddy."

His brother, the patron of young Joel, was, on the contrary, a practical planter, and his apprentice later described him as a "miscellaneous genius," who owned and successfully operated a plantation settlement, which comprised a hat factory, a tannery, a distillery, and a printing-plant. There

THE J. A. TURNER HOUSE AT TURNWOLD

were one hundred and twenty slaves on the plantation, and their quarters were ranged behind the J. A. Turner home. This house is also standing, and is less attractive in appearance than the old home. Perhaps it was not so angular and barefaced in the old days, for then it had "ells" on both sides, and in one of these "ells" was Joel's room. The other contained a portion of the paternal library which had been transferred from the old home and to which Mr. J. A. Turner had added many valuable volumes.

A large grove of oaks in the rear of the house sheltered the group of negro cabins, and screening the house from the main road was a semi-circle of stately cedars, whose dark green shafts were haunted by mocking-birds and other native songsters.

The heavy responsibilities of this plantation settlement did not prevent its master from interesting himself in politics. He was a member of the Georgia Legislature of 1860, noted for his eloquence and erudition; a student of the classics and a writer who modeled his style after that of Samuel Johnson. His paper, the "Countryman," was his hobby, and as a typesetter on this plantation sheet, young Joel had an opportunity to round off his meager education. He was made comfortable in

Mr. Turner's home, and, as was the custom with an apprentice, received his clothing and board during the term of nearly five years which he passed there.

In "On the Plantation" we read of his introduction to the printing-office, which was established in an outhouse: —

The printing-office was a greater revelation to Joe Maxwell than it would be to any of the youngsters who may happen to read this. It was a very small affair; the type was old and worn, and the hand-press — a Washington No. 2 — had seen considerable service. But it was all new to Joe, and the fact that he was to become a part of the machinery aroused in his mind the most delightful sensations. He quickly mastered the boxes of the printer's case, and before many days was able to set type swiftly enough to be of considerable help to Mr. Snelson, who was foreman, compositor and pressman.

The "Countryman" was probably the only newspaper ever printed on a Southern plantation. It was a success from the beginning, having at one time a subscription list of two thousand, and its editorials were quoted in all the papers of the Confederacy. There were no clippings from exchanges in its columns; instead, copy was drawn, when necessary, from three volumes selected by the editor from his library: La Rochefoucauld's "Maxims," Percy's "Anecdotes," and "Lacon."

The prospectus of the "Countryman" for 1864

displayed the slogan: "Independent in everything
— neutral in nothing"; and an announcement
followed:

This paper is a complete cyclopædia of the History
of the Times — The War News — Agriculture, Stock-
raising — Field-Sports — Wit — Humor — Anecdote
— Tales — Philosophy — Morals — Liberal and en-
lightened Religion as opposed to Sectarian Creedism
— Poetry — Politics — Art — Science — Useful re-
cipes — The Industrial and Mechanical Resources and
pursuits of the Country — Money and Market matters
—Literature — Genl. Miscellany — in short, everything that can amuse, instruct, or be of use to the general reader — all put up in a convenient form for binding and handling, at the low price of $10.00 per annum.
The publisher of the "Countryman" flatters himself
that his journal will not be excelled in the Confederacy
as a literary, miscellaneous, and news weekly.

The advertising columns of the plantation sheet
were used mainly by the editor himself, as an aid
in carrying on the manifold industries of his estate.
The hat factory figures conspicuously here, and the
inference is that it was a profitable business, —
indeed, we are told that demands for the hats came
from all over the South, and a dozen wool hats on
one occasion were sold for five hundred dollars in
Confederate money.

The following advertisements were selected at
random from three years' files: —

[29]

No hats made to order. You can find them of all sorts and sizes, ready made, at the hat shop. I will not trade in Eatonton.

Three fine beaver hats for sale — the last of the season.

Wool hats, rabbit hats, and mixed hats for sale, or for barter — barter preferred. Corn, meat, peas, lard, fur, rags, and wool wanted — Call at the hat shop.

Fur hats for sale, by retail. Call at the shop and get them, if you want them. I am not going to be hat peddler, and haul hats backward and forwards to Eatonton any longer. You have already imposed too much upon my good nature. Quousque, tandem, abutere, Catilina, patientia nostra? — J. A. Turner.

The advertising columns indicate that the pinch of the war was beginning to be felt and hence various commodities were scarce: —

Good jeans can be had at the house of the undersigned at twenty dollars per yard. — J. S. Bryant.

Let our good friends remember that they cannot better serve us than by saving rags for us to be made into paper, for which we will pay ten cents per pound. J. A. Turner.

Later the same advertisement offers twenty-five cents per pound. Another reminder of war is to be found in the announcement of the Quartermaster-

General of Georgia in the issue of February 23,
1864: —

Daughters of Georgia! I still need socks. I still have
yarn to furnish. I earnestly desire to secure a pair of
socks for every barefooted soldier from Georgia. You
are my reliance. Past experience teaches me that I
will not appeal to you in vain.

Young Joel was happy in the midst of these
plantation activities, and made himself at home
with his chief, the foreman of the printing-shop, an
Irish "tramp" printer, who had seen much of the
world and who regaled his apprentice with recita-
tions from "Richard III" and "Hamlet"; and with
the quaint little old master hatter who was "illit-
erate, but not ignorant," full of superstitions and
quaint tales of "North Ca'liny," his old home, —
a "born'd Baptis'," stubbornly grounded in his
creed.

Joel soon found a companion of his own age, a
neighborhood lad of fifteen, whose friendship was
worth a great deal to him, "for there was not a bird
in the woods nor a tree that he did not know the
name of, and something of its peculiarities, and he
was familiar with every bypath in the country
around. He knew where the wild strawberries grew,
and the chincapins and chestnuts, and where the
muscadines, or ' bullaces,' were ripest. He had a

tame buzzard that sometimes followed him about in his rambles; he tamed flying squirrels, and handled snakes fearlessly." It was he who initiated Joel into the mysteries of the coon hunt, with the help of his dogs, Jolly and Loud, and who accompanied the young printer in his sallies with the Turner harrier hounds.

It would have been hard for Joel to say which gave him the most pleasure — the out-door life of the plantation, or the hours of browsing in Mr. Turner's library; for the latter was not long in discovering the boy's passion for reading and he encouraged it. In the old dog-eared scrapbook I find a note from the patron to his apprentice: "When you are through with these two volumes, you can have others. I have about a dozen of Irving's works. 'Salmagundi' was in my father's library, but I think one of my sisters drew it. I will try sometime to borrow it for you. Take good care of my books and don't deface them."

Mr. Turner's knowledge of forestry and botany were also put at the service of the boy, and his eager mind absorbed a vast store of information not to be had in a village "academy" or a city "institute." Picture the modern child confined within the four walls of the average "graded school" and compare his opportunities with those of the lad whose schoolroom was a country printing-office on the roof of which the squirrels scampered about and the blue jays cracked their acorns! Not twenty steps from the office door a partridge had built her nest and was raising a brood of young; and more than once a red fox could be seen loping contentedly toward the nearby woods. Father once said: —

"As you may well believe, it was a great and saving experience for a youngster of that age. It was just lonely enough to bring me face to face with myself and yet not lonely enough to breed melancholy. I used to sit in the dusk and see the shadows of all the great problems of life flitting about, restless and uneasy, and I had time to think about them. What some people call loneliness was to me a great blessing, and the printer's trade, so far as I learned it, was in the nature of a liberal education; and, as if that was n't enough, Mr. Turner had a large private library, containing all of the best books. It was especially rich in the various departments of English literature, and it would have been the most wonderful thing in the world, if, with nothing to do but set a column or so of type each day, I had failed to take advantage of the library with its remarkable assortment of good books."

When the work and play of the day were ended

and the glow of the light-wood knot could be seen in the negro cabins, Joel and the Turner children would steal away from the house and visit their friends in the slave quarters. Old Harbert and Uncle George Terrell were Joel's favorite companions, and from a nook in their chimney corners he listened to the legends handed down from their African ancestors, — the lore of animals and birds so dear to every plantation negro. And sometimes whilst the yellow yam baked in the ashes, or the hoe cake browned in the shovel, the negroes would croon a camp-meeting hymn or a corn-shucking melody. The boy unconsciously absorbed their fables and their ballads, and the soft elisions of their dialect and the picturesque images of their speech left an indelible imprint upon the plastic tablets of his memory.

Here, too, he heard stories of runaway slaves and "patter-rollers." But Joel noticed that the patrol never visited the Turner plantation, and when, during the war, vague rumors of a negro uprising began to circulate, Mr. Turner only laughed, for he claimed that "the people who treat their negroes right have nothing to fear from them."

Thus passed the months and years at Turnwold, and it was during these colorful days that the creator of "Uncle Remus," of "Mingo," and "Free

A DAUGHTER (80 YEARS OLD) OF UNCLE GEORGE TERRELL

TURNWOLD

Joe " received those vivid and varying impressions
of the old régime, and of the customs of its mansions
and its cabins, — pictures of a period that passed
away long before he became known as a creator of
types rich in humor and poetry, and redolent of
the soil to which they were bound by a thousand
ties of love and sorrow, of bounty and privation.

CHAPTER IV

THE OLD SCRAPBOOK

REFERRING once more to the autobiographical sketch in "Lippincott's," we find the following paragraph: —

While setting type for the "Countryman" I contributed surreptitiously to the columns of that paper, setting my articles from the "case" instead of committing them to paper, thus leaving no evidence of authorship. I supposed that this was a huge joke; but as Mr. Turner read the proof of every line that went into his paper, it is probable that he understood the situation and abetted it.

Later on in his stay at Turnwold the young printer plucked up sufficient courage to submit contributions to the editor, and Mr. Turner became his literary mentor, and a frank and uncompromising critic of the boy's efforts. Between the leaves of Joel's old scrapbook is the following note, written precisely, and in ink, on the back of an old court summons (for paper was scarce then): —

For the first time since you sent in this article, I have found time to examine it, and though it has merit, I regret that I have to reject it, because it is not up to the standard of the "Countryman." In the first place, you have made a bad selection in the article you have chosen for a subject. That article is contemptible and beneath criticism. It borders on idiocy. Captain Flash did his paper injustice in publishing it. In the next place, there is want of unity and condensation in your article. It is headed, "Irishmen — Tom Moore," and then goes off on a great variety of subjects, and is too diffuse on everything it touches.

In writing hereafter, 1st select a good — a worthy subject.

2nd, stick to that subject.

3d, say what you have to say in as few words as possible. Study the 'nervous condensation' which you so much admire in Captain Flash.

All this is for your good.

J. A. TURNER

Aug. 21st, 1864.

The ambitious apprentice did not lose heart under the severity of such criticism, but continued his experiments until he produced something worthy of the select little sheet. In looking through the old files I have found a number of signed articles, mostly in sober tones and with little indication of the humor that bubbled and sparkled later on.

JOEL CHANDLER HARRIS

Doubtless young Joel was somewhat awed by the library of serious volumes and by his patron's admonitions, and felt that the "Countryman" was far too dignified a vehicle for the expression of the natural tendencies and effervescences of a fun-loving, green-horn printer.

One of his signed contributions is on the subject of "Death" and runs as follows: —

What is death, that we so much fear it? Is it the end of man? Is it an end to all his troubles? Is it a long, eternal sleep — and is this why we all dread it? — These are the questions that come looming up before the mind of every one. No one can tell why he actually fears death, yet the fear is with every one, as if by instinct and cannot be removed.

An Atheist fears death for this reason: His soul shrinks back with awe from the fathomless depths of a gulf that has been explored by many, yet no news of the dread land has ever been told. Many have traversed its wide domain, yet none have ever returned to relate the tale of what they saw. Many have had an audience of the terrible King; mothers have petitioned him to spare their infants; but he

"Has made their entreaties a jest";

and the soul of the Atheist sickens within him, at the thought of facing the terrible monarch that conquers all.

The Deist fears death for a far different reason. He believes that there is a just God, and the very justice dealt out by him causes the Deist to fear death.

THE OLD SCRAPBOOK

Death is but the beginning of life; and the grave is but a station house on the road to heaven. A person does not actually die. — The caterpillar enters his chrysalis a loathsome worm, but issues forth a beautiful creature. Man enters his coffin a weak, sinful being, and, if he puts his trust in God, issues forth entirely another creature; and, like the butterfly, he is robed with a gown of pure and beautiful colors, and inherits a pair of wings, if his deeds on this side of the grave merit the reward.

The painstaking efforts which won his admittance into the sacred columns of the "Countryman" were not Joel's first ventures in the field of writing. Before he came under the influence of Mr. Turner's criticism, and even before he began his apprenticeship at Turnwold, he had penned and penciled many a line in his dog-eared scrapbook — lines which reveal his budding personality with the naïf directness and wholeheartedness of extreme youth. For that reason and also because they give out an aroma of those far-away days of chivalric sentiment, these little tales, essays, and verses, written between the ages of twelve and fifteen, seem to me full of charm: the charm of boyhood with its turmoil of hidden feeling, obscure ideals, passionate preferences, and proud reserves.

The bashful boy confided his thoughts freely to the yellow pages of the little old book, and one finds there a fantastic medley of crude melodrama, sentimental verse, patriotic manifestoes, didactic essays, and foolish little skits, full of the rough fun of a boy in his early teens. Joel had not yet escaped from the spell of the high-flown romances of the period into the healthier air of Steele, Goldsmith, Scott, and Irving when he penned "The Comanche's Daughter," "The Bandit King," and "Allie Graham, or the Broken Heart." His "Bandit King" had his stronghold in the Apennines, and was "of giant stature, somewhat thin and *symetrycal*." His dress consisted of a "wolf-skin cap, the tail of which hung over his right shoulder; a dress coat of blue cashmere with gold buttons across the breast; pants of the same material with gold braid down the seam. A buck-skin belt was around his waist, and the butts of two revolvers could be seen protruding from behind the belt; also the silver handle of the far-famed Italian stiletto. A carbine hung to his back by a leather strap."

This human arsenal had a face that was "almost girlish in its expression," and his features were "elegant, not dark like the rest of his daring band. His nose was neither of Roman structure or of Aquiline — just enough of both to be beautiful. . . . His eyes were black and glittering, and if it were not for his eyes I should have said he was an American. . . . His manners were dignified and graceful to all, even to the lowest menial in his band. He was neither haughty nor indolent. This then was the celebrated robber bandit, Guilermo of the mountains. It was said he was extremely benevolent to the poor, giving to them half of what he took from the rich."

The young writer's love of the ridiculous found vent in a fragment called "The Darkey's Love; a Travesty on the Opera of Somnambule"; next he tried his hand on moral essays: "Sabbath in the Country," "Boys and Gambling," "Stability of Character"; then follows a debate on the relative mental capacity of man and woman, in which, I am glad to say, Joel eloquently defended the intellectual prowess of woman, a stand to be expected on the part of Mary Harris's son: —

"Mr. Chairman: The question which is under the consideration of this able and distinguished body is whether or not man is the intellectual superior of woman. I contend that he is not, by any means, or else why does he unbosom his trials and troubles to his wife and mother? Why does woman love to read books if she is inferior to man? Man is bold with his intellect, while woman never has the chance to show hers, or even if she has, she is too modest to make much use of it. . . . Look at the mother of

Washington — would he ever have been the great scholar and noble General that he was if she had had no intellect? Never! He would maybe have ended his life on the gallows or in the penitentiary if his mother had never had any intellect"; and so on.

A number of poems indicate that Joel was not too much taken up with fun and work to be entirely unmindful of the charms of sentiment. There are verses addressed to "Leone," to "Nelly White," to "Annie, in the Clover," and a mournful plea, "Bury Me in the Country."

"Nelly White" seems to have been a favorite with its youthful author, and it was many times refashioned and revised. In its final draft it was considered worthy of the "Countryman," and appeared in the issue of Sept. 27, 1864: —

NELLY WHITE
(Written for the "Countryman")
By JOEL C. HARRIS

The autumn moon rose calm and clear,
    And nearly banished night,
While I with trembling footsteps went
    To part with Nelly White.

I thought to leave her but awhile,
    And, in the golden west,
To seek the fortune that should make
    My darling Nelly blest.

For I was of the humble poor,
  Who knew that love, though bold,
And strong, and firm, within itself,
  Was stronger bound in gold.

And when I knelt at Mammon's shrine,
  An angel ever spake
Approvingly — since what I did,
  I did for Nelly's sake.

Again I neared the sacred spot,
  Where she and I last met,
With merry laugh, does Nelly come
  To meet her lover yet?

Again the moon rose in the sky,
  And gave a fitful light,
Which shone with dreary gleam upon
  The grave of Nelly White.

Between the leaves of the scrapbook I find a copy of a letter to the editor of the "Commonwealth," dated June 2, 1863 (it was in March of the same year that the essay on "Death" had appeared over Joel's signature in the "Countryman") which indicates that the budding writer was not content to be confined to the columns of Mr. Turner's paper. Without doubt the other papers were not so exacting and perhaps he found in them an opportunity to work off some of his more florid compositions: —

JOEL CHANDLER HARRIS

Eds. Commonwealth: —

Sirs: I send you an article for the "Commonwealth," which, if you see fit, publish, otherwise burn it up. On no account let my name be known. Hoping that you may soon receive a thousand reams of nice paper (which is the best wish that any paper can receive nowadays); I remain

Your friend,

J. C. Harris

P.S. I have an original composition for the "Commonwealth" entitled "A Night Hunt." Must I send it?

J. C. H.

There is also a personal memorandum, dated June 14, 1863: —

"Don't recollect when I finished 'Doodang.'[1] The 'Southern Watchman' copied it under the head of 'Select Miscellany' ! ! !—Finished 'Laughing Corpse' June 14th, have not sent it off, yet. Finished 'Gran'-pap' the same day. Have not sent it off yet, Will send it to 'Child's Index.' Finished 'A Night's Hunt' three weeks ago. Have not sent it off yet. No literary papers to send it to in the South, now that the 'Fireside' has stopped. I am

---

[1] It is interesting to note that one of the stories written by Joel Chandler Harris in the last year of his life was called "The Story of the Doodang."

engaged on a 'Burlesque,' though that is not its
name. It shall be in ridicule of the Yankees, and of
the South, *too*, for not advancing literature; do what
I can to help the cause along, people will not pat-
ronize *our* papers."

The war, whose gloomy echoes had penetrated
the quiet of middle Georgia, made a profound impression on Joel. He saw the young men of Putnam
County bid farewell to their families and depart
for the battlefields of Virginia. This scene called
forth an article from his pen entitled "The Recruits," and later on, when one of these boy soldiers fell before the Federal guns, his young friend
wrote an "obituary," full of boyish grief and indignation, of which the opening paragraph is as
follows: —

The Angels of heaven have recorded another deed
of murder committed by the minions of Abe Lincoln.
Edward S. Davis was killed in the battle of McDowell
by the Yankees. I knew the deceased well. He was a
bright, a brave and an impetuous boy (for he was only
a boy). He left school to join the Putnam Light Infantry, who were ordered to N.W. Virginia, where he died
bravely, battling for his country's wrongs.

Indeed, many of Joel's writings during the years
at Turnwold were inspired by the events of the war.
There is a patriotic ballad, "Ode to Jackson, the

JOEL CHANDLER HARRIS

Martyr of the South," and a play which was never completed, called "Butler, the Beast," referring, of course, to General Butler's occupancy of New Orleans. It begins: —

Enter Butler and William.

Butler : Well, William, have you sought the city on some pretence or other, to hang a man?

There is also a letter to Lincoln written in "cracker" dialect, which as far as I know is the first sample of dialect from Joel's pen. It is signed "Obadiah Skinflint." Obadiah tells President Lincoln that unless he evacuates Washington, in less time "than a sheep can skin a 'simmon tree," Jeff Davis will break his pitcher at the cistern. Obadiah continues: —

"You says you have n't got no floatin' battries. I don't kno' what the reason you ain't got none. W'y them thar skinatific Bobolitionists up thar could convert your old bull-hide boots inter floatin' battries in less than no time. But they'd have to work on them out er doors, fer they coudent carry them inter the house, they are so big . . ." etc.

Obadiah gets pretty rough with Mr. Lincoln before the end of the epistle and threatens to "draw his blood with a lead pill the first time he sets his peepers on him."

All this is so typical of boyhood, with its vivid

enthusiasms and passionate prejudices, that it
causes one to feel melancholy over one's world-
weary, judicial attitude of mind toward most issues. It is certainly indicative of the broad humanity and clarity of vision which the accumulation of
years brought to Joel Chandler Harris that, after
having passed through these turbulent times and the
later even more tragic and trying times of Reconstruction, with all the ardor and fire of a red-haired
rebel, he could, in his maturity and at the height of
his power as a writer, devote himself to delineating
that period with a moderation and a sense of pro-
portion which disarm the most suspicious critic.

The boy who in his youth so hotly denounced
Lincoln, later came to be a sincere admirer of the
genius and greatness of soul of the martyred
leader, and one of his most popular and spirited
stories [1] was to contain a study of the lamented
President unrivaled in its sympathy, vividness,
and veracity. I have heard father say more than
once that the greatest tragedy, next to the war,
that the South had ever experienced, was the death
of Lincoln.

Following the broken and meager records of the
old scrapbook, it is evident that Joel became more

[1] *The Kidnapping of President Lincoln.*

[47]

and more interested in his training as a printer and
"newspaper man" as the years rolled by at Turnwold. He grew to feel that he was of some importance on the plantation sheet, and after he ventured
to submit compositions to his patron and to profit
by his criticisms, and especially, after he was allowed to sign his name as a contributor, he felt a
natural pride of ownership in the little paper, a feeling which displays itself amusingly in a communication to a fellow journalist. This is addressed to the
editor of the "Illustrated Mercury," and, after the
usual preliminaries of polite correspondence are
disposed of, the youthful journalist continues:—

I like the "Mercury" exceedingly well, with the
exception of one thing, if I be allowed to be candid
— and that is the illustrations. After you get your
paper to paying, I hope you will discard them altogether. I am anxious for the "Mercury" to succeed, as I believe it is the only publication in the
State, with the exception of the "Countryman"
which does not model itself on the vile publications
of the North, as, for instance, the "Field and Fireside." I am afraid, also, that our Southern writers
are giving way to a wholesale imitation of Yankee
authors, especially the younger portion of those
afflicted with the *cacoëthes scribendi*. I shall do all

THE OLD SCRAPBOOK

I can to help the "Mercury," and if I can help it
by writing an article for it occasionally, I will do
so. Hoping that you may succeed in all your en-
deavors to establish an undefiled Southern literature, and that the "Mercury" may prove a blessing to the Confederacy, I remain,

Your well-wisher

JOEL C. HARRIS

Joel was now nearly seventeen years of age; his
apprenticeship to the printer's trade was completed; he was beginning to feel confidence in his
ability to express himself in writing, and the happy
sheltered days on the old plantation were drawing
to a close. Letters came to him from the outside
world — that world of conflict and bloodshed; one
from a comrade in the Quartermaster's Department at Macon, who tells him that "there have
been sad changes since the good old days now gone:
Eli Awtry and Jim Johnson were killed in the late
fight at Spottsylvania Court-House. I don't know
where Gordon Whiting can be; he was nearly dead
from consumption the last I heard of him. Old
Siddon you can't kill. Always foremost in the fight,
he has passed through a dozen battles unscathed."
His cousin, James H. Johnson, writes him from the
battlefield near Atlanta, where he is serving with

[49]

JOEL CHANDLER HARRIS

Baker's Brigade of the Thirty-seventh Alabama Infantry, and describes the "hissing of the minie-balls over the trenches, and the enemy within 350 yards of our works, their sharpshooters greeting us with unpleasant reminders."

Who can tell what was passing in Joel's mind as he read these messages from the heart of the great conflict? The time came when there was a raid on the outskirts of Eatonton, and the roll of the drums and roar of cannon drew daily nearer. More than likely the patriotic young rebel would have been drawn into the greedy maw which had swallowed up many of his friends, boys of tender age and home-bred habits, had not Johnston's defeat shattered the hopes of the Confederacy.

Prior to this disaster, General Sherman had swung loose from Atlanta and was making his way down through middle Georgia. "Before this vast host all sorts of rumors fled, carrying fear and consternation to the peaceful plantations. At last, one cold, drizzly day in November, Joe Maxwell, trudging along the road on his way to the printing-office, heard the clatter of hoofs behind him, and two horsemen in blue came galloping up. . . . They were couriers carrying dispatches from the Twentieth Army Corps to General Sherman." [1]

[1] *On the Plantation.*

THE OLD SCRAPBOOK

All was confusion and distress on the plantation after this. The horses and mules were hid out in the swamp, where they were later found and carried off by the Federal foragers, together with the supplies in the barns and smokehouses. Seated on a fence which bordered the Milledgeville highroad, Joel at length saw the Twentieth Army Corps, under the command of General Slocum, pass in review before him, a body of "tramping soldiers, clattering horsemen, and lumbering wagons" ploughing their way through ankle-deep mud. It seemed like a phantasmagoria to the boy; he could not believe it was real. There were no flying banners, no glittering trappings, and in the rear came a confused array of captured horses, mules, and cows, and wagon-loads of bateaux.

But it was real enough, with a melancholy and threatening reality, and when Joel climbed down from the fence, where he had been the butt of the soldier's jokes as they passed, and bent his steps toward Turnwold, he found everything strangely quiet and deserted. The stock was gone, and many of the cabins were empty, since numbers of the slaves had followed in the wake of the Federal army.

In the "Countryman" of May 9, 1865, appeared the following announcement, pathetic in its mingling of defiance and surrender: —

JOEL CHANDLER HARRIS

To My Patrons:

As an editor, I was once as bold as a lion. That was when I had a country. Now, it seems, I have none. Our people, it seems to me, are ready to bow their necks to take the yoke, Gen. Lee's army has been captured, and the balance of our armies, through their generals, are negotiating an abolition of our flag, and our country. If I cannot edit my paper as a freeman, I will edit none at all. Until I know the weight of the chains I wear, I shall publish a quarter sheet, but shall have nothing to say on political affairs. I will write upon no subject upon which I cannot freely speak my mind. All business matters between my subscribers and myself, will be adjusted, unless I am robbed of everything.

J. A. TURNER

P. S. Since writing the above, I learn that Gen. Johnston has surrendered to Sherman. Of course, therefore, we are an overpowered, and *for the present*, a conquered people. Before resuming the publication of a full sheet I shall have to wait and see what regulations my masters make concerning the press.

The closing paragraph of "On the Plantation" completes the forlorn record of the passing of the old order, but gives a hint of the hope and fulfillment that lay hidden in the new: —

The plantation newspaper was issued a little while longer, but in a land filled with desolation and despair its editor could not hope to see it survive. A larger world beckoned to Joe, and he went out into it. And

THE OLD SCRAPBOOK

it came about that on every side he found loving friends to comfort him, and strong and friendly hands to guide him. He found new associations and formed new ties. In a humble way he made a name for himself, but the old plantation days still live in his dreams.

CHAPTER V

THE war ruined Mr. Turner, as it did most of the Southern planters, and he died in poverty. On one occasion, when referring to the melancholy fate of the "old plantation" and the wrecked fortunes of his former patron, father paused for a moment and his face became clouded; then suddenly it cleared, and the familiar twinkle gleamed in his eye as he added: "It ruined me, too, for, you see, I trapped rabbits and sold their skins for twenty cents apiece. I would catch three or four every afternoon. I put the money in my trunk — it was a small trunk — and kept my clothes — I had n't many — under the bed. Well, all the money, being Confederate, of course went instantly and permanently out of circulation when Lee surrendered at Appomattox Court-House."

So the young printer found himself, at the collapse of the Confederacy, as penniless as when he went to Turnwold, and it became necessary for him to be "up and doing" again. But red-haired boys are not easily disheartened, and this particular one had already thought ahead.

OUT IN THE WORLD

Early in the preceding year, when he was little more than sixteen years of age, the idea of leaving Turnwold and seeking his fortune elsewhere had already occurred to him. One of his friends held a place on the Columbus, Georgia, "Times," and to him Joel wrote about the possibility of getting work on that paper. The young man replied in February, saying: "I should be delighted if you could come, as I am bored to death with the society with which I am compelled to associate. . . . Now, as to work: I can only say that I have tried in all the offices, and there is no empty case — all full at present, but probably there will be a vacancy in a short time, and if there is, nothing would afford me greater pleasure than for you to come and fill it. You can get a chance in Macon, no doubt, but you will have to work, work, all the time, day and night, and you would soon get tired of it."

Perhaps the prophecy in the concluding sentence dampened Joel's enthusiasm and determined him to stay on with the "Countryman," or it may have been that the thought of going farther away from his mother was distasteful to the boy; for during his apprenticeship under Mr. Turner, he had been able to see her from time to time. At any rate, he lingered at Turnwold until the disaster to his patron left him no choice about facing a change, and then, doubtless, the thought of work in Macon came back to him. In the terrible upheaval of his section and his State, personal changes must have seemed to the youth less than trivial, for there are no details to be found concerning his departure from Putnam County and his arrival in Macon.

We know, merely, that this prosperous town was his next home and that he was between sixteen and seventeen years old when he found a place as printer in the composing-room of the Macon "Telegraph." His old friend, Judge Bridges Smith, formerly Mayor of Macon, remembers Joel at this time as a slender youth, weighing not more than ninety pounds. He was silent and attentive, and determined to familiarize himself with the mechanical side of this (to him) large and important city newspaper. When he was not busy with his work of taking proofs and aiding the foreman, he was either reading or writing. Judge Smith tells of the newcomer's relations with his superiors: —

"Harry J. Neville, then city editor, often gave the studious apprentice work in his line. From the notebook containing memoranda of local events he selected such things as would suit Joe's style of writing, and then in some out-of-the-way corner the report was written. I remember some instances of Joe's 'filling-in' and will give one to illustrate:

OUT IN THE WORLD

In those days when a present of anything was made to the editors or printers, the paper gave a 'puff' in return. Over the way from the office was a beer saloon and 'billiard parlor,' as it was styled. On the opening night the proprietors of the saloon sent over a big bucket of beer to the printers. The local or city editor was not there on this occasion, but the 'puff' had to be written. The foreman called on Joe to handle it and he wrote it in a style entirely different from that of the local editor. In fact it was worthy of a better theme.

"In the office he was affectionately known as 'Pink Top,' because of his hair; but while the men thus spoke of him, and perhaps put too much work on him, every man was his friend and loved him.

"I remember when Joe 'completed his trade,' by joining Typographical Union No. 84. It was on a Sunday afternoon, in the little brick house that stood on Third Street, and was known as the Engine House of Young America, No. 3. To join the Union it was necessary to take an obligation, and Joe was so frightened that he was unable to repeat a word. Seeing his embarrassment, I said: 'Mr. President, Mr. Harris stutters.' He was therefore excused."

This slight impediment in father's speech remained with him through life, and in moments of embarrassment or excitement annoyed him greatly. It was partly due to this circumstance that he found it trying to meet strangers, for the "stutter" immediately became exaggerated in their presence, and there was not always at hand a thoughtful friend to extricate him from a painful situation, as Judge Smith did in this instance.

The days passed uneventfully in Macon, and the young "printer's devil" filled in his spare moments with independent work, sending his compositions to various publications. One of these was the "Crescent Monthly," of New Orleans, and as the result of his enterprise, a letter came one day from its editor offering Joel the position of private secretary. This was a great surprise to the young man, and he sought out the city editor, Mr. Neville, to ask his advice. The latter was aware of the young printer's talents and encouraged him to accept an opportunity to be near a man of culture in a cosmopolitan city. Joel studied over the proposition, nursed it, and sat up with it for days before he could make up his mind to accept it, but he finally did.

Father had pleasant memories of Macon days and Macon friends, and years after he left there, in a letter to one of his children who was having a happy time in the hospitable city, he wrote: "You can't tell me anything about Macon. I once lived

there, and liked it very much. The people are fine."
And when his old newspaper friend wrote him in
1905, congratulating him on his fifty-seventh birthday, his thoughts turned backward nearly forty
years and led him to write: —

DEAR BRIDGES: —
Among all the congratulations that have been
showered on me, with and without reason, none
touched me more than yours. It reminded me of
old times — the days when we worked as well as
loafed together — when we were young and
happy. . . .

The "Crescent Monthly" was published by William Evelyn at 82 Baronne Street, New Orleans,
and was devoted to "Literature, Art, Science, and
Society." Its editor was a gentleman of English
extraction, the same Captain Flash whose work
Joel had admired when a boy at Turnwold. As was
his habit, Joel continued to apply himself to creative work, though he must have been fairly well
occupied with his secretarial duties, and besides
contributing paragraphs and unsigned articles to
the magazine, he wrote freely for the New Orleans
daily papers. The following verses were published
in the "New Orleans Times" in January, 1867: —

JOEL CHANDLER HARRIS

THE SEA WIND

O sweet south wind! O soft south wind!
  O wind from off the sea!
When you blow to the inland ports of home
  Kiss my love for me.

And when you have kissed her, sweet south wind,
  Tell her I never forget —
For the pale white mists of parting tears
  Are floating round me yet.

Tell her I sit all day and dream
  Of the joys that time may bring,
Till the old love poems afloat in my heart
  Meet together and sing.

And the tune — O wind — that they sing and ring
  (With a burst of passionate rhyme)
Is "The Lover's Prayer" — a sweet, sad air —
  A song of the olden time.

Touch her lips lightly, sweet south wind,
  As I should, were I there;
And dry up the tears in her violet eyes,
  And play with her purple hair.

O soft south wind! O sweet south wind!
  O wind from off the sea!
When you blow to the inland ports of home,
  Kiss my love for me!

It was said (though I cannot vouch for the accuracy of the statement) that he also found time to prepare all but one of a series of lectures on English literature, delivered, with the applause of press, people, and students, by William Evelyn, the publisher of the magazine, before a female institute in New Orleans. He remained with the "Crescent Monthly" until it ceased publication.

While in New Orleans, father met Lafcadio Hearn, but their acquaintance was slight. I recall no details of it, but I remember that father once spoke of the unpleasant and sinister effect upon the beholder of that gifted writer's myopic eye. That Hearn's delicate and exotic imagination impressed the young Georgian is evident, for he did not lose sight of Gautier's translator, and after coming to Atlanta to live, he made reference to Hearn in the "Constitution," as follows: —

There is in New Orleans a man of letters who has already made his mark — Mr. Lafcadio Hearn, who has managed to translate the body and soul of some of Théophile Gautier's writing into English. Indeed, I am inclined to think that Mr. Hearn has imparted to his translations a sensitiveness, a delicacy, a spiritual essence not to be found in the originals. A ten minutes' talk with Mr. Hearn is among my most vivid recollections of a brief stay in New Orleans. He struck me as a man capable of putting versatility to new uses. He is a specialist in almost every branch of information. I hope to hear that he is writing a book which shall be a translation of the mysteries of his own mind and imagination.

JOEL CHANDLER HARRIS

It would be impossible for any one to live for long in New Orleans without bringing away pleasant memories of its famous restaurants, and they probably impressed the young man from middle Georgia, in spite of the fact that all his life he was a lover of simple fare, of corn bread and buttermilk, fried chicken and "collards." At any rate, he remembered witnessing the gastronomic ecstasy of a visitor over the delicate hot waffles of one of the famous French eating-houses — an article of food evidently before unknown to the stranger, who was so pleased with the crisp, brown discs that the waiter could not bring them fast enough to suit him. Finally, the gourmand beckoned the *garçon* to his side and made the following suggestion: "Say, bub, you might be able to hustle those little cakes along faster if you would tell the cook to cut out the *printing* on 'em. Tell him to just send 'em along *plain*."

In spite of the charm which the beautiful old city exerts upon all who visit it and which it undoubtedly exerted upon the imaginative young journalist, he was at heart a lover of simpler and less complex sensations than those offered by the cosmopolitan and softly glittering Creole city. He became homesick for the red hills and harsher air of his native State, and so took his way back to

OUT IN THE WORLD

Eatonton in May, 1867, to spend a short time with his mother, resting, — or, as he expressed it in a letter, "ruralizing in the places where grain grows and birds sing, . . . nursing a novel in my brain." But "nursing novels" brings no income to poor young journalists, and this one, after a brief indulgence in day-dreams, turned again toward Macon.

It was on the platform of a train in that city that he encountered an old friend, Mr. James P. Harrison, whom he had known in Eatonton, and who then and there persuaded him to go to Forsyth, Georgia. Mr. Harrison had recently bought the "Monroe Advertiser" in that town, and he offered Joel a position on his paper. Many years later father good-humoredly defined his duties on the "Advertiser": "I set all the type, pulled the press, kept the books, swept the floor, and wrapped the papers for mailing; my mechanical, accounting, and menial duties being concealed from the vulgar hilarity of the world outside of Forsyth by the honorable and impressive title of *Editor*. This often happens." The "Advertiser" was among the first, if not the very first one, of the country weeklies that had a regular local department. This, and several other features, soon gave it a prominent position among the leading weeklies of the State. Its owner not only recognized his young editor's ability from the beginning, but was sincerely attached to him, and invited him to live in his home. In fact, this friendship, formed back in the Eatonton days and renewed in Forsyth, was to last for a lifetime.

Joel's first paragraphing was done on the "Advertiser," and in this department of his work he was particularly happy. His clear, terse style and ready wit made him at once a popular paragrapher. His brief, pointed comments on public events or trivial happenings were a novelty to his readers and were copied all over the State. The "Atlanta Constitution" published a string of them under the heading "Harrisoniana," supposing them to be the production of Mr. James Harrison himself. Indeed, it was the success of these paragraphs that eventually gained the young man an editorial position on the "Savannah Morning News."

Working in the "Advertiser" officer under the instruction of the young editor was an apprentice, Turner Manry by name, a youth of seventeen years, whose home was in the country about seven miles from Forsyth. He came to the "Advertiser" to learn the printing-trade, and as he received no wages he, also, was taken into the Harrison home, and occupied the same bedroom with Joel. Mr. Manry, now living in Plain Dealing, Louisiana, and

WHERE J. C. H. LIVED WHEN HE WORKED ON THE "MONROE ADVERTISER"

Former home of Mr. James P. Harrison in Forsyth, Georgia

until recently a member of the Legislature from his parish, describes their unpretentious bedchamber as containing a bed, a pine table, two chairs, and Joel's trunk. The latter held "the finest of pleated-bosom white shirts, and unbleached English hose of the best quality, for Mr. Harris was very particular about his clothes, took good care of them, and was always neat." Mr. Manry goes on to describe the relationship between himself and his friend, one that extended over three years: —

"I never called Mr. Harris 'Joe,' though he was only twenty years old when I met him. As soon as I could set type, and got a little of the 'green' off, Mr. Harris took charge of me. He asked me what I had read, and as I had read only one novel, he got the 'Tale of Two Cities' for me from the Circulating Library. I would criticize the book to him, tell him how I liked it, and so on; and under his influence I cultivated a taste for good literature.

"As soon as I was competent to read proof, Mr. Harris entrusted me with all his corrections. He would compose all his articles at the case, even long ones. I remember one called 'A Fox Hunt in Georgia,' a column and a half in length; this, too, he composed at the case. He never signed his articles, and would not read in print what he had prepared, if he could avoid it.

JOEL CHANDLER HARRIS

"During the three years I was closely associated with him I never knew him during work hours to be absent from the office for even an hour. He was the fastest pressman on a hand-press that I ever saw. I usually rolled or inked the form. The roller was long enough to reach across the form, and the ink was distributed by turning a crank, mounted the height of the press, and looking very much like a clothes-wringer. Mr. Harris's work was always extremely neat, and he could say more in ten lines than some of the editors of those days could say in a column; consequently the 'Advertiser' had a large circulation. I saw about the first work of a literary character that he ever did. It was an index for the 'Living Writers of the South,' by James Wood Davidson.

"The 'Advertiser' received all the best magazines: 'Blackwood's,' the 'Living Age,' etc., and Mr. Harris kept up with them all. He was reading 'The Mystery of Edwin Drood' as it came out, and was greatly interested in it.

"In spite of his close application to his work, Mr. Harris found time to associate with other young men. He and some of the boys of the town had a club called 'Company Two,' and amusing references to this club sometimes appeared in the 'Advertiser.' He was full of fun and was fond of jokes: sometimes he stood me up in a chair and made me recite for him a string of foolish rhymes about 'Schneider and his Dog.'

"I remember when Mr. Harris received the letter from the 'Savannah Morning News' which completed his arrangements with that paper. His clothes had been taken out by the negro laundress the day before and they were not ready, so he asked me to pack his trunk later and express it to him, which I did. A few days after this I received a nice letter of thanks telling me that his editor (Colonel Thompson) was 'as gentle as a morning zephyr,' and further saying: 'If there is ever anything I can do to help you, or you want any books, let me know.'

"I can recall how thoughtful Mr. Harris was toward every one he came in contact with, especially those in a humbler position than himself. In watermelon season, knowing that I received no wages, he frequently gave me a quarter, and said: 'Here, Turner, take this money and go get us a McGough melon' (the best to be had in the market). He never cared to meet strangers, and avoided doing so when possible; but I remember enjoying the conversation between him and Mrs. Harrison and her sister-in-law, Mrs. Starke. Once Mrs. Harrison, whom we were very fond of, persuaded him to go to a Sunday-School picnic in his best clothes, and she borrowed one of his coats for me, so I, too, could go. We wore her 'colors' (she was a Methodist) and tried to outshine the Baptists.

"Mr. Harris regularly wrote his mother in Eaton-ton, and often sent her money — all he could possibly spare."

CHAPTER VI

TWO FRIENDSHIPS

FORSYTH brought good fortune to Joel in more ways than one. Not only did his work there lead to an important advance in journalism, but it was in this little Georgia town that one of the most fruitful and important friendships of his life was formed. I have mentioned that he made his home with Mr. James P. Harrison's family, and it was here that he became acquainted with Mrs. Georgia Starke, his host's sister, and her little daughter, Nora Belle.

Mrs. Starke was at this time a young matron, a woman of geniality and common sense. She was fond of books and had a cultivated and discerning mind. Her manners were unaffected and sincere and she was in full sympathy with youth. Joel was an awkward, country-bred boy of about nineteen, painfully conscious of his social deficiencies, handicapped by his tendency to stutter, and believing himself much uglier than he really was, for his red hair and freckled face had caused him to be the butt of many rough jokes. It was a critical period in the young man's life — a time when he was in danger of drawing more and more within himself as he advanced amongst strangers and retired farther from old friends who knew him well enough to make allowances for his lack of assurance and his congenital shyness.

At first, kind Mrs. Starke failed to make much headway with the reticent youth, who rarely spoke a word at table. Her friendly approaches caused him to blush furiously and to feel more ill at ease than ever. It was little Nora Belle who bridged over the awkward gaps in this difficult road to friendship. With childlike unconsciousness of Joel's timidity she clambered into his lap and putting her arms around his neck, called him "Ol' Fel'." And "Ol' Fel'" he remained to her for many a day, for he was always an easy prey to the charms of childhood. Thus little Nora Belle took possession of his heart without much effort and made herself at home there.

Gradually her mother gained the confidence of the sensitive young man and he revealed himself to her both in conversation and by letter perhaps more fully than he ever did to anybody save his wife. He visited Mrs. Starke and Nora Belle twice at the home of Mrs. Frances Harrison (Mrs. Starke's mother) in Milledgeville, Georgia, and once in Atlanta, at the home of her brother, Mr.

JOEL CHANDLER HARRIS AT 20
Photograph sent to his mother from Forsyth, Georgia

TWO FRIENDSHIPS

Z. D. Harrison. On the occasion of one of the Milledgeville visits, he was in the family sitting-room with a company of congenial souls when strangers were announced. The room was high up from the ground and had only one entrance. Mrs. Starke, seeing his embarrassment, said laughingly, "You are cornered now; I don't see how you can get away." But he *did* get away, by jumping out the window!

Mrs. Starke thought highly of her young friend's ability as a poet, and begged him not to neglect his lyrical gifts in the grind of newspaper work. Even after he had attained fame through his inimitable dialect stories she urged him to attempt poetry, but his invariable reply was: "I am no poet, and never will be. I can write only doggerel."

She also fostered in him his ambition to attain a clear, simple, rhythmic prose style and a command of English, and she did not hesitate to criticize him severely when the occasion warranted. Once he wrote to her in the slangy style often affected by unformed youths and she scolded him severely and expressed her strong disapproval of such a lapse. In June of 1870 there is a letter to Mrs. Starke commenting on Nora Belle's passing out of babyhood and mentioning "Ol' Fel's" intention of writing some verses for the little girl: —

JOEL CHANDLER HARRIS

Forsyth, Ga., 20 June, 1870

Dear Mrs. Starke: —

I should have written long ago, thanking you for Nora Belle's picture, and the other things which you were kind enough to send at the same time. But I have been trying to write a few verses for Nora Belle, and I thought I would finish them, print them, and write at the same time. I find, however, it is quite useless for me to wait any longer. I have written twenty different trifles for my little sweetheart, but none of them comes up to my standard of merit, or does justice to the subject, and I have destroyed them all in despair. The inspiration — or whatever you may please to call it — does n't come to me as usual, and I find myself in that most perplexing of positions — namely, the desire to write, without the ability. Don't laugh at me, please. My judgment has outgrown my power to perform, and I dare say I shall never be as well satisfied with anything I may hereafter write as I was with the first doggerel I ever wrote. So much by way of apology for my long delay in acknowledging your kindness.

I suppose Nora Belle has forgotten her "Ol' Fel," long ago; if so, he is extremely sorry, and trusts that her visit here, which is set down next month, may somewhat revive him in her memory.

TWO FRIENDSHIPS

She has no doubt grown to be quite a young lady
— or, rather, quite an *old* lady.

> Very truly your friend
> JOEL CHANDLER HARRIS

Perhaps after seeing his little friend, the poem
"wrote itself," for it was sent later: —

TO NORA BELLE

Of all the little fairies
That ever love caressed,
I know our little darling
Is the brightest and the best.
Oh! the neatest and the sweetest!
No tongue can ever tell
How much of love we lavish
On little Nora Belle.

She cannot reach the roses
That grow about her way,
But in her face are flowers
More beautiful than they;
And the sunlight falling round her,
Glows with a magic spell,
Shedding a golden glory
On little Nora Belle.

She is winsome, she is winning,
She is blithe and she is gay,
And she asks the wisest questions
In the most old-fashioned way;
And the lilies in the valley,
And the daisies in the dell,
Are not so pure and tender
As little Nora Belle.

JOEL CHANDLER HARRIS

. . . .

O rare sunshine and shadow!
That chase each other so —
That fall, and flit and flicker,
And restless come and go!
O winds from o'er the ocean!
O breezes from the dell!
Bring naught but health and pleasure
To little Nora Belle!

On the occasion of his visit in 1871 to Mrs. Starke and her mother, at the home of her brother, Mr. Z. D. Harrison, in Atlanta, Joel greatly enjoyed the beautiful singing of Miss Nora Harrison, the younger sister of his friend. It was on a summer night, and the listeners were seated on the grass under the magnolias, the moonlight filtering through the dense foliage of the trees and faintly lighting their milky blooms. The odor of the pale flower-discs, the mystery of the velvet shadows, the charm of the summer night, and the beauty of the song combined to stir the latent poetry in the soul of the young editor, and he afterward sent Miss Nora Harrison the following lines: —

A REMEMBRANCE
(*Atlanta*, 1871)
I

Soft, low and sweet, yet clear and strong,
Rose the rich volume of your song,
While on the languid August air
That swept your face and stirred your hair,

TWO FRIENDSHIPS

Invoked as by some magic spell,
Wild gusts of music rose and fell.
In the vague hollows of the night
The calm stars swung steadfastly bright;
A bird, belated in the gloom,
Fled nestward with bedraggled plume;
A star shook loose her fiery train
And swept across the sapphire plain.
Then all was still — except the strong,
Rich diatone of your sweet song.

II

I stood entranced; my soul was bound;
Melodious thralls enwrapt me round.
I lived again the wild, uncouth,
Dear, devious ways of my lost youth;
But floods of song swept in and drowned
The old-time singers, sorrow-crowned.
I saw once more the friends of old,
And heard their voices manifold;
And waste, wan years slipped slowly by,
With many a change of sea and sky,
With many a change of form and hue —
And left me happy there with you.

J. C. Harris

The correspondence between Joel and Mrs. Starke continues on into the Savannah days, and even at the risk of breaking into the continuity of the story it seems best to keep these letters together, so complete a revelation are they of the inner life of a young man, which, in the case of a youth of Joel's temperament, is not closely bound up with the ordered march of events.

JOEL CHANDLER HARRIS

The next letter in the series gives, in detail, his reasons for leaving Forsyth and going to Savannah: —

OFFICE MORNING NEWS,
SAVANNAH, GA., 9 December, 1870

DEAR MRS. STARKE: —

You cannot imagine how glad I was to receive your letter yesterday. It is something to be remembered by one's friends, is n't it? — and such remembrances as your letter are always very precious. It came just in time to relieve me of a serious attack of the *blues* — and in order to secure a repetition of the remedy, I write at once.

About myself: there is indeed very little to be said. I left Forsyth with much regret — and only after the most serious deliberation. If I had consulted my desires — my personal feelings, I mean — I would have remained on the "Advertiser"; but in this miserable world, personal predilections are often sacrificed for gain. It is a sad confession to make; but, in my case at least, it is true. The personal relations between Mr. Harrison and myself have been, throughout, of the kindest and most intimate character. There have been occasions, undoubtedly, when his impatient temper rendered me uncomfortable, because I am extremely sensitive; but I dare say that *my* shortcomings, to-

JOEL CHANDLER HARRIS AT 21

gether with the thousand and one imperfections which, through some bitter destiny, are a part of my nature, have to an infinite degree overbalanced everything. The cause of my leaving Forsyth was a matter of business simply, and had nothing to do with my friendship or personal feelings. I was offered a position as associate editor on the "News" at a salary which I could not refuse — and I therefore concluded to accept. I talked long and seriously with Mr. Harrison, and there was perfect confidence between us on the subject. I spoke fully and freely of my hopes and prospects and asked his advice on this matter. If there was any restraint at all — which I do not believe — it was altogether on his side. The position of associate editor on a leading paper like the "News" is not often tendered to a person as young and as inexperienced as myself — and I could not refuse. In speaking with Mr. H. I insisted upon and emphasized the fact that it was my *desire* to remain in Forsyth, but that I considered it my *duty* to come to Savannah. So anxious was I to impress this fact upon him, that besides alluding to it again and again in our conversation, I wrote him several notes embodying in each what I conceived to be a perfectly plain distinction between duty and desire. He afterwards came to Savannah to see me and to offer a proposition, the acceptance of which would take me back to Forsyth. In a day or two after he left, I wrote him a long letter, signifying my willingness to *accept the proposition* under certain conditions. I am pretty certain he received the letter; for I am in receipt of an answer to one mailed to a friend in Forsyth at the same time with his. From his silence, I judge he has made other and better arrangements.

I have thus given you a history of the matter as briefly and as clearly as I could. And if you have received even so much as a hint that I left Forsyth on account of a misunderstanding, I assure you it is a mistake. He treated me throughout with a kindness and consideration which I am not sure I deserved. Indeed, the whole family seemed to vie with each other in their kindness and in the expression of their goodwill. I never knew what a real friend was until I went to Forsyth, and it is no wonder that I look back upon my life there with the tenderest and most sincere regrets — regrets that I was compelled to give it up. My history is a peculiarly sad and unfortunate one — and those three years in Forsyth are the very brightest of my life. They are a precious memorial of what would otherwise be as bleak and as desolate as winter, and the friends whom I knew and loved there — whom I still know and love — will never lose their places in my heart — those dear friends who were so gentle, so kind, and so good — who were always ready to overlook my shortcomings and to forgive my awkward blunders. There is pathos enough in the recollection of these things to form an immortal poem, if one could only fashion it aright. But, for my part, I shall not try. Words are weak, at best, and it is only once in a century that they should be employed on such a sacred subject. That part of my life which is still in the future, I am willing to trust entirely to fate — or Providence; but I know that the coming years hold for me no such happiness and will duplicate no such dear days. I know in my soul that I will never again find such friends — tender and true-hearted, faithful and forgiving. Mr. Harrison, for aught I know, may have a very poor opinion of me — and I know I deserve nothing better — but whatever his opinion, I shall always remember him with feelings of the most sincere friendship. I do not easily forget. My surroundings here are pleasant to a degree that I could not have hoped for, and my success seems to be assured. But there is *something* wanting — something, I cannot tell what. I do not feel at home. The place lacks something.

After all, though, these objections are only nominal. The main point is success and advancement.

Whether I shall succeed ultimately, I cannot tell. I will do my best, and *then* if I fail, I will have the satisfaction of knowing precisely of what I am capable; and, you will agree with me that, in the vanities and egotisms of youth, knowledge of *that* sort is invaluable. In case of failure, I give place simply to some one who, perhaps, is infinitely better and worthier.

And Nora Belle! You cannot imagine how often and how tenderly I think of my dear little pet. It gratifies me beyond measure to know that she still remembers me. I will send the picture as soon as possible — and that means before many days. I think it would be at least prudence to send Wallace to Forsyth or Atlanta, where the air is better and the temperature more uniform. For the same reasons I shall emigrate to some higher spot during the summer season. I was thinking the other day of sending Nora Belle a Christmas present. Suggest something that she would appreciate. Your judgment is so much better than mine that I leave it to you; but don't disappoint me by refusing to name something. Say all sorts of sweet things to Nora Belle for me, and remember me to Wallace.

When you are writing to Forsyth or Atlanta, take occasion, please, to send them all my love — not even excepting proud Miss Nora.

LITTLE NORA BELLE

MRS. G. H. STARKE

MISS NORA HARRISON
("The Proud Miss Nora")

TWO FRIENDSHIPS

Don't fail to write to me. I have been without sympathy a good portion of my life, and your letters are very highly prized, I do assure you. Please remember that when you write to a "lonesome" boy like me, you are doing a missionary work.

I have no idea how long I shall remain in Savannah — the probability being that I shall gravitate towards that shining Sodom called New York; — but here, there, or elsewhere, please remember that I am always the same, and always your friend

J. C. HARRIS

Mrs. Starke was dismayed at the thought of her young friend "gravitating towards that shining Sodom called New York." Both her common-sense and her intuition recognized a talent in Joel which promised to unfold naturally in surroundings to which he was accustomed and in an atmosphere of friendly encouragement. She dreaded for him the cold impersonality of a great city and the inevitable suffering that his sensitiveness would subject him to amidst alien influences. She did not hesitate to express her fears to him and tactfully to guide his thoughts in other directions. Time proved her judgment sound, for it is doubtful if the special vein which finally yielded the young Southern writer so rich a return would ever have been worked if he had lost himself in the wilderness of New York journalism.

Adjustment to a new environment, in father's case, was always a painful process, and he doubtless passed through far more mental suffering in "casting off the old and taking on the new" than he gave evidence of to any but the most sympathetic friend. In the difficult days of fitting himself into his new surroundings and assuming unaccustomed authority in an old-established office, what a world of comfort and encouragement this correspondence must have afforded him!

The note of morbidity sounded in the following letter would be painful did one not feel that in the unrestrained confession of his acute sensitiveness the young man must have found exquisite relief. There could have been no safer antidote for the self-consciousness of youth than the sound common-sense and saving grace of humor which his mentor possessed in large degree.

MORNING NEWS OFFICE,
SAVANNAH, GA., 18 December, 1870

DEAR MRS. STARKE: —

Your letter was timely, and more welcome than you can possibly imagine. If there is anything that I do appreciate, it is a *long* letter from a friend. A short note always impresses me with the idea that it is written under protest, and because the writer could n't well get around writing *something*.

I don't expect to make any friends here — for the simple reason that I shall not try. I have n't room in my heart for them. My love, my friendship, and my esteem are exhausted on the few friends I already have. You see, I am conservative in my disposition and suspicious of new faces. I would n't give even the *memory* of *my* friends for the balance of the world. I have an *absolute horror* of strangers, and as for making friends of them *now*, it is not to be thought of. I am determined to put myself to the test at once — so that I may know exactly what is in me. In order to do this, I will have to trust entirely to merit for success, instead of depending upon the biased judgment of friends. By this means my capabilities — if I have any — will show themselves.

My letters are exact transcripts of my thoughts. They stand me instead of a "gift of gab," which most unfortunately, I do not possess; and when I wrote "proud Miss Nora," it was quite involuntary, and meant no more than if I had said it in a light, rattling way in conversation. That is my impression of her, at any rate. The truth is, I am morbidly sensitive. With some people the quality of sensitiveness adds to their refinement and is quite a charm. With me it is an affliction — a disease — that has cost me more mortification and grief than anything in the world — or everything put together. The least hint — a word — a gesture — is enough to put me in a frenzy almost. The least coolness on the part of a friend — the slightest rebuff tortures me beyond expression, and I have wished a thousand times that I was dead and buried and out of sight. You cannot conceive to what an extent this feeling goes with me. It is *worse* than death itself. It is *horrible*. My dearest friends have no idea how often they have crucified me. Of course no one can sympathize with such an inexplicable disposition. I can see how foolish it is, but the feeling is there, nevertheless, and I can no more control it than I can call into life the "dry bones," or bid the moon to stand still "over the valley of Ajalon." I recollect once when you came to Forsyth from Alabama, Nora Belle appeared to have forgotten me. She said "That ain't Mr. Harris; I know it *ain't* Mr. Harris," and refused to recognize me for some time. It was quite a small thing; but the best part of my life is made up of small things — and I pledge you my word I never got over it for weeks; indeed, it affected me for months afterwards, and I don't think I ever allowed my love for her to show itself to any great degree after that. I loved her all the same, but I kept it to myself. I will agree with (you) at once that it was very silly and very foolish in me to allow such a little incident to affect me; but in turn, I hope you will agree with *me* that such a disposition is a very unhappy one. At least that is my judgment after several years' experience. And this brings me back to what I was going on to explain before I dropped into the foregoing weary digression: namely, the expression I used in regard to Miss Nora. I really have the very highest respect for her and liked her a great deal better than she thought. Indeed, I considered her so much my superior in every way, and was so anxious to gain her good-will, that my awkwardness and clumsiness and confusion, together with my peculiar disposition, made me rough and repellant, and was no doubt the cause of the perfect and thorough contempt in which she held me. *She* was not to blame. It was simply my — shall I say fate? Her treatment of me was perhaps the best after all; for it showed me, more completely than a thousand years' experience could have done, what a coarse ungainly boor I am — how poor, small and insignificant. If you think, however, that I bear Miss Nora the least ill-will, you do me a great injustice. I do not love my friends because they love me — (I could never be sure of *that*, you know) — but because I must love some one. Besides, I look at the whole matter from Miss Nora's standpoint — I "see myself as others see me" — and the prospect is anything but flattering.

I am going to send Miss Nora a little book of poems in a few days, and some new music, and whether she accepts them with a good will or not, I shall at least have had the pleasure of *sending*.

This letter is all about self — self — self. That is the burthen, the chorus and the refrain — self — self — self. I beg that you will pardon such dreary dribble — and consider it confidential. I do not often tell my thoughts so precisely, and do not care to do so. If I were not sure of your hearty sympathy, I would never have written my little history so completely.

Well, you know what sort of message I would send Nora-Belle if I had any more room on this sheet. I will send the little present, and the picture in good time. I will probably spend two days in Forsyth immediately after Christmas.

Most sincerely and faithfully your friend

J. C. HARRIS

I forgot, in closing this dull letter, to ask you to write. That is understood, however. You can't make your letters too long.

TWO FRIENDSHIPS

MY DEAR FRIEND: —

Your long-looked-for and most welcome letter came to hand last night, and I cannot resist the temptation to answer it immediately, especially as I have a leisure moment or so. I dare say you will frown when it comes to hand and say to yourself, "There comes that irrepressible Mr. Harris! Why *can't* he be reasonable?" But what am I to do? Am I to suppress the desire to write to you, even when the spirit moves me? Indeed I shall not!

Do you really think it is a merit to be different from other people — to have different thoughts and ideas about everything? I have a suspicion sometimes that it is the result of some abnormal quality of the mind — a peculiarity, in fact, that lacks only *vehemence* to become downright insanity. I have been convinced for many years that the difference between lunacy and extreme sensitiveness is not very clear. Like the colors of the prism, they blend so readily that it is difficult to point out precisely where the one begins and where the other leaves off. I have often thought that my ideas were in some degree distorted and tinged with a coloring of romance fatal to any practical ambition. But if it be so, so be it. You may be sure that I shall cling to my idiosyncrasies; they are a part of me and I am a

[87]

part of them. They are infinitely soothing, and I would not be without them for the world. Why, sometimes — do you know? — I give myself up to the sweet indolence of thinking for hours at a time, and at such times I am supremely and ineffably happy — happy whether my thoughts are tinged with regret or flushed with hope. Not the least of my pleasures is the pleasure of melancholy. Sorrow is sometimes sweet — always sweet when it brings back to us, through the unexplorable caverns of the nights that have fled, some dear dead face — the touch of some vanished hand — the tone of some silent voice. Those who have not groped through the mystery of pain, who have not been wrapped about with the amber fogs of sorrow — have not experienced the grandest developments of this life, and from my soul I pity them.

Nearly akin to these things is another experience of mine, and it is very curious. When I was about six years old I went with my mother to the funeral of my grandmother, and the first words that the preacher said — and the only ones that I remember — have rung in my ears from that day to this. I have never forgotten them for a single moment; they are present with me at all times and under all circumstances. No matter what I do, what I say, or where I turn, those words are running in my mind like an undertone of sweet music. "*I am the Resurrection and the Life, saith the Lord.*" I often say it aloud, unintentionally and unconsciously. In my copybooks which I used at school, it is written and re-written hundreds of times. In my composition-book, it occupies every available place. "*I am the Resurrection and the Life, saith the Lord.*"

I suspected, from your long silence that you were either unwell or unusually busy — (you have a knack of being always busy, you know) — and I was content to be patient a little while. I knew your letter would come, and I knew that it was well worth waiting for. Upon my word, I wish that every lonely soul had some dear friend like you. I think the world would be infinitely better. If you only knew how precious your letters are — how they are read and re-read — you would not think the time spent in writing them altogether thrown away.

I enclose you a copy of "A Remembrance." When in Atlanta, I was under the impression that I had already sent you the verses, and so I told Miss Nora. It was certainly my intention to do so. It is crude enough, both in thought and expression; but the invariable result of all my attempts at elaboration is to consign everything to the waste-basket — and a convenient waste-basket, let me tell you, is in some sort a public benefaction.

Speaking of my attempts at verse-building reminds me to tell you that "Nora-Belle" has been copied from one end of the South to the other, and the western papers are now taking it up. I learn through a friend that General Toombs has spoken very highly of it — and through another that Paul Hayne, the poet, characterized it as "very fine."

I enjoyed myself rarely in Atlanta, and had what the ladies would call "a perfectly splendid time." I really *did* ask Miss Nora for her picture, and then had to take it *nolens volens*. The picture is not a good one, however, and I hope to get a better one in the summer.

My real reason for not attending Mrs. W——'s reception was that I had said something flippant about her book in my Georgia paragraphs, and I understood from a friend that it was her intention to take me to task about it. Another reason was, I did not wish to be in such a large crowd. I am never more lonely than when in a crowd.

It is probable that I will not be able to take any vacation until August. My plan now is to spend two weeks of it in Atlanta and two at home. I will try to get off the last week in July. Will you be in Atlanta in August?

Upon my word, this letter has spun out to a most

unreasonable length. You can get through it by installments, however.

Now, as always
Faithfully your friend
J. C. HARRIS

It so happened that Mrs. Starke and Nora Belle came eventually to live in Atlanta, and their friendship for father reached out and took in the entire Harris family, old and young, and expressed itself in many ways and during many pleasant hours of happy intercourse; and, fortunately, it persists to this day. Father never wearied of extolling their kindness to him in his "salad days," and that his memory of their good offices was ever a vivid and a grateful one can be seen from his assurances to Mrs. Starke as late as 1901 on the death of her mother: —

You may be sure that I have been sorrowing with you in the loss of your mother. I suppose that I should have written you a letter of consolation and sympathy — but I have received such letters myself, and there is too often a twang to them I cannot relish. I did better than that — I went into my own room, and remembered, one by one, all the old days when your friendship, your patience, and your unfailing kindness were my most precious possessions; and you may be sure that not one kindness — not the smallest was forgotten, or will ever be forgotten. I owe a great deal more to you than you would ever suspect, and what I owe is the best — the very best — that I have ever done or ever will do.

The last time I met Nora Belle, she was holding her head high. The dear girl is miffed, I suppose, because I could not go to Fern Bank. Well, she will never know how much I desired to go, and she would doubtless snap her fingers at any explanation I might make. She will never know — for she would never believe — how large a part she has played in everything I have done. The reason I know she won't believe it is to be found in a letter she wrote me many months ago, wherein she remarked that you had discovered some old letters of mine and felt as if you had *found* an old friend. *Found!* I was so certain that you knew you had never lost the aforesaid friend, that I laughed aloud.

Her first sweetheart sends his love to her and to you.

Faithfully your friend

JOEL CHANDLER HARRIS

CHAPTER VII

IT was in the fall of 1870 that father received from Colonel J. H. Estill the offer which led him to connect himself with the "Savannah Morning News." The sum offered him by the proprietor of that paper seemed to the young newspaper man incredible — forty dollars a week! "I read his letter twice before I could believe it. Forty dollars was enough to keep me for a year, in the way in which I had been accustomed to live. I was the biggest man in the world, I thought. I was to be associate editor, and to write editorial paragraphs, supposedly humorous — the kind that nearly all daily papers print now as a regular feature." [1]

One of father's old-time colleagues describes in picturesque terms the young man's introduction into the office of the "News": —

"I shall never forget the first night Colonel Estill brought Joe Harris up into the composing-room and sanctum and introduced him to us all. We thought at the time he was the greenest, gawkiest-looking specimen of humanity our eyes had

[1] Interview, by James B. Morrow, *Boston Globe*, 1907.

ever rested upon. He was of small stature, red-haired, freckle-faced, and looked like a typical back-woods country youth. His apparel hung upon his person as if thrown at him. He appeared awkward in his movements, but smiled pleasantly as he was introduced around.

"After Colonel Estill and Harris had left, we turned to Colonel Thompson and asked him 'what was that critter Colonel Estill had found? Was it human, or what?'

"Colonel Thompson replied that it was our new paragraphing editor; that Colonel Estill found him on a weekly paper at Forsyth. We then face-tiously asked Colonel Thompson 'how did Colonel Estill manage to catch him — in a fish-trap or a net?' It was the rule to poke fun at any peculiari-ties of a newcomer and we had undergone the same ordeal.

"But that night, when Harris's copy came up, we knew he was a writer of more than ordinary ability. He wrote a clear and beautiful hand, and the printers would shirk the hook to wait for his copy. . . . Every item from his pen sparkled with the keenest humor — he delighted to poke good-humored fun at public men or some institution popular with a rival city. I remember that the Augusta Canal was one of his themes, and Hon.

SAVANNAH DAYS

Benjamin Harvey Hill, then United States Senator, did not escape his witticisms. But everything Harris wrote was so nicely and kindly worded, that no one could take offense."

The "Morning News" in 1870 was the leading daily in Georgia. It had also a weekly and a tri-weekly edition. Its proprietor, Colonel J. H. Estill (himself a practical printer and one-time pressman on the paper, and at that time head of the Georgia Press Association), as a publisher had no superior in the State. Colonel W. T. Thompson, the editor, was a man of considerable literary reputation, the author of that delightful sketch of Georgia life, "Major Jones's Courtship," and of "The Chronicles of Pineville." Colonel Estill had taken over the "News" in 1867 when it was in a precarious condition, the result of war-time depression. Under his management it had become conspicuously successful, both editorially and financially, and its only rival in Georgia was the "Atlanta Constitution."

The press of Georgia in those days resembled a large family circle with all its branches and connections. Its members were on a familiar footing with each other, and many were the jokes and hoaxes circulated from paper to paper. If the jokes were sometimes rather rough and the hoaxes rather

silly, it was all a part of the spirit of good-fellow-
ship which gave early Georgia journalism a human
and personal character unknown to city journalism of to-day. The nearest thing approaching it
in modern papers are the various "columns" now
so popular in some of our metropolitan dailies.

The young paragrapher of the "News" had no
rival in his particular field, and he soon became the
center of good-natured persiflage and widespread
admiration.[1] He thrived and expanded in this atmosphere, and his high spirits never flagged and
his inventiveness seemed to have no bounds. In
the fashion of the time his friends of the press be-

[1] The following paragraphs, gathered at random from the "Morning News" of 1871–72, are representative of the talent of J. C. H.
in this special line: —

"The colored people of Macon celebrated the birthday of Lincoln
again on Wednesday. This is the third time since last October."

"A man named Lawson married Miss Rhoda Harris, in Forsyth
County recently, and then, in the most amorous manner, eloped
with a horse and buggy belonging to his father-in-law."

"A negro pursued by an agile Macon policeman fell in a well the
other day. He says he knocked the bottom out of the concern."

"The editor of the Atlanta Constitution asserts he is the owner
of four hundred acres of wild land in Florida. An editor that can't
tame four hundred acres of land in one season ought to sell it."

"There will have to be another amendment to the civil rights bill.
A negro boy in Covington was attacked by a sow lately and nar-
rowly escaped with his life. We will hear next that the sheep have
banded together to mangle the down-trodden race."

stowed upon him an assortment of obvious nick-
names: "Red-Top," "Pink-Top," "Our friend of
the ensanguined foretop," "Molasses-haired humorist," "Vermilion Pate," "Naughty Boy of the
Savannah News," etc.; and his paragraphs, copied
all over the State, were reproduced under such
titles as, "Harrisgraphs," "Red-Top Flashes,"
"Harris Sparks," "Hot shots from Red Hair-is."

Occasionally, a colleague of more partisan feeling than the rest ventured to protest against the
oft-repeated references to young Harris's auburn
locks:—

Whenever our friend Harris makes a hit at any of the
State papers, the editor of the worsted journal invariably falls back on that old, stale, weather-beaten and
worn-out repartee, "red head." J. C. has one consolation — if his hair *is* red, it is a durned sight *more than*
their articles are.

And a wit asks:—

Why is the red-headed department of the "News" like
the tail of a dog? Because that's where the *wag* is.[1]

---

[1] In a letter dated October 5, 1907, from his old friend, Thomas
E. Watson, author of the *Story of France*, the following reference is
made to the paragraphs and sketches of the Savannah days: " I
admire and love you as I have ever done since I was a poor school-
teacher in Screven County and read your paragraphs in the *Savannah News*. Tump Ponder's roan mule was so familiar to me that
when I finally met Colonel Tump himself, I inquired, first of all,
about the roan mule whose harness was put on with a long pole.
Many a laugh I had over those paragraphs of yours in the *News*."

[97]

JOEL CHANDLER HARRIS

Back of this incessant "jollying" was a real appreciation of the solid and original journalistic qualities of the latest comer on the "News." The following tribute from a Georgia paper is typical of many to be found in the two thick scrapbooks which record the passing of the years in Savannah: —

What shall we say of the bright, sparkling, vivacious, inimitable Harris? There is no failing in his spirit of wit and humor, playful raillery and pungent sarcasm. As a terse and an incisive paragraphist, he is unequaled in the South. One wonders at times that his fund of quips and odd fancies does not occasionally become exhausted, but the flow continues from day to day without sign of diminution or loss of volume. J. C. Harris is a genius of rare and versatile abilities. . . .

And again: —

Harris is the wit of the press. There is nothing waspish or malicious in the little bon-mots he showers upon the heads of his contemporaries, day after day. They are pure, chaste, and sparkling, with scarcely more of harm in them, but much more of brilliancy, than the shining drops of a June day rain. When he gets his hump up, however, and wants to help the "Colonel" drive an issue home, he puts an edge to his paragraphs, and they whistle through the air with the emphasis of a November sleet storm.

The breezy young paragrapher was the inventor of the "P. G. in G." ("Prettiest Girl in Georgia"), and stirred up over this amiable creature a contest which raged for weeks in the Georgia papers. Every town of any importance put forward candidates for the honor, and it was represented that the "editorial album" of the Savannah paper's "Naughty Boy" bulged with photographs of Georgia's choicest beauties. When the ingenious creator of the "P. G. in G." departed for a visit to his mother in Eatonton, it was rumored that he had gone so far as to undertake a particular and personal search for the elusive charmer.

Nevertheless, this "gay Lothario of the Press" succumbed to an attack of shyness when he was appointed by the Press Association to respond to a toast to the ladies at its annual banquet, and quietly withdrew before the toast was given. "And this is the man who says so much about the 'P. G. in G.,'" comments a fellow journalist. "Fie, Brother Harris! Ain't you ashamed? We never in our born days heard of a more diabolical case of ignominious desertion."

Next, he claimed to be the agent for a marvelous device called the "Chicken Torpedo," the invention of a Memphis man, which was warranted to blow up any person found in a henhouse after dark. As might be expected, after a few paragraphs by the "Naughty Boy" on the wonderful possibilities of the "chicken torpedo," floods of fake stories inundated the papers. One purported to be from a Baptist minister, in which he declared that "on arriving at his chicken-house, where a great noise was being made by the surviving chickens, he found that several had been maimed or killed by the explosion. A search was made for the 'chicken torpedo,' which was finally found in the wreckage of poultry. The body of the machine was blown to atoms, but its *two legs* were found intact, tightly grasped by a *huge, black hand,* which had been torn from the arm."

The rollicking inventions about this infernal machine of the barnyard earned for its "agent" a new collection of sobriquets: "Colonel J. Craw Harris, president and treasurer of the. Georgia Chicken Torpedo Company"; "Advisory Board and Actuary, Colonel J. Cataract Harris"; "Physician and Dental Surgeon, J. Charlemagne Harris," "Commissary of Subsistence, J. Chimborazo Harris"; "Traveling Agent, J. Codrington Harris," etc.

After exhausting the possibilities of the chicken torpedo, the "News" paragrapher led a "symposium" on the "Dolly Varden" style of dress, then in vogue, and celebrated its fascinations in verse: —

SAVANNAH DAYS

Vardens now are all the rage,
The theme of this revolving age —
No matter what — in everything —
The welkin loud is made to ring
    Of lovely Dolly Varden.

It's Dolly this, it's Dolly that,
A Varden skirt, a Varden hat;
Where'er you go, whate'er you hear,
It's all about some Varden queer,
    The taking Dolly Varden.

In calico 't was well enough,
But don't you think it's rather rough,
To know that she has thus crept in
To whiskey cock-tails, rum and gin,
    This naughty Dolly Varden.

The versifier, in answer to an imaginary correspondent, goes on to say: —

CLASSIE CLIFTON: — Don't worry us about the Dolly Varden mystery. Even before receiving your note of inquiry, we had subjected our file of Patent Office Reports to a rigid and searching scrutiny, but failed to find anything therein calculated to throw light on the subject. Your suspicion that the whole thing is an attempt on the part of dry-goods men to get off their old stocks of curtain calico is absurd. The specimens that we have seen are simply overskirts bound with satinet frills and cut with flowing sleeves, with nine flounces of plush lace worked on a crochet pattern. The whole is trimmed with a variegated bal masqué.

The young editor occasionally turned away from politics and nonsense to indulge his mood for poetry. Several creditable poems were the result of his stay in Savannah, the most characteristic, perhaps, being the following, written in 1870: —

JULIETTE

(Laurel Grove Cemetery, Savannah, Ga.)

Lo, here the sunshine flickers bright
    Among the restless shadows,
And undulating waves of light,
    Slip through the tranquil meadows.

The hoary trees stand ranged about,
    Their damp gray mosses trailing
Like ghostly signals long hung out
    For succor unavailing.

And marble shafts rise here and there
    In immemorial places,
Embalmed in nature's bosom fair
    And chiseled with art's graces.

'T was here, Juliette, you watched the skies
    Burn into evening's splendor,
And saw the sunset's wondrous dyes
    Fade into twilight tender.

And saw the gray go out in gloom
    Upon the brow of Even,
And watched to see the young stars bloom
    In the far fields of heaven.

So comes the winter's breath; and so
    The spring renews her grasses —
I lift my dazzled eyes, and lo!
    The mirage swiftly passes.

SAVANNAH DAYS

Dear child! for many a weary year
The rose has shed her blossom
Upon the tablet resting here
Above thy tranquil bosom.

And many a season here hath brought
Processions of new comers,
And many a wonder death hath wrought
Through all these fervid summers.

And naught remains of thee, Juliette —
Thy face, thy form Elysian,
Save what the whole world will forget —
A dreamer's dubious vision.

In addition to his usual work when his editor-in-chief, Colonel Thompson, went away for his summer vacation, young Harris sustained the whole editorial burden of the paper, "in such a way," comments a fellow editor, "that no one can detect the least deterioration. . . . He can turn away from his mad pranks and give a fragment of real philosophy, or a bit of genuine pathos, showing how able and earnest he can be when he chooses."

Father's friends of those days were not confined entirely to the newspaper circle of Savannah and other towns; he was on pleasant terms with his fellow boarders at the "Florida House," the "select" boarding-house of the city, partaking somewhat of the character of a hotel, in that it accommodated both permanent and transient guests. During the

"Reconstruction Period" its assortment of visitors was varied and interesting — Federal officers, Freedman's Bureau officials, members of theatrical companies, correspondents of the leading Northern newspapers, all mingled there with native-born Southerners. Mrs. Coolidge, the proprietress, was a woman of tact and experience, and under her ministrations a spirit of courtesy and tolerance prevailed around the board in spite of a great variety of opinions and wide divergence of principles.

Mr. Louis Weber, of Arkadelphia, Arkansas, was one of the guests of the "Florida House" in those days, and came to be an excellent friend of the rising young journalist. Of their association, Mr. Weber says: —

"Sometime in 1870 there appeared at the table of the Florida House a new boarder who attracted my attention; he could not have been called good-looking, with his reddish hair and mustache, but there was about him something which drew my interest. I learned on inquiry that he was J. C. Harris, associate editor of the 'Savannah Morning News,' and the writer of pungent and witty editorial paragraphs, which were then quite a novelty, and had won for him from the State press the title of 'the brilliant paragrapher of the Savannah Morning News.'

SAVANNAH DAYS

"Mr. Harris was not long in becoming a favorite at the table of the Florida House; plain in attire, unpretentious, almost shy in his modesty, yet his appearance at the table always brought a smile of welcome and a challenge for humor and banter.

"I occupied the front room on the fourth floor, and when Mr. Harris came to board at the house he was given the room back of mine. Not long after he took up quarters with us, the door connecting our rooms was kept open. My business (that of drug clerk and prescriptionist) was very confining and I rarely got to my room before 11 o'clock at night; and as Mr. Harris's duties kept him up until nearly midnight, I usually waited for him to come in before I retired.

"Ordinarily we discussed the news of the day, or took up the criticism of some new book, reading to each other. As a general rule the occupants of our flat were well behaved and observant of the proprieties, but occasionally the 'boy' spirit would break out and we would have some 'fun,' as Harris expressed it.

"I remember one night when Harris came in about midnight and found me still up; his expression was, 'Let's have some fun — let's play minstrels.' So we placed the chairs in a row, and the 'end man' began his banter. But the racket did not continue very long before the opening of doors told us that our landlady was aroused, so out went the lights and we were in bed in a twinkling. The next morning an aged couple who occupied the room below expressed themselves very forcibly about 'those boys who keep people awake at night.'

"Another night when we were returning from our work, just as we met near the entrance to the house, we saw another boarder approaching from the opposite direction. Harris's quick suggestion was, 'Let's have some fun; take hold of Berryman's arms.' I took hold of one arm, and Harris took hold of the other, and together we 'assisted' our friend upstairs. There was no limit to our noise, but our friend Berryman protested in vain. Harris kept up a succession of loud orders to the supposedly intoxicated boarder: 'Berryman, keep quiet; you will wake up all the boarders!' 'Berryman, put down that umbrella, it's not raining in the house!' So up to the fourth floor continued the disorderly procession, and from all indications there might have been half a dozen persons 'assisting' poor, sober Mr. Berryman up the stairs. From the start, the martyr saw that expostulations were vain, so quietly contented himself with accepting the situation until he was released; and, 'You boys think you are so smart,' was the only thanks he gave us for our trouble.

"I give these instances to show the boyishness of Harris's nature, which had to break out at times, although this was not his usual manner. He was shy about making close friends, and outside the 'Morning News' office force and myself he had few associates of whom I knew. On Sundays when I was not on duty at the drug-store, we would usually take a stroll on Bull Street, which was Savannah's popular promenade.

"Mr. Harris was no politician, and at the time of our association he was clearly out of sympathy with the ways of the politicians. In 1872, when the Democratic Party in convention in Baltimore adopted the platform of the Liberal Republican Party and nominated Horace Greeley as its choice for President, there was a great deal of dissatisfaction among the Southern people. The 'Morning News,' at that time, was the leader of political opinion in Georgia, and the country press usually followed its guidance. Colonel Thompson was away on his vacation and the control of the editorial page was left to young Harris.

"The latter did not like this Greeley business at all, and he did his best to forget it, keeping busy with his witty paragraphs and other more interesting matter. The country press and the local politicians began to worry, but Harris said, 'Let them worry.' Then the politicians became insistent that the 'News' should take its stand for Greeley, and got Colonel Estill, the proprietor, stirred up, but Harris stood pat, telling Colonel Estill that he (Harris) was left in charge of the editorial department until Colonel Thompson's return, and that he would not come out for Greeley. About this time Colonel Thompson came back, and the next day the 'Morning News' advocated the election of Horace Greeley as President."

Mr. Weber finally moved to Arkadelphia and left his "chum" toiling away at the editorial desk. But the latter did not lose sight of the sharer of his "flat" and his Sunday promenades. In 1903 there came to Mr. Weber in his Arkansas home a photograph bearing "Red-Top" Harris's autograph, and the following lines: —

"See the sweet smile? It is one of his tricks.
He's awful cute, and most fifty-six!"

CHAPTER VIII

ESTHER LAROSE

AMONG the guests of the "Florida House" in 1870–73 were Captain Pierre LaRose and his wife, Mrs. Esther Dupont LaRose. Captain LaRose was, as his name implies, a Frenchman — a citizen of Canada — who owned extensive farm lands in the Province of Quebec. There his wife and their three children spent the summer, but Mrs. LaRose was in the habit of joining her husband every winter in Savannah.

Captain LaRose had for many years carried on his business in the United States. In the early fifties he owned two steamboats, the John Tracy and the Edmund Lewis, which plied between Albany and Hudson, New York. He and his wife were living in Lansingburg in 1854 at the time of the birth of their only daughter, Esther LaRose. During the war, Captain LaRose ran his boat, the John Tracy, from Washington down the Potomac, carrying Federal mail and transferring Confederate prisoners and wounded soldiers. The latter lay on deck in the blistering sun (there were no awnings), and one day some of these poor sufferers begged, in their agony, to be thrown overboard.

Captain LaRose at once complained, on their account, to the officer in charge, which caused the latter on the return of the boat to Washington to report the humane Canadian as a Southern sympathizer. Captain LaRose was promptly placed in confinement in the Old Capitol, but when his wife arrived from the North and explained the circumstances to President Lincoln, who granted her an interview, he was released.

After the war the French navigator sold the John Tracy and the Edmund Lewis, and invested his money in the Lizzie Baker, and established himself in Savannah. His boat plied between Savannah, Georgia, and Palatka, Florida, and usually the owner accompanied her on her trips, though always a licensed navigator was in charge.

Captain and Mrs. LaRose lived at the "Florida House" during the winter months, and they had known their fellow boarder, the associate editor of the "Savannah Morning News," for nearly two years before their daughter Esther, a young girl of seventeen, who had been in a convent school in St. Hyacinthe, Canada, joined them. The parents regarded their young friend as a journalist of ability and a man of excellent habits, so they placed no

obstacles in the way of a friendship between the
two young people. Esther — or "Essie," as she
was called — was well educated, sang and played
prettily, and spoke English with a noticeable ac-
cent. She was small, dainty, and coquettish; her
dark eyes sparkled with innocent mischief, and she
wore her brown hair in ringlets. Her mother dressed
'her with French taste, and the piquant combination of modish figure and simple convent manners
made a deep impression on the young originator of
the "P. G. in G." The "Dolly Varden" costume
of the period must have been exceedingly becoming
to a young girl of Esther's type. Joel evidently
thought so, for after becoming well acquainted with
her he celebrated her appearance in a poem called

AN IDYL OF THE PERIOD

Oh, surely you have met her
At the Park or on the street —
She wears her hair in jaunty curls
And dresses deuced neat.

Her Grecian bend's a bouncer,
And her hat's the merest scrap
Of silk and straw and ribbon — but,
She does n't "care a snap."

She sports a Dolly Varden
Of yellow, red and green,
And skips along in bronzed bootees,
The neatest ever seen.

[111]

When she thrids the crowded pavement,
You can hear her flounces flap,
As she boldly swings her parachute,
But she does n't "care a snap."

The boys call her "a stunner,"
And many a love-lorn chap
Tips his beaver as she passes — but,
She does n't "care a snap."

And her epitaph will be,
When Death's cold hand shall rap
Upon her varnished chamber door:
"She never cared a snap."

ALEXIS.

The young rhymester probably admired Esther's
beauty more than he did her independence. She
had many "beaux," and could afford not to "care
a snap!" As time passed and Joel's interest deep-
ened into love, he had reason to believe that the
young girl favored him, but his native modesty and
lack of self-confidence kept him from pressing his
suit as ardently as a bolder lover might have done.
So when the sultry summer days approached, he
suffered the deep chagrin of seeing Esther depart
for Canada without having gained from her the
ultimate word.

It was natural that in this dilemma the morti-
fied lover should turn to his friend and confidant,
Louis Weber, and the latter tells how on one of

their customary Sunday promenades they turned aside into one of the beautiful old cemeteries of Savannah, and there, seated on a flat, weather-scarred tombstone, Joel unburdened himself. Probably the mere act of disclosing his love to a third person inspired the young man with the confidence he had lacked, for he very soon wrote to Esther and expressed himself in the manliest and most unmistakable terms: —

I began a journal the day after you left, and I have religiously put in its pages all my feelings and fancies. It was my intention to send you the journal for each week, instead of letters, but on reading it over, I find it contains much that would fail to interest you and much that I do not desire you should see, except under certain contingencies; and it depends on future developments whether I send it to you at all, or whether I consign it to the bottom of my waste-basket, along with a lot of other memorials.

I confess to you that I write this letter with many doubts and misgivings. I of course remember very distinctly that you said you would be glad to hear from me; but I also remember very distinctly that you contradicted yourself on several other occasions. However, you have the consolation of knowing that you need not reply unless you choose to do so. I can easily tell from the tenor of your reply — should you deign to favor me with one — whether or not you really desire to correspond with me, and I shall govern myself accordingly.

The week has been very dull to me, and I have spent my leisure time either in bed or in aimlessly wandering about the house. The parlor has a funereal appearance — the old sofa looks grief-stricken — the flowers on the center-table are withered — everything is gloomy. Even the pictures on the walls look down upon me mournfully as if they would say, "What have you done with her?" The rustle of the curtains sounds like a sigh, the piano is silent and everything wears an air of desertion.

Well, those who go are happier than those who stay, and I sincerely trust that you have not experienced that sense of utter loneliness which you left behind you.

There is no news to write, and if there was I would n't write it. Before I settle down to a regular correspondence — before I write you any of those long letters for which my friends give me credit — before I send you my journal — we must come to some understanding. You must answer my question. You can't put me off any longer. If it is, "No," so be it. Anything is better than this suspense. Don't say, "Yes," unless you mean it. *That* would be infinitely worse than "No" — would cause more misery hereafter than a thousand "noes." Be candid with me and settle the matter. You know very well that I love you. You know that I love you earnestly and seriously. You know that I am incapable of trifling with you. Knowing all these things, it is your *duty* to tell me whether you love me or not. If I am worrying you about this remember it is your own fault. You have given me every reason to believe that you *do* love me — otherwise I would never have confessed my own love for you. If you do *not* love me, your actions have been very remarkable — so remarkable, indeed, that I shall be quite at a loss to account for them.

You will observe that I am not writing from a sentimental point of view, and you may be surprised that I can express my love for you in such a plain, matter-of-fact way. The truth is, my love for you is plain, simple and direct, and is as far removed from that wild passion that develops itself in young men in their teens as anything possibly can be. It is faithful, tender and true; but it is not at all wild or unreasoning. If you were to ask me *why* I love you, my answer would be something like this: "Principally, my dear, because I can't

help it." And then you would look doubtful. Well,
so it is.

There is nothing in the world I desire so much as
to promote your happiness, and for that reason I
would not have you tell me "yes" unless you are
absolutely sure that you love me. Love is said to
be exceedingly selfish, but mine is not. I would
sacrifice my own happiness any day to secure yours.
I feel that there is nothing within the range of possibility that I would not do to make you happy —
and therefore it is that I know I love you truly.

Joel overcame his doubts about the expediency
of sending the "journal," and it followed the letter
in short order: —

JOURNAL TO ESSIE

Sunday, June 2, 1872

According to promise, I begin this evening a
journal of facts and fancies which I hope will interest you as much to read as it will me to write. I
daresay you will find it dreary enough. Men never
were and never will be good letter-writers. They
lack the intuitive tact and delicacy of woman.
They are bunglers at best — these men; and one of
their rough, off-hand letters, compared to the fancy-
laden missives that have their birth on the per-

fumed writing-desks of the ladies is as iron ore to exquisitely carved gold. In reading these prosy jottings then, I trust you will remember under what disadvantages, doubts and misgivings they are written. When you grow tired of them, you have only to give me a shadow of a hint to that effect, and they will be discontinued. They are written simply and solely for your pleasure, and because I — well, there is no use in worrying you with that old story again. If what I write will serve to fill up an idle moment in your life, or cause you to remember the friend you have left behind, I shall be amply repaid. It may be, however, that surrounded by your friends, acquaintances and relatives, you will have but little leisure and less inclination to let your thoughts drift Southward. Well, if it be so, so be it. I envy from my soul those who can forget, and pity those who remember. I read some verses in a newspaper the other day, that struck me quite forcibly. They were poor enough in their way, and yet the burden of the song was unspeakably touching. It ran in this wise: —

> "The world is round, the world is wide
> And hearts oft go astray —
> Yet those that go are happier
> Than those poor hearts that stay."

[117]

JOEL CHANDLER HARRIS

The verse is bungling and awkward, but the pathetic truth it contains lights it up with something nearly akin to the gleam of poetry. I sincerely trust that you are happier to-day than your friend who is writing these lines.

When you left yesterday, I was in my room — perfectly miserable. I did not realize the fact that you were really gone until I heard Mr. Weber tell you good-bye, and then — but it is useless to talk about it. *You are gone,* and all that I might say would fail to bring you back. I wanted to tell you good-bye, but I knew I would have to hide my real feelings and say something commonplace. I despise and detest those false forms of society that compel people to suppress their thoughts. If I had taken hold of your hand in parting I would have felt an irresistible desire to tell you how thoroughly miserable I was — how blank and desolate my life would be without you — and how patiently and faithfully I should watch and wait and long for your return. — I daresay you are laughing at me as you read. Well, laugh while you may. Some day you will discover that true love does n't grow upon trees. — But I am growing tedious. Good-night and pleasant dreams!

ESTHER LAROSE

Monday, June 3, —

I did not write all my experiences of yesterday. Somehow or other I have a suspicion that you will grow tired of my interminable small-talk, and this suspicion may cause me to omit from my scribblings many little occurrences that would be likely to interest you. I can judge, however, from your reply whether my long-drawn-out epistle is appreciated or not. If you write me a short, unsatisfactory letter, I will take it for granted that my so-called "Journal" is rather too prosy to suit your taste, and I will immediately cut it down to something like a sensible length. But, somehow, when I write to you, my ideas seem over-active and spin out into words with unusual facility. That must be my excuse, and if my poor words worry you, I can easily curb my "eloquence" (?).

Last night all through my sleep I saw a steamer tossing on the green waves, and a little girl on deck looking toward the South she was leaving behind. Alas! dreams are not true any more, and I doubt if the little girl turned her thoughts backward one time. She was glad enough to fly from the sultry heats of our languid summer.

I came downstairs this morning at the usual hour, and sat down in the accustomed place on the back porch. Once or twice I caught myself watching and listening for you. The parlor looked as gloomy as a grave. The sofa where we used to sit had a melancholy, desolate appearance, and the piano seemed to be ready to give out the most heartrending sounds. Even the curtains moved back and forth with a gentle, rustling sigh, and the pictures on the walls seemed ready to ask in querulous tones, "Where is she?" The very chairs looked lonely; the figures on the carpet seemed to be faded; and the flowers on the centre-table were dry and withered. The whole house is changed— the very air is full of regret. Something is wanting, and that something, *ma chère amie*, is yourself.

— By-the-by, these pages are not intended to be a journal of events. Far from it. They are intended to be a transcript, simply, of my thoughts and feelings, and they are written for no eyes but yours and mine — though I have no objection to your showing them to your mother. I shall write nothing that I desire to be kept from her. I may write some very foolish things, but nothing that it would be desirable to keep from her.

Joel's advice to Esther regarding the confidence that she owed her mother was typical of the absolute clarity of his nature. Then, and always, deception of any kind was a thing abhorrent to him. A love so guileless and self-effacing does not always meet with the appreciation it merits, but in this case, as in all the important crises of his life, destiny favored Joel (or, as he would have put it: "Providence took a hand"), and the woman he loved gave him the sign he craved.

A letter dated in January of the following year from Atlanta, where he had gone for a brief stay, gives untrammeled expression to his feelings: —

MY OWN DARLING: Contrary to promise and much to my regret, I could not write to you yesterday evening. When I arrived here, I found our interests in a precarious condition and I was compelled to set to work at once to recover lost ground. And yet I fear that I worked in a listless sort of way, for through it all my thoughts were continually recurring to you. I am afraid that some of the men who talked to me will think I am decidedly a strange fellow, for their conversation was all gibberish to me, and I found myself continually lapsing into listlessness.

To me, all that they said bore but one burden and that was you. It seemed as if I were dreaming, and my desires took but one shape — namely: the desire to be with you. Coming up·on the cars I really had the blues, — the first in years, and they were truly bluer than the bluest. I find I can have no pleasure at all away from you, and I shudder to think how dreary and how desolate my life would be without you. I think I have realized, in the past few hours, something of the unutterable sadness and loneliness that would be mine were we, by any mishap to be parted. . . . I have faith in you, and yet I sometimes ask myself if it is really true that you love me. There is no outright distrust, mind, but I often wonder if it *can be really true* that you care for such an awkward, unpolished person as myself. It seems so odd.

I feel and know that I am utterly unworthy of you, and I can thoroughly appreciate the sacrifice you will make in marrying me, when you might do so much better; but if there is any merit in love, then I am meritorious, for, my darling, I love you. I have no ambition that is not somehow connected with you and no thought that is not wholly yours. With you, I am happy and content —without you, I should be miserable indeed.

A few days later, he again writes: —

MY OWN DARLING: You cannot imagine — indeed you cannot — how very welcome your letter was. . . . My whole existence is so completely wrapped up in you that I would not care to live

ESTHER LaROSE HARRIS
Savannah, 1873

away from you. You often call me independent,
but, my darling, you never made a greater mistake.
I bluster about a good deal, but I am so wholly
and completely yours that I *could not give you up.*
. . . Waking or dreaming it is the same, and all
through the long days and longer nights your dear
face is constantly before me. The experience of
the past few days has taught me how impossible
it is for me to be happy away from you. I mix and
mingle with the larger crowd here, and my friends
show me every attention, but it is of no use. What
do I care for them?

The marriage of Joel and Esther took place in
Savannah, April 21, 1873, and the young man, who,
though rarely gifted and already widely known in
his profession, was yet so mistrustful of his own
merits and so sincerely convinced of his lack of
those superficial qualities which the world values,
entered into a companionship which, until the day
of his death, was to encourage his belief in himself,
to protect him from the inconsiderate intrusion of
the thoughtless, to relieve him of the undue pressure of irritating daily routine, and to surround him
with the affection and cheer and sympathy that
his sensitive nature so deeply craved. His Esther's
sprightliness acted as a curb to his more introspec-

tive tendencies; his timidity found relief in her self-possession; and her buoyancy and common sense helped him over many a crisis, both in his domestic and professional affairs.

In August the young wife visited her parents in Canada, and Joel later joined her for his vacation. The winter passed uneventfully for the young couple, and they had the pleasure of reading from the pen of a fellow journalist that, "Marriage has not quenched or dulled Harris's wit; he has launched out lately in a saucier and spicier style than ever"; and their friend, Henry W. Grady, wrote in his columns: "Marrying did n't do Harris a bit of good, but hanged if another twelve months don't tame him down. Just wait till *he* buys an eight-day ormulu clock!" [1]

[1] The wedding-present most in vogue in those days.

CHAPTER IX

EARLY DAYS IN ATLANTA

ON June 21, 1874, their first child, Julian LaRose, was born to Esther and Joel, and a little more than a year later, another son, Lucien, came to add to the happiness and responsibilities of the young parents. Father's love of children was one of his most marked qualities, and the development of these two little boys was a constant source of interest and delight to him. He once said: "I am fond of children, but not in the usual way, which means a hug, a kiss, and a word in passing. I get down to their level, think with them and play with them."

Later he was to express in his matchless stories his tenderness and sympathy for the universal child spirit, but even in the early days of his fatherhood, when it would have been but natural for his interest in childhood to confine itself to his own family circle, his love of young things was inclusive, and the joys and sorrows of youth moved him profoundly. One of his sweetest poems was occasioned by the death of a little girl, Addie Smith, of Blackshear, Georgia, who had relatives in Savannah. She was a child of unusual intelligence and had exhib-

ited a talent for writing. Father had been interested
in some of her little verses, and the news of her
tragic death by drowning while with a fishing party
on the Satilla River was a great shock to him. His
tribute to the child appeared in the "Morning
News" of June 24, 1876: —

IN MEMORIAM

(ADDIE E. SMITH, BLACKSHEAR, GEORGIA,
JUNE 24, 1876)

I

Dear child, a stranger mourning,
    Slips from the worldly throng
To weave and place beside thee
    This poor frayed wreath of song.

O'er him the seasons falter;
    The long days come and go,
And Fate's swift-moving fingers
    Fly restless to and fro.

O'er thee the west wind, sighing,
    Slow sways the slumbrous pine,
And through the shifting shadows
    The bright stars gently shine.

II

When springtime's murmurous gladness
    Filled all the listening air,
And old earth's rarest favors
    Bloomed fresh, and sweet, and fair;

When waves of perfumed sunshine
    Rolled o'er the ripening wheat,

EARLY DAYS IN ATLANTA

May laid her crown of blossoms
　　At Summer's waiting feet,

And Nature's pulses bounded,
　　As though infused with wine.
Life! was the season's token —
　　Life! was the season's sign.

And yet — ah, me! the mystery
　　Of this unbroken rest! —
June sheds her thousand roses
　　Above thy pulseless breast!

Bright hopes, nor fond endeavor,
　　Love's passion, nor Life's pain,
Shall stir thy dreamless slumber,
　　Or waken thee again!

The fragrance of the primrose
　　That opens fresh and fair
In the deep dusk of evening,
　　Still haunts the morning air.

The songs the wild bird warbles
　　With nature's art and grace,
Are wafted on forever
　　Through the vast realms of space.

Dear child, thy pure life's cadence —
　　A sad, yet sweet, refrain —
Shall wake the hearts now broken
　　To life and hope again —

And fall, a benediction,
　　When, at the day's decline,
Pale Sorrow, lowly bending,
　　Weeps at Affection's shrine.

JOEL CHANDLER HARRIS

It was in the same summer that a keen anxiety for his own children overtook him; the yellow-fever epidemic of 1876 broke out in August, causing consternation amongst the people of Savannah, and driving many of them to inland points. It was not possible for the young wife and her two babies to remain in the pest-ridden city, so there was no alternative for the provider of the family but to offer his resignation to Colonel Estill and hasten, with those dependent upon him, to the "high country." He had many acquaintances in Atlanta; there were well-established newspapers there; the city bade fair to be the most prosperous in the State; and its climate was notably healthy; so it was natural that the fleeing family should take refuge there.

The confusion and uncertainty of the moment must have been a sore trial to the young father, for it is not likely that he had been able to put aside funds against such an unexpected contingency. However, his sense of humor did not desert him, and when he arrived at the Kimball House he registered as follows: "J. C. Harris, one wife, two bow-legged children, and a bilious nurse." The party, so picturesquely described, remained at the hotel only long enough to get its bearings, but during these few days the Savannah editor's serene attitude in the face of uncertainty, and his fund of amusing anecdotes did so much to cheer up his fellow refugees and put their panic to flight, that when he asked for his bill he was told that he did not owe the hotel a penny. "Why, Mr. Harris," explained the manager, "we are indebted to you at least *three dollars worth*."

The Harrises left the Kimball House to accept the invitation of their old friends, Mr. and Mrs. James P. Harrison, to visit them at their home in Decatur, a few miles out from Atlanta. Mr. Harrison was then the editor of the "Christian Index and Cultivator," and father took up some work on this publication until he could reëstablish himself in his regular field.

One of his earlier friendships which he was now glad to renew was that with the talented young journalist, Henry W. Grady. They had become acquainted a few years before, when Grady, already editor of the Rome, Georgia, "Commercial," was only eighteen years old. Father described the circumstances of their first meeting as follows: —

"We had had some correspondence. Grady was appreciative, and whatever struck his fancy he had a quick response for. Some foolish paragraphs of mine had appealed to his sense of humor, and he pursued the matter with a sympathetic letter that made a lasting impression. The result of that letter was that I went to Rome, pulled him from his flying ponies, and had a most enjoyable visit. From Rome we went to Lookout Mountain (Tennessee) and it is needless to say that he was the life of the party. He was its body, its spirit, its essence.

"We found in our journey a dissipated person who could play the zither. Just how important that person became, those who remember Mr. Grady's pranks can imagine. The man with the zither took the shape of a minstrel, and in that guise he went with us, always prepared to make music, which he had often to do in response to Mr. Grady's demands." [1]

Mr. Grady had left Rome and established himself in Atlanta on the "Herald," which soon ceased publication. About this time (1876) Captain Evan P. Howell bought the controlling interest in the "Atlanta Constitution," and immediately offered Grady an editorial position. It was in the interim of the latter's departure from the "Herald" and his advent on the "Constitution," and shortly after father refugeed from Savannah, that the two friends met on the streets of Atlanta. It happened that Grady was in company with Senator Benjamin Harvey Hill, who, when he stood for Con-

[1] Introductory sketch to *Writings and Speeches of Henry W. Grady*, edited by J. C. Harris and published in 1890, by Cassell, New York City.

gress in the old Ninth District, had been the target
of some of the sharpest paragraphs of the "Savannah Morning News." It seems that during the
campaign Mr. Hill had been greatly annoyed by a
woman who dogged his steps and even tried to
force herself into his home. Among Harris's paragraphs was a pungent but good-natured reference
to this episode. The young writer had never met
Senator Hill, and when Mr. Grady presented him
to the Senator, mentioning that he was a yellow-
fever refugee, Mr. Hill drew out his pocketbook, and
taking from it the identical paragraph which had
so wittily commented on his dilemma, asked Harris
if he had penned it. Its author blushingly admitted
that he had. Upon which Senator Hill is reported
to have said: —

"Look here, young man, I own a block of stock
in the Kimball House, and you go there, register,
and tell the clerk to charge your board to B. H.
Hill just as long as you want to stay."

These may not have been his exact words, but
it was typical of the broad mind and keen appreciation of Senator Hill to enjoy a clever thrust even
when at his own expense.

The very day after Captain Howell engaged Mr.
Grady on the "Constitution," the latter carried
to his old friend, Joel Harris, an offer of twenty-

five dollars a week as editorial paragrapher. Colonel Thompson was anxious for father to return to the "News," but the epidemic had brought such disaster upon business in Savannah that he could not afford to offer the old salary, so it was decided that the Harris family should remain in the healthier atmosphere of the highlands. They therefore moved into an unpretentious five-room frame house on Whitehall Street, near the corner of Brotherton, and father took up his work on the paper which was to retain his services for a period of twenty-four years. Along with the paragraphing, he assumed the duties of telegraph editor, working a few hours at night, as there was little wire service then. This brought him an addition to his salary of five dollars a week.

His employment on the staff of the "Constitution" called forth many flattering notices from the Georgia press. I select one at random from the many at hand: —

For the past two or three weeks there has been such a decided improvement in the editorial conduct of the "Atlanta Constitution" as to occasion the especial comment of its readers. Its editorials are couched in such neat rhetorical utterances as to leave the impression that they are penned by a master hand. And this impression, it appears, is by no means erroneous. Mr. J. C. Harris, who made himself and the "Savannah

EARLY DAYS IN ATLANTA

News" so widely known, has been retained by the proprietors of the "Constitution," and will hereafter write
for that excellent journal. . . . We linger with delight
over Mr. Harris's paragraphic pleasantries descriptive
of events in Georgia, many of which paragraphs go
the rounds of the entire press of the country. His articles in review of the various social and political happenings of the day are remarkable for their clearness,
pungency and vigor, and would reflect credit upon a
much older man. As an essayist and book reviewer
we very much doubt if any excel him.

Shortly after the family settled in Atlanta, on
December 8, 1876, one day before father attained
his twenty-ninth birthday, a third son was born.
The baby was christened Evan Howell in honor of
the editor-in-chief of the "Constitution," who was
to become one of father's warmest and stanchest
friends.

As soon as the Whitehall Street home was made
comfortable, early in 1877, Grandmother Harris
came from Eatonton to join the family, and was
never separated from them again until the day of
her death. It can readily be imagined that the
Harrises were in narrow circumstances in those
days. One servant, Emma Beasley, a large mulatto
woman, lived in an outhouse on the place and did
the cooking and heavy work. The young wife knew
next to nothing about housekeeping or cooking, as

she had been brought up in ease and had never had to assist in the kitchen. In Savannah the family had boarded, so the necessity of being a "manager" never arose until she became the mistress of her own house with three small children to care for. [1]

It was a comfortable arrangement all round for Grandmother Harris to enter the family circle. She had remained in her little home in Eatonton during the years of Joel's apprenticeship at Turnwold, Macon, and Forsyth, except for one trip which she made to Randolph County, Alabama, to visit her sister. This was in war-times, and she wrote back to Joel that Yankee patrols sometimes came to their door and knocked, so near were they to the Federal outposts. Schooled by poverty, grandmother was the best of "managers," and

[1] Of these days mother says: "Even though I was doing without many things to which I had been accustomed, I did not feel poor, for I had 'father' and the children, and we were surrounded by refined people and good friends. The Howells were kind neighbors, and their children were devoted to little Evan, with whom they loved to play. Emma was a good cook and our meals though simple were well prepared. I still had plenty of good dresses from my trousseau and had them altered to fit the style. My parents were not able to help us then, for my father had lost his boat in the St. John's River. But even had it been otherwise Joel would not have accepted aid, for he was sensitive and independent. At one time, my father had offered to buy a newspaper for him in La Grange or Monroe, but Joel declined the offer."

knew all the ins and outs of domestic economy. It was she who taught her young daughter-in-law to cook and keep house, and her firmness and dignity were such that servants stood in awe of her.

She always kindled her own fire, for she was of the opinion that a negro servant scattered the ashes. On coming from Eatonton, she brought her feather bed with her, and she allowed no one but herself to "make" it. She kept her round, wicker sewing-basket near her rocking-chair and frequently busied herself with buttonholes for the children, using an open-top thimble; but she did not believe in "patching," as it was a "waste of cloth and thread"; and it remained for Grandmother LaRose, who had been more or less a "fine lady" all her life, to help "turn" garments and strengthen the weak places with squares of new material, when she came on occasional visits from Canada.

Grandmother Harris was fond of the children, but living alone had made her a little intolerant toward their boisterousness and mischievous ways, and she sometimes spoke severely to them. On the other hand, she told them stories of her childhood when she accompanied the family into Tennessee, through an Indian reservation; of how she rode on horseback and was not afraid of the red skins.

And she described how later when she lived all alone in the little house in Eatonton she kept a hatchet near her bedroom door for protection, and one night had occasion to throw it in the direction of a prowler who had "cut across" the backyard.

She added to an almost masculine courage a feminine tenderness for the glamour of the past, and after recounting adventurous episodes she sometimes drew from their hiding-place two jeweled garter-buckles which had belonged to her father, and a small medallion, containing a lock of his hair, and told the listening children how he had been a man of property until he gambled it away.

Of Grandmother Harris's appearance at the time they first met, mother says: "She was a woman of medium height, with a rather large frame; her dark hair [1] was parted in the middle, her eyes were hazel and her mouth was large. She wore percale house dresses made with 'paroda' waists and full skirts, and in winter a little shoulder shawl. Her best dress was made of black alpaca, cut in the same way. She never sat for a photograph, for, as she said, 'I have seen old photographs hidden away in attics or given as playthings to children.'"

From the first day of her entry into the family she

[1] In her youth Mary Harris's hair had been red, but following an attack of fever it turned quite dark.

JOEL CHANDLER HARRIS

Atlanta, 1877

was her daughter-in-law's firm friend. Although the least meddlesome of persons, when the occasion arose she was not afraid to speak her mind freely. In the South of those days newspaper men were more or less convivial, and for a time after settling in Atlanta father "drank with the boys" more than grandmother thought good for him. So she called him into her room one night and told him that the quality of his work was suffering, and that he now had three boys for whom he was responsible, and that she wanted him to leave off drinking altogether. He listened respectfully, took what she said in good part, and followed her advice.

Such was the family circle during the years between 1876–80 — years of strict economy and mutual sacrifice, but lightened by love and harmonious understanding. The first grief to overtake the household was the death in May, 1878, of little Evan Howell. Father had contracted measles, which he gave to all three children, and the baby never recovered from the effects of this disease. He was taken into the country for a change and given the best medical attention, but in his weakened condition he fell a victim of the maladies of teething, and his little life flickered and went out.

The poor mother felt it was best to take Julian and Lucien to her parents in Canada for the hot summer months, and their father mourned the little one alone. In a letter written soon after mother's departure, he tells of his sad nightly home-comings, and of how in his dreams he hears the empty cradle rocking. Happily these dreams were not to endure, for another little baby came to fill the cradle in September of the same year, Evelyn, the fourth boy.

Early in 1879, in addition to his other work, father was conducting a column called "The Lounger" in the weekly "Sunday Gazette," in which he wrote on nature, literature, the stage, and topics in general. This brought in a welcome increase to the family funds and earned much appreciation from the public. The column was a favorite not only with the subscribers of the "Gazette," but of a wider circle. An appreciative reader comments: —

These paragraphs are written in a style singularly easy and elegant . . . there is no name attached to the "Lounger's" column, but there is only one man in Georgia who could have written them — Joel Chandler Harris. . . . There is about them something which reminds me of the best English writers of a generation ago. Indeed, they are strongly like the essays of Charles Lamb, and have, at the same time, a crispness — a touch of the dramatic — which we have seen nowhere but in Bret Harte.

Particularly interesting, in that it demonstrates

EARLY DAYS IN ATLANTA

the strong sense of responsibility which father always brought to his work, was a paragraph, devoted to the function of an editor, which appeared in "The Lounger": —

An editor must have a purpose. He must have in view some object beyond the mere expression of an opinion or the publication of a newspaper. The purpose may be moral, social or political, but it must be well defined and pursued constantly. I shudder when I think of the opportunities the editors in Georgia are allowing to slip by. It grieves me to see them harping steadily upon the same old prejudices and moving in the worn ruts of a period that was soul-destroying in its narrowness. Between you and me, there never has been a time when an editor with a purpose could accomplish more for his State and his country than just at present. What a legacy for one's conscience to know that one has been instrumental in mowing down the old prejudices that rattle in the wind like dry weeds! How comforting to know that one has given a new impulse to timid convictions! But an editor with a purpose can do more than this: he can sweep away all false conditions in society and politics and bring his fellows back to the sweet simplicity of the ancient days. Provided he be earnest. That is everything. What if it require a generation of time to reform a generation of men? The flight of a swallow is swift, but it conveys no idea of permanency. A good writer need not be an editor, but an editor needs to be a writer, and a vigorous one; but no gifts of intellect will compensate the lack of a purpose. Let him play the politician if he will, but always as an editor. In the South, John Forsyth made an impression that will be permanent; in the North, Samuel Bowles. These men were editors with a purpose, and whatever part they took in politics was subservient to that purpose. In the South to-day we sadly need the resurrecting hand of editors with a purpose; who will supply that need?

The answer to this question was soon to be furnished by the editorial work on the "Constitution" of Henry W. Grady and Joel Chandler Harris himself. The combination was a peculiarly happy one, for in the exercise of their respective talents they supplemented each ᴐother. A contemporary expressed it aptly when he said: —

On the "Constitution" we have two opposites, Harris and Grady. Harris is retiring, never speaking unless spoken to, but the words flow as freely from his pen as is possible. Grady, on the other hand, is gifted with extraordinary conversational powers; his tongue moves with the rapidity of a needle on a sewing-machine. But when he attempts to write, he is less facile, and sometimes the words stick.

The devotion of both men to their section was passionate without being irrational, and it bred in them an earnest desire for a complete reconciliation between the North and the South, and an obliteration of that bitter feeling remaining as an aftermath of Reconstruction days. Their patriotic impulses gave life and force to the editorial columns of the "Constitution," and won for it a national reputation as the most important organ of the "New South."

Grady was later to put to the service of his country his remarkable oratorical gifts, and in his famous speech before the "New England Society" in New York, in December of 1886, he did more, perhaps, than any other Southern man to bridge the gap created by war, and to rekindle feelings of mutual sympathy and tolerance. Harris, on the other hand, carried on the work of reconciliation with his pen, not only in the columns of the "Constitution," but later in his stories of Georgia life. It remained for his warm friend, Colonel Theodore Roosevelt, to say in an address on the occasion of one of his visits to Atlanta, during his term as President: —

"Where Mr. Harris seems to me to have done one of the greatest services is that he has written what exalts the South in the mind of every man who reads it, and yet what has not a flavor of bitterness toward any other part of the union. . . . There is not an American anywhere who, on reading his writings, does not rise up with a more earnest desire to do his part in solving American problems aright."

CHAPTER X

FATHER was in the habit of saying that his career as a writer was wholly "accidental." His insistence on this point was, of course, largely due to his humble estimate of his talents. But the lover of "Uncle Remus" who has fallen under the spell of the old man's humor, tenderness, and dramatic force, is inclined to disagree with the author's own theory of his success, and to believe that aside from all accidents, happy or otherwise, he was bound to fulfill his destiny as a creator of characters that "wind themselves around our hearts and owe little to circumstance."

After the enthusiastic reception by the public of two volumes of "Uncle Remus" stories, their author was asked to contribute to an "experience meeting" of writers in "Lippincott's Magazine." Under the title of "An Accidental Author," this is what he wrote, in part: —

The "Countryman" was published on a plantation, and it was on this and neighboring plantations that I became familiar with the curious myths and animal stories that form the basis of the volumes accredited to "Uncle Remus." I absorbed the stories, songs and

[142]

myths that I heard, but had no idea of their literary value until, sometime in the seventies, Lippincott's magazine published an article on the subject of negro folklore, containing some rough outlines of some of the stories. This article gave me my cue, and the legends told by "Uncle Remus" are the result. . . .

This was the accidental beginning of a career that has been accidental throughout. It was an accident that I went to the "Countryman," an accident that I wrote "Uncle Remus," and an accident that the stories put forth under that name struck the popular fancy.

It was some time in 1878 that there occurred in the course of father's work an incident which became the means of releasing this rich store of myths and legends which had slumbered for years in an obscure compartment of his memory. Sam W. Small had been conducting in the "Constitution" a column of anecdotes and sketches in which a negro character, "Uncle Si," figured. When the "Constitution" changed hands, Mr. Small withdrew from the paper, and Captain Howell applied to his new editorial assistant, asking him to carry on the series if possible. This, father was not inclined to do, but he agreed to furnish something in another line. "Uncle Remus's" songs, sayings, and fables was the result. Prior to this time father had contributed several "songs" in dialect to the "Constitution." The first of these was a "Revival Song," the one beginning: —

"Oh, whar shill we go w'en de great day comes,
Wid de blowin 'er de trumpits en de bangin' er de drums?
How many po' sinners 'll be kotched out late
En fine no latch ter de golden gate?
No use fer ter wait twel ter-morrer!
De sun must n't set on yo' sorrer,
Sin 's ez sharp ez a bamboo-brier —
Oh, Lord! fetch de mo'ners up higher!"

It appeared in the "Constitution" of January
18, 1877, and made a genuine "hit." In spite of the
fact that it was copied far and wide, in November
of the same year there was printed in the "Editor's
Drawer" of "Harper's Monthly" a mangled version of it, purporting to be the product of a man in
Ilion, New York. It was introduced with the following paragraph: —

From Ilion, New York, where they make so many
guns, comes this camp-meeting hymn of our colored
brethren.

In the Ilion version the second line read:

"Wid de blowin' of de *trumps* and de banging of de *guns*."

Needless to say, the dialect was absurdly garbled.

The "Constitution" carried the story of the
theft, and commented wittily on the changes from
the original: —

It will be noted that in Ilion "Uncle Remus" has been
re-inoculated with Fourth-of-July enthusiasm and has
been made to predict the opening of Judgment Day

with "de banging of de *guns*" — a sort of national salute to Gabriel and his "*trumps*," of which he will have a full hand, as we well know.

Other "songs" were contributed throughout 1877, and, as before stated, character sketches of the old man followed in 1878–79, together with the animal stories, including the one about the Tar-Baby. Of all the "Uncle Remus" legends written during twenty-five years and gathered into five separate volumes, the "Tar-Baby" story is perhaps the best loved. Father received letters about this story from every quarter of the civilized world. Missionaries have translated it into the Bengali and African dialects; learned professors in France, England, Austria, and Germany have written, suggesting clues as to its source; it has been used to illustrate points in Parliamentary debates, and has been quoted from pulpits and in the halls of Congress.

The great popular success of the legends was a matter of strange surprise to their author. It was "just an accident," he said; and added, "all I did was to write out and put into print the stories I had heard all my life"!

When asked by an interviewer if any particular negro suggested "the quaint and philosophic character which he had built up into one of the monuments of modern literature," he replied: —

JOEL CHANDLER HARRIS

"He was not an invention of my own, but a human syndicate, I might say, of three or four old darkies whom I had known. I just walloped them together into one person and called him 'Uncle Remus.' [1] You must remember that sometimes the negro is a genuine and an original philosopher."

On being asked how the legends happened to be put into book form, their author continued: —

"The representative of a New York publisher came to see me, and suggested an 'Uncle Remus' book. I was astonished, but he seemed to be in earnest, and so we picked out of the files of the 'Constitution' enough matter for a little volume, and it was printed. To my surprise, it was successful." [2]

The publishing firm was that of D. Appleton and Company, and its representative was Mr. J. C. Derby. The book appeared in December, 1880, and in the previous May the following letter was printed in the "New York Evening Post," in the columns of which paper many of the "Uncle Remus" stories had been copied: —

---

[1] Mr. J. T. Manry, who worked under father in the office of the *Monroe Advertiser* at Forsyth, is of the opinion that the name "Uncle Remus" was a souvenir of the Forsyth days. The "town gardener," who once belonged to Dr. A. H. Sneed, the village postmaster, was called "Uncle Remus," and Mr. Manry recalls that the old negro's name appealed to father's imagination at that time.

[2] Interview by James B. Morrow, syndicated in numerous newspapers.

UNCLE REMUS

A NOTE FROM "UNCLE REMUS"

To the *Editors of the Evening Post:*

I do not know whether the circulation of the "Evening Post" covers all creation, but I do know that since you were generous enough to take up Uncle Remus and introduce him to respectable literary society, so to speak, we have received more than a thousand inquiries covering the points given below. I mention this because it might seem to you that I am endeavoring to use your columns for advertising purposes — a suspicion which would do me injustice. . . . I feel that if the "Evening Post" had not taken up Uncle Remus, his legends would have attracted little or no attention; and but for a kind letter from Mr. —— I am sure I should not have had the courage to seek a publisher. The information is asked for by people who, almost without exception, say that they have seen Uncle Remus in the "Evening Post." I could not find time to reply to one twentieth of the letters.

In response, then, to these inquiries, will you permit me to state through your columns: —

1. That Messrs. D. Appleton & Co. will shortly issue "Uncle Remus's Folk-Lore" [1] in book form;

2. That it will be illustrated by Mr. Frederick S. Church;

3. That the series will not previously be completed in the "Atlanta Constitution."

Gratefully yours

J. C. HARRIS

ATLANTA, GA., May 19, 1880

[1] The volume referred to was issued under the title, "Uncle Remus: His Songs and His Sayings."

JOEL CHANDLER HARRIS

Father took great interest in the illustrations for the book, as will be seen from the following letters to Mr. Church:—

CONSTITUTION OFFICE,
ATLANTA, GA., May 17, 1880

MY DEAR SIR:—

Permit me, through you, to congratulate myself that you have consented to illustrate the plantation legends of Uncle Remus. I was afraid you were too busy to give your attention to such trifles. The success of the book will depend upon these illustrations, and I trust, therefore, that you will not enter upon it as a task, merely, or allow yourself to be hurried. Just such another opportunity of catching that incongruity of animal expression that is just enough human to be humorous— just such another opportunity of interpreting the roaring comedy of animal life— will never occur again while the world stands; and if you can succeed here as you have elsewhere (and as no other artist has ever succeeded) in catching and expressing the humor that lies between what is perfectly decorous in appearance and what is wildly extravagant in suggestion, your illustrations will be something more than memorable. If you will bear in mind that the stories are perfectly sane and serious— that they are related by the south-

ern negroes with all sincerity—you will have no
difficulty in catching the curious idea that underlies the legend.

The fox of the stories is the gray fox—not the
red. The rabbit is the common American hare.
The bear is the smaller species of black bear common in portions of Georgia and Florida.

I presume the Messrs. Appleton have left it to
your discretion as to whether the illustrations shall
be full-page or whether they shall be embodied in
the sketches. They should be profuse, in any event.

I must congratulate myself once more, and you
must permit me to say, in addition, that with your
name upon the title-page, I have no doubt of the
success of the book.

I send this through Mr. Derby.

Very truly yours

J. C. HARRIS

In the artist's reply he puts the question, "What
is your idea of 'Miss Meadows an' de gals'? . . .
perhaps they mean just *Nature*, in which case I
should depict them as pretty girls in simple cos-
tumes, making a charming contrast to the ludicrous
positions of the animals."

ʳ Father was greatly taken with this suggestion
of Church's, and he adopted it with characteristic

deference, again emphasizing his rôle as mere "compiler" of the stories: —

THE CONSTITUTION, ATLANTA, GA.
EDITORIAL ROOMS, June 11, 1880

MY DEAR MR. CHURCH: —

My relations toward the sketches you are illustrating are those of a compiler merely; consequently I cannot pretend to know what is meant by Miss Meadows. She plays a minor part in the entire series, as you will perceive when the concluding numbers have been sent to you. Why she is there, I cannot say, but your conception will give to the sketches a poetical color (if I may say so) which will add vastly to whatever interest they may have for people of taste. By all means let Miss Meadows figure as Nature in the shape of a beautiful girl in a simple but not unpicturesque costume. As it is your own conception, I know you will treat the young lady tenderly. How abundantly you justify my anxiety to get you to illustrate these queer relics! I feel sure that no one else would have ever dreamed of investing them with poetical interest. I trust you will not change your intention in this respect, but if you do, please let me know; otherwise, I shall allude to the matter in the preface, and give you due credit for the conception.

UNCLE REMUS

There are several sketches yet to come, but to save you the trouble of plodding through the MS., I will send the outlines to your address. I appreciate the difficulty of obtaining variety, but nevertheless I trust to your versatility to obtain more than twelve drawings. At the very least I hope you will be able to furnish an initial piece to each sketch. I wish you could get the photograph of Moser's ideal portrait of Uncle Remus, which I have already forwarded to the Appletons, and study the type so as to illustrate the story of the war which is to follow after the sketches in the volume. The story will afford you an opportunity to make at least two effective drawings.

Moser's conception of the negro is perfect, whatever technical defects there may be about it. Moser will make two drawings in wash; one a corn shucking scene and the other a plantation frolic — each illustrating a song. I wish you would see them when they get to New York, and tell me what you think of them. If they are not technically up to the mark, I don't want them engraved, but you can take the idea and work it over in your own style, the conception in neither case being original with Moser. Each is a part of my own memory and experience, and each has been drawn under my supervision. Thanking

[151]

you for your kindness in replying to my letter, I remain,

Yours very truly

J. C. HARRIS

The drawings were, after all, not entirely satisfactory. Father appreciated their fanciful charm, especially those in which "Miss Meadows an' de gals" figured, but the animal delineations fell short of what he had in mind; and in Mr. Moser's sketches of the negroes he found "the spirit good, but the art crude." Not until Mr. A. B. Frost brought the skill of his pencil and the inimitable inventiveness and vigor of his imagination to bear upon Brer Rabbit and Brer Fox did their "compiler" feel a thrill of satisfaction — I might say of enthusiasm. He expressed this later on when he wrote to Frost, "You have breathed the breath of life into these amiable brethren of wood and field.`. . . The book was mine, but you have made it yours, both sap and pith."

It seems a commonplace now to speak of the "success" of "Uncle Remus," since for two generations the old man and his "amiable brethren of wood and field" have been the dearest friends of thousands of children all over the world — for the book has been translated into many languages. But it may not be known that the collected stories were a conspicuous success from the day they appeared on the market. The book had· passed rapidly through four editions when Mr. Derby wrote, December 8, 1880, "The firm are well pleased with the success of 'Uncle Remus'. . . . Mr. Charles A. Dana, of the 'Sun,' told me in my office last week, ' " Uncle Remus " is a great book. It will not only have a large but a *permanent* sale.'" The book was favorably noticed in every paper of any importance in the country, and scientific publications devoted columns to its value as a contribution to folk-lore.

The stress laid upon this aspect of the stories always amused father. He once had occasion to write a review of some folk-tales of the South-west, and in this connection he said: —

"First let us have the folk-tales told as they were intended to be told, for the sake of amusement — as a part of the art of literary entertainment. Then, if the folk-lorists find in them anything of value to their pretensions let it be picked out and preserved with as little cackling as possible."

Certainly Uncle Remus was capable of following his own advice, for the quality most conspicuously absent from the tales is pedantry.

"It is but fair to say that ethnological considerations formed no part of the undertaking which has resulted in the publication of this volume," wrote the author ir the introduction to the "Songs and Sayings." Nevertheless, he had most carefully investigated the genuineness of all the tales, and in every case had sifted out the variants and had taken pains to retain the version which seemed to him most characteristic, after which he proceeded to give it "without embellishment and without exaggeration."

Whether or not father had anything more than a passing interest in folk-lore *before* the stories were published, he certainly made some study of the subject later on. He was a subscriber to the "Folk-Lore Journal," published in London, and his library was well stocked with the folk-lore of different nations; but never for one instant did the humorist and imaginative writer separate himself from his "bump of locality" and get lost in the complicated mazes of ethnic or philologic investigation, — for which let the sophisticated and overwise children of the present generation be duly grateful!

It may not be amiss to introduce at this point a letter written to an Englishman in 1883, since it refers to one of the stories in the "Songs and Sayings," the Appleton publication of 1880. The English edition of this volume was published in London in 1881 by David Bogue, and has, to this day, as devoted an audience as that of the American edition.

ATLANTA, GEORGIA, U.S.A.
1883: 28 June

DEAR SIR:

A note from Mr. Brander Matthews informs me that you are interested in at least one of the Uncle Remus legends — the Crayfish and the Deluge. The history of that legend, as far as my knowledge of its genuineness extends, is this: I heard it told a number of times from 1862 to 1865 on the Turner Plantation (Putnam County — Middle Georgia) each time by a negro. The Remus legends, it should be said here, were not written with an eye to their importance as folk-lore stories. I had no more conception of that than the man in the moon. The first one was written out almost by accident, and as a study in dialect. It was so popular that I at once began to ransack my memory for others. My friends ransacked their memories, and the result was the book as it is printed — and another volume still to be printed, specimens of which you will find in the July "Century Magazine." But in order to make assurance doubly sure, I took the pains to verify every story anew, and, out of a variety of versions, to select the version that seemed to be most characteristic of the negro: so that it may be said that each legend comes fresh and direct from the negroes. My sole purpose in this was to preserve the stories dear to Southern children in the dialect of the cotton plantations.

To return: The crayfish story was told me by negroes on the Turner Plantation many times during the war period. It was recalled to me by a suggestion from the Editor of the " Savannah Daily News," who overheard it on the coast, and by other friends, and I then searched for it until I found it among the negroes of this — the Northern — section of the state. Since the publication of the book I have found a variant in which the Mud Turtle is substituted for the Crayfish.

I enclose with this a letter written some weeks ago to Mr. Laurence Gomme. I had decided not to post it for fear that the gentleman might be disposed to regard it as a presumptuous effort to intrude the Remus book upon his attention — notwithstanding the fact that my relation to the stories is that of a compiler merely. Pray consider the letter as a postscript to this.

I shall be glad to give you any information you may desire in regard to the negro legends, or to serve you in any way, not merely because I am interested in the study of comparative folk-lore, but because the enjoyment I have obtained from some of your poems has made me your debtor.

Very truly yours

JOEL CHANDLER HARRIS

THE CONSTITUTION, ATLANTA, GA.
EDITORIAL ROOMS
ATLANTA, GEORGIA, UNITED STATES
9 June, 1883

DEAR SIR:—

I have just been reading in the "Folk-Lore Journal" "The Hare in Folk-Lore," by William George Black, F.S.A., and his treatment of the subject has suggested to me the propriety of calling your attention to my little book "Uncle Remus and his Legends of the Old Plantation." (London: David Bogue, 1881.)

It is a misfortune, perhaps, from an English point of view, that the stories in that volume are rendered in the American negro dialect, but it was my desire to preserve the stories as far as I might be able, in the form in which I heard them, and to preserve also if possible, the quaint humor of the negro. It is his humor that gives the collection its popularity in the United States, but I think you will find the stories more important than humorous should you take the trouble to examine them. Not one of them is cooked, and not one nor any part of one is an invention of mine. They are all genuine folk-lore tales.

Since the publication of that book, I have interested myself in the matter, and, with the assistance of friends and correspondents in various parts of the Southern states, I have been enabled to gather seventy or eighty new ones. Pardon this letter. I am interested in the negro stories only as their compiler.

Very truly yours

JOEL CHANDLER HARRIS

G. LAURENCE GOMME, F.S.A.
Editor Folk-Lore Journal, London.

Before leaving the subject of the first volume of "Uncle Remus" stories, I cannot refrain from quoting a paragraph of the introduction, in which father touches on the prowess of their hero, Brer Rabbit, proceeding to link up his salient characteristics with the psychology of the negro. It is in reference to the almost invariable conquest of the fox by the rabbit that the author says: —

"It needs no scientific investigation to show why he (the negro) selects as his hero the weakest and most harmless of all animals, and brings him out victorious in contests with the bear, the wolf, and the foe. It is not *virtue* that triumphs, but *helplessness;* it is not *malice,* but *mischievousness.*"

Indeed, the parallel between the case of the "weakest" of all animals who must, perforce, triumph through his shrewdness, and the humble condition of the slave raconteur is not without its pathos and poetry.

Finally, the reader not familiar with plantation life is counseled to "imagine that the myth-stories of Uncle Remus are told night after night to a little boy by an old negro who appears to be venerable enough to have lived during the period which he describes— who has nothing but pleasant memories of the discipline of slavery — and who has all the prejudices of caste and pride of family that were the natural results of the system." I have been asked many times if my husband, the eldest son of the family, was "the little boy" of the stories. He was not; and strangely enough, father never told these stories to his own or any other children. His rôle was to record, not to recount. In a letter to Joe Syd Turner, one of his old playmates, and the son of Joseph Addison Turner, of Turnwold, written in 1883, shortly before the publication of the second volume of "myths and tales of the old plantation," father said: —

"Did it never occur to you that *you* might be

JOEL CHANDLER HARRIS

the *little boy* in 'Uncle Remus'? I suppose you have forgotten the comical tricks you played on old George Terrell, and the way you wheedled him out of a part of his gingercakes and cider. Lord! those were the wonderfullest days we shall ever see."

CHAPTER XI

THE aftermath of the appearance of "Uncle Remus: His Songs and His Sayings," demonstrated to father, with peculiar force, one thing: that he was to be educated in the subject of folk-lore whether he willed it or not! I am certain that when "Uncle Remus" received his first greeting from the English-speaking public, his creator was ignorant of the fact that variants of the legend were to be found among so many of the primitive peoples.[1]

Concerning the number of communications from various parts of the globe which came on the heels of the first volume of tales, father once said: —

[1] In his admirable monograph on "Dialect Writers Since the Civil War," Professor C. Alphonso Smith, head of the Department of English of the United States Naval Academy, states that variants of the "Tar-Baby Story" have been found among the Indians of North America, the natives of the West Indian Islands, the Indian tribes of Brazil, the natives of Cape Colony, amongst the Bushmen, amongst the tribes of the lower Congo, in West Central Africa, amongst the Hottentots, and in the "Jatakas," or "Birth Stories" of Buddha. An officer of the United States Army stationed at Jolo, Philippine Islands, in 1907, wrote father that he had heard variants of the Uncle Remus stories from the Moros, a Mohammedan tribe inhabiting the lower islands of the Philippines. One of these legends, referring to the alligator, was recounted to this officer by Hadji Butu, chief adviser to the Sultan of Sulu.

JOEL CHANDLER HARRIS

"To be frank, I did not know much about folk-lore, and I did n't think that anybody else did. Imagine my surprise when I began to receive letters from learned philologists and folk-lore students from England to India, asking all sorts of questions and calling upon me to explain how certain stories told in the rice-fields of India and on the cotton-fields of Georgia were identical, or similar, or at least akin. Then they wanted to know why this folk-lore had been handed down for centuries and perhaps for thousands of years. They wanted to know, too, why the negro makes Brer Rabbit so cunning and masterful. These letters came from royal institutes and literary societies, from scholars and from travelers. What answer could I make to them? None — none whatever. All that I know — all that we Southerners know — about it, is that every old plantation mammy in the South is full of these stories. One thing is certain — the negroes did not get them from the whites: probably they are of remote African origin."

In the introduction to the first volume, father says in regard to his method of gathering the tales: —

I have found few negroes who will acknowledge to a stranger that they know anything of these legends; and yet to relate one of the stories is the surest road to their confidence and esteem. In this way, and in this way only, I have been able to collect and verify the folk-lore included in this volume.

In a letter, dated December 14, 1880, from James Wood Davidson, for whose volume, "Living Writers of the South," father had prepared an index when general factotum of the "Monroe Advertiser," the writer said of "Uncle Remus": —

"It is the only *true* negro dialect I ever saw printed. It marks an era in its line — the first successful attempt to write what the negro has actually said, and in his own peculiar way. After so many dead failures by a hundred authors to write thus, and after the pitiful *niaiseries* of the so-called negro minstrels, 'Uncle Remus' is a revelation."

Father, however, did not claim to be the pioneer in this field; he justly and generously maintained that the first accurate and artistic depicter of the negro was the young Texan, Irwin Russell, who died in the early days of his promise, and whose book of verses, "Christmas Night in the Quarters," portrays the negro with sympathy and fidelity. Father wrote the introduction to the edition of Mr. Russell's poems published in 1888, and in a letter to Miss Russell, thanking her for a photograph of her brother, he said of the latter: "No man the South has produced gave higher evidence of genius during a period so short and so early in life. . . . I have always regretted most deeply his untimely death. Had he been spared to letters, all the rest of us would have taken back seats so far as representation of life in the South was concerned."

But Irwin Russell made no attempt, in his short career, to perfect himself in the dialect of the negro. It was in the truth and flavor of negro characterization that he excelled. Either because of the fineness of his ear or the accuracy of his memory or the wonderful assimilative power of his mind, or the combination of all three, father obtained an early and a complete mastery of the dialects of the American negro. In an interview in 1881, Walter H. Page, now American Ambassador to the Court of St. James, says: "I have Mr. Harris's own word for it that he can *think* in the negro dialect. He could translate even Emerson, perhaps Bronson Alcott, in it, as well as he can tell the adventures of Brer Rabbit."

And Thomas Nelson Page, now American Ambassador to Italy, who has himself so beautifully depicted certain phases of life in the South during and following the Civil War, accurately appraised father's knowledge of the "old-time" negro and his vernacular when he wrote: "No man who has ever

written has known one-tenth part about the negro
that Mr. Harris knows, and for those who hereafter shall wish to find not merely words, but the
real language of the negro of that section, and the
habits of all American negroes of the old time, his
works will prove the best thesaurus." [1]

Such appreciations as this and others from his
colleagues were, of course, gratifying to father,
who, nevertheless, in his almost incredible humility,
was skeptical of all praise. But the tributes that
pleased him most were those that came from children, or from men and women who found their
childhood memories revived by these legends of the
old plantation. Amongst the latter is a note dated
November 27, 1880, from Alexander H. Stephens,
himself a Georgian and formerly vice-president of
the Confederacy, in which he says: "My father
had an old family servant whose name was Ben.
He came from Virginia, and was quite lame from
rheumatism, from my earliest remembrance. Often
have I sat up late at nights in his house, and heard
nearly every one of those stories about Brer Rabbit, Brer Fox, and Brer Terrapin, as you have reproduced them. In reading them, I have been
living my young life over again."

[1] "Immortal Uncle Remus," an article in the *Book Buyer*, December, 1895, on the appearance of the "Frost" edition of *Uncle Remus:
His Songs and His Sayings.*

JOEL CHANDLER HARRIS

And in a letter from Harry Stilwell Edwards, of Macon, Georgia, is found an interesting picture of a gathering on the plantation of one of his friends: "I had occasion to visit Miss —— on a distant plantation some days since, where I surprised a curious assemblage. The lady sat in the midst of a group of pickaninnies and was engaged in reading 'Uncle Remus' to the most delighted audience you ever saw: the little devils were grinning and giggling, the last mother's son of them, and my advent was doubtless the most unwelcome thing that could have happened. . . . The scene gave birth in my mind to many odd thoughts: a Southern girl reading to little negroes stories which had come down from the dead fathers of their race."

On an occasion when the creator of "Uncle Remus" was asked to give to a child an outline of a typical plantation legend, he took out his pad and wrote: —

"I remember the story where Brer Tarrypin wanted to learn to fly. He had seen Brer Buzzard sailing in the air, and thought he could sail, too. So he persuaded Brer Buzzard to take him on his back and give him a start. This was done. Brer Buzzard carried Brer Tarrypin in the air and dropped him. He fell, kerplunk, and nearly killed himself. He was very angry with Brer Buzzard, not because he failed to fly, but because Brer Buzzard failed to show him how to light. Says he: 'Flyin' is as easy as fallin', but I don't speck I kin learn how to light.'

"If you don't know what this means, ask some grown-up person. Before you begin to fly, be sure and learn how to light."

Following the appearance of "Uncle Remus" came many requests from editors for more of the negro tales, and in the "Century Magazine" for June, July, and August of 1881, appeared three stories under the title, "A Rainy Day with Uncle Remus." "Mr. Fox as an Incendiary" and "How Mr. Fox Failed to Get His Grapes" were those that appeared in the initial numbers of the "Critic" in February and April of 1881.

Sometime during the course of this year a letter had come from Mark Twain, expressing his admiration for "Uncle Remus," and proposing that father should visit him in Hartford at some early date, adding that he would like to discuss some outlines of negro fables which he had, one in particular being a "ghost story." Father replied to him as follows: —

JOEL CHANDLER HARRIS

The Constitution, Atlanta, Ga.
Editorial Rooms 4 August, 1881

My dear Mr. Clemens: —

You have pinned a proud feather in Uncle Remus's cap. I do not know what higher honor he could desire than to appear before the Hartford public arm-in-arm with Mark Twain. Everybody has been kind to the old man, but you have been kindest of all. I am perfectly well aware that my book has no basis of literary art to stand upon; I know it is the matter and not the manner that has attracted public attention and won the consideration of people of taste at the North; I understand that my relations toward Uncle Remus are similar to those that exist between an almanac-maker and the calendar; but at the same time I feel very grateful to those who have taken the old man under their wing.

The ghost story you spoke of is new to me, and if I dared to trouble you I would ask you to send me the outlines so that I might verify it here. I do not remember to have heard it, but I do not by any means depend upon my own memory in matters of this kind. It is easy to get a story from a negro by giving him a sympathetic cue, but without this it is a hopeless task. If you have the story in manuscript, I would be very grateful to you for a sight

of it; if not, I will try and find it here in some shape
or other.

While I am writing, I may as well use the gimlet
vigorously. — I have a number of fables ready to
be written up, but I don't want to push the public
to the wall by printing them in the magazines
without intermission. I must ask your advice.
Would it be better to print the new fables in a volume by themselves, or would it be better to bring
out a revised edition of Uncle Remus, adding the
new matter and issuing the volume as a subscription book? I am puzzled and bothered about it.

Glancing back over these two sheets, I am compelled to admit that you have escaped lightly.
Nevertheless, you cannot escape my gratitude for
your kindness to Uncle Remus.

Sincerely yours

JOEL CHANDLER HARRIS

In his reply, Mr. Clemens commented on his
friend's modest estimate of his abilities: —

"You can argue *yourself* into the delusion that
the principle of life is in the stories themselves and
not in their setting, but you will save labor by stopping with that solitary convert, for he is the only
intelligent one you will bag. In reality the stories
are only alligator pears — one eats them merely for

the sake of the dressing. 'Uncle Remus' is most deftly drawn and is a lovable and delightful creation; he and the little boy and their relations with each other are bright, fine literature, and worthy to live. . . . But I seem to be proving to the man that made the multiplication table that twice one is two."

Mr. Clemens offered some advice regarding the publishing of a second volume of tales and sent the outline of the "ghost story" (called in his version "The Golden Arm"), which had been told him in childhood by his "Uncle Dan'l," a slave of sixty years, before the flickering blaze of a kitchen fire. Father was familiar with a variant of this story and afterward developed it in the dramatic "Ghost Story" told by 'Tildy, and incorporated in "Nights with Uncle Remus." Mr. Clemens was anxious for father to appear with him in readings, and followed up this letter with a request that father meet him in New Orleans, where he was to stop for a few days in the course of a trip down the Mississippi River with Mr. Osgood, the publisher, to discuss this and other matters. Father replied: —

I will gladly meet you in New Orleans unless some unforeseen contingency should arise. In regard to my diffidence, I will say that the ordeal of appearing on the stage would be a terrible one, but my experience is that when a diffident man does become familiar with his surroundings he has more impudence than his neighbors. Extremes meet. At any rate, your project is immensely flattering to me, and I am grateful to you for even connecting me with it in your mind. I appreciate the fact that, if successfully carried out, it would be the making of me in more ways than one. It would enable me, for one thing, to drop this grinding newspaper business and write some books I have in mind. I only hope you will see your way clear to including me in the scheme in some shape or fashion. A telegram three or four days in advance of your arrival in New Orleans will enable me to be on hand promptly; and you might mention the name of the hotel provided you settle that matter in advance also.

Gratefully yours
JOEL CHANDLER HARRIS

In his "Life on the Mississippi," Mr. Clemens tells of this meeting in the chapter entitled "Uncle Remus and Mr. Cable": —

We were able to detect him among the crowd of arrivals at the hotel counter by his correspondence with a description of him which had been furnished us from a trustworthy source. He was said to be undersized,

[171]

red-haired and somewhat freckled. He was the only man in the party whose outside tallied with this bill of particulars. He was said to be very shy. He is a shy man. Of this there is no doubt. It may not show on the surface but the shyness is there. After days of intimacy one wonders to see that it is still in about as strong force as ever. There is a fine and beautiful nature hidden behind it, as all know who have read the Uncle Remus book; and a fine genius, too, as all know by the same sign. I seem to be talking quite freely about this neighbor: but in talking to the public I am but talking to his personal friends, and these things are permissible among friends. He deeply disappointed a number of children who had flocked eagerly to Mr. Cable's house to get a glimpse of the illustrious sage and oracle of the nation's nurseries. They said: —

"Why, he's white!"

They were grieved about it. So, to console them, the book was brought, that they might hear Uncle Remus's Tar-Baby story from the lips of Uncle Remus himself — or what, in their outraged eyes, was left of him. But it turned out that he had never read aloud to people, and was too shy to venture the attempt now. Mr. Cable and I read from books of ours, to show him what an easy trick it was; but his immortal shyness was proof against even this sagacious strategy, so we had to read about Brer Rabbit ourselves.

As for the project of a joint appearance before the public of these three well-known writers, — a project which had so appealed to father in the first place, — it never came off. It was inevitable that the impediment in his speech and his "immortal shyness" should combine to make it impossible for "Uncle Remus" to recount the exploits of "Brer Rabbit" from the platform.

The success of the first book and the consequent addition to the income of the family was not the only conspicuous piece of good fortune that visited the household during the closing months of 1879 and the year of 1880. On December 29th of the former year the birth of their first daughter, Mary Esther, brought great joy to her parents. Father, especially, had ardently wished for a little girl, and the realization of his hopes at a time when his success as a writer seemed assured must have appeared to him as a peculiarly happy omen.

The time soon came when three vigorous boys and a little baby sister filled every nook and cranny of the Whitehall Street cottage, and the state of the small house resembled somewhat the simmering kettle that threatens to boil over. Acting on Captain Howell's advice, father therefore began negotiations for the purchase of five and a quarter acres of land, on the western outskirts of the town; it was known as the "Broomhead property," and upon it there already stood the crude shell of a home. The land bordered on a fine tract of pine woods, sloped agreeably from the rear toward the street; was across the road from a beautiful spring; and seemed in every way desirable for the home of a growing family. The price of the land was twenty-five hundred dollars, and arrangements were made by means of which monthly payments could be made on it.

Mother had always wanted a spick and span new house, and when father took her to West End for the first time to inspect the property, she was on the verge of tears. The original three-room house had been built in a hit-or-miss style, and the person who owned it immediately before it came into father's possession had confirmed its nondescript character by adding three rooms in front. It was in a ramshackle condition when mother first saw it — full of rat holes, and almost hidden from view by a crop of giant ragweeds. The interior had been rendered lugubriously hideous by an application of dark green paint. The kitchen was in the basement, and its only means of connection with the dining-room was by a flight of steep narrow stairs.

The young wife's disappointment was somewhat modified by the attractive nature of the surroundings, the health-giving aroma of the nearby pine woods, and the feeling of space; and she philosophically looked forward to various improvements as soon as the family purse warranted. So the rat holes were mended, plenty of whitewash was applied, and the forlorn house was made habitable if not beautiful. The family moved in toward the end of the summer of 1881.

At this time the street cars stopped several blocks short of the house, and every morning at half-past eight o'clock father walked through the oak grove which lay between the house and the end of the car line, and boarded the little mule car which landed him, after a leisurely half-hour's ride, near the "Constitution" office. Arriving there, the associate editor first attended a sort of "staff frolic" in the editorial rooms, as it was Mr. Grady's habit to devote the first few moments of the day to an exchange of pleasantries which sometimes culminated in a gale of fun; for Grady, Howell, and Harris relished a spicy joke or a rollicking story as a gourmand relishes his *hors d'œuvres*. After this breezy prelude came the real editorial parley. If a "policy" was outlined by the directorate of the paper, father listened attentively and went about his work unhampered by explicit directions, for his colleagues knew his temperament and were satisfied that no mistakes would be made in the execution of their suggestions.[1]

[1] The editorials in the *Constitution* that afforded father the most pleasure in the writing were those that partook of the character of

[175]

JOEL CHANDLER HARRIS

At noon father left off work and jogged back to West End behind the street-car mules with their jangling bells. He was well acquainted with the drivers, "Grandpa" Bennett, "Dutch" Reynolds, "Bill" Plunkett, and others, and many a time at the noon hour he took the reins from the driver who happened to be in charge, and guided the animals while their erstwhile master emptied his lunch-basket. If the meal was in progress when the car arrived at the end of the line, father would get down, uncouple the linch-pin, lead the team around front, couple up again, and turn the conveyance over to "Grandpa," "Bill," or "Dutch," as the last drop of buttermilk — often furnished by mother — or crumb of corn-pone disappeared; then away through the oak grove and across the terraces to his own midday meal. After an hour's rest he was ready to return to the office, where he worked until late in the afternoon. His stories were written at home during the evenings, usually

essays, on subjects such as "Bird Songs," "The Old Letter Box," "Knowing Your Neighbors," "A Melodious Mimic," "Water-ground Cornmeal," etc. Of these his old friend, Thomas E. Watson, the author of the *Story of France*, wrote him: "Why have you never scrapped up a selection of those little prose-poems you wrote when you first went to the *Constitution*? I remember also those sketches of the country post-office in Putnam County, and I still think that Bret Harte wrote nothing better. A volume of such selections would go down to future generations along with Irving's *Sketch-Book*."

in his bedroom, at a plain pine table, but sometimes
by the fireside in the family sitting-room.

Of the impression made, at this time, by father
upon a stranger, Mr. Walter H. Page, who called
upon him at the "Constitution" office, gives a
picturesque account: —

Passing through a dingy doorway and ascending two
flights of more dingy stairs, I entered a still more dingy
room, on the door of which a dingy placard was stuck,
with this information, "Editorial Rooms." And there
I found an individual apparently at sea in an ocean of
exchanges, but quite calmly smoking a cigar, with the
air of a man who owns the whole day and has no need of
haste. I thought he must be the "devil" of the office
who was amusing himself with yesterday's papers before the gentlemen came down.

"Is Mr. Harris in?"

"Yes."

"I should like to see him."

"My name is Harris."

"I mean Mr. Joel Harris, one of the editors of the
'Constitution.'"

A sly twinkle came into the fellow's eye as he rose
and asked, "What may I do for you?"

"Are you the author of 'Uncle Remus'?"

A little laugh bubbled up inside him, he extended his
hand, offered me a seat, and looked as much confused
as I felt. I must have said something about how much
delight Boston people had got from "Uncle Remus,"
for he replied, with a blush and much confusion: —

"They have been very kind to 'Uncle Remus.'"

It was impossible to believe the man realized what he

had done. I afterwards discovered that his most appreciative friends held the same opinion: that Joe Harris does not appreciate Joel Chandler Harris. . . .

A little man, just turned thirty-one, with red hair, a fiery, half-vicious mustache, a freckled face and freckled hands. His eyes are all that belong to Mr. Joel C. Harris; all other things, hair, complexion, hands, chin and manner, are the property of Joe Harris.[1]

Father, was of course, unknown to me in those days, but I suspect that Mr. Page's picture was a fairly accurate one, with the exception of a single detail — the *hands*, which this description slights. Father's hands were the most beautiful I have ever seen — small, sensitive, perfectly modeled, and scrupulously cared for.[2]

The first spring after the family moved to West End, there was laid out a garden, which occupied

[1] "The New South," *Boston Post*, September 28, 1881.

[2] The adjective "unkempt" was once or twice applied to father's appearance by interviewers. This was misleading. He was, on the contrary, exquisitely neat, and even fastidious in the choice of his clothing. His suits were always of the best material and excellently tailored, and even on the hottest summer day he looked fresh and comfortable. It may be recalled that back in the days when he was a poor young journalist in Forsyth, Mr. Manry noticed his "fine, white, pleated shirts, and English socks of the best quality." On this point mother says: "When Joel was a young man he kept up with the fashion, his best suit being, in the style of those days, a cutaway coat and vest of black cloth and trousers of dove-colored material. His business suits were of dark material. As he grew older he became averse to changing from one style to another, but he was always scrupulously neat."

CHLOE

For many years the milker at West End. Often mentioned in the stories and letters

a large portion of the western side of the property. The master of the house was always greatly interested in its cultivation, and one year, amongst other produce, one hundred and seventeen bushels of sweet potatoes were raised. There were three cows which found abundant pasturage in the Bermuda lot back of the house, and the children gradually accumulated all kinds of pets.

"Mandy" Henderson presided over the kitchen, and her sister Mattie, later a "spiritual healer," was the nurse. Chloe Henderson came from her home in the country twice a day to milk the cows, walking two miles down what is now the Cascade Road to West End. Chloe was a "character," and undoubtedly furnished father with material for many of his stories. She was very religious and could not be persuaded to live out of sight of her church, the "Philadelphia Baptist." She was eventually the mother of twelve children, and one or two of them were usually in service around the place, as yard boy or house boy. I mention the servants thus specifically because they played their part in the family life with a certain vividness, and became attached to the fortunes of the family in a way which is rare nowadays; also because they figure in many of the character sketches and are frequently mentioned by name in father's letters.

Those servants who remained with the family for a length of time became devoted to "Marse Joel." He had a knack with them, and knew how to deal with them humanly. His comprehension must have been a help to mother, for she was, of course, unused to negro servants when she began housekeeping.

"Mrs. Absalom" expressed father's viewpoint in "Gabriel Tolliver," when she said: "Well, you need n't be too hard on the niggers; everything they know, everything they do, everything they say — everything — they have larnt from the white folks. Study a nigger right close and you'll ketch a glimpse of how white folks would look and do wi'out ther trimmin's."

In fact, both father and mother were tolerant and genial in their relations toward all with whom they came in contact, and even in its humblest days the West End home was a *real* home, and one felt unmistakably, the moment one crossed the threshold, that "subtle essence, as mysterious as thought itself" — the essence of kindliness.

CHAPTER XII

WE have seen how back in the Forsyth days the obscure young editor took an interest in forming the literary taste of his greenhorn assistant. This wish to be helpful was characteristic; father never forgot the immense value to him of Mr. Turner's encouragement when he was a crude, unlettered youth, and when young writers applied to him for advice he gave it to them with earnest kindliness, always marveling that they thought it worth while to apply to a "cornfield" writer.

A young woman who lived in the foothills of North Georgia, and had abundant opportunity to observe the mountain types, sent father some sketches of mountain life which interested him very much. Acting upon his advice the author of these sketches, Miss Matt Crimm, continued to cultivate her talent and later found entrance into the pages of the "Century" and other leading magazines. The letter that follows was written upon the receipt of some of her earliest compositions: —

JOEL CHANDLER HARRIS

MY DEAR MISS CRIMM: —

I am glad indeed that you did not misunderstand the purport of my hastily written note. The fact that you have returned to the assault shows that I did not wound your sensitiveness, and I feel profoundly grateful to you for assuring me of that in your kind note. You have no lost ground to regain. Uniformity in literary effort is the result only of years of experience and patient apprenticeship — and the result of all experience and all apprenticeship is this: that it is better to do one thing well than a score of things ill. Ruskin says he frequently spent two hours in adjusting and balancing one sentence in his "Modern Painters," and his style has made him famous. I think if I had the time to engage in literary work, this system of rewriting and readjusting with regard to all the niceties of language and the rhythm thereof would be a most delightful occupation. Did you ever try it? Your own style is a marvel of simplicity for a young writer, and, like your handwriting, is without femininity. It is not less attractive on that account, you may depend.

I know you are capable of better work than the sketches you have been sending — capable of better work in that line. Why do you persist in dash-

[182]

ing them off by way of experiment? Why not elaborate them, if not in rewriting them, at least in your mind? It will be no trouble for you to attract attention in the " Constitution " provided that what you write deserves attention. Permit me to suggest a series of "Street Car Studies," or something in that line —something about people and things with which you are perfectly familiar. It is a great step toward success when a young writer gains his or her consent to treat of things with which he or she is familiar. It is worth while to remember also that what is really great in literature is the Commonplace. Shakspeare is commonplace from beginning to end, and so is Thackeray. Did you ever notice the terrible meaning Mrs. Browning gives to commonplace thoughts? But my opinion is worth nothing if you cannot verify it, for I am in no sense of the word a literary person.

The sketches you send will appear in Sunday's paper — probably. I say probably because I have no control over the events that, frequently, late at night, crowd my own matter to the wall. You would be astonished to learn how much matter is put in type that never appears in print.

Wishing you a happy New Year, I am

Sincerely your friend

J. C. HARRIS

[183]

JOEL CHANDLER HARRIS

Father's growing reputation exposed him to situations that were sometimes embarrassing. Mother was usually at hand to spare him as much as possible from the intrusion of strangers, but sometimes even her intervention failed of its object and father's natural defenselessness before the pleas of youth laid him open to imposition. One of these occasions, not without its element of humor, resulted in the following letter to Mr. Alden, of "Harper's Magazine": —

ATLANTA, GA., March 6, 1882

DEAR MR. ALDEN: —

Pray permit me to explain. Some time ago a young lady called on me and insisted upon reading several rhymed versions of the "Uncle Remus" stories in the coast dialect. Suppose I had not gone into ecstasies over them? What would have been the feelings of the lady? She would have accused me of envy, and I should never have heard an end of it. Then she asked me to give her a letter to some magazine, and I thereupon addressed a note to you in self-defense.

One of the miseries of my position is that people hereabouts think I have great influence because of the accidental success of the "Remus" trash, and I am constantly embarrassed in that way. All this, however, is no excuse for troubling you, and I write to explain and to beg your pardon. There was no escape for me.

Very truly yours

JOEL C. HARRIS

During 1881–82 father continued to contribute "Uncle Remus" stories to various periodicals, and wrote many of the "Plantation Ballads" that were includèd in the volume of 1892, published by Houghton Mifflin Company under the title, "Uncle Remus and His Friends." These were contributed, in the first instance, to the "Critic," "Our Continent," the "Century" and "Harper's" magazines.

Robert Underwood Johnson, of the "Century," in commenting on some of the "ballads" sent him early in 1882, writes: "They are very soil-y and are part of the history you are making of a fleeting epoch." [1] Mr. Johnson, in the same letter, calls attention to the stir being made amongst the philo-

---

[1] Of the ballads written during 1882–83, and collected in the *Uncle Remus* volume of 1892, father's favorite was the one called, "O, Gimme de Gal." The editor of the magazine to which it was submitted thus commented on it: "It is a little too 'niggery.' Have you not another a little more ideal than that, to substitute for it?" Fortunately no substitution was made, as the song's realism is the very quality that makes it a cotton-field classic. In a letter to the poet, Paul H. Hayne (year not given), in reference to a selection from the "Ballads" for an anthology, father said: "I would suggest 'The Plough-Hand's Song' as perhaps the most characteristic."

logists by "Uncle Remus," and suggests that his creator write a paper on comparative folk-lore, under the title of "Uncle Remus in Other Lands." This was never done, for the story-teller in father resolutely kept the lid clamped on the folk-lorist.

A significant paragraph in the same letter refers to a paper on "The Mocking-Bird" submitted sometime early in the year, but returned to the author for slight alteration. Mr. Johnson writes: "We like the 'Mocking-Bird,' and in your humility of soul you must remember that it is accepted in good faith. Send it back when you can. If by any chance you should drop below your best standard — why, what are editors for? We shall certainly be frank with you; — frank in appreciation and in criticism." But even such reassuring comment failed to convince father that the article in question was up to the magazine's standard, and the editor of the "Century" inquired late in the year if the "Mocking-Bird" was "pigeon-holed." Evidently it was, for not until sometime afterward did it appear in the "Constitution" as an editorial. In this form it was widely copied.

Father had been approached by a publisher with a request for a life of Thomas Jefferson to be written in a "serio-comic" style. The idea appealed to him, but after considering it from all points, he reluctantly abandoned it. His reasons for this decision were given in a letter to Miss Gilder, dated May 9, 1882: "I had hoped to write a life of Jefferson for Holt's series, but it will be impossible. The subject is an attractive one, but it is to be feared that a humorous treatment of so serious a matter would put the politicians after me; and yet, if I had time, such considerations would not stand in my way. I mention this because I saw in the 'Critic' some weeks ago an announcement that I was writing on Jefferson."

In June of this year father set out for New York with Captain Howell, intending to go on to Boston after he had viewed the sights of the former city, and also to make the promised visit to Mark Twain at Hartford. The travelers stopped at the old St. James Hotel on Broadway at 26th Street, and Mr. Robert Underwood Johnson, of the "Century Magazine," very thoughtfully provided the "cornfield" writer with an itinerary for a day of sightseeing. I give it because it conjures up a vivid picture of the New York of thirty-five years ago: —

Itinerary for Thursday

1. Ride down Broadway from Delmonico's on top of stage and ask driver to point out things. A cigar would arrange it with him.

2. Visit Tribune building. Introduce yourself by inclosed card to Mr. Lyman.
3. Walk to Astor House and on down Broadway to Equitable building. Go to top by elevator for view of city and vicinity (bay, rivers, Brooklyn, Jersey City, Staten Island, and the Narrows).
4. Go into Trinity Church, down Wall St., to Stock Exchange. Lunch here, and on to the Wall St. Ferry, and down South St., to the Battery, past the freight shipping. View of Brooklyn Bridge.
5. Castle Garden and the Battery. Go into Castle Garden to see immigrants and inspect arrangements. Walk along West St., north, to some big Ocean steamer.
6. Ocean Steamer. For 25c, a sailor will show you over a steamer. Try to find one of the new *big* ones. Thence go by Ninth Ave. El. R.R. to 59th St.
7. Central Park. Get Park-carriage at 8th Ave. entrance and 59th, and ride around and get out at nearest point to 5th Ave. entrance and 59th St. (Obelisk, Museum, etc.).
8. Walk down 5th Ave. to 45th St., past Vanderbilt house, Cathedral, Windsor Hotel.
9. Ride down 5th Ave. from 45th to your hotel on stage.

— And, may you have a clear sky and a good digestion!

R. U. J.

I do not know if father had the temerity to follow out Mr. Johnson's programme. Somehow I can't picture him riding down Fifth Avenue on top of a

'bus. It is so much easier to visualize him behind
the mules on the old West En'd car!

The travelers were offered most courteous attention by publishers and literary men, a banquet was
arranged in their honor at the Tile Club, and father
was cajoled into being present, though he went
with many misgivings. One of his fellow guests on
this occasion has given me a few details of the evening's entertainment. He tells how father "made
a hit" with everybody, but could not be induced to
make a speech or tell a story. Finally, Mr. F. Hopkinson Smith, the artist and writer, came to the
rescue and told one of the "Uncle Remus" stories.
Father expressed his delight and said, "That's
much better than I wrote it, Mr. Smith." After
the affair, everybody was in a particularly jovial
mood, and several of the crowd accompanied
"Uncle Remus" up Fifth Avenue toward his hotel.
When abreast of the Farragut statue, Abbey, the
artist, stood on his hands on the pavement and
saluted, whilst his small change poured out of his
pockets and scattered itself on the ground. Just at
this juncture father had been telling one of his companions what an unusual evening it had been and
how wonderful it was to see so many distinguished
people acting like "everyday" folk and enjoying
themselves in the fashion of school-boys. But Mr.

Abbey's prank must have made him feel that the mischievous spirit of his acquaintances might soon turn itself loose on him, so when his gratified companion asked, "Why did n't you tell us all this at the dinner, Mr. Harris?" father stammered in amazement, "What! Make a speech before all those brilliant fellows! No, sir! All I can do is to tell you *good-night!*" And with this he made a dash for his near-by hotel, the others chasing him and shouting after him. But he ran up four steps at a time and disappeared from sight!

A few days later, Mr. Gilder, of the "Century Magazine," called at the hotel and left with Captain Howell an invitation for another gathering which he accepted for himself and father, the latter being out. Captain Howell relied upon diplomacy to carry out the plan and did succeed in extracting a promise from father that he would go. But on recalling the ordeal of the Tile Club, and fearing that he might again be called upon for a speech, he found his courage failing him, and just before the hour appointed for the feast, he hastily packed his valise, left a note for his traveling companion, and departed for Atlanta!

Mr. Clemens wrote reproachfully to him later in the summer, saying, "Hang it! Why did you go back on us so?" and referred to a friend's report of his "admirable stupefaction at the Tile Club and his yarn afterward about the coon and the rabbit," to all of which father replied: —

THE CONSTITUTION, ATLANTA, GA.
EDITORIAL ROOMS, 12 September, 1882

DEAR MR. TWAIN: —

How can you call my stupefaction at the Tile Club dinner admirable? I suffered the agony of the damned twice over, and when I reflected that probably Mr. Osgood was prepared to put me through a similar experience in Boston, I thought it would be better to come home and commit suicide rather than murder a number of worthy gentlemen by making an ass of myself. Still, you will not escape. I shall have to go to Canada anyway, and I'm going by way of Hartford. Next Spring probably.

Did Mr. Osgood send you the notice of "The Prince and the Pauper"? That notice expressed my ideas more fully, and I think, by George! that Mr. Howells had it framed in front of him when he wrote the "Century" sketch.

Faithfully yours

JOEL C. HARRIS

True to his promise, father *did* stop over a day in Hartford on his way to Canada the following spring, and enjoyed the long-deferred visit with Mr. Clemens.

In October of 1882 father was in correspondence with Mr. Osgood, of the firm of Boston publishers, in regard to a second "Uncle Remus" book. The tales which followed the first volume, and which had appeared during 1881–82 in periodicals and newspapers, continued to delight the ever-increasing circle of the old man's friends. So father began systematically to tap all possible sources for more stories, and to verify the legends of the coast negroes which he had heard. For help in the latter undertaking he applied to an old newspaper associate, Mr. R. W. Grubb, of Darien, a Georgia coast town, in the following letter: —

3 February, 1883

DEAR GRUBB: —

Is n't there some one connected with your office who would be willing to piroot around among the negroes of Darien and gather me the outlines of the animal and alligator stories that form the basis of African mythology? I have a whole raft of stories current among the cotton plantation negroes, but there is another whole raft current among the coast negroes. Can't you get some one, who has the knack, to get in with some old negro, male or fe-

JOEL CHANDLER HARRIS AT 34

male, and secure me a dozen or more specimens? There are a number of stories in which the alligator figures, which I would like to have. All I want is a reasonably intelligent outline of the story as the negroes tell them, and for such outlines I would be glad to pay what the collector may consider reasonable and fair. The only way to get at these stories is for the person seeking them to obtain a footing by telling one or two on his own hook — beginning, for instance, with the tar-baby. There are few negroes that will fail to respond to this.

You see, dear boy, I am always sponging on your good nature, and I can never get a chance to repay you. I owe you ten thousand thanks for your kindness in one shape and another, and I would take it as an additional favor if you would tell me how I may help you in some way. In any event, I am grateful to you, and I show it by trying to sponge on your good nature again.

Faithfully yours

J. C. HARRIS

Mr. R. W. GRUBB,
Timber Gazette, Darien, Ga.

Mr. Grubb put father in touch with Mrs. Helen S. Barclay, of Darien, who had for long been interested in the coast legends, many of which she had

gathered from the old "body servants" of the
Pierce Butler estates in the neighborhood of Darien.
It was on these estates, which included an island
opposite Darien, that Pierce Butler and his wife,
Fanny Kemble, the actress, resided for a time.

Several dialects were spoken amongst these old
negroes, all quite different from that of the cotton-
fields in the "high country," and especially individual was the "gullah" of the Butler Island negroes, many of whom had been brought direct from
Africa, and some of whom were said to have been
cannibals in their own country. They were ridi-
culed by the Darien negroes,who looked down upon
them as benighted heathen. In a letter to father
early in 1883, Mrs. Barclay wrote: "I have,
through the kindness of a friend, given you two of
the real old nursery tales of alligators; and from my
washerwoman, who 'use ter b'long ter Butler
estet,' I have heard a true tale of a 'dead gose
(ghost) wha' I bin see wi' my own two eye.' This
I have written in her own language as nearly as
spelling can reproduce it." Mrs. Barclay commented on the mannerisms of these old island
slaves and regretted that she could not reproduce
the "lowering of the voice to a subdued and sly
monotone at such points in a story as 'Brer Rabbit
he *watch* um,'" which, she remarked, was full of

the subtlest humor. Again she said, "The 'Ya-a-s' in the mouth of one of the old-time coast darkies surpasses by far the shrug of the German or the 'Je ne sais pas' and uplifted hands of the French."

. Mrs. Barclay was a student of the folk-lore of other countries, and in referring to the legends of the Hartz Mountains she wrote that some incidents in these stories had led her to believe that "Miss Meadows an' de Gals," of the negro legends, might signify *Nature*, an interpretation which had already been hazarded by Mr. Church.

From Mr. Charles C. Jones, Jr., of Augusta, Georgia, outlines of other coast legends were obtained — tales which he had gleaned from the negroes of his old home in Liberty County, and some additional "up-country" myths were furnished by Mr. John Devereux, then living in North Carolina, — stories which he had heard in his childhood from his "Uncle Tony." In regard to his contribution, Mr. Devereux has written me, "I had been familiar with these stories from childhood and I sent Mr. Harris the bare outlines of several, leaving it to his genius to make 'these dry bones live.'"

In the introduction to the second volume, "Nights with Uncle Remus," published by Houghton Mifflin Company, in 1883, and in which the tales gleaned during 1881–82–83 were incorporated,

father describes most graphically a scene on the
platform of the little old station at Norcross,
twenty miles north of Atlanta, where he had occasion to wait for a belated train in the summer of
1882. A number of negroes who had been engaged
in working on the railroad were loafing near by, all
apparently in high good humor, cracking jokes and
indulging in boisterous laughter. Father drew near
one of the group in time to hear him make a reference to "Ol' Molly Har'" (Brer Rabbit's wife).
This, of course, interested the creator of "Uncle
Remus," and, after listening unobtrusively for a
few moments, he addressed himself in a low tone to
one of the negroes and began to narrate the Tar-
Baby story, by way of a "feeler." The negro's attention was caught and held, and he showed his
pleasure in loud comments, such as, "Dar now!"
"He's a honey, man!" "Gentermens! git out de
way, an' gin 'im room!"

This caused the other negroes to draw close and
to listen attentively, and father continued with the
story of "Brer Rabbit and the Mosquitoes," giving
all the necessary accompanying pantomime. This
so delighted his audience that all began telling
stories, and "for almost two hours, a crowd of
thirty or more vied with each other to see which
could tell the most and best tales."

Among these father recognized many of the tales
he had already gathered, but some were new. It is
likely that "Uncle Remus" took pains at this time
to extract a promise from one or two of the more
intelligent of this younger generation of story-
tellers to send him other outlines, for I have found
several fragments of tales scrawled in almost unde-
cipherable characters on scraps of paper and signed
"Jim" or "Buck." One outline sent from Senoia,
Georgia, in 1881, I give as characteristic of the
form in which many of the legends came to their
"compiler": —

"Mr. Harris I have one tale of Uncle Remus that
I have not seen in print yet. Bro Rabbit at Mis
Meadows and Bro Bare went to Bro Rabbit house
and eat up his childrun and set his house on fire and
make like the childrun all burnt up but Bro Rabbit
saw his track he knowed Bro Bare was the man so
one day Bro Rabbit saw Bro Bare in the woods
with his ax hunting a bee tree after Bro Rabbit
spon howdy he tell Bro Bare he know whare a bee
tree was and he would go an show and help him
cut it down they went and cut it an Bro Rabbit
drove in the glut while Bro Bare push his head in
the hole Bro Rabbit nock out the glut and cut him
hickry. Mr. Harris you have the tale now give it
wit I never had room to give you all you can finish it."

JOEL CHANDLER HARRIS

This outline was elaborated and shaped into the story, "The End of Mr. Bear."

On March 1, 1882, a second daughter, Lillian, had been born, and the year that ushered in this little girl was to close tragically with the death of her older sister. Mary Esther, or "Rosebud," as she was called, was a beautiful, blue-eyed little creature with fair hair and a round, rosy face — an active and a precocious child, the dearly-loved first daughter who had brought "good-luck" to the family. She was seized with diphtheria shortly before she attained her third year, and after a few days' illness, mother and father suffered the profound shock of seeing this little "Rosebud" droop and die like a tender plant cut off at the root by some hideous, unseen canker.

CHAPTER XIII

"MINGO," "BLUE DAVE," AND OTHERS

LONG before father had any idea of utilizing the negro legends he had cherished the hope of writing a novel of Georgia life; even so far back as the Forsyth days he had written a friend that he was "nursing a novel in his brain." But the pressing necessity of supporting a family had kept him at the newspaper grind so steadily that the project was neglected until 1878. In the "Weekly Constitution" of March 12 of th.tt year, "The Romance of Rockville" was announced — "a serial story to run several months. . . . The scene will be laid in Georgia, and it will embody the peculiar features of life and society in the South, anterior to the war." However, during the appearance of this serial, the "Uncle Remus" stories were inaugurated, and for nearly three years they absorbed father's time and energy to the exclusion of everything outside his routine work, and not until 1882 did he have leisure in which to write other stories of country life. The first of these, "Mingo," he submitted to Mr. Osgood for criticism and the publisher expressed his appreciation of it. In replying to his comments, in October, 1882, father wrote: —

"I am glad you like 'Mingo.' I am finishing up a short moonshine sketch entitled 'Teague Poteet.' I like it a great deal better than 'Mingo,' but that may mean it is worse. I think myself it will be better to begin with the Remus business." [1]

"Mingo" appeared in the Christmas number of "Harper's Magazine" (1882), and attracted considerable attention as being the work in a new field by the creator of "Uncle Remus." The "New York Tribune" asserted that "in the 'poor whites' of Georgia, Harris has found material as fresh and picturesque as anything in the delightful experiences of 'Uncle Remus,' and he has handled it with the ease, mastery, and grace of a natural artist." The contrast between the native gentility of the old negro, "Mingo," and the uncouth and almost savage traits of "Mrs. Feratia Bivins," the "poor white" woman, whose fortunes and those of her little granddaughter the former slave had elected to follow, is developed in sure and masterful fashion, and the story culminates in a burst of elemental

[1] The volume brought out by Osgood in 1883, *Nights with Uncle Remus*. Mr. Osgood had advised father to continue with sketches similar to "Mingo," in which he had great faith, but considered it better to follow up the success of the first volume of negro legends with another before attempting to bring out a volume of "Georgia Sketches."

MINGO, BLUE DAVE, AND OTHERS

hatred and rage on the part of the injured white
woman, which lays bare, in truly Dantesque fashion, the passions that seethe under the crust of
social conventions. In my opinion, "Mingo" ranks
with "Free Joe" as being the best of father's short
stories of rural life.

Sometime in 1882 father sent "At Teague Poteet's, a Story of the Hog Mountain Range," [1] to
the "Century Magazine," writing to Mr. Gilder:
"Enclosed you will find a sort of whatshisname.
I'm afraid it is too episodical to suit serial publication — but after all, life itself is a series of episodes.
Perhaps something else is the matter. If you don't
find it available, you can at least give me some
helpful suggestion." Mr. Gilder was pleased with
this two-part story and proposed to announce its
serial publication as a "novelette." But this, to
father, seemed too pretentious, and he registered a

[1] In a biographical sketch, prepared by Mr. Erastus Brainerd for
the *Critic* sometime during 1885, he gives the following account of
the genesis of "Teague Poteet": "The trial of two United States
deputy marshals for the killing of an old man, who was guilty only
of the crime of having a private still for 'moonshine,' was progress-
ing in Atlanta when the subject of proper names as titles of stories
came up in the *Constitution* office. Taking up a Georgia State direc-
tory the speaker's eye fell on the name of *Teague Poteet*. He suggested to Mr. Harris that if he merely took that name and wove
around it the story of the moonshiner's trial, it would attract as
many readers as 'Uncle Remus,' and it was suggested that he make
a column sketch of the subject for the next Sunday's *Constitution*.
From this simple beginning 'Teague Poteet' grew after several
months' incubation."

[201]

protest. From the editorial office of the "Century" came the following reply: —

"What a modest fellow you are about your work! We shall, of course, respect your wishes in the announcement of your story, but all your protestations do not convince us that this is not a novelette. . . . I am afraid that in your modesty you think I am not sincere in what I have said of the merits of the piece. Such modesty is so *rare* that I forgive you the imputation. . . . As I think over the story I find it has left a very definite impression and a very agreeable human feeling . . . the whole Poteet household is full of life, and the heroine is not sentimentalized nor lifted out of her plane. . . . The MS. is not a 'failure'; it is definitely accepted in its present shape, in the belief that you can easily strengthen it."

Father never got to the point where he could accept with complete confidence the praise bestowed upon him. He was almost morbidly doubtful of the merit of his work, was easily discouraged, and required a good bit of "boosting" from his publishers. In one letter, Mr. Johnson of the "Century" staff advises him to get a copy of Emerson's "Self-Reliance," and read it for his "literary dumps"! In another, he refers to father's insistence on his "lack of culture," and comments kindly and most sensibly: "The best American fiction is the outcome of what you call 'lack of culture.' Bret Harte, Cable, and Mrs. Burnett had little or none, and you can see culture gone to seed in James. . . . Don't have any fears on that score, but be thankful you have individuality and native force."

The two stories already mentioned, together with "Blue Dave" and "A Piece of Land," were brought out in the spring of 1884 under the title of "Mingo," by Osgood in Boston, and by David Douglas in London. With the exception of the Hog Mountain story, they depicted phases of rural life in middle Georgia.

When sending a copy of the book to a friend, in July of 1884, father wrote: —

I took the liberty of mailing you, a few days ago, a copy of "Mingo." I have no right to attack you in this manner, but you are not defenseless — you are not bound to read it. Indeed, it is not a book for young men. It is intended to please the aged and the half wits of our time — those who are suffering for want of sleep. Under the circumstances you can hardly be prepared to believe me when I assure you that I am,

Faithfully yours
JOEL CHANDLER HARRIS

JOEL CHANDLER HARRIS

In connection with these Georgia sketches, it is interesting to turn to an article on "The American Type," contributed by father to the "Current," a Chicago periodical, in 1884, shortly after the publication of "Mingo." When approached by the editor for something under this title, father had written (June, 1884): "I fear my ideas will strike you as crude. I think, for instance, to give you a whiff of my smoke, that 'The Story of a Country Town' is one of the best American stories that has ever been written, though it is one of the most inartistic. I think, moreover, that no novel or story can be genuinely American, unless it deals with the *common people*, that is, *country people*. If you say so, I will elaborate such ideas as I have and send them to you."

The editor replied: "That is just squarely on the line of what I should be glad to get. There is no nonsense about that sort of Americanism." So, working from that point of view, father shaped an article in which the following paragraphs appear: —

The American character is seen and known at its best in rural regions; but it is a fatal weakness of American literature that our novelists and story-tellers can perceive only the *comic* side of what they are pleased to term "provincial life"; for it is always a fatal weakness to see what is not to be seen. It is a remarkable fact that the most characteristic American story that has

thus far been written should approach rural life on the
tragic side. This is the "Story of a Country Town,"
by E. W. Howe.

In closing, father sums up: —

The point of all that has been herein said is that, no
matter what phase of American life the novelist may
choose to depict, he cannot fail to reproduce the true
American type if he but faithfully portray the human
nature that underlies all types of life; the human nature (to take an instance at random) that makes Mrs.
Poyser as common to Georgia as to New England, to
Maine as to Kansas.

Another little boy, Linton, had been born to the
family in July of 1883, and, in the following summer, mother took the baby, together with the other
children, to Canada to spend several weeks with
her parents. Grandfather LaRose had had the misfortune to lose his steamboat, the Lizzie Baker,
when it struck a shifting wreck near the bar of the
St. Johns River. There was no marine insurance on
the boat, but undoubtedly its owner could have
recovered damages on account of the obstruction
of the channel had he pushed his claim with sufficient persistence. But his lawyer, Hon. Julian
Hartridge, of Savannah, died at this juncture, and
grandfather became discouraged over the affair,
bade farewell to Savannah, and established himself
permanently on his farm near St. Éphrem d'Upton,

in the Province of Quebec. So it was only at rare intervals that the grandparents could see the children. For this reason it became the established custom for mother to make a yearly pilgrimage to Canada.

The sales on the two "Uncle Remus" books had brought in enough money for the enlargement and improvement of the West End home, so during mother's absence the work was undertaken. Two rooms and a spacious porch were added in front. Mother's room was enlarged, as was the dining-room, and a kitchen and porch were built adjoining the latter. At the same time father had a little "study" built for himself above the front hall, at the head of a winding stair. This architectural feature gave the needed effect of height to the house, but aside from its æsthetic value the upper chamber served very little purpose. Father could not make himself comfortable so far away from the life of the family, and continued to write in his bedroom or near the sitting-room fire, whilst the "study" was relegated to the base uses of attic and storeroom!

When the family returned in the fall, their delight in the "new house" knew no bounds, but they were distressed at father's appearance, as he had grown so thin during their absence that the children hardly knew him. Shortly afterwards he began making frequent trips to Lithia Springs, about twenty miles from Atlanta, and under the combined influences of change, rest, and the excellent mineral water, he began to gain flesh, and gradually grew quite rotund, which greatly improved his appearance and made him look much younger.

In March of 1883 father had written a letter to his old playmate, Joe Syd Turner, of Eatonton, in which he made the following request: —

May I pester you a little for the sake of old times? I am anxious to get a sample of the musical instrument peculiar to the negroes called the "Quills." It is a classical affair, too, and has attracted attention as Pan's pipes. Roughly, it is something like this:

[Follows a sketch of the instrument.]

That is to say, reeds tied together with waxed twine. But you have seen the affair hundreds of times. Indeed you have listened with me while Fountain (or Fontaine), one of your father's negroes, played upon it. It ought to be easy to get, and yet I am afraid I am asking you too much. I have seen hundreds of these instruments in Putnam. The Spivey negroes, the Marshall negroes and Andy Reid negroes — all on river plantations and therefore convenient to cane-brakes — were much given to the quills.

If you can, pray buy me one of the instruments and send it by express.

Faithfully yours

J. C. HARRIS

Father was preparing for the "Critic" an article to be entitled "Plantation Music and the Banjo," hence his request of Mr. Turner. This same article caused quite a commotion on account of the following statement: —

The banjo may be the typical instrument of the plantation negroes, but I have never seen a plantation negro play it. I have heard them make sweet music with the quills — Pan's pipes; I have heard them play passingly well on the fiddle, the fife and the flute; and I have heard them blow a tin trumpet with surprising skill; but I have never seen a banjo, or a tambourine or a pair of bones, in the hands of a plantation negro. My experience was limited to plantations in the counties of Putnam, Jasper, Morgan, Greene, Hancock and Jones. In these counties there were hundreds of Virginia negroes, — negroes of every stripe and kind. I have seen the negro at work and I have seen him at play; I have attended his corn-shucking, his dances, and his frolics; I have heard him give the wonderful melody of his songs to the winds; I have heard him fit barbaric airs to the quills; I have seen him scrape jubilantly on the fiddle; I have seen him blow wildly upon the bugle, and beat enthusiastically on the triangle; but I have never heard him play on the banjo.

After its publication, not only the "Critic," but a number of New York daily papers received communications from readers claiming with varying degrees of courtesy that "Uncle Remus" did not know what he was talking about! The "New York Tribune" printed a little story about Mr. Cable's opinion of father's statement, in which he was quoted as saying: "I have listened half a night to negroes sing to their banjo in Louisiana. But it is possible that Mr. Harris never saw a negro with one. It is a fact that where you find one negro with a banjo, you find a hundred with a fiddle."

But the popular idea of an old-time negro represented him as being forever in the attitude of "picking a banjo," and this cherished delusion was not to be easily dissipated, so the musical "tempest in a teapot" continued to hum and buzz! I had occasion recently to ask Mr. Cable if he recalled the "controversy," and he replied: "Your father was quite right in the statement he made as to the banjo not being an instrument much in use among the negro slaves in our Southern States. Why he should have had to defend his statement, I do not now recall, but I remember that it was so."

One of father's warmest friends at this time was

JOEL CHANDLER HARRIS

Colonel Richard Malcolm Johnston, who under the name of "Philemon Perch" wrote "Dukesborough Tales" and other delightful Georgian sketches. Colonel Johnston was, like father, a native of middle Georgia, a favorite in the households of that section, and a welcome guest at dinner-parties, for there was no such *raconteur* in that part of the State as he. In his "Oddities of Southern Life," Colonel Henry Watterson tells how in the days when Colonel Johnston lived on his plantation near Sparta he was the central figure about which gathered lawyers, jurors, and litigants, when, at the close of the day's work, all came together around the hearths of the country taverns for story-telling and social converse. The end of the war found the bulk of his property gone and he taught English in the University of Georgia for a time. Later, he moved to Baltimore where he began to write his charming stories of Georgia country life, and where he also gave dialect readings. In fact, it was he who first read the "Uncle Remus" stories in public, before a Baltimore audience in 1884.

Not only was he greatly interested in father's development as a writer (he was many years father's senior), but he loved him as tenderly as a younger brother. Writing to father on one occasion he refers to himself as "the old man who, old as he is, loves you very much, and rejoices in your youth, and that without feeling like complaining of his old age." He recalls visits to the home in West End, and says: "I love to go there and stay all night and see how happy you are and ought to be. I wish you and I could take together sometime a turn in Hancock and Putnam Counties. . . . I went to my native place last year, to see it, and to have the graves of my family repaired. Oh, it did my heart so much good!"

All during 1884 there was much correspondence between father and Colonel Johnston in reference to a play which they planned to write together. A letter dated August 26, 1884, calls attention to a notice in the "Baltimore Sun" relative to their project, and Colonel Johnston adds: "This spurs me on mightily; I wish to gracious I could be with you. We could work this up together in a month or six weeks."

In fact, the scenario *was* written, and the characters outlined (it was to be a play of Southern life), but for some reason, which I have been unable to discover, the work never reached completion. Colonel Johnston wrote of "troublesome business affairs" which absorbed his attention and prevented him from making a prolonged stay in Atlanta; and father's mistrust of his own ability to work out a sustained plot probably deterred him from proceeding alone in the work.

This was not the first time, nor was it to be the last, that father dallied with the drama! The desire to write a play seemed to persist, and occasionally it cropped out in experiments.

CHAPTER XIV

DURING the latter half of the eighties the routine of father's work proceeded in almost uninterrupted fashion. The merit and popularity of his writings kept pace with his growing fame, and he was approached by the majority of the leading publishers and editors of magazines for contributions; and in April, 1885, a letter came from Major J. B. Pond, who proposed that "Uncle Remus" read some of his own stories on tour. "There is no trouble about capturing an audience after you have once started. . . . The people, including the children, are calling for you, and that has not happened to any other author of late years. *No* will not do for an answer." Thus wrote the famous "lyceum" originator, and his request was backed up by Thomas Nelson Page, who had already appeared before audiences as a dialect reader. Mr. Page proposed a joint tour, and suggested jocularly that if he could induce "Uncle Remus" to consent to the plan, in all probability the two Southern writers "might in a couple of months lay by enough of our Yankee cousins' gold to compensate us for some we have furnished

[213]

them." But father was proof against these temptations and declined without any apparent regrets.[1]

These were the early days of Colonel S. S. McClure's publishing activities, and in May of 1885 the author of "Uncle Remus" was requested by that energetic and versatile literary promoter to contribute to his "Octave" of short stories by the best American writers, and also to send him a story to head the series of "100 stories by 100 authors in 100 days." About the same time the Century Company proposed a contract by means of which the newspaper grind could be dropped and the writer guaranteed an agreed income from work to be done exclusively for this firm. In short, it would seem that now father could easily have slipped out of the journalistic harness and settled into a pace better suited to his temper and strain. That he did not take advantage of these opportunities to free himself for exclusively creative work can be explained only by his abnormal lack of confidence in himself as a "literary man."

How often, in his correspondence, does he insist that he is only a "journalist" or a "corn-field

---

[1] Major Pond later made a second proposal, telegraphing an offer of $10,000, if father would consent to read with James Whitcomb Riley and Mark Twain. On receipt of the offer, father remarked to a friend, "I would not put on a dress-suit every night in the winter for $10,000, much less go on a stage and make a fool of myself."

SKETCH SENT TO J. C. H. BY MR. JOHN H. GARNSEY

On the occasion of a visit to New York in 1900

writer"! So hypnotized was he by this *idée fixe* that a little incident which occurred about this time caused him no end of amazement. An instinctive joker himself, he was quick to relish a joke at his own expense, and when in 1883 Eugene Field, whom he greatly admired, set going through the daily papers a fantastic story about his friend's birth and early life, father entered into the spirit of the thing like a boy.[1] Later, however, Field carried the joke a little farther, and stated that the now famous "son of missionary parents" was the richest American author, having gained an enormous sum by his writings, which he had invested in "Atlanta Constitution" stock, Central of Georgia Railway stock, and a tract of the finest timber land in the State! To father's unbounded amazement this story found credence amongst a number of people,

---

[1] "Joel C. Harris has had a strangely romantic career. His father was a missionary, and it was at the small town of Booghia, on the South Coast of Africa, that Joel was born. He was educated by his father and acquired a wonderful acquaintance with foreign languages. He is an adept Sanskrit scholar and is deeply versed in Hebraic and Buddhist literature. The sweetly quaint legends of Indian and Judean mythology have found their way into his simple Southern tales, and the spirit of his philosophy is identical with the teachings of Moses and Buddha."

Another version of the tale was: "Joel Chandler Harris, the Southern dialectician and *littérateur*, sails for Africa in December, it being his purpose to revisit the little coast town of Joel, where he was born of missionary parents January 13, 1842. Mr. Harris lost a leg in the battle of Lookout Mountain. His career has been full of incidents."

and even in Atlanta, where the simplicity of "Uncle Remus's" life was well known, a young man was one day heard to name Joel Chandler Harris as the South's richest citizen; and this in perfectly good faith!

Eugene Field could not have hit upon anything so far removed from the bounds of possibility as this (so thought his victim), and when begging letters followed upon the heels of the story the astonishment of the "most modest author in America" began to be tinged with annoyance. At least one request furnished occasion for a laugh; it came from a man living in a small Georgia town, and he wrote: "Le' 's be up and doing! I'll head the list with $5.00 for my father's tombstone. A little tombstone is all that is needed. What will you give?"

During 1885 father furnished to the "Youth's Companion" five articles under the general title, "Negro Customs and Superstitions"; these included three new "Uncle Remus" stories and some "ballads." For some reason their author was not satisfied with them, and when, in 1900, the editor asked for other stories, father replied: —

DEAR MR. EDITOR: —

I am very fond of the "Companion," and it has been coming into my house for fifteen years. I have often wished to appear in its columns and on one occasion, at the request of the editor, did contribute some sketches. But they were out of tune with the rest of the paper. They constituted a discord. Says I to myself: "If they jar on me, what must be the feelings of the editor and the readers?" So I sent no more. The truth is, my literary clothes-line is so near the ground that I should despair of suiting you. I candidly think that your editorial policy is too refined, but it has been eminently successful. I'm simply complaining because it shuts me out. Sterne's Starling wanted to get out; whereas I want to get in. You have sent me a circular. But what would you personally suggest in regard to the line of contributions that might be expected to develop under my heavy hand?

Yours sincerely
JOEL CHANDLER HARRIS

In March of 1886, following a suggestion of the editors of the "Century Magazine" [1] a joint trip was arranged for father and Mr. A. B. Frost, the illustrator, in search of "types" in the Georgia highlands. The explorers chose Marietta, about

---

[1] Though father did not agree to the contract proposed by the Century Company, most of the work done by him from 1885 to 1890 appeared in the *Century Magazine*.

twenty miles from Atlanta, for their point of departure, but the direction taken was ill-advised, and Mr. Frost describes it as "an amusing trip from the fact that absolutely nothing happened. We went from Marietta to some God-forsaken little town and found nothing there but a marble quarry. We could get nothing to eat, and no train back to Marietta till late in the day. It was an absolute blank, and amusing on that account. Afterwards I went to White Path and saw the real mountain people, just such people as Mr. Harris wrote about."

Father spent parts of many summers in the shadow of the Georgia mountains, and he loved their wild, primitive beauty, their clear, chattering streams and their exquisite flora as only a native of the dear old State could love them. Some of his best work deals with the lives of the primitive people of pure Anglo-Saxon blood who inhabit these mountain fastnesses, and one of the most interesting stories of this type was published during 1886 in the "Century," whose editor, Mr. R. W. Gilder, in referring to it wrote: "I have been reading and re-reading your wonderful little story, 'Trouble on Lost Mountain.' When it comes out you will find yourself approached in all directions by the envious and the ambitious. . . ."

FREE JOE AND DADDY JAKE

What a wave of homesickness sweeps over me
as I turn to this tale of simple highland folk, from
whose cabin, "poised on the shoulder of Lost
Mountain," blue Kennesaw could be seen behind
its atmospheric trappings, and whose tragic little
story unfolds itself out there where, "in the cold
air, or the wide skies, or in the vast gulf of night,
there was nothing to suggest either pity or com-
passion—only the mysterious tranquillity of Nature"; for "the majesty of Kennesaw was voiceless, its beauty was forever motionless. Its silence
seemed more suggestive than the lapse of time,
more profound than a prophet's vision of eter-
nity, more mysterious than any problem of the
human mind." [1]

The stories written between 1884 and 1887 were
to be gathered into the volume published by Scribners in 1887, under the title "Free Joe, and Other
Georgian Sketches," and published in London by
George Routledge. The story which gave the book
its name was the author's favorite amongst his
works. It is the tale of a former slave — a "free
nigger" during slavery — "a black atom, drifting
hither and thither without an owner, blown about

---

[1] "Trouble on Lost Mountain": In the volume entitled *Free Joe,
and Other Georgian Sketches* (Scribners, 1887). Kennesaw Mountain
is visible, on a clear day, from the hills surrounding Atlanta.

by all the winds of circumstance, and given over to shiftlessness." The tale of this forlorn creature and his little dog Dan, outcasts from the plantation hearths, scorned by the slaves, hated by the overseers, and whose only friends were the "poor whites," Miss Becky and Marse Cajy, is one of the most poignant and solemn arraignments of "man's inhumanity to man" in the annals of fiction. Its brevity, its simplicity, its unforced pathos — all combine to achieve an impressiveness and a fatefulness rarely found within the compass of so short a tale.

"Little Compton," the second story in the volume, gave father a good deal of trouble in the writing. He was overworked all during the spring and summer of 1886, a season of exceptionally exciting events in local politics, and naturally he felt the strain most when he turned to his literary work. "Little Compton" did not "go off" as readily as such work usually did, and when it was submitted to the "Century" Mr. Gilder suggested several changes in construction and a different climax. These suggestions were acted upon and the story was greatly strengthened, but the following letter indicates the fatigue under which the work was done: —

FREE JOE AND DADDY JAKE

22 July, 1886

My DEAR MR. GILDER: —

I forward by express to-day the revision of "Little Compton." Your letter in regard to its weak points paralyzed me, but I have tried hard to profit by every suggestion you made. I know that it is much better now, but I do not know whether you will find it available. It still seems to be desperately thin. The additions are made in pencil; but I hope this is no objection, for a pen cramps both my thoughts and my hand. For several months I have been suffering with fatty degeneration of the mind — and local politics. In other words, the newspaper grind has been harder than ever, owing to various circumstances. . . . I am in the agony of finishing a story which I had intended to call "An Easter Girl," but I have compromised on "Azalia." It will make probably a three-part story in the "Century."

Faithfully yours

JOEL CHANDLER HARRIS

"Little Compton" brought to its author many friendly letters from Northern admirers who appreciated the spirit of the story as developed in the portrayal of its hero, a "Yankee" living in a Southern town during Civil War times.

JOEL CHANDLER HARRIS

"Aunt Fountain's Prisoner"[1] was also a story of the Civil War, whose hero, a wounded Federal soldier, was nursed back to health in a Southern home and eventually married the only daughter of the household. The closing paragraph emphasizes a belief which father many times expressed both in fiction and editorially: "He gave me a practical illustration of the fact that one may be a Yankee and a Southerner, too, simply by being a large-hearted, whole-souled American."

In a letter to Mr. Gilder in September of this year, father wrote: "I am lying — or rather, I am telling the truth — flat o' my back at home, where I have been for three weeks, the result of false pleurisy and overwork on the paper. We have just passed through a hot campaign in Georgia, as you will see by the papers."

As soon as he was able to travel, the convalescent went to his beloved mountains, so beautiful in the early fall, and on his return had better news to send his publisher: "The mountain air has revived me, and I have returned to work much improved. My experience has taught me that it is best to take a vacation every year — a fact that I have ignored

---

[1] In *Free Joe, and Other Georgian Sketches.* First called "Uncle Fountain's Prisoner." "Uncle Fountain," or "Fontaine," was the name of one of the Turner slaves who had been a friend of the boy Joel.

heretofore. Next summer I am going to start early and stay late, if the Lord spares me."

The story, "Azalia," which closes the volume of 1887, had in it an episode which caused an interesting interchange of opinions between writer and publisher. A Boston girl goes to the town of Azalia in the piney woods of Georgia to recuperate from an illness, and there becomes acquainted with the "tackies," or "poor whites," of the turpentine regions. One of them, a forlorn creature, conceives a hopeless passion for her and finally dies. When the girl visits the cabin of his mother after his death, she is overcome to find that the poor bereaved woman has built a little contrivance of boards like a trap which, when lifted from the ground, reveals her only souvenir of the dead son: the mark of his footprint in the clay. Mr. Gilder was greatly pleased with the first draft of the story, made a few suggestions, and then added: "The story of the footprint I heard only a few weeks ago. I think P——, of Frankfort, told me about it. I am glad to see it in literature." Father replied: —

20 December, 1886

My dear Mr. Gilder: —

Your letters in regard to "Azalia" have been received. I'm glad you're somewhat pleased with it, and I'm willing to adopt any suggestions you may make in the way of bettering it, for all your suggestions heretofore have been to the point. With respect to the footprint episode: It was given to me by Mrs. Crawford, of Columbia County, who gave me leave to use it. I felt free to do this because it is beyond the invention of any man. It is a touch of nature that no imagination would have ventured to think of. Where Mrs. C. got it, I don't know, but the impression she left on me was that it was told her by her husband, who carried some of those piney-woods tackeys to war. However, I'm not afraid to use it, nor any other similar episode that may fall in my way. When human nature goes to invention, her inventions are the property of the first to use them. That is my feeling about it. I may be wrong, but I think not.

Yours

JOEL CHANDLER HARRIS

Perhaps Mr. Gilder did not fully agree with these theories; but I am inclined to think that father exaggerated the difference of opinion (if there was one), for the next letter indicates that his sensitiveness was touched: —

FREE JOE AND DADDY JAKE

24 December, 1886

My dear Mr. Gilder: —

Mr. Buel referred to the episode in Edwards's "Two Runaways," and I have heard that there was some such episode in real life. But is n't that what you want? Come! Are you going to confine us all to inventions of our own? Are we, who are working in a comparatively new field, to take no advantage of the legends, the traditions and the happenings with which we are familiar? Are you going to say to us, "If you have nothing to invent, pray send us nothing"? If you are, you may put up the bars against one and against all the rest of us at once.

As for me, I have no new situation to invent, and if I should invent one it would probably be weak and ineffectual. Take "Azalia." The Footprint business, as I have already said, was given to me by Mrs. Crawford. That is beyond invention. It is real. It belongs to human nature. It is mine if I re-create characters that would be apt to employ it. So with the death scene which you extol. Do I make it natural — obvious? If so, it is mine. I shall never hesitate to draw on the oral stories I know for incidents. The thing is, do I make my poor characters conform to the requirements of human nature?

JOEL CHANDLER HARRIS

The most a writer can do now-a-days is to try to invest his characters with a certain nobility of purpose, a certain pathos, that shall relate them to human nature, or to a series of incidents that belong to human nature. Why should Edwards (for instance) claim to have invented the main coincidents of the "Two Runaways"? They might readily have happened, and no doubt they did. If they were possible, we may be sure they happened; if they were impossible, why put them in literature at all?

The greatest literary men, if you will remember, were very poor inventors. If your grandmother was a Scotchwoman, as mine was, you have some idea of the debt that Sir Walter Scott owed to tradition.

But all this is too long. If your letter is intended to convey a slight intimation that the footprint business in "Azalia" is "below the belt," you need have no hesitation in returning the vile affair. Perhaps I can do better next time.

JOEL CHANDLER HARRIS

The "vile affair" was, of course, *not* rejected for that or any other reason, but father was a little uncertain about its ending, as is shown in the next letter, and retained the story for several months before he finally yielded it for publication: —

FREE JOE AND DADDY JAKE

27 April, 1887

MY DEAR MR. GILDER: —

Now, about that story: My dear Mr. Man, I think you must be mistaken about the climacteric. Consider the situation! Here is a young woman who has lost her only brother. Her grief for his death — she knows he is dead — is sincere, but the shock of it is past. Suddenly she discovers that the brother whom she mourns as both dead and lost, has received a decent burial in this out-of-the-way place. She is astonished, of course, but her astonishment gives no basis for a scene, for with her knowledge of the fact there must also be a feeling of gratification. Turn it as I may, this seems to be the inevitable conclusion. I have rewritten the part several times, but each time I have been disgusted with my attempt to make a sensation out of what ought to be a perfectly natural scene. Yet I am so sure of your judgment, and so doubtful of my own, that I will hold the copy back until I hear from you further.

Faithfully yours

JOEL CHANDLER HARRIS

Not until the end of May, 1887, did the story go to the "Century" in its final form, followed by this letter: —

JOEL CHANDLER HARRIS

26 May, 1887

My dear Mr. Gilder: —

The "Azalia" business went forward a day or two ago, and you have received it by this time. Kemble suits me. Pray ask him to treat my decent people decently, and with some refinement. But he can't make the Tackies too forlorn. Beg him also to give the old negro man some dignity, and to remember the distinction between the Guinea negro — as he is in New Orleans — and the Virginia negro as he is in Georgia.

Yours faithfully

Joel Chandler Harris

"The shaping" of "Azalia" had been a matter of enough argument between the writer and the editor to cause the former still to regard it suspiciously, and when it came to putting the stories in book form the author wrote to the publisher: —

Atlanta, Ga., 10 October, 1887

My dear Mr. Scribner: —

Unless you can conjure up some significant *general* title, let it go as you say, "Free Joe and Other Georgian Sketches." I see that Mr. R. H. Stoddard says that "Azalia" is "exquisite and pathetic," but if that affair isn't trash from the word go, then I don't know what trash is. There's no use to wait for "Ananias." It is worse than "Azalia."

Faithfully

J. C. H.

One of the sequels of the publication of "Azalia" was a letter from a lady in Colorado, which contained a statement that must have caused the author to feel that the long arm of coincidence was reaching across the continent with a gesture of incomparable irony. She wrote: —

"My sister has just called my attention to the fact that the name 'Jedediah Kingsbury' in your serial story, 'Azalia,' belonged to a great-aunt of our own, who, like your character, was the author of the 'sure-enough book' mentioned by your genial 'Mrs. Haley.' My great-aunt did, indeed, go South, where she taught school before the war, and compiled a dictionary as mentioned in your novel. I would like to obtain one of these dictionaries; and any information concerning her, personally, would be of much interest to us."

Poor father must have felt that he was the victim of a sort of literary secret service, ever ready to pounce upon his episodes and correlate them with their prototypes in real life! However, the resur-

[229]

rection of Aunt Jedediah Kingsbury, so "pat" on the heels of the *footprint* episode, was one of those delicious compensations that make up for the vexations of story-writing!

In 1889, the Century Company brought out "Daddy Jake, the Runaway, and Short Stories Told after Dark." "Daddy Jake" was a three-part story of the pursuit, on a flatboat down the Oconee River, by Lucien and Lillian (the little children of Dr. Gaston), of their dear old friend Daddy Jake, the carriage driver, who in a fit of justifiable anger had struck the overseer on the head with a hoe handle. Thinking he had killed the man, the old slave ran away and took refuge in a canebrake on the banks of the river, where, in the company of other runaways, he was finally found by his adventuresome little friends, who brought their willing captive back in triumph. For the old man was only too happy to return when Lucien told him that "Papa was n't mad and the overseer was n't killed," to which Daddy Jake replied: "Well, I'll be blest! W'at kinder head you reckon dat w'ite man got? Honey, is you *sholy sho* dat man ain't dead?"

The other stories in the volume were "Uncle Remus" tales which had appeared in the "Youth's Companion," "St. Nicholas," and "Century Magazine." "Daddy Jake" was very popular and has passed through twelve editions.

In this same year the Osgood publications passed into the hands of Houghton, Mifflin & Company, and father had a letter from Mr. H. O. Houghton, of that firm, expressing gratification in the prospect of handling "Uncle Remus's" books, and referring to a meeting of the two in Atlanta several years before in a way which throws a side-light on father's timidity toward strangers. "I am afraid," wrote Mr. Houghton, "we were both of us a good deal in the condition of Lady Avonmere, who got snowed up in the woods of California, and was not able to find her path to civilization. She accidentally met a grizzly, and said she did not know which was the most frightened, she or the grizzly, as she ran one way and the bear the other!"

It was sometime during this period that the International Copyright Bill was passed, largely through the influence of the Authors' League. Father had, of course, been much interested in the passage of this bill, and, at Mr. Gilder's request, had sent the following paper, bearing on the subject, to be published in the "Century Magazine," previous to the presentation of the bill: —

JOEL CHANDLER HARRIS

To the Editor of the Century: —

I have been asked to give my ideas in regard to the movement in favor of international copyright that is to be pushed in Congress this winter. The movement is important, but my ideas are worthless. As a sort of one-horse literary man, I should say that the Hawley bill ought not to be insisted on, but as a practical person, with some little knowledge of the methods of legislation, I should say that a straight-out copyright bill would have no chance whatever. There are other interests that claim recognition when the matter of copyright is up for consideration, and though the claim is preposterous in the extreme, these interests are powerful enough to make their influence felt in Congress — far more powerful in this respect than the Authors' League. Now, whether a fact is absurd depends on the point of view, but a fact is a fact from any point of view. Indeed, a fact is so much of a fact that even the authors ought to recognize it when they meet it in the road. If anything is more important than one fact, it is a drove of facts, and the drove of facts that the authors must deal with have snouts as long as a razor-back hog and are full of bristles.

It is well to bear in mind that although the Dorsheimer bill was fired into Congress without consideration or consultation, it was promptly antagonized and practically defeated. It was defeated by the "pirates." This is what some of the authors said. It was defeated by Philadelphia publishers. This is what some of the experts remarked. As a matter of fact, it was defeated by a coalition of the most prominent publishers in this country — a coalition that worked somewhat in the dark, but always to the purpose. The same coalition will defeat the Hawley bill, or any other bill that fails to recognize the supposed interests of those who are in the habit of pirating. The coalition is not simply one of publishers, but of printers and binders — manufacturers.

Now these are the facts that ought to be recognized. It is to the interest of the Authors' League to recognize them. Why not undertake a compromise? Why not win these antagonistic interests over to the support of international copyright? Why not prepare a bill that will compose the difference between apparently conflicting interests? Naturally, these ideas are provincial, but provinciality is sometimes another name for common sense.

JOEL CHANDLER HARRIS

Father's views were not exactly in line with the ideas which prevailed in the League (the majority favored no compromise), therefore his paper was not used, but I give it because it is characteristic of the writer's inherent common sense and his ability to see both sides of a question.

CHAPTER XV

WEST END DAYS

THE beginning of 1890 found the West End home comfortably filled; even the little room at the top of the house now had an occupant, for in 1885 another little girl, Mildred, had been born; and in 1888, Joel Chandler Harris, Jr., had arrived to complete the family circle.

A friend of the family at this period describes mother as "in the early thirties and looking as fresh and girlish as the bright-eyed, vivacious ladies of her land alone can look"; and says of father, "His red hair has grown much darker, his freckles have paled, and his mustache shades a mouth from which come hearty laughter and delightful anecdotes when only home folks are about."

Grandmother Harris, now more than seventy years old, was pictured as "a plain, honest old lady, who calls nothing to her aid to soften the marks of time. . . . Her form is bent and her face slightly furrowed, but her hair is smooth and abundant, her eyes clear and her laugh hearty. . . . She is an entertaining talker, bright and graphic in description, and without any touch of the meandering,

[235]

digressive style of story-telling that afflicts so many old ladies. . . . Her famous son is still the same Joel to her that he was in boyhood. His achievements in literature do not surprise her. She tells how he used to say in childhood, 'Just wait, mother. I will write stories myself some day.'"

In the kitchen "Aunt Celie" had taken the place of "Mandy" Henderson, and her round, cushioned body and shiny, good-humored face, beaming under a red turban from which dangled huge brass moon-shaped earrings, made of her a veritable "Sis Tempy." Celie, of course, was very pious, and one of her children was named "Ananias," "atter de proffit, an' *not dat owdacious liar*," she explained emphatically. Chloe still made her twice daily pilgrimage, to milk Mayflower and Nita, remaining at home so short a time before and after the birth of her numerous progeny that it was always a shock to mother to see her back at work, strong and hearty as a native of the primeval jungles. In speaking of those days the good old soul said to me recently: —

"Miss Essie sho' wuz good ter me. She ain't nuver say er cross wu'd ter me. Ef dar wuz ennybody what wuz cross 't wuz me, an' 't wuz mo' 'n onct I oughter bin knock down, I 'speck. But Miss Essie she ain't nuver say er wrong wu'd. . . . Bofe

THE HOUSE AT WEST END

on us, we had our chilluns right erlong tergedder. Fust, me I'd ketch up wid Miss Essie, den she'd ketch up wid me! An' at de las', w'en little Marse J. C. wuz bornded, I had one er my little boys."

The cottage home had had time since its days of renovation and remodeling to become an integral part of its surroundings. Its foundations were hidden by flowering shrubs, and the low, latticed arches of its porch were screened by rose-vines and wisteria, the pale lavender blooms of the one being followed in June by the glorious golden flowers of the other — amazing masses of "cloth-of-gold" against the glossy green of its own foliage interlaced with garlands of English ivy. A long row of venerable apple trees bounded the southern extremity of the lot, and in early spring their blossoming boughs sheltered many song birds. In the shafts of the dark cedars bordering the front walk mockingbirds nested, and during the moonlit nights of early summer their thrillingly beautiful notes could be heard far into the small hours of the morning. On either side of the house were rose-beds fringed with violets, and father himself pruned the bushes and cut the flowers. The velvety "jacqueminots" were his favorites, and during their time of bloom the house was filled with the fragrance of their rich red blossoms. In the back yard the children's pets found accommodation, and two dogs, "Nero" and "Mingo," the latter an English bull-terrier, had their kennels near enough to the house to be conveniently tended. It was part of the home routine of Julian and Lucien to get up early on alternate mornings and chain these watch-dogs which were regularly turned loose at night, for West End was still sparsely settled and prowlers were an occasional menace. Two canaries, "Bo-peep" and "Nelly Bly," hopped about their cages out of reach of the innumerable cats, offspring of the venerable mouser, "Mrs. Kitty Banks." The children "raised" fancy chickens, pigeons, guinea-pigs, and rabbits, and father insisted on the most conscientious care of these birds and animals: if a pet were neglected that pet must be forfeited, was the rule of "Snap-Bean Farm." [1]

Every phase of life about the home was of interest to father, and in the midst of his work he would often get up from his writing-table and stroll into the sitting-room to listen to the chatter of the children or the gossip of neighbors. If mother had a new dress or hat, he was as interested in it as she; if a church "bazar" was to be held at the house, none of the details bored him; the annual Catholic

---

[1] Called so by father in playful imitation of the "Sabine Farm" of Eugene Field.

festival that took place on the lawn surrounding the house was a matter of lively interest to him, and when the church members and friends and neighbors gathered on these occasions, he mingled freely with them, his soft hat on the back of his head and his hands in his pockets. He once said, "I like people who are what they are, and are not all the time trying to be somebody else"; consequently he was at home in the company of unaffected people. But let a pretentious person, a "high-brow" or a lion-hunter, appear on the scene, and not even Brer Fox could "lay" as "low" as his creator! Particularly was father averse to bogus culture, and on this point once wrote: "Culture is a very fine thing, indeed, but it is never of much account either in life or literature unless it is used as a cat uses a mouse — as a source of mirth and luxury. It is at its finest, in this country, when it is grafted on the sturdiness that has made the nation what it is, and when it is fortified by the strong common sense that has developed and preserved the republic."

Father enjoyed the comforts of his home, its cheer and freedom; its bountiful but simple table; its warmth in winter and its "coolth" in summer, sheltered as it was by overhanging eaves and plentiful trees. He liked to sit on the porch late in the afternoons and watch the birds, or stroll about in the vegetable garden, or take the hose and water the roses, those aristocrats of the flower-plot which especially appealed to him. On one occasion he writes to the girls: "The mildew is getting on my rosebushes and I'm fighting it with sulphur, and there's no telling which is going to come out ahead, me, or the sulphur, or the mildew. I felt right sorry for myself when I first found the mildew, but I'm feeling better now. Chloe had all her young ones here this morning picking strawberries. They picked the milk bucket full and two boxes. So you see we are having very gay times in Wes' Een', Atlanta, Georgy."

And again, he writes of the bounty of the garden and the flower-plots: —

"During the past few days we have been fairly feasting on home-made strawberries. To-day we had three shortcakes for dinner, and two large bowls full of berries left over for supper. Will have almost as many more to-morrow: and all this from the little patch you saw when you were here. I set out 500 new plants in March, and next year (if all goes well) we'll have enough berries to supply the neighborhood. To-day we had green peas for dinner out of our garden, being somewhat ahead of anybody in West End, although we planted later

SNAP-BEAN FARM IN 1900

than our neighbors. This must be just luck, for I take no special pains with the garden, leaving it pretty much to Banks.

"The weather is warm, and we have a profusion of roses. La France seems to be outdoing herself this year, giving us some buds larger than I have ever seen from a hot-house, and delightfully fragrant. I trimmed the bushes very close in March, and now they are paying me back. I never saw so many buds. But for the cold weather and high winds, the flowers would have been more perfect, but they are perfect enough for me. I'm not grumbling — which reminds me that J. C. has placed a 'grumble-box' on the dinner table. Whoever grumbles must place a copper in the box."

Summer, with all its out-of-door pleasures, was the season that he liked best, but cold weather he detested, and once during a very cold spell he wrote to one of the children: "The thermometer and the mercury caught hold of each other's hands and went down nearly to zero. I hope they liked it; I'm sure *I* did n't. If I had the tropic zone here I'd sleep with it to-night, much as I dislike to sleep with strangers."

Yet even bad weather failed to make him grumble audibly; he might be uncomfortable, but he could joke even about rude Boreas: —

"The weather is bad — clouds, rain, and snow. I tried to have the blues, but somehow they did n't 'take.' When I feel like I ought to have the blues, so as to do like other people, something is sure to happen to take my mind off and set me to laughing. A lady once told me she thought it would be dreadful if she could n't have the blues; and there are a great many people who are never happy unless they are unhappy."

Indeed, father dwelt often upon the virtues of cheerfulness and contentment, and said to his girls once: "When you grow up, be contented; don't be carried away by vain things; be good-humored and good-tempered, and knock disappointment in the head with a smile. Oh, it is so easy to be contented, and yet there is so little of it in the world."

The only thing in the routine of the home that annoyed him was "house-cleaning." He had a theory that sweeping merely sent the dust from floor to ceiling, and that the vicious circle was complete when the dust settled back again and the sweeping had to be done all over! When Chloe appeared upon the scene at house-cleaning time, and put her abounding energy behind the broom, the master of the house shuddered, and removed himself as far as possible from the whirlwind campaign. After one of these upheavals, he wrote: —

WEST END DAYS

"We have had so much house-cleaning lately that it is too nice to believe in, but we can't help ourselves. We are obliged to live in it or camp out next door to the street, but this would be an invitation to burglars. And so mamma prefers to sleep in the mansion, though really, the dust and dirt are horrible. Nobody knows where they come from. Chloe carries out seven bale-fuls every Friday and mamma sweeps out seven bale-fuls every Saturday. I suppose this is the way to enjoy life, but as for me, I'd prefer to live in a house that did n't have to be swept but once every fifteen years."

However, he rejoiced in mother's energy, even if it *did* often take the odious form of directing such domestic "drives," and he said to the girls: "Mamma is enthusiastic, and I am glad of it. When we lose enthusiasm, appreciation goes with it, and then the joy of living is taken away."

Though appreciating thoroughly the society of his friends, father abhorred formal gatherings, and could rarely be induced to be present at one.[1] On the occasion of Captain Howell's silver wedding in 1886, his affection for his old friend led him to promise to attend the celebration, and he dressed and accompanied mother to the front gate of the

[1] Father's old friend, Thomas E. Watson, once wittily said of him that he was "plainly incapable of adjusting himself to the human miscellany."

Howell place. From there he could see the bright lights shining through all the long windows of the old mansion and numbers of persons passing back and forth. The intimations of the scene were too much for him; the thought of the crowd and of meeting strangers paralyzed him, and he fled, leaving mother to make his excuses! On the occasion of another "silver wedding" he was less canny, and actually found himself in the midst of the festivities, an account of which he wrote to one of his children: —

"I went to Dr. T.'s silver wedding and found myself the observed of all observers; in fact, I had to stand in the same room with the middle-aged bride and groom, and hold a reception of my own. Mrs. Z—— talked one ear off, and the rest of them marched off with the remains of the other. I never heard so much talk in my life. Some woman caught hold of the lower corner of my vest, and held on as though she was afraid she'd drown if she turned loose. You may be sure that I had a surfeit of all this. Enough is enough and too much is a plenty. It was all mighty funny to me. As I was going, Dr. T. whispered that he wished everybody would go but me. He and his wife must have been tired, for they stood up, as I did, all the time. When I got out, I panted right heartily and felt as if I had done a day's ploughing. And yet in spite of this, I rather enjoyed the affair, for it enabled me to see with my own eyes how foolish nice women can be." [1]

One form of social contact which father thoroughly enjoyed was the time spent with his West End friends on the street-car each morning in going to town. The schedule was a twenty-minute one, and on account of the considerable interval between cars, the same crowd usually found it convenient to ride on the same car day after day. This group numbered, amongst others, Colonel George W. Adair and his son Forrest, Captain Evan P. Howell, Dr. Sidney Holland, and Major Joseph Van Holt Nash, Sr., all *West-Enders.* Thus the 8.30 A.M. West End car was as much a "special" in its way as the "Congressional Limited," and woe betide the stray traveler who boarded it lacking a sense of humor, for he or she was more than likely to be made the victim of a good-natured joke. Once on his way to take the car father picked

---

[1] On the occasion of the marriage, in June, 1889, at Washington, Georgia, of Miss Annulet Andrews to Mr. J. K. Ohl, now editor of the New York *Herald*, to the great surprise of everybody father consented to be Mr. Ohl's "best man." Both Mr. Ohl and Miss Andrews were connected with the *Constitution* and father was very fond of them. This was such an extraordinary departure from his regular custom that no one dreamed it could be accomplished, but it was. Mr. Ohl carried his "best man" to Washington and the ceremony took place as planned.

up a pair of blue-glass eyes which had fallen out of
a doll's head, and absent-mindedly put them in his
pocket. Sitting in front of him on this particular
trip was a sedate elderly woman and her little
granddaughter. Father knew the lady only by
sight and as one who stood greatly upon her dignity
and at once the impish idea occurred to him to try
the effect of the glass eyes on the little girl who
peered at him from time to time over her grandmother's shoulder. So he closed his own eyes, and
after a fashion held the doll's eyes in place with the
muscles of his eyelids. When next the little one
peeped at him, she was startled to see a pair of
glassy optics where before she had noticed only the
mild blue eyes of a stout, placid gentleman.

In alarm she whispered to her grandmother,
"Gran'ma, that man's got the *funniest* eyes!"

"Sh! sh! child, don't comment on people,"
warned her grandmother.

But before long the lady herself shot a well-bred
glance in father's direction. There was nothing
unusual to be seen. In a few moments the glass
eyes were readjusted, just in time to meet the little
girl's second stare with a particularly uncanny
glitter. Again she whispered excitedly: —

"Gran'ma, I tell you that man *has* got somethin'
awful the matter with his eyes."

"Why, child," replied the astonished lady, "you must be crazy. What are you talking about?"

And when she could safely do so, she again glanced at father only to see a perfectly normal individual, looking dreamily out of the window. This comedy kept up for several minutes, until the lady began to suspect from the demeanor of the regular 8.30 West-Enders that she was being made the victim of a joke. Upon which she haughtily arose from her seat and casting a disdainful look in the direction of the offender left the car with her bewildered little charge in her train.

Such jokes as these, indulged in now and then, occasionally acted as boomerangs. Once at night-fall father, who was standing near his front gate, saw one of mother's acquaintances approaching, and the spirit of mischief prompted him to pull his soft felt hat over his eyes, turn his coat-collar up around his ears, and step forward toward the lady in the attitude of a tramp asking for money. Taken by surprise the lady failed to recognize him, became frightened, and turned and ran back up the street. Father was immediately seized with compunction and ran after her to reassure her, but she, thinking that the "tramp" was in pursuit, only ran the faster, and did not stop until she heard her name called by a familiar voice. By this time the crestfallen "tramp" was so out of breath and so overcome with confusion that he could make only an incoherent explanation. The result was that the offended lady whispered around the neighborhood that she '*did* believe Mr. Harris had been drinking when he ran after her that way'!

Oftentimes the conversations on the street-car furnished father with hints for his editorials. At one point on the line was a factory which made sewing-machine motors, and it was thought that this company furnished excellent opportunity for investment. In passing it one day, some one asked Colonel Adair if he had any stock in it. "Did you ever get on a drunk?" was his answer. "Do you know the symptoms of a drunk?" he continued, — "of a *patent* drunk, for instance?" And he enlarged on the subject of people who get drunk on *patents* and untested inventions. Father listened to the conversation and later used the expression "patent drunk" as a text for a humorous editorial.

He also wrote character sketches for the "Constitution" based on street-car anecdotes, one of these being a most amusing account of Colonel Adair's "attack of the grippe." It seems that Mrs. Adair (always called by her husband "Old Miss") was in the habit of putting away the blankets in pepper to preserve them against moths. One night in early fall, before she had thought it necessary to have the winter bedding freed of its medication, the colonel felt the need of extra covering, so he ordered one of the servants to get out a blanket. The negro boy hastily placed the pepper-impregnated covering on the bed and shortly afterward his master was seized with a terrible fit of sneezing. "Old Miss," hearing the noise, appeared in the doorway and ordered a hot mustard foot-bath and some quinine pills for the sufferer, who by this time was convinced that he was coming down with a bad case of the grippe. After a half-hour of dosing and coddling, the colonel was put back to bed and snugly tucked in, when lo, and behold! the sneezing began again, and this time both the negro attendant and "Old Miss" joined in the chorus. For a few moments the bedroom rang with sneezes; then it suddenly occurred to the lady of the house that this highly infectious form of grippe had its origin in the pepper-box!

Nearly all the old West-Enders are dead now, but Colonel Adair's eldest son remembers the "good old times" on the "West-End Special," and in addition to the stories already given has told me how father once protected himself against a talkative old gentleman who for some time persecuted him with his attentions on the daily rides back and forth between West End and the center of town. This individual had an unspeakable habit of working his false teeth up and down, with uncanny clicking noises which punctuated his long-winded stories. For some reason he had selected father as the object of his attentions and nearly bored him to death. One day he seated himself next to his unhappy victim and began torturing him; father sat in a listless and dejected attitude, paying as little attention as possible to the old gentleman's harangue. By and by a paper bag containing grits which the boresome one held on his knee sprung a leak and the fine, white grains of hominy trickled steadily on the floor. The old gentleman was so deeply interested in his own conversation that he was totally unaware of the accident, and as his tale waxed longer his supply of grits grew shorter and shorter. Father kept his eyes fixed on the white pyramid which was piling up with increasing rapidity, but never a word did he say. Just as the old bore drew near his journey's end, he emphasized a point in his discourse by bearing down rather heavily on his sack, and thus discovered for the first time that it was nearly empty. In astonishment he glanced at father, whose eyes were still glued to the floor.

"Why did n't you tell me that my hominy was running out?" he demanded indignantly, as he realized that father must have known about it for some time.

"Well," stammered the latter, in a weary tone, "I thought you were doing it on purpose."

This was the last time he had to submit to the old gentleman's unwelcome attentions.

In contrast to his attitude toward a too talkative person was father's effort to make friends with "Old Man Gregg," a silent and rather morose old Irishman, a veteran of the War of 1812, whose pension kept him in a little house on one of the side streets near the end of the car line, where he lived in the company of his dog "Paddy" and his pet king snake. The old fellow had little use for his contemporaries, but he tolerated the boys of the neighborhood who flocked to see his tame snake; and he sometimes condescended to talk Gaelic for their entertainment. The veteran's independence of character attracted father, and after a few advances on the part of the latter, they became excellent friends, for when father made an effort to get next to people he was irresistible — he was so human and unassuming, so genuinely kind.

Mother tells an incident which reveals how these qualities endeared him to those who knew him well. One of his West End friends, the brother of Colonel Richard Malcolm Johnston, dropped by the house one evening when the family was seated on the porch and asked father to take a little walk with him, as he had "something to tell him." When mother later asked if Mr. Johnston had told him any bad news, father stammered awhile, and finally replied, blushing vividly, "Why, no. He — he just wanted to tell me how much he loved me." Father was very fond of Mr. Gus Culberson, one of his neighbors, and when Mr. Culberson's younger brother, Hubert, married and settled near by with his young wife and baby, father one day saw the mother sitting on the porch holding her little girl in her arms. He walked up the steps and sat down near Mrs. Culberson, and after a few commonplaces were exchanged, his hostess remarked that she was sorry her husband was not at home. Father replied that he did not come to see her husband. "Well," said Mrs. Culberson, "I am so pleased that you came to see me." "But I did n't come to see you, exactly," answered the guest. "Then," she asked quizzically, "would it be out of the way for me to inquire what you *did* come for?" "Not at all," he replied; "I came to see the baby!" And for some time he sat near by, silently studying the little one, presumably to his own satisfaction and to that of the young mother!

As time passed, father became more and more

attached to his West End home, and rarely left it for a visit or a vacation. He wrote one of the children who was in Canada: "Home is a great place when you look at it from a distance. I think it is a great place, no matter how close I am to it, and I never expect to be as far from it as you are now. We had some cantaloupes for breakfast this morning and they were monstrous good. And I had a dish of figs besides. Yes, siree! home's a fine place, and don't you forget it."

And again: "I prefer to stay where I can see the lawn and the flowers, and hear the birds, and run the chickens out, and chunk old Ovid out of the flower-beds."

It would not be seemly for me to cite any instances of father's numerous acts of charity and kindness toward those less fortunate than himself — those whose miseries constantly knocked at his heart. In a letter to one of his children he said: "The happiest people are those who never try to be rich, and I thank heaven that I never had any real desire for riches. Yet I should like to have a surplus so as to help the unfortunate." He disliked the term "deserving" as applied to the poor, and his utter lack of condescension toward his fellow creatures was expressed in one of his earlier editorials when he wrote regarding his conception of charity:—

JOEL CHANDLER HARRIS

"You will observe that although I have the frog securely fastened I never tighten the line to study his antics. I know very well he would make an ineffectual struggle to escape, and finally become comfortable again. If I am thus tender of the feelings of the frog, you may be sure of carefulness when the hook is baited with a human creature. How can I tell whether it is myself or some one else that is dangling at the end of the line? We all have our weaknesses, and for my part I never did envy your strong man, who is above every sort of temptation. There is something wrong about him somewhere."

So it was not surprising that his sympathy and benefactions were extended alike to those whose honest efforts entitled them to help, and to "bums" and chronic beggars. "Organized charity" would have regarded his system with disapproval, but the knowledge of this fact did not disturb father's serenity, for he never greatly concerned himself with modern methods.

CHAPTER XVI

FATHER AND SON

IN March of 1890 father accompanied some friends on a fishing trip to Florida in order to escape the disagreeable "breaking-up" season between winter and spring, which he so much dreaded. He had a good time, and, as he expressed it, "helped eat the fish that his friends caught." A pleasant feature of the trip was a short time spent in St. Augustine, and of this he wrote mother: —

24 March, 1890

MY DARLING GIRL: —

We have been having a great time here. Mr. Flagler, the proprietor of the Ponce de Leon, seems to have singled me out for his courtesies. I have been with him all day, and he is sitting by me now, while I am writing. He has made some wonderful changes here, so they say, and an Englishman who has been all over the world says that the Ponce de Leon is the finest hotel in the world, being a combination of the good points of all.[1]

[1] The occasion of father's visit to the Ponce de Leon Hotel was another instance of his sense of humor running away with him. His punishment overtook him in due time and he tells of it in a letter to his friend, John Henderson Garnsey, in 1898: —

"A man from Florida called on me some time ago, and, after

JOEL CHANDLER HARRIS

I am well, and, as Irwin said, if I have any fault in the world it is in being too good. I have seen Mr. Chauncey Depew, and about the first thing he said to me was, "I hear you have a boy who is a smarter man than his daddy." I told him that this was mere rumor, but he continues to believe it. If I have a chance to write to you again, I'll do so. My partner is Dr. R. D. Spalding. We got up this morning and went to church in the oldest Catholic church in America, and this was my first attendance on morning mass — early mass. The doctor says I am a right nice man, and has just written to his wife that he is fortunate enough to have me for a partner. Give my love to all, and beg the boys to be good.

Your affectionate

JOEY

some conversation, asked: 'Where did Flagler get the idea that you were a drinking man?' I was shocked and surprised, and could give no explanation. Days afterwards the truth flashed on my mind. Several years ago I went to Florida with Captain Howell and a lot of other Atlantans, and Flagler sent a special train to Jacksonville for us. He seemed to take to me, and addressed himself almost wholly to my ears as he showed us over the hotel. He carried us into the grand parlor, and began to expatiate on the *cost* of the paintings. One was especially voluminous in price. 'Yes,' said I, 'it is certainly fine, *but where is the bar-room ?*' He must have thought I was after liquor, instead of trying to call him away from the *price* of the pictures. I judge he has never forgotten the episode. You see the cornfield journalist ruined himself with the author and inventor of crude petroleum and Ponce de Leon hotels."

FATHER AND SON

The compliment paid Julian by Senator Depew must have tickled father, for he was ambitious for his eldest, who had begun to "compose little tales," which appeared regularly in the paper issued by the boys of the military school which he was attending. Father held to the theory that a contact with new people and new surroundings was an excellent thing for an ambitious young person, and advocated "neighbor-knowledge" as being quite as important as that imparted in schools, meaning by "neighbor-knowledge" an exchange of ideas between the people of different sections. Julian was now nearing his sixteenth birthday, and had begun to concern himself about a "career" and to fidget about going to work, turning over plans for training in a newspaper office one day and the study of law the next; so father thought he could not do better than to send him to Grandfather LaRose's farm, near St. Éphrem d'Upton in the Province of Quebec, for a protracted stay. There he could have the benefit of rigorous exercise in a bracing climate, could mingle with new people, acquire "neighbor-knowledge," study French, and fit himself both physically and mentally to make the great decision when the proper time arrived. So in July, 1890, a slight, erect figure in the cadet uniform of the Gordon Military Institute set out alone for Canadian territory, carrying his "grip" and feeling very important at the prospect of taking in the sights of Washington and New York *en route* to the land of the "habitans."

Father had arranged with Mr. E. W. Barrett, the correspondent of the "Atlanta Constitution" (now editor of the "Birmingham Age-Herald"), to meet the young traveler in Washington and show him the city, but when the train pulled in and Julian alighted, his escort was nowhere to be seen and the boy independently set out for himself. He wandered about for part of a day, not being particularly impressed with the wonders of which he had heard, especially when he saw a number of *crows* flapping across the sky. No truly metropolitan city could be infested by *crows*, thought the young Georgian, so at the end of a few hours and in a somewhat condescending mood, he boarded his train and set out for New York; and, in the careless fashion of youth, he neglected to telegraph home the news that he had reached Washington in safety.

On arriving in New York he left the Desbrosses Street Ferry, strolled along until he came to an eating-house, and went in and ordered for his supper a dish of lobster salad. This delicacy must have symbolized to the young man from an inland town all the mystery and grandeur of the great seaport, and there could have been no question about the appropriateness of his choice had not he yielded to a home-bred habit and demanded at the same time *a glass of milk.* The waiter, a fatherly individual, politely suggested that the combination was ill-advised, but the youth felt competent to settle such a trifling matter as a choice of dishes, and replied that he "was used to lobster and milk," and made good his boast by partaking heartily of the spread.

The result was that shortly afterward he succumbed to a violent attack of ptomaine poisoning — called colic in those days — and his would-be adviser led him unresistingly to a bedroom above the restaurant and called in a doctor. After several hours of acute misery, a meek, white-faced youngster set out with uncertain steps in the direction of the railroad station, robbed of all desire to see the sights of a treacherous city which now seemed to him to be full of pitfalls for the inexperienced. Upset by his illness, again he failed to wire his parents of his safe arrival, and when he reached St. Éphrem d'Upton twelve hours later, he little dreamed what consternation and anxiety raged on his account in the West End home.

The telegram from Mr. Barrett stating that he had failed to see Julian in Washington was received by mother in the middle of a very hot afternoon, and in her distress of mind she ran several blocks to the old Wilson pond where father and the other boys were in swimming. Standing on the bank she wildly signaled to them and wailed, "O Joey! Joey! Julian is lost! Why did we ever let him take that trip alone!"

The outcome of this comedy of errors is given in the following letter and clipping: —

DEAR JULIAN: —

I enclose a clipping from the "Washington Post," one of many of that kind that have appeared in the newspapers during the past week. Please have it inserted in the "Upton Bugle" or in the "St. Hyacinthe Poppy." You can imagine what a charming episode it has been to us all — how pleased your mother was when a telegram from Barrett came, announcing that you were not in Washington, and that you could not possibly have arrived. It was a beautiful scene — one long to be remembered; a scene such as can only be found (with this exception) in books.

To add to the anxiety of your friends here, J. W. Todd telegraphed from Central, S.C., on his way back, that no such passenger as Julian Harris had been on his train.[1] This telegram I kept from your

---

[1] Julian could never understand the obtuseness of the conductor and it still remains a mystery to him how a youngster in the uniform of a military school could have been so completely overlooked!

mother. What an easy matter it would have been to send a telegram from Washington that you were going through!

Well, I trust you will have a good time. You have arrived at the age when carelessness and indifference to the feelings of others have taken possession of you, as they do of all youngsters, but try to be as respectful to your grandfather and your grandmother as possible. Bear in mind that they have lived long out of the world, so to speak, and try not to treat them with that superciliousness so often affected by boys of your age. Remember that learning is merely an accomplishment and not a virtue, and if they seem to you to be ignorant, bear in mind that, in turn, you will seem to be ignorant to your descendants.

Remember, too, that we love you, that we and all who know you expect great things of you — remembering this, let every act of yours bear some definite relation to your self-respect.

We are all well here. The place is just as you left it, except the hole made in the air by your absence, and it is a pretty large one, too.

I am waiting for those long letters.

Your

DAD

JOEL CHANDLER HARRIS

WHERE IS THIS BOY?

Joel Chandler Harris's Son Missing on his Trip to Washington

Julian Harris, the sixteen-year-old son of Joel Chandler Harris (Uncle Remus), of the "Atlanta Constitution," is badly wanted by his father and friends.

A few days ago Mr. E. W. Barrett, correspondent of the "Constitution" here, received a letter from Mr. Harris stating that his son, Julian, would leave Atlanta Sunday morning for Canada, to visit relatives. He would reach Washington Monday morning, and would stop over three or four days before proceeding on his journey. Mr. Barrett was asked to kindly look after the young man, and to show him such favors as might be necessary and convenient. The letter stated that he would stop at the Metropolitan.[1]

Mr. Barrett notified the clerk at this hotel to say to young Mr. Harris to remain at the hotel until he came in from Takoma Park, about noon Monday. When Mr. Barrett went to the hotel at the time named, he was told that no such party had arrived. This appeared strange, and when Mr. Barrett reached the Capitol he found a telegram asking if Julian had arrived safely. An answer was sent, saying that he had failed to reach Washington, or else he had gone to some hotel other than the Metropolitan.

This telegram caused Mr. Harris, Captain Howell, and other members of the "Constitution" staff to become alarmed, and since its receipt a large number of messages have been sent to Mr. Barrett to spare neither

---

[1] There was some misunderstanding on this point. Julian's expectation was that he was to be met at the train, and he recalled no mention of the Metropolitan or any other hotel by his father.

time nor money in ascertaining the whereabouts of the young man. He had left Atlanta Sunday morning, and his failure to reach Washington could not be explained.

All day yesterday efforts were made to learn something of him, but without avail. Late in the afternoon Mr. Barrett notified detective headquarters, and left a description.

The young man is of a quiet, retiring disposition, and no one who knows him would for a moment believe that he has concluded to run his trip on his own schedule and to suit himself.

Father's tender heart ruled him even in the midst of his justifiable irritation toward the thoughtless boy who had been the unwitting cause of such a disturbance, and he wrote another letter which he sent along ahead of the first one to salve its sting: —

6 July, 1890

MY DEAR BOY: —

I wrote you a letter last Sunday, but as it was written while I was still suffering from the strain which my uneasiness and anxiety placed on me, I did not mail it. I will send it to you this week, for there are some things in it that you ought to see; but in reading it you must bear in mind that it was written under the pressure of excitement. I received your letters enclosing a piece headed "My Trip." The difficulty is that it is not about your trip at all, but is only an episode of your trip. When you send me a real letter for the paper I will put this episode in it. Can't you take time to write about 1200 words for the paper? But you must certainly improve your handwriting. Get some wider paper — get foolscap and larger envelopes. I could hardly read your letter at all. When you write, don't be in a hurry. Another thing: you must learn how to talk French. You will never have another opportunity. Don't disappoint me in this. It will be a great pleasure to me to hear you talking French to your mother when you return. You must help your grandfather and grandmother all you can. You can make yourself useful in a thousand ways.

With the $14 you can get your grandmother to take you to St. Hyacinthe, and to Montreal. I will send you some money later on, so that you can buy you a suit of winter clothes and an overcoat.

There is no news at home. One day with another, it is the same as when you left. Such points as I think may interest you I will give in another letter. But don't be alarmed when you receive my famous letter of reproval which I will mail to-morrow.

Your affectionate

DAD

Father was anxious that the novel impressions of Canadian farm-life should stimulate Julian to express himself in writing, for he was convinced that the boy had the journalistic gift, and as Mr. Turner once encouraged him, so he now encouraged his eldest: —

July 20, 1890

DEAR JULIAN: —

Your last letters show a great improvement over the first, not only in writing, but in expression. I suppose you wrote the first in a great hurry, being anxious to get out and around, and make your influence felt on the worthy *habitans* of the Province of Quebec. I see from your various letters that you are having a good time, and that is what I want you to have. Are you keeping up with your shorthand? And are you perfecting yourself in spoken French? I remind you of these things in order that even during your play you may have an eye to your future. But I am not a great success as a lecturer, and if I take that attitude occasionally it is because I have more interest in your future career than I have ever had in my own.

A dog caught one of Tootsie's [1] bantams the other night, and the next night he sat up for him. When the dog appeared, the gun was lying across Tootsie's lap, and he cocked it and pulled the

[1] Lucien, the second son.

trigger at the same time, so that, with a terrific explosion, the whole load went into the calf-pen.

Tootsie, however, is coming out in great shape. He has been moping about the house and reading ever since you left, until the other day, when he joined a "literary society." Friday evening he was invited to a party given by Ivy and Alice May Lee. He decked himself out in a new hat and a pair of patent-leather pumps (having on his clothes, of course) and appeared on the festive scene in great shape. It was said that Tootsie was the life of the party, full of wit and humor. He certainly made a fine impression. Buck, Lucien, Joe Swartz, and Evelyn slept last night in a litter out under the smoke tree, and they say they had a fine time. Evelyn has learned to swim a few strokes, but he is afraid to take advantage of this fact. Linton still has one or the other of his feet wrapped in a dirty, greasy rag, and he presents a picturesque appearance wherever he goes. Sometimes he hides the rag with a dirty old sock. Mildred has become a great elocutionist. She went to the school exhibition, and can now repeat all the songs and dialogues she heard there, and she does it with surprising accuracy. J. C. is right now in the middle of the whooping-cough. He stands up under it very well, but he is having a tough time.

FATHER AND SON

The boys will tell you all the juvenile news when they write — if there is any. The cows are holding up well, but I expect they are eating their heads off. I am afraid to make a calculation.

My dear boy, I am neglecting my work to write you this stuff, and I must stop. Write to me when you spare the time from your arduous duties, and give my love to all.

Your affectionate

DADDY

It would seem that the boy responded quickly to encouragement and made an effort to do justice to his opportunities; this naturally gave much pleasure to his "Dad," who had an engaging way of mingling advice, praise, and tender home messages in every letter: —

MY DEAR BOY: —

Your last letter was charming. I was so proud of it — of the style and the expression — that I showed it to Mr. Reed.[1] His remark was "That boy is a good writer." Then after a while he said, "He is a splendid descriptive writer." This is very gratifying to me, and I tell you about it in order to

---

[1] Wallace P. Reed, on the editorial staff of the *Constitution* and one of father's warmest friends.

encourage you to do better all the time. Do you know what genius is? It is large talents united with the ability to take pains — native ability wedded to persistent industry.[1] If you will only take pains you will make a tremendous success in everything you go at.

I suppose that by this time you are getting somewhat homesick, and we are still missing you. The baby is always asking about Bubber Ju-ju, and your mother and I sit on the porch after supper and wonder what our young man is doing. Still, we know that you are enjoying yourself, and that is enough.

Meantime, write something about Upton and the people you meet up with — the impressions they make on you — and don't forget the folklore stories that are to be found in that neighborhood. Get your grandpa to help you on this.

Your affectionate

DAD

Julian did his full share of work on the farm — he helped garner the hay crop, milked several cows morning and evening, sawed wood against the

---

[1] On another occasion father wrote one of his children, "Writing is an easy matter, but fairly good writing is a matter of hard work, and the very best, like Cardinal Newman's, is simply the outcome of the most abject painstaking."

early fall weather, and "picked" potato bugs off the big potato patch when the annual ceremony of sprinkling the crop with holy water failed to do the work of Paris green.

Then, too, he practiced his short-hand and wrote accounts of his doings for the "Constitution," so when he failed to respond promptly to welcome home letters, father was not too hard on him: —

3 August, 1890

My dear Boy: —

I have written you two letters since hearing from you, and this is the third. I suppose you are too busy to write to an old man, whose letters are uninteresting. This is a perfectly natural feeling. I don't like to write letters myself, and I never do unless I feel it to be my duty. You are probably too young to understand what duty means. It gets to be a bigger and more important word as one grows older.

I have n't had time yet to patch your letters together. Mr. —— has been on a tremendous drunk, winding up in the calaboose, and this has been supplemented by a "booze" on the part of Mr. ——, who has just turned up while I am writing. He looks sad and sorry. Ah, Lord! I trust you will never fall into such a muddy ditch. I don't see how the Almighty can ever forgive an intelligent human being for making a sot of himself. You will see that I have had very little time of my own except at night, and the weather is too warm then for work. The "Century" has just accepted the story I was writing in the spring [1] when I had to drive you boys out of the room. It will make fourteen pages in the magazine, and will appear in the December number. If it was n't so hot I could make a great deal of money by this literary work. I think next year I'll stay in Canada during the three hot months and try to do some literary work.

I hope you are keeping up your short-hand, as you promised, and I shall be very much disappointed if you don't learn to speak French fluently. I have n't time to write a long letter, especially as I have n't heard from you lately.

Be good to yourself.

Your affectionate

DAD

Julian's grandfather thought it would be a good plan for him to have several months' instruction in the Frères Maristes College in order to improve his French, and the boy fell in with this idea.

---

[1] "A Conscript's Christmas." This, together with five other stories, written during 1890, was published by Houghton Mifflin Company, under the title *Balaam and His Master*.

FATHER AND SON

Father agreed, but his wise suggestion that these months in Upton were to be considered merely as a preparation for a life in a less limited environment indicates that his ambition for his eldest son was always on the alert: —

1 September

DEAR JULIAN: —

I enclose you sight exchange on New York for $50. This will leave you some money over, and I want you to take care of it as well as you can. You will have enough to go to the French School if you are still in that mind. I think it is a very good idea. It will be a very poor return for me, and a great disappointment to boot if you come back here with only a smattering of French. I want you to know the principles of it thoroughly, so that you can enjoy its literature.

You ought to be able to explain to your grandfather that you will have to begin the business of life next year, and that you cannot afford to remain in Upton any longer unless you propose to settle there. He will understand that. No youngster who has any promise of a career can afford to bury himself in Upton, or in any other country place. Not that I object to the country places. I think it is quite as important as any other part of his education that a boy should be brought up in touch with the rural regions, and that he should appreciate them to the fullest extent. That is the reason you are in Upton now. When you get as old as I am you may want to go back there and live — having discovered that life has very little to offer outside of the contentment of home. It will be time enough for you to spend a longer season in Upton when you have made this and other discoveries.

I am now trying to look at life through your eyes, and I frequently catch myself mapping out a proud career for you. But this will be a vain imagining unless you have that within you which will enable you to resist the various temptations that are spread out before a young man. The real success in life is the will-power that enables one to resist these.

But I am not much of a preacher, and this is not intended to be much of a sermon — being merely a roundabout way of saying that your future is altogether in your own hands. I am not much of a Puritan myself, and I have tried to so conform my views to yours as to enable you to say that I have never denied you anything that would tend to give you real pleasure. All that I ask in return is that you won't drink whiskey or other spirits.

Your
D<small>AD</small>

FATHER AND SON

Father was, indeed, not given to "preaching," which accounts in part for the comradeship that existed between him and his children. When he did think it necessary to administer a dose of advice, he always flavored it with humor and thus robbed it of its unpalatable quality. "This thing of giving Information and Advice, and making believe that everything in life is very, very serious, is tiresome to me," he once said; and he went on to tell of an old gentleman who thought he took an interest in him as a boy and wrote him long, dull letters, and to cap the climax presented him with a copy of Cobbett's "Letters to Young Men." "It was all very dreary," he commented, "and I know now that it turned me against the man. But if he had sent me cheerful letters, I should have regarded him as a benefactor."

The early fall brought a great anxiety to the family in the illness with diphtheria of Linton, now seven years old. This little boy was Julian's especial favorite, and father made as light of the affair as he could in writing about it, knowing the effect that the dread word "diphtheria" would have on the older boy. Even in the midst of his anxiety, he took pains to send the absent one all the news of Snap-Bean Farm: —

JOEL CHANDLER HARRIS

15 September, 1890

DEAR JULIAN: —

I have not written sooner for several reasons. In the first place you owe me a letter; you have never answered the one in which I enclosed a draft on New York. I suppose, however, your school and your work keep you pretty busy. In the second place, Linton has been very sick. He is still very sick, but the doctors think he is improving a little. In addition to the tonsilitis which your mother wrote you about, he has had polypi in his nose. In other words, a polypus in each nostril. I have heard of this disease, but never saw it before. A polypus is a sort of growth in the nostril — in,the case of a man gristle; in Linton's case a sort of pulpy flesh, not greatly different in appearance from the lights of a chicken, though a little darker. I suppose these polypi have been growing in Linton's nose for some months, and that they were greatly aggravated by the tonsilitis.

This afternoon Dr. H—— cut them out, and I judge from the size and length that they must have extended throughout the nostril. The operation would have been a very painful one, but for the use of cocaine, but Linton says it did n't hurt him at all, and he seems to be very much better. He is very hoarse, and his throat is still very sore, but he

[274]

is bright and patient under it all. He gets mad sometimes when we irritate him with our attentions and anxiety, but altogether, he is the most courageous and patient chap I ever saw. You may judge from all this that he has been very sick. He is still very sick, but has retained his strength and nerve to a remarkable degree.

The calves are both in good condition, and so are your fowls, so far as I know. Your celebrated game has renewed his feathers, and not his courage if he ever had any. He does n't stay around where old Buff can trample on him. Lucien has a three-ounce bantam that tries to train Maripo in the art of scrapping, but the great chief refuses to come to time. The Pekin ducks are the only game fowl on the place except Linton's hen. I think I will write to my friend ——, of Fort Valley, in October, and get a trio of games — the real article.

Your affectionate

DAD

With a blighting suddenness, which was so often characteristic of the disease in those days before anti-toxin was generally used, the end came to Linton a few days after the preceding letter was written. This was the most heartbreaking grief that had overtaken the household; Linton's gentle,

[275]

affectionate, endearing nature was plainly shown by the sweetness of his expression and the soft beauty of his large brown eyes. He had inherited mother's charm of person and father's responsiveness to natural influences, and his little soul was sensitively attuned to all that was lovely around him. Father was terribly affected by the untimely end of this child, and the letter announcing the tragic event to the eldest brother came straight from the depths of a tortured heart: —

22 September, 1890

MY DARLING BOY: —

In the midst of my grief and despair I can scarcely summon courage enough to write you of the death of Linton — your little brother and partner. If there had been time, I would have telegraphed you money to come home on, but the change came so suddenly that there was hardly time to send for Dr. C——. The trouble was not with his throat — that was getting along very well — but with his heart. Though his throat was improving all the time, he never seemed to rally, and at the last, too late to apply any effective remedy, we discovered that his heart was affected.

The change took place late Saturday evening; he was bright Friday, looking at his cigarette pictures and talking about you; and at 5 o'clock Sunday morning he died, without a struggle and with no pain whatever, like a tired baby going to sleep. From beginning to end he made no complaint, and was never fretful nor irritable, and the last words he said were, "I feel better."

It is a great blow to us as it must be to you. I have always fancied that you cared more for him than for the rest — perhaps it was only a fancy, but I know that you were chiefly in his thoughts, although you were away.

Of such dispensations as this, we have to make the best. So I am told. But I should like somebody to tell me how. While we are thinking about it, let me advise you to take Linton for your pattern so far as his patience was concerned. I cannot write you a long letter, and I hardly know what I have written.

Your mother sends her dearest love, and we both bless you, and trust that heaven may guard you safely.

Your affectionate

PAPA

In the "Constitution" of the day following that of Linton's burial was a tribute to the little one written by father himself, in which he tells in simple

and touching fashion something of the boy's graces
of person and character. Only those who have
known the immeasurable grief of losing a child can
appreciate the solace that comes with the ability
to pour out the soul in words of love and appreciation as an offering to the adored little creature who
is no more: —

THE DEATH OF A LITTLE BOY

At the funeral services of little Linton Harris, in West
End, yesterday, the floral offerings were less remarkable
for their quantity than their quality. The rarest blooms
that the season affords were there, sent by those who
knew the little fellow in life. With him the love of flowers was something more than fancy — it was a passion
that gave to his young life a beautiful ardor and a delicate refinement that are not to be acquired by artificial
aid.

In the early spring it was a favorite remark of his that
he proposed to hide in the bushes and watch the roses
bloom. That he discovered this secret there can be no
doubt, for he carried the knowledge of it in the wise,
mysterious, and unfathomable depths of his beautiful
eyes. But the secret was inviolate. Whether told to
him by the singing birds, the droning bees, or the va-
grant wind, it went no farther. But it was not alone the
secret of the rose that he learned. There was no flower
of the woods or fields so shy that it hid from him. At
his timid but familiar knock Nature opened wide the
door of her vast storehouse.

It is natural that the hand that pens these lines should
permit itself to be swayed by partiality in touching on

the characteristics of the little boy that is dead; and yet
an old man, a distinguished writer, and one of the most
accomplished scholars the South has produced, was so
attracted by the rare personal characteristics of the
child that he wrote him long and affectionate letters.[1]
Another old man, long buffeted about by the world, and
who has seen all of life that is worth seeing, fell to weep-
ing like a child when he heard that the little boy was
dead. An old negro woman who had nursed him went
away from the house where he lay dead with the tears
streaming down her face.

As with these, so it was with all who knew him. Possessed of singular beauty and grace, his life and character were more beautiful and graceful still; shy and diffident, he was yet the manliest and brightest little fellow
ever seen. There was some nameless attraction about
his personality as perceptible as the perfume of a flower,
and as elusive. He touched all hearts and led them captive. His life was as perfect as a poem, as pure and as
sweet as a strain of music. He carried life and sunshine
everywhere he went.

Even Death, laying aside his dart, took the little boy
gently to his bosom, where he lay smiling.

Julian was completely overcome by the news of
the death of his little "partner" whom he did indeed love more tenderly than any of the other chil-

[1] Colonel Richard Malcolm Johnston, who wrote of Linton:
"That little boy, so meek, so simply childlike, with something almost melancholy in his look — whose soft eyes seemed as if they
were looking, almost yearning for the unknown, which was soon
to come, and be very blessed in its coming. That little one who is
now wiser than all the sages of all times, and who was my friend."

dren, and father's reply to his letter indicates that he feared that the boy's mind might dwell too constantly and sadly on the loss of his little brother. So he does what he can to divert his thoughts into other channels: —

6 October, 1890

DEAR JULIAN: —

If anything could possibly have that effect, your beautiful letter has drawn you closer to your mother's heart and mine. A boy of your age may sometimes have such tender and true sentiments in his mind; but I think it would be difficult to find a man of any age capable of giving them more beautiful expression. All this we are proud to know and we hope that the gift of expression will grow in you.

Dismissing other things, let me suggest to you that you have a very rare opportunity to claim for your own the literary field that is richer and broader in French Canada than in any other portion of the globe. That field has still to be filled. It has been touched on here and there by awkward and adventurous hands. Fiction based on the lives and characters of these quaint and simple people could be made more picturesque than any I know of. Think about this and study the *habitan* in his native simplicity. You may be able to make a mint of money.

I think your grandfather is right about the law. There is in it the certainty of recompense to a bright mind, and it could be made the handmaid of literature. But this is a matter you will have to decide for yourself. It will do you no harm to take a turn at the newspaper business, for you have plenty of time to be a lawyer or anything else.

Your affectionate

PAPA

Our love to all.

Later father advises Julian to keep a journal and write in it his daily experiences and observations, with notes on the *patois* or dialect spoken by the farmers. "To do this," he adds, "may seem monotonous to you now, but it would be invaluable to you hereafter, and some of the simplest notes would be of great aid to you, particularly if you propose to get your bread by the sweat of your brow. I hope all this is not tedious to you. I am not lecturing, nor issuing orders. I am merely making suggestions. . . . I am sure that your experience on the farm and in the neighborhood generally will be worth a great deal to you hereafter. The work you have done will insure you a sound and strong

[281]

body, and that is worth more than all the education you could get. I think you are almost too young to jump into the newspaper business, but just the right age to do what you are doing. Write me your views."

And, always wary of the danger of preaching, he continues: "I am not a great success as a lecturer, and if I take that attitude occasionally it is because I have more interest in your future career than I have ever had in my own."

When Julian's observations began to bear fruit, father wrote as follows: —

Sunday, November 16, 1890

DEAR JULIAN: —

Your letter in to-day's paper is admirably done. Mr. Reed praises it very highly. The error in the headline is mine. I had it *Les Habitans*, but our Greek proof-reader changed it to *Habitant*, and left the plural. *Habitant* is the dictionary word, but *Habitan* is the Canuck dialect, and it ought to have been spelt so throughout the letter. Speaking of this, you ought to jot down in your notebook the words and phrases of *patois* that you hear — the speech of the common people. They will be of immense importance to you hereafter if you should dabble in literature, and they will be interesting if you should not. You can certainly make notes of what you see and hear — the thousand and one little intimations and suggestions that float in the air — the traditions that are cropping out among the older people. I think you could find your Aunt Josephine a perfect mine of these things. Why do I pick her out? Because she is not French, and everything she has heard struck her as strange and queer at first, and has stuck in her memory.

I am sending you a book about Emerson. It is time you were beginning to take a little interest in thoughtful things, and you will find in this little book some remarks on style that may be profitable to you. Another thing — when I make a remark or suggestion, don't take it too seriously. You are old enough to have discovered, or, at least, to have suspected, that, except in the matter of morals, it is impossible to map out a young man's career by means of advice. All that I can do is to give you some of the results of my own experience. I am much more interested in seeing you grow up strong-bodied and clean-minded than I am in your career. A clean-minded man will be everything that he should be. I should like to see you with a will strong enough to resist all forms of temptation. Your career will then take care of itself. And yet I should n't like to see you puritanical and narrow-minded. I want you to grow up to be a wholesome, hearty, liberal-minded man. You have individuality enough to make your impress on the public in various ways, and when you get a little older you will know which way to choose.

Be good and write soon to your loving

PAPA

As the winter weather made itself felt in Georgia, thoughts of Julian's welfare in the much severer Canadian climate caused father some apprehension, and led him to write: —

You wrote about not wearing your overcoat on a very cold day. Do you know that you have to take care of yourself in that climate? An attack of pneumonia might undermine your constitution and destroy your health entirely. Don't let your high spirits lead you into taking risks. Mark Twain told me that the first winter he spent in the North he wore no overcoat at all, and he has been paying for it ever since, with rheumatism of the loins. But, alas! behold the force of habit! When you are home, I am hectoring you, and when you are away, I am "lectoring" you, or words to that effect. I saw Pearl and Ruby to-day. They are certainly beautiful girls, but as I don't know t'other from which, I can't say which is the beautifullest. I'll say this, though, — they are the prettiest girls for miles around. I had never seen them before.

Did you know that our friend X—— is in jail? I have a suspicion that you found out something about him long ago, for I remember that you dropped him very suddenly. It is a pity that a man who could be useful to himself and to others should allow his depravity to get the better of him. I hope you won't fall into any bad habits. The boy that can conquer himself at your age can conquer the world. Everybody that I know is constantly asking about you — how you are getting on, and sometimes these questions are asked by people who are strangers to me. It is very gratifying to me to know that you have made an impression on people. Lord, Lord! don't disappoint 'em, and don't disappoint your mammy and daddy. (More "lectoring.")

Next Tuesday I'll be 42 years of old, a fact that goes to prove my great 40-two'd. (Laughter and applause.) Lucien seems to be getting along better at Gordon than he did anywhere else. The discipline is good for his health. Your letter was too much for him. We laughed at him so that he got mad, and has been pouting at you, but he vows that he wants to see you mighty bad: and it's the truth. I believe he thinks more of you than he does of anybody in the world. Not long ago, a country rooster, who goes to the academy took a notion that he ought to whip Lucien. So one evening he waited for Tootsie and sent after him. Whereupon Lucien went out and cuffed him round considerably. Shortly afterwards the T—— boy — Ed — who is not as large as Lucien, concluded that he could whip him; so he sent up after Tootsie, and challenged him. Lucien told him he did n't want to fight him on account of his size, but T—— whaled Tootsie over the head with a stick, and Tootsie lit into him and smashed him in the face and swept the road with him. It is the general opinion that the boys will let Tootsie alone after this. They seem to be mad because he wears military clothes and puts on airs. Write soon to your

DAD

Christmas drew near and found the eldest still far away, absent for the first time at holiday season. It was characteristic of father to try to let the exile know how each member of the family, from the oldest to the youngest, had been full of thoughts of "Bubber Ju-ju": —

MY DARLING BOY: —

We were all very much pleased at getting letters from you to-day. We were not getting uneasy, but just a trifle restless at the failure to hear from you.

I suppose the boys and the other children had a very good time Christmas. They say they did. And then, when the keen edge had been taken off of expectation, and there was something of a lull in the hurly-burly, we sat around the fire and talked about you. You see there was something missing, and in its place there was the big hole caused by your absence. I think it was felt by all. I made a few remarks about it myself, but your mother and Lucien and Evelyn — in fact all of them had something to say about Julian and Bubber Ju-ju. The big hole is still here — in the daytime, but mostly at night when we are sitting in my room after supper. Lucien is especially loud-spoken in his desire to see you.

Just at this present time your mother is rocking J. C. to sleep, and he remarked a few moments ago that he wanted Bubber Ju-ju to come home right now, right to-night. I observe that you have been having some such feeling, and you boldly announce that you are about to be homesick and want to take the necessary medicine at once. I am not at all sorry to see you hoist the signal of distress. I was beginning to fear that there was no place in your mind for homesickness, and that would be very bad — for us who love you. I used to read about a man who loved to travel merely for the pleasure of coming back home again, and I have often thought that he was a man who knew how to enjoy life.

I hope you have not forgotten that your visit was protracted at your own suggestion. I thought, and still think, that the suggestion was a good one. Your contact with new scenes and new people, and your struggle with the language of all Gaul will be of much benefit to you in the long run. The language itself will open up a new literature to you.

I think the last of April or the first of May would be a good time for you to come home. In fact, if I had my heart's desire you would be here now, but I console myself with the idea that you are making your stay there count for your own good. Lucien took a two days' hunt in the country last week — no, this week — going with Ovid, and stopping at the house of Mr. Tom Powell ten miles out on the Sandtown Road. He was very successful, killing a good deal of game. He brought home two rabbits and a squirrel.

But I am getting tired. This is the first letter I have written since last year, and I am out of practice.

Write soon to your

Affectionate

D<small>AD</small>

FATHER AND SON

As winter waned and memories of springtime at Snap-Bean Farm filled the thoughts of the young man, he began to yearn for home and so expressed himself. His father was not displeased, and replied: —

I gather from the tone of your letters that you are getting somewhat homesick. Indeed, I have been afraid that you would n't get homesick, a condition of affairs that would have betrayed a hardness of heart and an unregenerate spirit altogether out of keeping with your character. I think you have been very brave in sticking it out so long, and it has given your mother and me great pleasure to know that you have made such progress in French. This being the case, I am ready, whenever you please, to discuss the precise date of your homeward voyage; and it is a date which I shall leave to you to set, merely remarking that we are about as homesick to see you as you are to see us. Your mother thinks I ought to appoint the date myself; but I tell her that it is better for you to do so, in order that all your arrangements may be made to fit. I shall expect you to tell me in your next letter when you desire to start from Canada, so that I may send you a cheque in time to meet your views and wishes.

[289]

Mayflower has a baby calf, another heifer —
and this is about all the local news that occurs to
my mind.

The "New York Sun" of Sunday had a sketch
and portrait of your dad. The sketch said I had
married a Miss *La Bosse*. I shall write to the editor
and say that your mother was not *La Bosse* before
I married her, but that she certainly is *La Bosse* now.

I did n't tell you what I thought of your New
York letter because I took it for granted that its
appearance in the paper would satisfy you in regard to my opinion of it. I thought it was very
good, for it was a very difficult piece of work to do.
You certainly have a knack with the pen, and you
will have a "fetching" style if the reporting business does n't destroy it forever. I may be wrong,
but I believe that reporting is death to the literary
style if it is persisted in, or if it is n't accompanied
by some higher work. But what is the use of my
running on in this way? You will be what you will
be, and your success is in your own hands to make
or mar.

Your affectionate

D<small>AD</small>

It seemed to be just as inevitable for Julian as it
had been for his father at sixteen to "stick his head

into an ink-fountain," so when he came home he went on the "Atlanta News" as a "cub" reporter, and after making good there, found a place on the "Constitution." Before his twenty-first birthday he was news editor of that paper, and when, at twenty-four he became managing editor, father realized, perhaps with regret, that the executive talents of his eldest son would probably turn him aside indefinitely from the development of any literary gifts he may have had.

CHAPTER XVII

FRUITFUL YEARS

LITTLE LINTON was Grandmother Harris's favorite amongst the grandchildren, and his death was a great shock to her; she mourned him deeply and began to fail perceptibly as the winter waned. The overflowing spirits and active mischievousness of Julian and Lucien sometimes annoyed her, as was not unnatural in the case of an old lady of nearly seventy-five years; the irrepressible Julian had written her from Canada, "This letter is to serve as a sort of lovelink between you and me, though I feel sure no 'link' of any sort is needed, for the further off I am the better you love me." But the quiet, gentle, thoughtful little boy with brown eyes had ensconced himself in the dear old lady's heart and become her faithful little companion to such an extent that she never quite rallied from his loss. Her lowered vitality was not proof against the changeable weather of early spring, and in March she contracted bronchial pneumonia. There was not much hope for her from the beginning, and when she realized that the end was near she called mother to her bedside one day for a last talk. She

[292]

expressed her wishes regarding the disposition of her little trinkets and keepsakes and apportioned the famous feather-bed to Lillian, whom she called "Pods." [1]

After disposing of her simple possessions she took mother by the hand and said, "Essie, if you never have anything worse to reproach yourself with than your treatment of me from the first day I came into your home, you may rest easy about your life in the hereafter." Shortly afterward she breathed her last, and was placed beside the three little grandchildren who had preceded her into another life. It must have been a comfort to father to feel, as he mourned the fearless and loyal soul who from his earliest recollection had been to him the symbol of the very essence of motherhood, that Death had forever linked her destiny with that of the little ones whom he so tenderly loved.

The previous December (1890) when Julian was still in Canada, father had written him: "I suppose you think I have been very neglectful, but I

[1] "Pods" had long before been told that when grandmother died she was to have this treasure, and as the child had never seen any other feather-bed and therefore regarded her grandmother's as something rare and sacred, she probably referred to her expected legacy oftener than discretion warranted. At any rate, her grandmother once looked at her accusingly and said, "Pods, I believe you want me to die so you can get my feather-bed right away."

have been writing every night on the new story, and now it is nearly done. S. S. McClure has offered me $2,500.00 for the serial rights of the story, and I have written to him that he can have them if he'll pay $2,000.00 cash down, and $500.00 in July. This will be a right snug sum to make in two months, won't it?"

The story referred to was "On the Plantation," called, at that time, "Joe Maxwell." It was syndicated by Colonel McClure and published serially during 1891 in a number of newspapers. Later the Appletons bought the book rights, American and foreign, for which they paid $2300. "On the Plantation" is the story of the boy Joel's life at Turnwold, facts mingled with fancy, of which the author says in the introduction, "That which is fiction pure and simple in these pages bears to me the stamp of truth, and that which is true reads like clumsy invention"; and he advises the reader to sift the fact from the fiction and label it to suit himself! The story was dedicated "To the memory of Joseph Addison Turner, lawyer, editor, scholar, planter, and philanthropist."

"On the Plantation" is one of the most spontaneous and fascinating records of a boy's life ever written, and a perusal of Joe Maxwell's story is a delightful way of becoming acquainted with the life and customs on a middle Georgia plantation before and during the Civil War. The reviewer of the "Dial" said of it at the time of its publication in book form: —

It is a pity that in this day of many books there is so little room for such a fresh and genuine one as this. Such books are covered up and lost sight of under scores of new publications that ought never to have been issued. . . . A hundred volumes of to-day might well fail and disappear to make room for one fresh, wholesome, genuine book like this; full as it is of the odors of the woods and fields, full of kindly and picturesque sketches of simple and unconventional people, both white and black, full of truth and nature, but with no overstrained and degrading realism, no sensational working-up of effects.

Intermingled with the fascinating reminiscences of plantation life are vivid pictures of Joe Maxwell's friends — old Mr. Wall, the hatter, who tells the story of

"Ningapie! Ningapan!
Who up an' killed the Booger Man ";

of the slave Harbert who rivals "Uncle Remus" when he takes a notion to talk about the owl and the jay-bird, or to sing the hog-feeder's song; of Jim-Polk Gaither, the country boy who takes Joe on hunts after old Zip Coon; and of the deserters from the Confederate army, who, in their hiding-place in a lonely cabin, listen to Mink the runaway slave tell of the "Ole Mammy Sheep" and "De Big Injun Man." Finally, after giving us a wealth of colorful episodes, the author observes that to say more would be to carry a "simple chronicle" too far, for it was not his intention to tell of "the healing of the wounds of war; the lifting-up of a section from ruin and poverty to prosperity; the moulding of the beauty, the courage, the energy, and the strength of the old civilization into the new; the gradual uplifting of a lowly race."

In the early summer of 1891 father again went to New York on a brief business trip. He called at the offices of the Century Company, in regard to certain of his stories which were appearing in the magazine, but for some reason (possibly because he did not make clear who he was) he failed to gain admittance to the editorial sanctum. A reference to this incident occurs in a letter to one of the editorial staff later in the summer: —

20 July, 1891

MY DEAR JOHNSON: —

I was away when your letter arrived, and since then I've been so busy with our interior politics — the Alliance — the third party — the legislature — and the Lord knows what else — that I

JOEL CHANDLER HARRIS AT ABOUT 43

have n't had time to write. I'm sorry I did n't see you when I was in N.Y. I called for that especial purpose, but I judged from the tone and air of Messrs. Scott and Chichester that there was too much business going on in the Century building for a Georgia cracker to fool with it, so I took my hat in my hand, made a bow and left. I know how things are; I don't want to be bothered when I am busy, and I know how to sympathize with others who live in the channels of botheration. I judge that Messrs. S. & C. took me to be the editor of the "Constitution," whereas I am only a hireling — having nothing whatever to do with its management or its policy.

Faithfully yours

JOEL CHANDLER HARRIS

In the same year "Balaam and His Master" was brought out by Houghton, Mifflin & Company, a volume comprising six tales of life in Georgia, before and during the Civil War, all of which had previously appeared in the "Century" and "Harper's" magazines. The English edition of this book was published simultaneously in London by Osgood, McIlvaine & Company in their series of "Red Letter Stories."

Additional "Uncle Remus" stories continued

to appear during 1891–92 in a syndicate of newspapers — the "New York Sun," "Boston Globe," "Philadelphia Times," "Washington Evening Star," "Chicago Inter-Ocean," "St. Louis Republic," "San Francisco Examiner," "Louisville Courier-Journal," and "New Orleans Times-Democrat." These stories, together with some plantation ballads and character sketches, were collected and published in 1892 by Houghton, Mifflin & Company under the title "Uncle Remus and His Friends," and the book was embellished by A. B. Frost's drawings, which were full of humor and fancy, and at the same time possessed a realistic quality that made the animals seem "jes' like folks."

The introduction to "Uncle Remus and His Friends" is most interesting in the contrast which it furnishes to the somewhat technical nature of the introductions to the two preceding volumes of "Uncle Remus" tales, in both of which a good deal was said about the origin of the legends. Father calls attention to this change of mental attitude on his part when in this third "introduction" he writes: —

But the folk-lore branch of the subject I gladly leave to those who think they know something about it. My own utter ignorance I confess without a pang. To know that you are ignorant is a valuable form of knowledge, and I am gradually accumulating a vast store of it. In the light of this knowledge the enterprising inconsequence of the introduction to "Nights with Uncle Remus" is worth noting on account of its unconscious humor. I knew a good deal more about folk-lore then than I do now. . . . Since that introduction I have gone far enough into the subject to discover that at the end of investigation and discussion speculation stands grinning.[1]

When we are young we are prone to be very sure of ourselves, but as we grow older, Time's pendulum manages to knock in the head any illusions as to our infallibility. In common with the rest of humanity, father had passed through this mental transformation, and his natural modesty only made him abnormally skeptical of what he had once known! Then, too, he had always had a horror of pedantry, and perhaps he had become a little wearied by the letters from learned professors who insisted upon his authority as a folk-lorist.[2] At any rate, this

[1] In a letter to one of the children, father once wrote: "When old people find out how foolish they have been, they are called wise; when they discover how foolish they *are*, they have reached the pinnacle of wisdom."

[2] That even in the early days Joel Chandler Harris regarded lightly his reputation as an authority in this department of knowledge is shown in the following excerpt from a letter published in the *Critic* in September, 1882, regarding a collection of American Indian myths: "I am not specially well versed in folk-lore, but I presume this collection will possess scientific value. . . . It would be a wonder if any contribution to myth-literature could be made that would not

JOEL CHANDLER HARRIS

apparently "round-about face" attitude is not hard to understand when we recall that "Uncle Remus" was avowedly the story-teller, and not the philologist. His interest in the folk-lore side of the legends was incidental, but his interest in their human side was *perennial*.

The delight of "Uncle Remus's" audience in the possession of a fresh volume of tales was mingled with regret at the announcement in the introduction that the good old man was making his last appearance: —

> It is not an easy or a pleasing ceremony [wrote the author] to step from behind the curtain, pretending to smile and say a brief good-bye for Uncle Remus to those who have been so free with their friendly applause. No doubt there is small excuse for such a leave-taking in literature. But there is no pretense that the old darky's poor little stories are in the nature of literature, or that their retelling touches literary art at any point. All the accessories are lacking. There is nothing here but an old negro man, a little boy, and a dull reporter, the matter of discourse being fantasies as uncouth as the original man ever conceived of. Therefore let Uncle Remus's good-bye be as simple as his stories; a swift gesture that might be mistaken for a salutation as he

be promptly traced, historically or psychologically, to the Aryan sun-myth — as, for instance, if a South American cotia creeps in at one end of a hollow log and out at the other, or if Brer Fox runs Brer Rabbit into a hollow tree, we have the going down and the rising of the sun typified. And really the sun-myth does nobody any harm; if it is quackery it is quackery of a very mild kind."

"আমি শুনেছি, মাংসকে ধূলোর উপর দিয়ে টা'ন্লে, তা' আবার টা টুকা হয়।"

A HINDU ARTIST'S ILLUSTRATION FOR ONE OF UNCLE REMUS'S
STORIES

Brer Rabbit getting Mr. Man's Meat

takes his place among the affable ghosts that throng the ample corridors of the temple of dreams.

More than a decade had passed since "Uncle Remus" made his first bow to the audience which was to gather him so wholly and entirely to its heart. The old man had brought fame to his creator and comfort to the Harris family, and it must have been with a feeling of sadness that he was finally dismissed to the "temple of dreams." The two little children who had been creeping on the floor or haltingly taking their first steps in the Whitehall Street cottage when the dusky Æsop began to recount his fables were now asleep beneath the green sod of Westview, and their two older brothers were nearing manhood. Their father had suffered and enjoyed many things during those busy and eventful years, but his nature had retained the buoyancy of youth while developing the tolerance and acceptance of middle life. He deeply believed, as did the two old men who watched over the body of Meredith Featherstone, that "all events — the accidents that bereave and the maladies that slowly consume — are alike timely and providential," [1] and good fortune had but opened his heart wider to the poor and wretched, whilst sorrow had resolutely

---

[1] "The Making of a Statesman." (Joel Chandler Harris.)

closed the door against bitterness and cynicism. The fame which had come to him had made the West End home the object of interest and curiosity on the part of strangers, but its master pursued the routine of his life in the same old simple way, becoming daily more attached to Snap-Bean Farm and the interests of his growing family.

Lucien in his turn had been sent to his grandparents in Canada, and in a letter addressed to him in the early fall of 1892 father wrote: —

"There is quite an interest in sparring among the boys. Julian issued an open challenge at the tennis grounds the other day to spar any of the boys to a finish, and the challenge was promptly accepted by Charley Sayre. There will be fun when they come together, for both have a motive (in the charming W——). I have said nothing, but I think Julian will do him up. I don't know whether to stop it or not, but I think I'll just let it go ahead. If Julian should happen to get knocked out, it will be a good lesson for him. Would n't it take the starch out of him?"

Evidently Julian was not the only member of the family who had a sentimental motive for boxing and other doings, for the following letter, also to Lucien in Canada, has quite a lot to say about the latter's interest in a certain young lady: —

FRUITFUL YEARS

4 September, 1892

My dear Boy: —

I don't think I've written to you this week. I've been so busy with a preface for the new Uncle Remus Book that I have n't had time for much else at night. And there has n't been anything to write about. It is about as dull in West End as I ever knew it, and C—— S—— has added to the general dullness by giving a birthday party at night. Did I say dull? It is a time of gloom, with the G——'s swarming across the lot at meal-time and Mrs. R—— shooing at your bantam roosters, and J. C. rolling down the woodpile, and the ducks nibbling at the young turnips, and Malsby's baby howling like a freight engine.

You say you would be surer of certain matters if you were at home. I'm not so certain about that. You are terribly suspicious; you seem to be unable to put yourself in her place. Well, I have taken an interest in the matter because I advised you to hold off, and by my comments, some of them in fun and some in earnest, made you more suspicious than you would have been otherwise. Consequently I have gone out of my way to find out the true inwardness of things. I have written you only what I know to be true. I may be wrong, but I think that girl is true from first to last.

The great thing about her is her independence — not in the way you think, but her indifference to the small matters over which other girls giggle. She told Julian the other day that she was writing to you, and she was n't ashamed for me to know that she wanted your picture. That's the reason I like A. Z.,[1] because there is nothing small, or mean or foolish about her.

By the way, when do you propose to take your flight southward? How long do you propose to remain in the land of the skinned eel and the peeled potato? If you stay until Christmas, don't you want to take a short course with les Frères?[2] It is for you to say. I'm sorry there's no news. When there's no news I fall to preaching and that is what makes you tired. Well, old men must be excused; lecturing and preaching seem to be their forte. My love to all, especially to yourself.

Your affectionate

DAD

When father did preach, which was rarely, he did it very tactfully, always tucking in a little praise, so that sensitive young souls might not be too cruelly hurt. Again in writing to Lucien he says: —

---

[1] This young lady four years later became Lucien's wife.

[2] Les Frères Maristes, the school which Julian had attended in Upton.

FRUITFUL YEARS

My dear Boy: —

When it comes to writing, you are as punctilious as a Parisian; you stand on your dignity. I said the other day I would write again in a day or two, and because I did not, you have "*saved* yourse'f on yo' dignity," and refuse to write. Sweet youth; if I had as much time at my command as you have, I would write at least twice a week, if not three times. Take notice that my letters are four times as long as yours and five times as dull. Mix all this with your thinking apparatus, and make a solemn promise to yourself to write to your old Dad at least twice a week, even if you don't write but 17 or 18 pages at a time. I think you have improved a great deal in your writing — in the style and spelling. Try to write just like you talk, only round it off into sentences. In a roundabout way I have heard that you have made a decided impression on the folks who live where you stay.

By being as nice and as clever as you know how to be you can always make a good impression anywhere you go: You know how your own folks (except me) misunderstand you when you give way to your foolish little temper; strangers will misunderstand you even worse. My plan has always been to *conceal my feelings* about *small* and *unimportant* matters, and be genial and funny even when

I did n't feel like it. A little practice goes a long way. I have got so now I feel genial all the time.

Lucien had thought over the offer about a year in the French school at Upton and decided against it, so father thought it would be best for him to return before Christmas: —

5 October, 1892

MY DEAR BOY: —

You missed writing a letter according to your programme last week. So did I. The truth is I was troubled for two or three days with your disease — headache. Last Friday I had to go home and stay there. Of course I am lonesome without you, but not selfish, so I want you to have all the enjoyment you can. I hurried up the cheque because I did n't know what your headache would develop into. Just put the cheque in a safe place and it will be just as good when you want to come home as it is now. But don't stay away from us simply to show you are not homesick. There is nothing unmanly in such a feeling; on the contrary, I should think there was something wrong about you, or your mother and me, if you failed to be homesick. I should think that either we had treated you very badly, or that you were heartless; therefore I trust

[306]

you have been homesick, and that you have at least a trace of the feeling still left. If you have n't, your ma and I are deep in the blue soup. You can stay until your visit is out, which will be about the first week in December, — supposing, of course, that you want to spend Christmas here.

There is just one thing for you to do about the A. Z. matter, and that is to use your own judgment. But, honestly now, don't you think you are giving too much importance to the whole business? Devote your attention to growing and getting fat, and don't let your self-consciousness toot out like a pot leg. It does n't make the slightest difference in the world whether A. Z. is trying to fool you or not. It does n't make any difference whether she succeeds or not. In fact, it is all child's play, a joke, a dream, a delusion, something for you to gossip about when you get old and your dewlap hangs down on your bosom. If she's all right, she is; if she's all wrong, she is; and nothing will change it, for the good Lord had his hand in it long before the foundation of the world. You have the free will and she has the predestination, and these terms of theology will fit any case in the round world, especially a case of male and female measles, which we sometimes call love.

You don't take my advice in these things, although you ask for it, and I'm frank to say that I know of no earthly reason why you should, for the whole business is like a hanging bird's nest — very much in the air. Now, dear Tootsie, don't take all this too seriously. There is a good deal of nonsense in what I have written, but the moral I want you to get out of it is, that it is n't healthy to be in any great strain about A. Z., or any other girl. They are all like a young bird — more craw than meat. But in this you'll have to row your own boat. Your dad can't help you much, and it is n't necessary that he should.

There had never existed any barrier of fear or formality between the boys and their father, so it never occurred to them to hide their love affairs from him. "Tootsie's" continued to be "very much in the air" for some time, but it settled down into something permanent finally, and "A. Z." remained the lady of his choice.

In the fall of 1893 occurred the terrible Sea Island hurricanes, which spread terror and devastation throughout the islands lying off the Atlantic coast from Savannah to Charleston. Clara Barton, head of the American Red Cross, hurried to the seat of the disaster, took up her headquarters in

Beaufort, and began organizing relief work in which she was helped by citizens from the neighboring coast towns and by funds from all over the country. The editors of "Scribner's Magazine" were anxious to carry a full account of the disaster and the relief, so Mr. E. W. Burlingame telegraphed to father asking if he could arrange to cover the story. The idea interested him and he wrote in reply: —

ATLANTA, GA., October 31, 1893

MY DEAR MR. BURLINGAME: —

Your proposition is a very attractive one to me, and I have taken two days to consider it. But I don't see how I could undertake it before the 15th of November, as I have other work under way that must be finished by that date. That would probably be too long a delay for you — and yet I could get files of the New Orleans papers containing ample accounts of the storm on the Gulf coast. These could be worked over. You could send the artist direct to the Gulf coast, and he could then come to Atlanta. From here I could go with him to Savannah, thence to Port Royal and to Charleston, and so to the Sea Islands. I am a tolerably rapid writer, and knowing what was coming you could hold open space in the February number; or, may be March would n't be too late.

JOEL CHANDLER HARRIS

I wish I was out of the newspaper business so I could devote my whole attention to stories and magazine work, all of which, as matters are, I have to do at night after my day's work is over.

Yours faithfully

JOEL CHANDLER HARRIS

Mr. Burlingame fell in with the above suggestions, so, as soon as possible, father set out for Savannah, from which point he covered most of the islands between that city and Beaufort, in company with Mr. Daniel Smith, the illustrator. From the latter place he wrote on November 20th to Mr. Burlingame: "Owing to the kindness of friends here we have been able since last Friday to go over an expanse of territory that could not be reached by the ordinary methods in less than a fortnight. A tug-boat was placed at our disposal Friday, and on Sunday we had the use of the steam launch at the naval station. In these boats we have been able to see a great deal that the newspaper correspondents have been left to guess at."

Even with such facilities for covering much territory in a short time, the trip was beset with difficulties, to one of which father referred when he wrote: "If you are going to make a tour of the islands, the first thing the pilot does is to close his compass box. He has and can have no sort of use for that instrument. The waterways are so crooked, the channel is so devious, that in the course of an hour the prow of the boat heads to all points of the compass. It is impossible to say whether you are going away or coming back, and the pilot must depend entirely upon his familiarity with the channels"; which, needless to state, were at this time stripped of many of their oldtime landmarks.

Once ashore, the only means of locomotion was a kind of two-wheeled sulky, drawn by a gaunt little island pony. Picture father and Mr. Smith crowding into the narrow seat of this little vehicle while the negro guide seated himself without more ado on the shaft in front of the singletree, leaning against the pony! Mr. Smith, who was from New York, and to whom these preparations looked far from practical, thoroughly doubted the boy's ability to remain seated in such a precarious position.

"Are n't you afraid you will fall?" he asked.

"I been deer 'ready, suh," replied the negro sententiously.

"What does he say?" asked Mr. Smith.

"Why," replied father, "he declares that he has occupied that position on many previous occasions."

Whereupon Mr. Smith dubiously took the reins and urged the pony forward.

JOEL CHANDLER HARRIS

"Don't fahs, now," exclaimed the guide.

"What does he mean?" queried the New York man.

"He says, don't go so fast to begin with," interpreted father.

"Well," said the artist, "the stenographers ought to get hold of this lingo. It beats the Pitman system."[1]

Mr. Smith told me lately what a knack father had with these island negroes, how much at home he seemed with them and how readily he obtained all the information they had to give in their strange vernacular. Father had, twenty years earlier, studied their speech and characteristics in order to portray them in the character of "Daddy Jack," the queer, little old dried-up coast darky who visited "Uncle Remus" occasionally, and who told the "little boy" stories of the "critters" during the interludes of courting "Tildy."[2] On this trip to the devastated regions, father was interested to note the great improvement which had taken place in the Sea Island type since he had first encountered it. "They are still different from their brothers in the upland plantations," he wrote, "but the Gullah

[1] "The Sea Island Hurricane," *Scribner's Magazine*, February and March, 1894.
[2] *Nights with Uncle Remus*, "African Jack," and others.

[312]

element is nearly wiped out, and the Congo type
is rapidly disappearing. They are not so gay as the
upland negro, they do not belong to the same
tribes, but they are gentler, they are more unaffected, and there is a flute-like note in their
voices, a soft lilting intonation at the close of their
sentences, that is indescribably winning."

Two thousand of these poor creatures were killed
outright, and thirty thousand were left destitute
beside the ruins of their homes before the hurricane had spent itself. Father described them as
good-humored in the face of their affliction, with
a kind of good-nature that "was not gayety, nor
carelessness, but the good-humor that nestles close
to patience, and that sometimes holds sorrow's
hands."

Of the work of the Red Cross father wrote,
"Everywhere I went I found that the Red Cross
Society had been there before me. There was no
point so remote that its agents had not visited;
there was not a case of sickness that had not received attention." He particularly noted the tact
and wisdom which led Miss Barton to press all
able-bodied survivors into service, forcing them to
help themselves and their maimed and exhausted
fellows. All who could use tools were given hammer,
saw, nails, and lumber, and were set to building

houses for the homeless; and in every direction were to be seen the boats of the blacks, and their little carts carrying relief far and near.

Another article of importance which father contributed during 1893 to "Scribner's" was "The Mystery of the Red Fox," an account of the introduction of the red fox into Georgia, which concluded with a spirited and enthralling description of an old-time fox-hunt near Eatonton. The author was very fond of describing fox-hunts, and other graphic stories of this favorite Southern sport are to be found in "On the Plantation," and "How Whalebone Caused a Wedding." [1] I have found, bearing on the "Red Fox" story, the following letter from father's old friend, Mr. Dennis, the veteran hunter who in days gone by had so often allowed Joel and Hut Adams to drag the skin before his hounds: —

FRIEND JOSEPH: —

Yours of the 2d inst., to hand. The first red fox ever seen in Putnam County was seen and ran by Mr. John R. Respess, of this county, on the first Monday in Jan'y 1845.

Yours very truly
H. J. DENNIS

[1] In *Tales of the Home Folks in Peace and War.* Houghton, Mifflin & Company, 1898.

FRUITFUL YEARS

Mr. Dennis figures in all father's hunt tales, with his famous dogs "Rowan" and "Flirt"; likewise does another old friend, Matt Kilpatrick, with his equally famous hounds "Music" and "Whalebone." "The Mystery of the Red Fox" proved immensely popular, and its author received more than a hundred letters from readers, begging him to write a series of hunting stories.

Father's only book of translations, "Evening Tales," from the French of Frédéric Ortoli, was made about this time. His account of this undertaking as given in the introduction to the book is of sufficient interest to reproduce in part: —

Once upon a time Mr. Wendell P. Garrison, the literary editor of the "Nation," sent me a picture he had found in a catalogue of French books. It represented a very interesting scene. There were the Tar-Baby and Brother Rabbit as natural as life; but Brother Fox was missing. His place had been supplied by Brother Billy Goat, whose formidable horns and fierce beard seemed to add to the old episode a new danger for poor Brother Rabbit.

The picture was an advertisement of "Les Contes de Veillée," by Frédéric Ortoli. After a while the book itself came to hand. . . . It was examined, and in some sort relished, laid aside for future reference, and then forgotten.

But one night, after supper, the children of the house were suddenly missing. . . . There were no voices to be heard on the lawn. There was no rippet taking place in

[315]

the bedrooms. . . . The silence was so unusual that it created a sudden sense of loneliness.

But the investigation that followed showed that the youngsters had merely made a temporary surrender of their privileges. Their mother was reading to them some of the stories in M. Ortoli's book, and they were listening with an intense interest that childhood can neither affect nor disguise.

I begged permission to make one of the audience . . . and the lady, who was and is the center of the family circle, graciously made room for one more listener; and thus it happens that this little volume of M. Ortoli's stories is in the nature of a family affair. The lady, for the benefit of the intruder, was pleased to go over the stories again, and to read them more slowly, and thus they were put in their present form.[1]

There were fifteen of these tales, some about animals and some dealing with fairies and humans, in all of which, as in the "Uncle Remus" legends, the triumph of craft over brute force was celebrated.

The year 1893 ended with a letter relating to a project which father was nursing in his brain — one upon which he must have lingered with enthusiasm, since it dwelt with plantation life in his beloved Putnam County: —

28 December, 1893

MY DEAR MR. BURLINGAME: —

I have in mind two or three articles on Middle Georgia under the title, "When Cotton was

[1] *Evening Tales.* Chas. Scribner's Sons, 1893.

King." The subject lends itself readily to illustration, both practical and humorous. Middle Georgia was and is the center of the most unique — the most individual — civilization the Republic has produced. "Georgia Scenes," "Major Jones's Courtship," and all that is racy in "Simon Suggs," [1] and Colonel Johnston's characters, all came out of Middle Georgia. I could do this in the spring — laying the groundwork for it in the meantime. Think it over.

Yours faithfully

JOEL CHANDLER HARRIS

As far as I know this scheme was not developed, which was a pity, since it probably would have resulted in a work of flavor and charm, as well as of historical value.

[1] *Georgia Scenes*, by Judge A. B. Longstreet; *Major Jones's Courtship*, by Colonel W. T. Thompson, *Simon Suggs*, by J. J. Hooper.

CHAPTER XVIII

THE "LITTLE MR. THIMBLEFINGER" SERIES

"ONCE upon a time there lived on a plantation in the very middle of Middle Georgia a little girl and a little boy and their negro nurse. The little girl's name was Sweetest Susan. . . . She was seven years old. The little boy's name was Buster John. . . . Buster John was eight. The nurse's name was Drusilla, and she was twelve. . . . She was more of a child than either Sweetest Susan or Buster John, but she was very much larger. She was their playmate — their companion, and a capital one she made."

In this way the author of "Uncle Remus" introduced to his little friends a new set of playfellows who were to entertain them with their adventures through a series of six books.[1] The first two of these recounted happenings in Little Mr. Thimblefinger's queer country behind the spring, where the visitors met Mr. Rabbit, Mrs. Meadows, Chickamy Crany

---

[1] *Little Mr. Thimblefinger* (1894); *Mr. Rabbit at Home* (1895); *The Story of Aaron* (1895); *Aaron in the Wildwoods* (1897); *Plantation Pageants* (1899); and *Wally Wanderoon* (1903) — all published by Houghton, Mifflin & Company, Boston, except the last mentioned.

Crow, Tickle-my-Toes, and other quaint people. The Grandmother of the Dolls was responsible for their falling in with the cute little man, "not above four inches high," who wore a dresscoat and velveteen knickerbockers and a little hat like a thimble, with a feather stuck in one side.

"How do you get to your country?" inquired Buster John.

"The nearest way is by the spring," replied Mr. Thimblefinger.

"Can I go too?" asked Sweetest Susan. "And Drusilla?"

When they were told that one and all could go, they wondered how they could get there.

"Right down through the spring and under it," replied their quaint little guide; but Drusilla objected: "Well, you'll hatter 'scuse me, . . . dat water's too wet fer me"; and Sweetest Susan feared she would drown. But Mr. Thimblefinger revealed a great secret. Precisely at nine minutes and nine seconds after twelve o'clock the water of the spring was as dry as air; and so at the magic moment the adventurous youngsters plunged through the spring and out into the marvelous country behind it — the country "next door to the world." And there they heard as strange and delightful tales from old Mrs. Meadows and Mr. Rabbit as any told by "Uncle

Remus" — stories of the "Looking-Glass Children," "The Strawberry Girl," the "Witch of the Well," "The Three Ivory Bobbins," and others about Brother Bear and Brother Lion and Brother Terrapin.

In the introduction the author stated that the stories in "Little Mr. Thimblefinger" belonged to three categories, and explained that some were gathered from the negroes, but were not embodied in the tales of Uncle Remus because he was not sure they were negro stories; some were middle Georgia folk-lore, no doubt originating in England; and some were merely inventions. He jokingly told his own children, on one occasion, that Little Mr. Thimblefinger first appeared to him in a nightmare which was the result of eating rabbit-pie!

Most of the summer of 1894 was given up to writing the first book of the series, and in the spring of 1895 the second, "Mr. Rabbit at Home," was published. The Mr. Rabbit of this series was quite a different person from his crafty namesake of "Uncle Remus" fame. He was "a tremendous creature, grizzly and gray, and watery-eyed from age. He sat in a rocking-chair and smoked a pipe." Drusilla and the children, who had heard of the other Mr. Rabbit since they were "knee-high," were frightened at this strange beast. "Le's go back," said the little black nurse. "Dat ar creetur bigger dan a hoss. Ef he git a glimp' er us we er gone!" But when Mr. Thimblefinger reassured them and Mr. Rabbit invited them into Mrs. Meadows's house "in a voice that sounded as if he had a bad cold," and referred to Drusilla as the "tar-baby," their sense of humor was tickled and they drew near, whereat Mr. Rabbit began to tell them a story, and so the adventure proceeded.

When these books came out it was suggested by certain reviewers that there was a noticeable resemblance between them and the "Alice in Wonderland" series. This amused father very much, for he had never read the famous stories by Lewis Carroll; he had been so often told that his and Carroll's work were somewhat similar that he purposely refrained from reading either of the "Alice" books.

The "Thimblefinger" series was very successful; "Drusilla," especially, became a great favorite, and she is, indeed, one of father's most vivid and piquant characters. "Drusilla is always responsive, always convincing, always herself," said one critic. Her comments on the stories told by Mrs. Meadows and Mr. Rabbit are characteristic; she does·n't like those "what move along too slow fer ter suit" her, nor those with "too much kingin'" in them; and of the "Woog," who crushes fairies, she says: —

JOEL CHANDLER HARRIS

I may n't look like no fairy, but I don't want no Woog fer ter be cuttin' up no capers 'roun' me. I tell you dat, an' I don't charge nothin' fer tellin' it. Black folks don't stan' much chance wid dem what knows 'em, let 'lone dem ar Woog an' things what don't know 'em. Ef you all hear 'im comin', des give de word, an' I boun' you'll say ter yo'se'f dat Drusilla got wings. Now you min' dat.

In the latter part of 1895 the "Story of Aaron" appeared, carrying on the adventures of Sweetest Susan, Buster John, and Drusilla, but no longer in the "country back of the spring"; their friend Aaron made life on the Abercrombie plantation so interesting to them that, for the time being, they forgot about Mrs. Meadows and Mr. Rabbit. In the "Sea Islands' Hurricane" articles father called attention to the Arab strain in many of the old Georgia negroes, and spoke of "Old Ben Ali, who left a diary in one of the desert dialects of Arabic." This diary came into the hands of the son of Dr. Goulding, the author of "Young Marooners." Father went on to explain that Ben Ali was never a slave in the ordinary meaning of the term, but a foreman on his owner's plantation, and as fierce a taskmaster as a negro ever had. It was this same Ben Ali who suggested the character of Aaron, the hero of the second and third books of the Thimble-finger series, and together with his black stallion,

Timoleon, he creates a dramatic and mysterious effect.

It seems, when in Mr. Thimblefinger's queer country the children had been asked if they knew a slave named Aaron, that Buster John replied that Aaron was the foreman of his father's field hands. Then said Mr. Rabbit, "If you want to learn the language of the animals go to Aaron, son of Ben Ali, take him by his left hand, bend the thumb back, and with your right forefinger make a cross mark upon it."

The slaves on the plantation stood in awe of Aaron for several reasons: he was unlike them in appearance, being tall and of a majestic mien, with a well-shaped head, a sharp black eye, thin lips, and a finely shaped nose; and his hair was thick and wavy. The fact that he held aloof from the other slaves gave rise to various stories: that he was a conjurer, a partner of the "Old Boy," etc., and these superstitions were strengthened by his ability to manage the black stallion Timoleon whom no other negro could approach. The children remembered the advice of Mr. Rabbit and hunted Aaron out in his cabin one day, made friends with him, and induced him to tell them of his father, Ben Ali, who had been a slave-raider in Africa, and who, in his turn, was captured and sold as a slave and brought to America. These confidences led to others, and before long the children had won from him the secret of the language of animals, which enabled them to hear from the mouth of the Black Stallion, the White Pig, and Rambler the track dog, the story of Aaron's life on the Abercrombie plantation and elsewhere long before they were born; of how he loved their crippled uncle, "Little Crotchet," whom he risked his life to save; of the cruel treatment meted out to him at the hands of old Gossett, and of his final flight to the swamp.

"Aaron in the Wildwoods" [1] takes up the story of the Arab's life as a runaway in the mysterious swamp "where the cow-itch grew, and the yellow plumes of the poison-oak vine glittered like small torches"; where "the thunder-wood tree exuded its poisonous milk, and long, serpent-like vines wound themselves around and through the trees, and helped to shut out the light"; and where the

[1] In November, 1896, father had written Lillian: "Did you know I've nearly finished another book — *Aaron in the Wildwoods?* No doubt I told you something about this in a former letter. I'm always gossiping about my poor little affairs. They pester me almost as much as Ovid's fleas pester him, and I'm always lifting one hindfoot and dragging the other, trying to scratch myself on the back, as Ovid does. And it tickles me as much as it does Ovid for somebody else to scratch me on the back. Oh, you don't know what preposterous frauds WE AUTHORS are: I mean *we authors!!* The books are getting some very nice notices — better than they deserve, for when all is said, I know how far they fall below what I want them to be."

"night-birds gathered to sleep during the day, and all sorts of creatures that shunned the sunlight or hated man found refuge."

Any imaginative child on reading this fourth book of the series is swayed by the fascination of the swamp's mystery, by the power and cunning of the majestic Arab, or by the charm of the picturesque and gentle Little Crotchet galloping here and there on the Gray Pony. But the older reader senses something more; he perceives the hunted slave, an outlaw in the gloomy swamp peopled with wild, uncanny creatures, becoming the humble instrument of mercy to Little Crotchet, the slave of Pain, who in his turn conveys to all who come within his reach the lesson of uncomplaining acceptance and brave endurance. This aroma of "good in everything" becomes more and more perceptible in the writings of father's middle age and invests them with a perfume of ripeness and benignity. In this atmosphere of harmony and good-will the cynic feels ashamed and the pessimist gathers courage. *Belief* is their keynote — belief in the beauty of the world, in the inherent soundness of humanity, in the unconscious power of the humble, in the mercy of God, and in the reality of things unseen.

When Little Crotchet's tutor begged Aaron to

teach *him* how to talk to animals, Aaron shook his head: —

"Too old," he explained. "Too old, and *know too much*."

"It's another case of having a child's faith," suggested the teacher.

"Most, but not quite," answered Aaron. "It is like this: The *why* must be very big, or you must be touched."

"There must be some real reason why I should desire to learn the language of animals. Is that it?"

"Most, but not quite," Aaron responded. "You must have the *sure-enough* feeling."

"I see. But what is it to be touched? What does that mean?"

"You must be touched by the people who live *next door to the world*," said Aaron.[1]

An interesting sequel to the publication of "Aaron in the Wildwoods" was a letter from a lady connected with "Munsey's Magazine," asking further information about the Arab and stating that her family once owned an Arab slave who bore the same name. Father replied with an account of the Arab, Ben Ali, Aaron's father, who was owned by the Gouldings, and Miss Leach responded as follows: —

"I am very glad to hear your story. I had always supposed that my family owned 'the only' Arab.

[1] *Aaron in the Wildwoods.* Houghton, Mifflin & Company, 1897.

He came at fourteen to this country in a slave ship, was educated by my great-grandfather, was named Aaron, and had peculiar gifts. He never spoke to the negroes except as a master, and, indeed, tradition says he dominated my great-grandfather. At forty he decided that he was tired of being a slave, announced his intention of leaving, obtained a large sum of money (for those days) from his master, with passports, and went to Canada. He wrote letters as long as my great-grandfather lived and then we lost sight of him. You can readily see how the title of your story startled me. I am sorry it is not our story. I should like to feel that I had so much touch with your delightful stories."

After the completion of "Aaron in the Wildwoods" father undertook to write, for the American Book Company, the story of his native State, to be used as a textbook, and to be one of a series entitled "Stories from American History." As early as 1887 he had been approached with a request for such a book, which was to be, as the publishers expressed it, "the real story of your State in brisk, entertaining, and stirring narrative — the story of the people for the people — connected, historical, and picturesque — with a dash of fiction, if need be, to give it thread." In the preface to the volume, as published under the title of "Stories of Georgia," the author suggests that "every person interested in the growth and development of the Republic should turn with eager attention to a narrative embodying the events that have marked the progress of Georgia," because, he explains, "it was in this State that some of the most surprising and spectacular scenes of the Revolution took place"; for in one corner of Georgia a desperate stand was taken which, if it had ended disastrously, "the battle of King's Mountain would never have been fought, Greene's southern campaign would have been crippled, and the struggle for liberty in the South would have ended in smoke."

The narratives in the book comprise spirited accounts of the leading events in the history of the State from the invasion of De Soto to recent times, and abound in delightfully human character sketches of Nancy Hart, Generals James Jackson, and Elijah Clarke; the negro patriot, Austin Dabney; of Eli Whitney, the inventor of the cotton gin; of the two famous Indian chiefs, Alexander McGillivray and William McIntosh; of Governor Joseph E. Brown, and others.

Of unusual interest and dramatic quality is that chapter called "A Daring Adventure," which tells of the exciting capture by the "Yankees" of a train and engine near Atlanta in 1862, and of its

pursuit and recapture by a crew led by Captain
W. A. Fuller, of the Confederate Army, and Anthony Murphy, who followed it first on a hand-car
and later on a superannuated locomotive. The
"Yankee" soldiers who ran away with the train
were caught and put in prison in Chattanooga;
later their leader [1] and seven of them were tried
and hanged, six were exchanged, and six escaped.
It was, perhaps, the most daring and thrilling event
of the kind in the Civil War, and "but for the recapture of the train with the 'Yankees,' the Fed-
erals would have been able to strike a severe blow
at the Confederacy's main source of supplies much
earlier than they were afterwards able to do." [2]
The details of the story were obtained by father
from the leaders of the pursuit, Anthony Murphy,
superintendent of the railroad shops in 1862, and
Captain W. A. Fuller, acting conductor of the train,
both residents of Atlanta, and old-time friends of
the author.

During the spring and summer of 1895 the "Free
Silver" campaign was in full blast and the "Constitution" was one of its most enthusiastic sup-
porters. Father's editorial duties, therefore, were
unusually heavy, and his literary work was more or

[1] J. J. Andrews, an active spy in the Union service.
[2] *Stories of Georgia.* American Book Company, 1896.

less interfered with. One of the projects which it would have been agreeable and profitable for him to have considered had he not been so snowed under with routine work at this time was that suggested by Colonel S. S. McClure: a series of five articles on Stonewall Jackson for the McClure Syndicate. Colonel McClure made father a liberal offer, and the work would have been particularly congenial, for father had an unbounded admiration for General Jackson as a man and a leader, but he did not see his way clear toward attempting it.

Of course, it was well known that father wrote most of the "Free Silver" editorials for the "Constitution," so the opponents of the "Silveroons," as they were called, delighted to hurl verbal brickbats at "Uncle Remus." Some of these "flings" took a decidedly humorous turn; for example, the "Washington Post" published the following paragraph: —

Joel Chandler Harris, the financial editor of the "Atlanta Constitution," receives his salary of $450 per week in bright, silver dollars. Mr. Harris will touch no other kind of money, and if the "Constitution" office does n't happen to have silver on hand, Mr. Harris will allow his salary to accumulate until a supply is laid in. Last week, while attempting to carry home three weeks' salary, Mr. Harris was so unfortunate as to seriously wrench his back. He has been confined to his home ever since, but the "Post" sincerely hopes he will soon be able to be out and at his desk. The cause of free silver cannot well spare Mr. Harris.

As can readily be inferred, any sort of political campaign was more or less a trial to father, for his interest in politics was not perfervid. He once said to an interviewer, in reply to a question about his political convictions: "I am not a politician. I am a Democrat on election day, but that is as far as I go." [1]

The fifteenth anniversary of the appearance of "Uncle Remus; His Songs and his Sayings," was commemorated this year by D. Appleton & Company, in the publication of a beautiful new edition of the book with numerous Frost illustrations. Great was father's delight in these inimitable drawings, and he expressed his appreciation of them in a dedication of the new volume to the artist, in which he generously said: —

---

[1] My husband says on this point: —
"I can recall only two occasions when father appeared to be really interested in so-called politics. The first time was when free silver was the campaign issue. He read extensively on the subject — *Coin* being a part of his sixteen-to-one list of authorities. Although I was barely twenty-one, I differed with him in his views, and our discussions drew out the fact that his principal interest was humanitarian, so to speak. He thought that free silver would be the salvation of the poorer people, and believed that political conspirators and capitalistic highbinders had combined to debase silver and force down the market price of the white metal."

It would be no mystery at all if this new edition were to be more popular than the old one. Do you know why? Because you have taken it under your own hand and made it yours. . . . Because, by a stroke here and a touch there, you have conveyed into the animals' quaint antics the illumination of your own inimitable humor, which is as true to our own sun and soil as it is to the spirit and essence of the matter set forth. . . . The book was mine, but now you have made it yours, both sap and pith. Take it, therefore, my dear Frost, and believe me faithfully yours.

Mr. Frost responded most feelingly and gracefully when he wrote: "The dedication in 'Uncle Remus' is the most beautiful, lovely thing that ever happened to me in my whole life: not that I accept the gift you make me, not by a mighty long way. But I do accept most heartily the feeling that dictated it, and I love you for it, old man!"

Father had been asked to write an appreciation of the second "Jungle Book" for the Christmas "Book-Buyer," which he did with pleasure and zest, for he greatly admired these stories. It was appropriate that "Uncle Remus" should pay a tribute to the creator of "Mowgli," and he touched on Kipling's peculiar gift as would have been expected when he wrote: —

Now, as of old, the elemental in man rhymes with the elemental in all things else, and Mr. Kipling's genius touches the center of it all with a swing, a vigor, and a fearlessness that cannot be matched in modern literature. There is no mincing here. A swish and a slash, and the stroke goes home. . . . Since the days of Uncle Æsop the animals have been parading about and making speeches, sometimes feebly and sometimes to good purpose; but never have they been caught in the act, as it were, by a more facile or a stronger hand than in these jungle tales.

On father's birthday came a letter from Mr. Kipling in his Vermont home thanking "Uncle Remus" for his good words and telling how, as a boy, the friend of "Mowgli" had relished "Brer Rabbit" and "Brer Fox": —

WAITE, VERMONT, December 6, 1895

DEAR MR. HARRIS: —

I am taking the liberty of sending you with this a copy of the "Second Jungle-Book" — which I see with delight you have been good enough to praise in the Christmas "Book-Buyer." This makes me feel some inches taller in my boots: for my debt to you is of long standing.

I wonder if you could realize how "Uncle Remus," his sayings, and the sayings of the noble beasties ran like wild fire through an English public school when I was about fifteen. We used to go to battle (with boots and bolsters and such-like) against those whom we did not love, to the tune of *Ty-yi-tungalee : I eat um pea, I pick um pea*, etc., and I remember the bodily bearing into a furze-bush of a young fag solely because his nickname had been "Rabbit" before the tales invaded the school and — well, we assumed that he ought to have been "bawn an' bred in a briar-patch," and gorse was the most efficient substitute. And six years ago in India, meeting an old schoolmate of those days, we found ourselves quoting whole pages of "Uncle Remus" that had got mixed in with the fabric of the old school life.

One thing I want to know badly (you must loathe the people who pester you with this kind of thing), but from what nature-myth or *what* come "Miss Meadows and the girls?" Where did they begin — in whose mind? What do you think they are?

I hope you will not think yourself in any way bound to answer this note — except, please, about Miss Meadows, and a post-card would do for that. I know Christmas must be a very busy season with you, so I will not trespass on your patience.

With all respect and admiration,

Believe me

Very sincerely yours
RUDYARD KIPLING

To JOEL CHANDLER HARRIS, ESQ.

LITTLE MR. THIMBLEFINGER SERIES

The closing days of the year had been enlivened by a visit from mother's cousins, Mr. and Mrs. Richard Green, of Troy, New York, and father regrets their departure in a characteristic way in the following letter: —

9 December, 1895

DEAR DICK: —

Your letter came just in time to enable me to celebrate my forty-seventh birthday by writing to you: and likewise to Sophia — for we can't leave these women out of anything, not even out of the bed. We have missed you both to a degree that would hardly have seemed possible before I knew you. Even the yaller cat and the "nudder" cat — as Sophia called it — are not kicking up as many pranks as formerly. Edward, the white-eyed Butler, is more subdued and does n't knock down and drag out things as he used to do when you were here. And we all sit around the fire at night and think about you. It is just like I told Sophia — if you two had half as much pleasure out of your visit as we did, you 'll want to come again before another twelve months is gone. We take it for granted that ~~society~~ (see that! I wrote "society" when I meant Sophia!) — we take it for granted that Sophia is too busy talking to do any writing. But she 'll get over that after a while, and then she'll send a long letter all about the men that sit around at your house and play cribbage and cuss. Well, when Sophia gets through talking we'll be glad to hear from her, and when you both get tired of that Trojan climate we'll be glad to see you again. We've had some pretty cold weather here, down to 20°, but now it is warm and raining. I suppose Essie will write to Sophia some of these days, and then, if Sophia is as fluent with her pen as with her tongue, we'll hear all the news. But I'm not making fun of Sophia. The Lord knows I wish she were here to do some talking now. The place would be livelier. News is lacking. Tootsie is smacking his lips over his approaching marriage, and his mamma is going about with her feathers ruffled same as a setting hen that has fallen in the rain-barrel.

Give our love to all our kinnery, and tell Sophia to write when she can. Do you write, also, when you have time; anything you say will be interesting because it will keep us in touch with people we like. All send love, including

Yours faithfully

JOEL CHANDLER HARRIS

December, 1895, had brought several pleasant events in its train, but none so happy or important as Lucien's marriage on the 11th of the month to "A. Z."! There was no sadness attached to the event in the prospect of giving "Tootsie" up, for the young couple were to remain at Snap-Bean Farm for a few months at least.

CHAPTER XIX

THE FIRST NOVEL

In 1885 father's friend, Mr. Erastus Brainerd, of the "Philadelphia News," had prepared an article, "Joel Chandler Harris at Home," for the "Critic," and in the course of the correspondence which the article necessitated, Mr. Brainerd wrote: "In what you have done I am sure no one will fail to recognize the feeling of poise and reserve force which is always present in the best work, and which always excites the reader's desire to follow a sustained effort on the part of an author who has exhibited his powers as you have done, albeit within the limits of the short story. I hope you will one day be moved to essay a novel which shall reveal the life which you know so well, but which is unknown at the North and unrealized at the South. 'Mingo' contains the germ of what I mean, and while 'Mingo' is complete in its way, it lacks the comprehensive view which would be more impressive if elaborated. I only hope you can be persuaded to undertake a novel."

Undoubtedly the project of writing a novel had long been under consideration by father; the way

had been paved, after a fashion, by the "Thimblefinger" series. But he had a deep-seated convic-
tion that the handling of a sustained plot would
be beset with difficulties; and in his lack of self-
confidence, doubtless the difficulties magnified
themselves mightily.

It is obvious to a student of father's writings
as a whole that his conspicuous gifts are those of
humor, of vivid characterization and of poetic in-
sight, and the ability to environ his people with an
atmosphere of reality: his folks are real folks who
live and move in a real world, where their tenderness, humor, and shrewdness color all their actions.
If, on the other hand, the student perceives a
faultiness of structure, a failure to bind together
tightly and cunningly the loose ends of plot, then
let him reflect that the writer for more than thirty
years had been a victim to the routine of newspaper work, and that, deprived of the leisure of
unbroken hours, he had had scant opportunity for
the cultivation of the technique of his craft. Perhaps if the author of "Mingo" and "Free Joe"
had felt it possible to give up his editorial work
years before he did, in a more abundant leisure he
might have developed his art at the point where he
felt it weakest, thus gaining that mastery in crafts-
manship which the novelist must possess. But that

is another story! We only know that the time had come when he was in a mood to respond to his old friend's urging, and attempt a novel of Georgia life.

In a letter dated April 1, 1896, to his eldest daughter, Lillian, a student at St. Joseph's Academy, Washington, Georgia, he writes: "I am about half through my story, having written 50,000 words in spite of my illness. But it is no good; I can't write a long story. I put all my strength in the episodes and leave the thread of the main story hanging at loose ends." [1]

The work was carried rapidly on to a conclusion, and on April 19th, he wrote to Mr. Burlingame: —

ATLANTA, GA., 19 April, 1896

DEAR MR. BURLINGAME: —

I have also tried to write another long story — not for fame or money, but merely to get some characters out of my head. It falls naturally into

[1] In November, 1894, in a letter to Mr. E. L. Burlingame, of *Scribner's Magazine*, referring to a three-part story submitted at that time, Joel Chandler Harris expresses sentiments similar to the above when he writes: "The affair represents a good deal of hard work, but not in the direction of giving it *literary form*. There is something so painful in modern literary form — outside of Mr. Stevenson's inimitable stories — that I have forsworn all efforts in that direction. . . . My whole aim has been at *life* and *character*, and I have purposely left the *style* to take care of itself."

twelve parts of 6000 words, each part containing two chapters. I did n't write it to worry you with, but to give peace and rest to some Georgia characters that have been capering about in my mind for years.[1] Mr. B——, of the "Ladylike Home Journal," says that the magazine editors don't want any more long serials. I sympathize with them in this, and mention the matter with diffidence. Please consider it unmentioned if you have already laid your serial plans for next year. I have my doubts about the story anyway. It is called "Sister Jane and Her Neighbors."

Thanking you again, I am

Yours faithfully

JOEL CHANDLER HARRIS

As it was not convenient for "Scribner's" to handle the story serially during 1896, father submitted it next to Houghton, Mifflin & Company. In due time a response came from one of the editorial staff pointing out certain faults in construction and weaknesses in plot, but adding, "We admire greatly your treatment of the two delightful old

---

[1] I have found amongst other papers a memorandum bearing the following notes: "Sister Jane was written 1. To get rid of a number of people — critics call them *characters*, but to me they are *people* — who were capering about in my mind. 2. To take out of the mouth of my mind the bad taste of some pessimistic books I have read."

[341]

gentlemen [1] who sing their duet from time to time. They seem to us a distinct contribution and even more than 'Sister Jane' they appear to embody the fine charity which is the impulse of the story." Father had dreaded just this criticism, and he winced under it, despite the praise of the character drawing which he must have known was merited. He felt the justice of the editorial stricture and was quite ready to cry "peccavi," yet he continued to insist that his chief aim had been at life and character. To which his publishers replied that they, too, agreed in thinking the construction of the book its less forcible claim to attention, yet they wished to point out certain weaknesses which would be liable to call out criticism. On the other hand, they added, "We are not sure that you recognize as strongly as we do how clear is the characterization, and how faithful a picture you have drawn of one form of society."

But father continued to feel very timid about the whole affair, and it was not until he received a letter from Mr. Walter H. Page, who had been asked to read "Sister Jane," that he felt in any wise "boosted up" about this first novel. Mr. Page wrote: —

"I have you to thank for a very memorable day. Early one Sunday morning I took 'Sister Jane'

[1] Grandsir Roach and Uncle Jimmy Cosby.

out into Boston Common, and there she proceeded to unfold herself. Except 'Uncle Remus' himself, no Southern characters have walked from life into a book quite so naturally or unblurred, it seems to me, as 'William Wornum,' 'Sister Jane,' and the two old fellows from the country.

"In answer to your question which you asked me some time ago, namely, What is the matter with the book? let me say that it needs to be put in type and printed. That is my prescription for it."

This very human and matter-of-fact advice settled the question and removed the writer's doubts; Mr. Page seemed to know just what sort of tonic father needed, and later on, when connected with the firm of Doubleday, Page & Company, he had a way of getting the very best out of him, but that, also, is another story! Another good friend who had a hand in steering "Sister Jane" into port was Mr. John Henderson Garnsey, of Joliet, Illinois. Mr. Garnsey visited Snap-Bean Farm several times and was warmly attached to father and all the family. Indeed, he always referred to the mistress of the house as his "other mother."

"Sister Jane," said Mr. Garnsey to me recently, "came very near going into the waste-basket once. After it was written and Evelyn had typed it neatly, it did not seem to 'read right.' One evening

JOEL CHANDLER HARRIS

Mr. Harris called me into his room, — the front one with the books on the floor, on the mantel, on the chairs and stool, — placed a chair by the little table and asked me to read the typed manuscript, sheet by sheet, as he went over it, ostensibly, to correct errors. 'If it's trash say so, and I'll tear it up,' he commanded. Two evenings were spent — memorable ones, too — and the story interested me. I told him that I felt that I knew William Wornum, the narrator — felt as if he were an old friend. 'That's just the trouble,' said Mr. Harris, 'I'm afraid some one will find out who he is, and ruin me.' Well, we discussed the story pro and con, timidly on my part, because my literary attainments or judgment could not come within miles of his, and he was finally induced to put the manuscript in shape for the printer. He vowed that the cyclone was in the wrong place in the book — in which I agreed with him, and he finally switched it from its place and made it the climax."

Houghton, Mifflin & Company brought out "Sister Jane" in 1896, and one of the first copies received by its author was sent to Mr. Garnsey; it contained the following inscription: —

To John Henderson Garnsey, this book, which he was first to read and commend. It goes with the affectionate regards of his friend, Joel Chandler Harris.

"WHAT DREAMS MAY COME!"

A fantastic of St Valentine, '99 ___ ?

SKETCH SENT TO J. C. H. BY MR. JOHN H. GARNSEY

On reading a news item to the effect that the "Uncle Remus" stories were to be dramatized.

THE FIRST NOVEL

In a letter to Mr. Garnsey dated February 14, 1897, father wrote: "'Sister Jane,' did very well, selling 3000 copies by the first of January. But to show I can do better, I am on another long story. The 'New York Times' and 'Tribune' roasted 'Sister Jane,' but the rest of the papers treated her very gently, some giving her high praise."

And again, to Mr. Garnsey: "'Sister Jane' is still selling, but Lord! it's poor stuff. No doubt that's because the brother [1] represents my inner — my inner — oh, well! my inner spezerinktum; I can't think of the other word. It is n't 'self' and it is n't — oh, yes! it's the other fellow inside of me, the fellow who does all my literary work while I get the reputation, being really nothing but a cornfield journalist. Mrs. Cornelia [2] — a mighty pretty name that! — will agree with this when she knows me. And that's the trouble. I wish I could trot the other fellow out when company comes. But he shrinks to nothing and is gone. But the cornfield journalist pursues me and stays on top."

The keynote of "Sister Jane" is *charity*, charity for poor Mandy who was so deeply wronged, charity for her nameless child, and charity even for her seducer. In the words of Grandsir Roach, "Charity! Why, William, what does Paul say?

[1] William Wornum.   [2] Mrs. Garnsey.

[345]

Look it up in the Bible! Why, take charity out'n religion an' what in the name of common sense would be left? Nothin' but the dry peelin's. It'd be like takin' corn out'n the shuck. Shucks'll maybe do for steers an' dry cattle, — but you give shucks to creeturs what's got any sense an' they'll snort at 'em an' walk away from the trough."

The character in the book which was, perhaps, of most interest to the author was that of Jincy Meadows, the strange creature who bore the name of "half wit," and coaxed birds from out the bushes with his whistle and who loved to play at "make-believe." Between him and William Wornum (whom father had designated as "the other fellow inside of me") there was an indefinable sympathy, for William, too, had the "whimsies" and in *his* world of make-believe had lived Jincy's experiences over a thousand times. In regard to Jincy father once wrote to Lillian: "I enjoy gossip because it gives me a clue to character, and there's nothing richer than human character. To me the most serious person is the most humorous if I can but get him to open his mouth and speak freely, and sometimes the most humorous are the most serious: you remember Jincy in 'Sister Jane.'"

But let us leave novel-writing and all its botherations for a while and see what was going on in the domestic circle at Snap-Bean Farm. During 1896 there were gaps in the family despite the fact that Lucien had brought his young wife into the home for a few months stay. Julian at twenty-one had got a temporary leave of absence from the "Constitution" and had gone to Chicago to study the newspaper game under Mr. H. H. Kohlsaat on the "Times-Herald" (now the "Record-Herald") and Lillian was a pupil at St. Joseph's Academy at Washington, Georgia. Julian made contributions from time to time to the "Constitution" and the "Alkahest," and concerning one of the latter, his father wrote him, May 20, 1896: —

My DEAR BOY: —

I have just read the "Alkahest," or, rather, your story and squibs in the "Alkahest." You tell Evelyn that you are sorry your name was signed to the story — but it is by far the best thing you have done in that line, and shows a development that both pleases and astonishes me. I enjoyed it immensely, and yelled at the close. It is very neat, very deft, and yet strong and vigorous. The squibs are perfect — bright, snappy, and telling. I don't know when I've been so proud and pleased. In fact I'm prouder than if I had done it myself. It speaks to me of great possibilities for my young

man. Your letters to Evelyn are in the right key.
Having my shrinking, doubting, self-effacing disposition, he needs bracing, and you are just the
chap to do it. That's the way Turner (in Putnam
long ago) and Evan Howell (in Atlanta) braced me,
and it does a world of good.

Your affectionate

DAD

All send love.

Father's interest in Julian's progress was no
greater than that felt toward the eldest daughter
who had been placed with the good Sisters of St.
Joseph, and the series of letters to Lillian which
follow give a graphic picture of home happenings
during the year. Mother had just made a little
visit to Lillian, and on her return father writes: —

7 March, 1896

MY DEAR DAUGHTER: —

Confidentially, between you and me, *entre nous,
sub rosa* (likewise, nix cum a rous), I'm the most
worthless and forgetful daddy you ever had. I get
absorbed in my work, and forget to send your
papers when they should be sent. And then, when
you fail to get them, you sit and bite your fingers
and say to yourself that you are forgotten; and
then along comes one of the dear Sisters — or two

of them — and they see you looking doleful. Then this dialogue occurs: —

Sr. M. L. — That child is not feeling well. I think she ought to have a pill.

Dr. B. — *A* pill, did you say? Two at the very least. See how she droops! It's her liver. Two pills, *of course.*

Sr. Sacred Heart (at foot of stairway). Did I hear you say "liver"? Three pills for the liver. Don't forget — three.

Chorus behind the scenes

Oh, a *doctor* must be a *cheerful* giver — (treble)
One pill for a *shake* and *two* for a *shiver* — (alto)
And *three* for that *awful* thing the *liver* — (bass)

Consequently you must be feeling very much better. All your commissions shall be attended to — the new films, the development of the old ones, et cettery, and so forth. Right now I intend to do these academic chores the first thing in the morning. If I'm the same man I was I shall probably forget it and then abuse myself for being such a heartless, cruel monster as to forget any errand that a young lady desires me to undertake — especially when that aforesaid young lady is so well and favorably known to me.

I declare, your mamma is a perfect martyr — such adventures — such experiences — such waiting for trains — such awful spectacles of engines lying sprawling, their eyes knocked out and their boilers cold — such going without dinners and things! It would take a whole letter to relate them. But there were some streaks of sunshine amid the general gloom. She had seen you and she had seen the Sisters, and she enjoyed every moment of her stay there. It was only when she started away that gloom began to gather. It was quite four o'clock when she arrived, and there was an expression in her face — well, I'm glad I was n't a railway schedule! She says she had an elegant time at the convent, and she talks about it even when I want to go to sleep.

Why, of course I received your report and appreciated the wonderful record you are making. But don't study so hard as to give you a distaste for your textbooks. Health, my dear, — health, — that is the main thing at your age. Still, I like your reports; they are a great satisfaction to me, and if you can get such records and not overtax your mind, all right.

Your affectionate
DADDY

A vacancy in the kitchen brought Chloe temporarily into the house, for she was willing to turn her hand to anything at "Miss Essie's" bidding, and a portion of her large family came along to assist.

25 April, 1896

MY DEAR DAUGHTER: —

You know Mattie is gone. Well, Chloe and her family are cooking for us. The greater part of last week, we had in the kitchen Chloe, Lizzie, Ed, Rufus, Johnson, and the mule and wagon. Of course they were not all in the kitchen at once, but off and on — relays and reliefs. I don't know whether Johnson or the mule made up biscuits, but certainly one or the other. Chloe seemed to be hard run even then, and so I told Banks[1] that he had better come and bring his wife and family to help Chloe and her family cook for us this week.

My regards to Sister Bernard, and say to her that I am glad and grateful that she is praying for a special favor to me. I think I know what it is, and the idea is growing more and more pleasing to me every day. Say to her that if she had been raised a Protestant she would know how hard it is to root out of the mind the prejudices and doubts and fictions that have been educated into it. This is the task I am engaged in now. There are only small and

---

[1] Banks was for many years the gardener at Snap-Bean Farm.

[351]

insignificant weeds in my mind at this time, but I
want to have them all cleared out and thrown over
the fence in the trash-pile. My regards also to Sister Mary Louis.

Your affectionate

D<small>AD</small>

The last paragraph of the preceding letter is of
peculiar interest, since it is the first intimation in
father's letters that his thoughts were bent seriously
toward embracing Catholicism. He had never been
a member of any church, nor had his mother,
though her people were Methodists. Grandmother
was a student of the Bible all her life, and from
childhood had instructed father in its lessons, but
had never attempted to instill creed or dogma.
Father's preoccupation with the doctrine of Catholicism began with his study of the works of Cardinal Newman to which he often referred with deep-
est admiration.

2d of May, 1896

D<small>EAR</small> M<small>ISS</small> B<small>ILLY-ANN</small>: —
Weather cold; wind blowing a gale from the
nor'west, thrashing out the roses, and making thin-
skinned people feel as if they had lost home and
friends and country; old Annabel ailing; calf so
poor that it falls down when it tries to bleat; hens

[352]

deserting their nests, and allowing their eggs to get cold; birds pecking at the strawberries; bucket falling in the well; J. C. cutting a hole in the toe of his Sunday-go-to-meeting shoes; donkey trying to climb the wire fence; pigeons gobbling up the chicken food; apples rotting; stove smoking; dry-goods bill heavy; bonnet bill heavier; street-cars behind time; Chloe trying to get in the stove to cook; Rufus dropping plates from the ceiling; milk bill growing; cow-doctor's bill coming in; dust blowing everywhere; kitten getting its tail under the rocking-chair; Brader with his hair soaped smooth on each side; the pony wallowing himself black; planks falling off the fence; Lizzie helping Chloe to harden the biscuit —

Now, how do you suppose I can find any news to write while all this is going on? More than that, how do you suppose I survive the infliction? Well, I'll tell you Billy-Ann: I laugh at it. I'm just as happy, almost when things are going wrong, as I am when they are going right; and for a very good reason. It doesn't amount to a row of pins. There's nothing funnier than to see small troubles disappear when you laugh at them. They seem to get ashamed of themselves and run away.

I went to see Mildred confirmed this afternoon and enjoyed it very much. More than a hundred were confirmed, I think, and among them three or four colored people. At the close the Bishop delivered a little address, and in the course of it made a remark that caused me to laugh. He said: "If all people were good Christians it would put a stop even to the scandals in Atlanta." I dare say our enterprising town appears to be very lively to outside folks, especially to those who live in Savannah, where everything goes on in a sort of mild dream. I remember running to catch a street-car when I first went to Savannah. The people in the car looked at one another and whispered, and one old lady in a corner said to a companion, "If you think he's crazy, let's get off."

Savannah folks don't like Atlanta. I got even with some of them the last time I was there. The train arrived about 8 o'clock A.M., and I went to a restaurant to get my breakfast. The waiter seated me at a table where there were three old gentlemen. I knew one of them, but he did n't know me. While waiting to be served I turned to him and said: "What town is this?" He shuffled about with his feet. "I did n't catch your remark, sir," he replied. "I asked the name of the town; it is a very pretty place." He regarded me with amazement, but finally told me it was Savannah. One of the others leaned his elbows on the table

and asked me what part of the country I was from.
"Atlanta," I replied. Well, I wish you could have
seen their faces! The old gentleman to whom I had
first spoken swelled up in the most comical manner,
and ordered the waiter to carry his breakfast to
another table; whereupon I made myself known
to him, and I never saw a man enjoy a joke more.
In fact, he paid for my breakfast.

My regards to Sister Bernard and Sister Mary
Louis. And please remember that I'm your affectionate Queen of the May.

Vacation-time came round and "Billy-Ann"
returned to Atlanta, so the home chronicle was
suspended until fall.

During the summer of 1896 father worked on
short stories and prepared articles bearing on the
South for the "Busy World" department of "Harper's Weekly." He also wrote, for a new department in the "Atlantic Monthly," articles on literature and nature. One of these, "At the Wren's
Nest," which was not submitted until 1898, told
the story of the housekeeping of two little wrens
in the letter-box near the gate of the West End
home. This little episode, which was afterwards
rewritten for the "Uncle Remus Magazine," gave
to the home place the name by which it is best

known to-day: "The Sign of the Wren's Nest."
On Lillian's return to St. Joseph's the amusing
annals were resumed: —

25 October

MY DEAR DAUGHTER: —

We are all pretty well, now, except mamma, and
her ailment is n't serious. She was fooling with
the stove-pipe in the hall yesterday, and it came
unjointed in some way, and about twenty-eight
pounds of soot, or *sut* (as we say in Georgia)
poured down on her devoted head and face. She
looked like Dinah in the minstrel show, only worse.
She was so black that the whites of her eyes appeared to be as big as the doorknobs in Julian's
room. When she first washed her face she looked
worse than ever. She had to go in the tub head-
foremost, and then, as a final effect, — something
lah-de-da, you know, — nothing would do her but
she must put some ammonia in the water for her
face. So she poured it in and poured too much, and
when she got through with that, her face looked
like a boiled lobster. Then on top of that she
smeared her matronly countenance with vaseline;
and this made a beautiful moonlight effect by gas-
light, showing the lights and shadows of home life
in West End. (Edited with notes by that well-

known humanitarian, Joel Chandler Harris, author of the beautiful song, "Don't Make any Noise; Mamma's Bathing.")

Now, you think all that's funny, and it is (on paper), but you wouldn't have enjoyed it if you had been here. For I know mighty well I had to crawl under the bed, and the three cats went out at the back door with such velocity that the carpet smoked — or it may have been the soot rising. And you ought to have heard the racket, when I (from under the bed) asked: "Aunt Dinah Harris, why did you want to crawl into the stove-pipe?"

And even at the supper-table, there was considerable gloom when I remarked, casually, that there are more than seven hundred different ways of getting dirty respectably. I was told to go somewhere and select me a perfectly clean wife. I answered that the Church does not allow divorces. The reply was that I was not a Catholic — to which I answered that having become (as it were) a brother-in-law of the Church, with the hope and expectation of a closer relation when I felt good enough, I felt bound to conform to the rules in so far as I could. Well, it was a great time.

Your loving old

D<small>AD</small>

JOEL CHANDLER HARRIS

A letter of October 27th announces an important event, the birth of the first grandchild: —

27 October, 1896
10.30 o'clock (night)

DEAR LILLIAN: —

Your nephew is now sleeping soundly in Alleen's room. He weighs seven pounds, and was born at 9 A.M. He seems to be about 81 years old, but will get considerably younger in a few days. Everybody is happy, and all send love to you, including

Your affectionate

DAD

Say to the Sisters that the apples were shipped Monday, freight prepaid. I hope you'll all enjoy them.

Father entertained the highest opinion of the value of the Sisters' influence on their pupils and often expressed himself in terms similar to those of the following letter: —

Sunday evening, November, 1896

MY DEAR DAUGHTER: —

Mamma enjoyed fixing the box as much as you did the eating of the contents; and I think Mattie enjoyed cooking the stuff, for she went about it

[358]

very cheerfully, and seemed to take a great interest in the matter. And we are all glad that you like it. Your report is perfectly splendid, as the girls say. The first one was good enough for me, but this beats it out of sight. And now you say you are going to excel even this magnificent record! Well, please, marm, permit one little 99 to slip in somewhere, so that I may know that the report comes from a real human being.

But, seriously, I am very proud of the report and so is your mother, and we thank our stars that we were fortunate enough to have an opportunity to place you with those devoted Sisters, who have the art of developing young minds. More than that, we are grateful that Providence so arranged it that you might be under the especial supervision of Sister Mary Bernard, who seems to have the gift (and it is a heaven-born gift) of imparting something of her own knowledge and exquisite culture to her pupils. I knew from the third letter I received from you that you had fallen under some sweet and yet powerful influence, and that you had begun to learn how to *think* and think *right,* which is the end and aim of all education.

Of course, my famous portrait of the baby was a caricature. He is a very nice-looking baby, but he seems to me to be always in trouble. When he's

not crying, the expression of his face shows that he
has something on his mind. He works his hands and
blinks his eyes, and appears to want to know why
he came to this country anyhow — a country
where everybody seems to have the colic and live
on soothing sirup, and where the whole population
has to be joggled on somebody's knee in the most
terrific manner if it so much as whimpers. He's
crying now, and somebody is jolting him up and
down in the most fearful manner. If he holds together awhile longer he will make a famous foot-
ball player, and will be able to emerge from a railway collision serene and smiling.

Your affectionate

D<small>AD</small>

Lucien had begun building a home on the far-
western corner of the farm, and it was not long
before he carried his little family to its own headquarters; not too far away, however, for the grandmother to run across lots for a morning call on the
lusty-lunged youngster who continued to thrive
in spite of colic and soothing sirup.

CHAPTER XX

AMUSING ANNALS OF SNAP-BEAN FARM

THE months rolled by as usual in West End, and "Commencement" time approached at St. Joseph's Academy. Father sent a letter to Lillian the last of May, 1897, to announce his intention of being present at the "closing exercises": —

30 May, 1897

DEAR BILLY-ANN: —

Your report is horribly good. It makes cold chills run over me to think of the amount of vitality you must expend to get a perfect report. And yet I suppose I should be disappointed and disgruntled if you were to send me a poor report. Mamma intended to write, but she has had a very bad cold. One day, she was too ill to sit up, and even now she talks in a wheezy tone of voice. Under the circumstances, it has been practically impossible for her to do anything except sniffle and try to clear her throat.

Quite a cat-(no, a dog)-astrophe happened in our neighborhood last night. Roy had a stray dog named Patsy, which he was very fond of. He and

Grace and our children were playing on the sidewalk when Patsy made the mistake of getting under a street-car. You have heard Mildred squeal? Well, she and Grace squealed in concert, but Patsy never heard them. Mamma heard the extraordinary squealing, and she knew — she just knew — that J. C. had been hurt. She knew it because she had been feeling all the afternoon that something had happened. And would n't I go and see about it? — because if it was J. C. she just could n't bear to go and find out herself. But we soon learned that Patsy was no more, and everything quieted down again, except the still small voice of Miss Laura who was trying to learn to ride a bicycle in front of the gate.

I have a new bull-terrier pup, white with a speck of brindle on the right ear. His forgiven name is *Muldoon.* He threatens to be a very fine dog of his kind, though he will never be as beautiful as *Mingo* was. The old cow is no better. She is a wreck. I'm sending her out to a swamp near Chloe's, where she may drink branch water and feed on various "errubs" (which is Chloe's word for herbs) and so, perchance, recover. J. C. went to his first professional game of base-ball yesterday, and was absolutely charmed by it. I think I'd enjoy such things myself if I could make up my mind

to go and see them. I "have n't done a thing"
(as the boys say) but forget your films again, and
now I'm afraid you'll think I'm too stingy to buy
them. But it is n't that. It's just pure forgetful-
ness. I'll try and remember to get them the first
thing in the morning. If there is anything else you
need to complete your *tout ensemble* (as we French
say) let us know. If you are to read an essay, you
will need a piece of blue ribbon to tie it with, and a
fan to hide your embarrassment. I'll come down
on the 21st, so as to get a good front seat where I
can make faces at you when you come forth on the
scene. This is all I have to say at this time, except that the baby is blooming, and the strawberries are nearly all gone. Likewise the dry
weather continues with some small promise of rain
to-night.

My regards "to all inquiring friends," especially
to Sister Bernard and Sister Mary Louis.

Your affectionate

DADDY

Mildred went to the convent school with Lillian
when the latter returned in the fall of 1897, and
father's letters to the girls kept them in touch with
all the home happenings. Mildred was a very active youngster, with her father's red hair and love

of pranks. She liked to romp and climb and gallop over the lot on the donkey, hence her nickname, "Tommy."

3 September, 1897

MY DEAREST TOMMY: —

Your letters are very cute indeed — cute and short. I notice you say that my letters are "dear." That would be true if they were written for publication — $20, $30, and $50 a thousand words. The publishers sometimes think they are too dear. Mamma says she can't write to-day. She has a bad cold and id dalking through her doze. She says: "Dell de girls I ca'd wride do-day; by doze is stobbed ub." Says I: "I hobe you don't wride wid your doze; I don't wride wid bine." She would have said something in reply, but she had to sneeze, and while she was preparing to do so I made good my escape.

Toodie[1] is looking peaked and puny. He has been sick again on account of his teeth, and had to have the doctor. But he's better to-day — in fact, well enough to come down here. Still, he is not lively, but fretful, and has lost some flesh. We'll soon have cold weather, and then Toodie will be all right. I showed him your picture to-day and he

[1] Little Stewart, the grandbaby.

[364]

took it and kissed it, and then looked at me and said "Ai?" "You are right, young man," said I, "she's the girl that loves you." "Ah?" And so on and so on.

One afternoon not long ago, while your mamma was up town, Nelly[1] chewed her rope in two, and got loose. Rufus chased her around awhile, but she finally went out at the big gate. Rufus would have gone after her but it was getting late, and I told him to let her alone. Then I shut both gates, intending to get rid of the donkey for good and all. But it was not to be. Just then mamma stepped from the car and asked me what I was doing at the front gate at that time of day. Nelly was then standing under the electric light at Frazier's. I pointed in that direction. Then there was a scene! "Rufus! why did n't you send Rufus after her? I never did see such a man. That's the way! Something always goes wrong when I'm away." Then mamma rushed to the house, flung her hat on the bed, and rushed out again with J. C. The upshot of it was that they drove the donkey back in triumph. I never will get rid of that donkey. She sticks to us like a redbug. Would n't the sisters like to have a donkey warranted to eat a panel of fence a day. I think Nelly would enjoy the picket-fence around

[1] The children's donkey.

the academy. The pickets are so small she would n't have much chewing to do.

From your devoted

DAD

Poor Mildred suffered an acute attack of home-sickness about this time, and the result was a "poem," on the subject from father, calculated to transform "weeps" into smiles: —

September 22, 1897

An Ode on Weeps

(All rights reserved.)

They say that Mildred cried, O, and cut up such a dido
  The sisters knew not what to do.
Said Sister Sacred Heart, "I 'll try and do my part,
  And help her out with my boo-hoo."

But Sister Mary Bernard, who from Northern lands had
    journeyed,
  Declared that she would help out too;
Said Sister Mary Louis, (a correspondent cu'ous),
  "I 'll drop a letter in her shoe."

And there never was such doin's, such weepin's and boo-
    hooin's
  Seen in St. Joseph's house before.
And Father O'Brien comes creepin' up and pryin',
  "And," says he, "I 'm not denyin' that this is real sighin',
But when it comes to cryin',
  Just watch me rise and walk the floor."

[366]

AMUSING ANNALS OF SNAP-BEAN FARM

Now, that 's the news that comes here, from a little bird that
    hums here
And he said it was a sight to see
Sweet Mildred a-cryin' and all the rest a-sighin'
    With hearts as full as hearts could be.

    (Carefully copied from the New Edition of Poems
    by W. Shakespere. *London: Lovingood, publisher.*)

A little comedy of the guinea-pig pen followed,
also with a view toward cheering up the lonesome
Tomboy: —

26 September, 1897

My dearest Tommy: —

As I was passing through the back yard yesterday afternoon, I heard considerable noise at the
guinea-pig pen. I thought at first the young ones
were squealing for something to eat, but when I
crept nearer I found that the little white one was
talking. At first I could n't understand what he
was saying, but after listening a while I managed
to catch some of the words, and presently I had no
difficulty in understanding what was said. The
young ones caught sight of me, and one of the brown
ones started to run.

"What do you want to run for?" said Old
Whitey. "Why, pa, there's that old man watching us. What is he going to do?" "Just what he
does every day. I'm not afraid of him." "Well,
I am, pa — he looks so big and rough." "That's

[367]

because he's a man, my daughter, I'm not so smooth myself." "Oh, look at him, pa! What is he doing now?" cried another of the brown ones. "Taking a chew of tobacco my son. I'd like to have some myself." Then the little white one began to talk again, as if in answer to a question I did n't hear. "That great big girl that used to come here and kick up such racket? Well, I heard somebody say she'd gone off to school. Goodness knows! I hope she'll learn how not to tickle my nose with a straw." "She never tickled *my* nose," said one of the little brown ones; "but I remember she flung an apple at our house and it nearly scared me to death." "Why, she did n't throw the apple," explained the old white one, "it dropped from the tree."

"Pa, what does 'dropped from the tree' mean?" asked the brown one. "Oh, don't ask such foolish questions; go to bed!" exclaimed the old white one. "But that girl could throw," he went on, turning to his wife. "I believe you!" said the old lady; "I saw her fling something they call a ball, and it hit Rufus on the shin." "You should n't say *shin*, my dear; that is naughty. You should say *chin*," remarked the old man solemnly. "Much *you* know of *shins* and *chins*," snapped the old lady. "But, ma," said the little white one, "why did they call her Tommy?" "Well," replied old Mrs.

Guinea Pig, "that was because she could throw rocks and play ball better than the boys could." "I liked her well enough until she said one day that my eyes are red because I drink too much beer," remarked the old white one. "Well, I don't know but it's true," said the old lady. "You certainly do act mighty funny sometimes. I hate for our children to see you go on so. For my part I'll be glad when the Tommy girl comes back. She won't be gone long. I remember that when J. C. forgot to give us something to eat, she used to come out and give us some herself."

"That's so," said the old white one; "but I think she thought more of that brat on the other lot than she did of us." "Why, that brat is her nephew," said the old lady. "Ma, what is a nephew?" asked little Whitey. "Oh, some kind of a blood cousin," said the mother. "Watch!" cried one of the little ones; "there comes that abominable dog. They call him Muldoon. He'll stick his nose against this pen once too often." "Oh, he's got a new collar," cried little Whitey. "Yes, indeed," exclaimed the mother. "They think a great deal more of him than they do of us." "Well," said Old Whitey, "his day will soon be over. There are some young chickens in the pen next door, three brown ones and a white one."

"Oh, ma! look at the big old man laugh," cried one of the brown ones. "Make him go away." "Don't bother," said the old lady. "How can I do anything penned up in this place?" About that time, an apple fell on the box and the whole crowd disappeared like a flash.

Your affectionate

DAD

Next comes Billy-Ann with a request that she may exchange letters with one of the neighborhood boys, a friend of the family for many years. The reply shows her father's sympathy with young folks and, at the same time, his courteous regard for the authority of the Sisters: —

DEAR MISS PODS: —

First, about Charles. You know perfectly well that we have no objection to your corresponding with him. Yet, at the convent, it is a different matter. We, as well as you, must be governed by the rules. If the Mother Superior decides that this particular case is an infraction of the rules, and that it would be a bad example for the other girls, or set them wondering why *you* should have a young man correspondent, and thus give them an idea that they are the victims of partiality, then it would be better not to correspond with Charles.

You see the question has a wider bearing than your own personality, and the Mother Superior must judge of its importance. You must remember that very few girls have been raised as you have — on perfectly familiar and confidential terms with their fathers and mothers, and fewer still have been taught to discriminate between the romance of fiction and the realities of life. You have read pretty much everything you have desired to read; yet I have been particular that the *most* you have read is sound and sweet at the core, and therefore wholesome. This has been done so quietly, that you have never known that the process was going on. This great plot has been going on and you never suspected it. You remember that there was something of a fuss made three or four years ago about your reading the newspapers. As you know, I did n't make any fuss about it, for I knew and still know that even the sensations in the newspapers carry their moral with them. Up and down the columns of the newspapers it is writ large: "Be good! Men, women and children, be good!"

Whoa! Wait ! — let me get my foot out of the stirrup. Now! — My goodness! I was on my high horse. Yet, high as he is, he should be mounted sometimes. To conclude the matter — the question is not whether it is wrong for Lillian Harris to correspond with a young man who is almost like one of our own family, but whether the fact of the correspondence will be a good example for your friends and companions. *That* question the Mother Superior must decide, and you may be sure she will decide it correctly from her point-of-view.

Your loving

DADDY

Some time in 1891, mother's young niece and namesake, Esther LaRose, had come from Canada to be a member of the family at the "Wren's Nest." She was older than either of the girls; nevertheless, they were like three sisters, and father and mother looked upon her as one of their own children. In the fall of 1897, while she was on a visit to her grandparents in Canada, her uncle wrote her as follows: —

DEAR ESSIE: —

There is no news in this neighborhood, not even any new cats. Why this is so I can't imagine. We have never gone for so long a time before without new cats; but now they are all old and sore-eyed. When there is an improvement in this respect I'll let you know. We have lots of okra going to waste with nobody to eat it. And the long drouth is on, and the grass is dying, the leaves turning yellow, and everything going to show that the year is coming to its close.

I hope you sometimes think of me with love. I send you mine, and hope it will reach you and make you happy.

Your affectionate

UNCLE

In November there goes to Essie another letter which refers to an event that had taken place during the previous month. Julian had returned from Chicago in due time, and had again taken up his work on the "Constitution," as night editor. I had become engaged to him early in 1896, before he went to Chicago, but on account of the ill-health of my mother, our marriage was deferred indefinitely. My mother grew much worse in the winter of 1896 and did not live to see the spring. The following October, Julian and I were quietly married and he came to live with me in the house where I was born, since it was impossible for me to leave my younger brothers and sisters. My parents had, of course, known Julian's father, but up to the time of my engagement I had never met him. I shall never forget how gentle and loving his manner toward me was from the first day I knew him.

[373]

Both he and mother seemed to feel that I was especially in need of their affection, since I had so recently lost my own mother, and my heart was theirs from the beginning. Father could not resist teasing us a little on the subject of lover's raptures, yet it was always done with so much geniality that we had no doubt of his sympathy and understanding. In fact, no one could doubt, when regarding the merry and kindly twinkle of his blue eye, that he, too, "had dwelt in Arcady."

Monday, 7th November, 1897

DEAR ESSIE: —

We have received two or three letters from Julian, who seems to be in the seventh heaven. His honey-moon is a very full one. It just drips with sweets and confections and things of that kind. He says he has found out she is more perfect than he thought she was, which means, I suppose, that he has discovered an unsuspected mole between her shoulders, or a dear little dimple on her arm. These lovers are great people. Won't you join us and be happy for a fortnight? I think you'd like it until you got tired of it, and then, like all the habitans, you'd want to get out in the yard and shake the dust out of a rug, or hang a ruffled petticoat on the clothes line. Your last letter to your

JOEL CHANDLER HARRIS
About 1897

Aunt Essie was a perfect model so far as the feeling of it goes. She's going to make believe she thinks it all taffy but I could see she was very proud of it and appreciated it to the utmost.

There is nothing here that I can call news: I don't weigh any less than I did, and as for Chloe — well, the Lord help us all! I don't know what's about to happen to Chloe. She's not cooking now, and for the simple reason that if she wanted to take off or put anything on the stove, she'd have to back up to it, like the wagons back up to the house when they want to throw coal in the cellar.

So you see we are living in strange times, and queer happenings are about to take place.

Give the folks my love, and tell the Captain that there's no such good luck for him as your staying in Canada. We are not going to spare you yet awhile even to *Du Priez*.

Your loving

UNCLE

Essie returned to Atlanta in time for the holidays, and concerning the preparations for Christmas, father wrote in late November to Lillian and Mildred: —

JOEL CHANDLER HARRIS

I don't know, dear gals, how in the world I'm to finish this letter. Finish it! I don't know how I'm to begin it. I've made an awful discovery — just simply *awful*. You could n't guess it — no, not if — not if each of you was eight inches taller and weighed twenty pounds heavier; not if you were to guess until your tongues were tired and your heads aching with the same ache. It's just simply too terrible to think of; but I must tell it; I never could keep a secret, especially from my dear gals. Then listen: that fruit-cake I wrote you of — it's old and wrinkled already, and no wonder! — that fruit-cake is a confirmed toper, a wretched inebriate, a habitual sot. I never would have found it out if I were any less cunning than I am — if I were less shrewd than old man Tallow Rand [1] used to be.

Mamma says to me, says she, "Cephas, have you any whiskey?" At once I began to suspect something, but not a muscle betrayed my agitation.

"Well," says I, "as likely as not there may be a thimbleful or two in the bottle. But who's ill?"

---

[1] Mamma says I have the name spelled wrong; that it should be Talleyrand — one word; but I don't see why we can't spell French names in English.

"Nobody; I just wanted some for cooking purposes," says she.

"Aha!" says I to myself, "I smell a rag burning somewhere"; but not a quiver of an eyelid betrayed me. "Then we are to have mince-pie for dinner, or the stuff you call Trifle?" says I.

"If you have no whiskey, Cephas, say so, and I'll order a bottle through the grocer," says she.

"I'll bet you a quarter you want it for that fruit-cake," says I, not dreaming that my suspicions were correct.

"I do," says she. "It must be kept moist and soft, till Christmas, and whiskey is the thing to keep it so."

So the secret was out! Every week or two the fruit-cake must have its dram, and it drinks so heartily you can almost hear it hiccough. It may happen that we'll have to send the cake to the Keeley Institute, the place where they reform poets and other geniuses. I says to mamma, says I, "you needn't accuse anybody of nibbling at that cake if you find it broken. A tipsy cake can't walk any straighter than a drunken man, and if it gets up from that box it is sure to fall back and break."

And mamma says, says she, "Cephas, if you had married any other woman" ("Heaven forbid!"

[377]

says I) "you would n't go on with that kind of nonsense."

> The Fruit-Cake fumed at the young Mince-Pie;
> "My friend, I fear you 're 'fresher' than I."
> Then he up'd and laughed, did young Mince-Pie;
> "With that, dear sir, I quite agree:
> I 'm young and warm, but, then, you see,
> I 'd rather be 'fresh' than 'full,'" says he.
> And then he bowed to the old F.-C.
> And "the table groaned," and the crock*ree*
> Cracked itself with laughter free
> And the dishes joined in the Fruit-Cake spree.

My goodness! if Sam Jones [1] knew the habits of our fruit-cake he'd make a prohibition speech on it. I know the sisters won't expose us, and I hope the girls won't tell. Sh —! I hear somebody coming now! Keep right still — (no, "still" might remind one of the dram) — keep quiet, and pretend you're reading — don't laugh! — Thank goodness! it was nobody but J. C. coming to tell us good-night. I feel right ticklish when I have a big secret like this. Essie's gone to bed, too; she does n't know a word about the condition of that cake.

Your loving

DAD

How the years fly! Here's Lillian sixteen years old, and it seems only a few pages back that we

---

[1] The well-known revivalist.

were recording the arrival of the first baby born in the West End home! Just because Billy-Ann *is* sixteen, father does not mean for Tomboy to feel slighted, so he writes: —

Sunday evening, 6th March, 1898

SWEET LITTLE TOM: —

My mind is made up. I have determined to write you a letter all to yourself, and send it to you in an envelope all by itself. I can see Billy putting on all sorts of airs because she is so old as to be sixteen; I can see how she holds herself. "I thank you, Mildred," says she, "you must treat me with more politeness hereafter. Remember, child, I am now sixteen." Oh, but these sixteen-year-olds are awfully stuck up. *I've* seen 'em; I've watched 'em out of the corner of my eye (when mamma was n't looking, of course), and I know how they carry on. It is quite aggravating, enough to discombobble the minds of young ladies of eleven and twelve and thirteen. Yes, and I've seen something else, too. I've seen the same sixteen-year-olds very jealous and envious, oh, perfectly green with envy when the young ladies of eleven and twelve come to be sixteen. It is easy to guess why. It is because those who were once sixteen have grown to be twenty and twenty-one; yes, you may count it up yourself —

twenty-one. They are almost old maids, and oh, would n't they give just anything to be sixteen again! Let us hope that Billy is enjoying herself now, for in three years and five months, dear Tommy, you will be sixteen, and then you can do some crowing — (ahem! please excuse the slip; I mean you will be enjoying the honor that Billy now wears).

Now, although it may seem a long time to you at present, three years and a half will fly by very rapidly. By that time you will be in the graduating class — or maybe you'll graduate the month before — and *then* there'll be hot times in the old town where (as Chloe says) "we lives at." You write very cute letters, and your handwriting is improving, and you say yourself you are getting along finely in music, and so forth; so what is there to grumble about? Oh, pardon me! you think June has gone lame. Well, you are very much mistaken. June will arrive on schedule time, and you'll enjoy your vacation all the more for having exercised a little patience — especially when you are obliged to exercise it.

Mamma will of course send a hamper basket of stuff for Easter, and I hope Sister Bernard — no, Sister Doctor Mary Louis — will lay in an extra stock of cholera drops and paregoric and other medicines calculated to soothe and regulate a pair of night mares imported into Washington, from West End. If there's any news here I haven't heard it. J. C. threatens to write you. The dogs got in a fight with another dog one night recently and tried to pull him in two. He didn't like this operation, and uttered his reproaches in a very loud tone of voice. He said they were bad neighbors and very inhospitable. When he did get away he ran through the empty barrels and over the loose shingles, making such a racket that mamma declared the parlor chimney had fallen in.

Heighho! I don't know anything else, except to say that this is from

Your loving

D<small>AD</small>

Violet time arrives again at the "Wren's Nest" — the time when all the neighborhood children were welcome to come and pick the dark purple California beauties until their little knees ached:

Sunday evening, 13 March, 1898

S<small>WEETEST</small> T<small>OMMIE</small>: —

The rain falls drizzle-drizzle, when it doesn't come mizzle-mizzle — and it is very welcome, too, for the garden, and the roses, and the sweet peas all need it. Violets by the basketful! We had 'em all picked clean yesterday, and now they look as though not one had been pulled. I believe two come when one is taken away. The tulip-beds at the front door are green, and the first thing we know we'll have 'em all blooming. The babies are getting on famously. Stewart can say a good many words. He did n't come to see us all last week. His mamma says it was on account of his teeth, but he seemed to be just as well as if he had all his teeth or none. Chubby[1] says very little, but seems to be doing a great deal of thinking. Sometimes he laughs to himself, and when I ask him what the joke is, he merely blinks his eyes and pretends not to know what I'm talking about. Oh, he's a shrewd one, Chubby is. And he's so fat he looks like a bologna sausage painted white (or pale pink).

Nelly, the donkey, has been ailing, but she's better now; in fact, she's able to holler back at Rosser's donkey. Rosser's yells out, "A-h-h-h-e-r-! what-er-are er-you er-doin', er-over-over er-there, er-anyhow-er-ow, er-ow?" And Nelly replies in language that I fear is not always polite. You see I am writing another "private letter" to you. I'll tell you why. The fact that Lillian is sixteen reminds me that some day *you'll* be sixteen, and then I'll have to be on my P's and Q's with you. So I may as

[1] Stewart's little brother, three months old.

well begin practising now. Lillian used to receive
private letters from me before you went to Washington, and I think you deserve to receive some.

Your report has not made its appearance yet.
Don't be afraid to send it because it is imperfect.
We are all imperfect. Besides, it will be time enough
for you to get to your books in earnest when you
are a little older. I'm glad to hear you are moving
along in music. Some day when you are grown
you'll be very glad you went to St. Joseph's Academy, and you'll remember the patient and gentle
sisters as long as you live—you'll remember them
with love, and wonder how they could manage so
many girls young and old so quietly. I think you
write very clever letters. I'd be glad to have them
a little longer occasionally. There are lots of
things about yourself you could tell me, or your
mother. When you take up your pen just say to
yourself, Now I'm not going to write; I'm just
going to talk to papa and mamma just as though
they were sitting here listening to every word I
put down." That's the way I do when I write to
you and Lillian. You know, of course, that I do
most of my talking with the pen.

My kindest regards to the sisters.

Your loving

DAD

JOEL CHANDLER HARRIS

In the next letter father has something more to say of the "fellow inside me" — that fellow who was too patient by half, else he would have gotten rid of his rival, the fag who wrote pot-boilers, long, long ago!

Sunday night, 19 March, 1898

Here I come a-runnin' for to say howdy to my dear gals and pass the time of day. And I want to say here, right at the very beginning, that Lillian's composition is fine — not because she wrote it in half an hour, but in spite of that fact. The idea is good, and it is happily carried out. Indeed, I was surprised, for the piece has humor in it, and it is very rare for young girls of seventeen to display humor. But Lillian must remember that the very best things are the result of much thought and very hard work — though some people don't have to think as much or work as hard as others.

As for myself — though you could hardly call me a real, sure enough author — I never have anything but the vaguest ideas of what I am going to write; but when I take my pen in my hand, the rust clears away and the "other fellow" takes charge. You know all of us have two entities, or personalities. That is the reason you see and hear persons "talking to themselves." They are talking to the "other fellow." I have often asked my "other fellow" where he gets all his information, and how he can remember, in the nick of time, things that I have forgotten long ago; but he never satisfies my curiosity. He is simply a spectator of my folly until I seize a pen, and then he comes forward and takes charge.

Sometimes I laugh heartily at what he writes. If you could see me at such times, and they are very frequent, you would no doubt say, "It is very conceited in that old man to laugh at his own writing." But that is the very point; it is not my writing at all; it is my "other fellow" doing the work and I am getting all the credit for it. Now, I'll admit that I write the editorials for the paper. The "other fellow" has nothing to do with them, and, so far as I am able to get his views on the subject, he regards them with scorn and contempt; though there are rare occasions when he helps me out on a Sunday editorial. He is a creature hard to understand, but, so far as I can understand him, he's a very sour, surly fellow until I give him an opportunity to guide my pen in subjects congenial to him; whereas, I am, as you know, jolly, good-natured, and entirely harmless.

Now, my "other fellow," I am convinced, would do some damage if I did n't give him an opportunity to work off his energy in the way he delights. I say to him, "Now, here's an editor who says he will pay well for a short story. He wants it at once." Then I forget all about the matter, and go on writing editorials and taking Celery Compound and presently my "other fellow" says sourly: "What about that story?" Then when night comes, I take up my pen, surrender unconditionally to my "other fellow," and out comes the story, and if it is a good story I am as much surprised as the people who read it. Now, my dear gals will think I am writing nonsense; but I am telling them the truth as near as I can get at the facts — for the "other fellow" is secretive. Well! so much for that. You can take a long breath now and rest yourselves.

Your loving

DAD

More hints of the ever recurring springtime pageant on the farm, and gossip of Sunday afternoon visitors: —

Sunday evening, March 20, 1898

DEAR BILLY-ANN: —

The weather is really too fine for letter writing. It is warm, and yet not too warm. The tulip beds — where we used to have pansies — are beginning to make a brave show, and in the poplars the mock-ing-birds are singing. The violets have been a real show. One day during the week, in fact, three or four days, they have been a mass of bloom. All the neighbors have been picking at them, and still thousands are left. People going along the street have stopped to gaze at the extraordinary display. Everything looks so fresh and green and promising that I am beginning to feel gay and kittenish like a colt in a barley patch. — At this point, Julian and Julia have just walked in.

After Supper

I don't mean of course that they walked in after, or for supper. Like all country folks, I instinctively say "evening" when I mean afternoon. I began this letter about four o'clock. It is now half-past seven, g. m. Julian and Julia stayed till sundown, and while they were here, Lucien and Alleen came in. Ellinor came, too, and she and J. C. had a boisterous time running around the house.

Julian and Julia are looking well, and seem to be very happy. Julian's dignity is gradually wearing off. Like all married men, he has discovered that his wife walks on the ground as other folks do. Consequently he feels more chummy than he did. Of course this is a discovery that all lovers make for themselves after they marry. It is not disillusion; it is simply that they feel more "at home" with each other — and you know a human being of either sex could not possibly feel at home with a *real angel.*

Well, we had a very pleasant time. The mocking-bird gave a concert, the roosters crowed, and the cows lowed. As usual, I have nothing of startling importance to relate in regard to that branch of society belonging to maidens of sixteen. These maidens seem to be skipping along the same as ever, putting on great dignity when a young man comes on view, and unbending again as soon as he is out of sight.

Your loving

DAD

And later there is news of the babies and the inevitable bug-a-boo of spring cleaning!

Sunday evening, 30 April, 1898

DEAR TOMMY! —

Your letter full of busses was received; and you must imagine that mine has twice as many, though I do not mark the places. Toodlum — Boo and Chubby were here to-day. Stewart is smart and boisterous, while Chandler is sweet and quiet and fat. Alleen and Lucien took dinner and supper here to-day, and are still here as I write. The babies are at home and asleep. J. C. had seven more little bantams to hatch yesterday, and they are behaving very well for such young chickens. They have already learned to wipe their mouths, using blades of grass as napkins, and young as they are, they return thanks every time they take a drink of water. I wish that little hen would show people how to train their children as well as she has trained hers. Of course, I did n't mean *my* children — especially my *girls* — but other folk's children.

J. C. went out beyond the Stewart farm in Fritz's pony cart yesterday and brought back a load of sweet shrubs. To-day he rode with Fritz and Roy to Grant Park and made arrangements to swap some of his guinea pigs for black ones. He has four tee-nine-chy ones, and they are very prettily marked. Julian and Julia were here this afternoon, and they seemed to enjoy themselves. Louise came with them. I was to go to Mayor Collier's last Monday night (with mamma) to play whist, but the wind blew and the rain fell, and we could n't go. So we are to go to-morrow evening if nothing happens to prevent it.

Mamma continues to have general spring house cleaning twice a week, and I heard her say to-day that she was only waiting for good weather to have a *genuine* spring cleaning. I don't know where I'll go nor what I'll do. If I were a housekeeper I would n't live in a house that had to be turned upside down every day to get the dirt out of it. A *genuine* spring cleaning means that Chloe, and Johnson, and John, and Lizzie, and Rufus, and Banks and Ca'line are to come in to the tune of one of Sousa's marches, played on the piano by Essie, tear up the carpets, knock down the plastering, break the clocks, and drop a stove in the back porch. Mamma has made no attempt, as yet, to sun the bath-tub, but I'm expecting it every day. When it happens, I'm going to have the chimneys taken down and dusted. When this is done, I'll have the wood-pile cleaned and polished with that perfumed stuff they use on the stoves. And then I'm going to have all the dirt swept out of the garden — I think a clean garden — a garden with no dirt at all in it — is one of the loveliest sights on earth.

Well, this is all for this time.

Your loving

DAD

It was about this time that the newspapers were buzzing with the talk of war with Spain, and Lillian asks father's views on the subject: —

AMUSING ANNALS OF SNAP-BEAN FARM

DEAR BILLY-ANN: —

I think it would be impossible to give you any clear idea of my views on public affairs. Events follow each other so swiftly, and circumstances follow so hard on one another's heels, that mere "views" go for nothing. There may be no war with Spain, after all. On the other hand, war may be declared before you get this letter. Whatever is done must be done quickly. A war means the ruin of Spain; though, for the matter of that, it is ruined now. The Cuban revolution was brought about by the oppressive taxes levied by the Spanish government. The Cubans were taxed on everything. This was unjust, and yet Spain was obliged to raise money to pay the interest on its bonds and to carry on its government. The Spaniards are out of date with the times. Once they laid claim to this whole continent, and actually held a large part of it. They held Mexico and all South America. And all has been lost to them by reason of their pride and folly.

In old times Catholics believed that a monarchy was of divine origin. This belief was held because all the Catholic countries were governed by kings or queens. It was a very natural belief. The Pope himself not very long ago wrote a letter to the bish-

[391]

ops of France and warned them that they owed
their political allegiance to whatever form of government the people found satisfactory. He did this
because the bishops were opposed to the republic.
I gather from the Holy Father's letters (or ency-
clicals) to American Bishops that he admires the
American republic. He is a very great statesman
(aside from his holy office) and ranks — in my mind
— even above Gladstone.

I can't tell you how long the war will last if it
comes. War is one of the demons that are hard to
pacify when once they break loose. We cannot
wipe out the Spanish navy in a day — or we could
n't if their ships were manned by real men instead
of pompous mannikins. I never have liked any of
the Spaniards except Don Quixote and Sancho
Panza — and the first was crazy, the second a
clown. But I'm sorry for the poor little king. He
is a small boy. I've a great mind to send him a
Thimblefinger book. It is so silly for a child to be
"a-kingin' it," as Drusilla says. He should be
playing marbles with other small boys. You see I
have written you quite a dull editorial essay, as
becomes one who is addressing a mature young lady
of sixteen.

Your loving

DAD

AMUSING ANNALS OF SNAP-BEAN FARM

Not often did father touch on anything pertaining to his craft in his letters, but on May Day he writes to Lillian a little essay on the difference between style and diction, in which he refers to the works of one of his favorite writers:—

May Day, Sunday, 1898

DEAR LILLIAN:—

The Gleanings came to hand, and I read your account of the pottery tour with great pleasure. It is particularly well done, and the reason is very plain. You had something to write about, you knew what you wanted to say, and you said it, briefly and clearly. There are two secrets of good writing that I will whisper in your ear. One is to write about something that interests you because you know it; the other is to be familiar with and believe in the ideas you propose to write about. One secret refers to description, and the other to views, feelings, opinions. Combined, or separate, they relate to everything that has been or can be written in the shape of literature. So far as merely correct diction is concerned, that can easily be acquired, especially by those who have a knack or gift of expression.

In nearly all the books and magazines that I read, diction is called style. Why, I don't know, for the two come together and combine only in the works of the very greatest writers, as, for instance, Hawthorne — or, to name a greater still, Cardinal Newman. I have just been reading some of the Cardinal's works, and I am simply amazed at the beauty, power, fluency and vividness with which he uses the English tongue. In discussing the dryest subjects, he frequently thrills the mind with passages of such singular beauty as almost to take one's breath away. In these passages you cannot separate the style from the diction, for they are fused.

Nevertheless, style is one thing and diction is another. If some one should compel me by force to explain the difference between the two, my answer would be something like this: Diction is the body — the flesh and bone — and style is the spirit. But some years ago, that able Heathen, Mr. Herbert Spencer, had something he wanted to say about diction, and so he wrote it out and called it An Essay on Style, and ever since then the Heathens, the Pagans, and not a few who call themselves Christians, have persisted in referring to diction as style — just as our Northern scholars refer to the "*provincialism* of the South," when they mean the *provinciality* of the South. Dear me! I hope I am not wearying you with all this; more than all, I hope I have made myself understood. It is so easy to be vague and hazy when talking about writing as a gift and as an art. A person who has the gift must acquire the art, and that is to be done only by long practice.

You will never learn English grammar from the books. All you can learn is the parts of speech, and the dozen or more pages that deal with inflections. English grammar proper cannot be written. The worst English is written by those who call themselves grammarians. An article or a book may be grammatically perfect and at the same time be written in vile English. You will learn more from Latin grammar than you will from English grammar. And you will learn most of all by reading the best English books. — But really you will think some one else has taken your popsy's place in writing to you; but it's the same old fellow, subdued and sobered by the fact that you are now more than sixteen, and still looking puny.

It's a good thing I've filled up this letter with all that talk about — By the by, permit me to congratulate you on that "bumpety feeling." *That* was quite a stroke. It tells the whole story, and gives the necessary touch of humor to light up the description. Don't be afraid of such passages. Well, as I was going to say, if I had n't filled this letter

[395]

up with all this highfalutin talk about style and diction, it would have been a very poor letter indeed, for there's nothing to write about; no news; no nothing. The cow begins to holler for Chloe at the same time every afternoon, and Rufus, in the matter of shoes, has graduated from No. 8's to No. 9's, and feels that he has won a victory.

Regards to the sisters, and love to Burdeene.

Your loving

DAD

CHAPTER XXI

"TALES OF THE HOME FOLKS" AND "AUNT MINERVY ANN"

IN April of 1898 father had written Lillian: "I am glad you were pleased with at least one page of the new book. I certainly wrote the few lines thereon with greater pleasure than all the rest gave me. It was just a whim of mine to make a little secret of the matter. I thought you would like it best if you came upon it unawares. At first I had only one line, 'To My Daughter Lillian,' but when I made the title 'Tales of the Home Folks,' the publishers wanted to know if I could include the Canadian story under such a title. Then I added the rest of the dedication — 'who will know why,' etc. You know — because your mother is a French Canadienne and all your home folks are on that side. The book you received was the first bound. It will not be published till the 9th of April, next Saturday."

"Tales of the Home Folks in Peace and War" was the full title of this book, and it comprised twelve stories which had appeared during the course of two or three years in "Scribner's," "Lippincott's," "The Cosmopolitan," and "McClure's" magazines. The story referred to in the letter to Lillian was "The Belle of St. Valérien," and the dedication of the book ran thus: "To my daughter Lillian, who will know why I have included in the 'Tales of the Home Folks' the little skit about our friends in St. Valérien."

Of one of the stories, "The Comedy of War," Colonel McClure had written father some time previous to the publication of the book: "Do you remember that splendid story I published entitled 'The Comedy of War'? Did not that Irishman, O'Halloran, have any other adventures? It seems to me he is too good to waste on one short story. Cannot you give me four or five short stories like 'The Comedy of War'? . . . If you could have the same character in the heart of the stories, or as a central figure, it would make a capital book, and we could publish it, giving you a good royalty. . . . We are short of short stories, and I turn to you."

And later, Colonel McClure reminds him of the *O'Halloran* scheme, and urges him to begin at once on the work. But father was very busy at this time with the "Stories of Georgia" and "Sister Jane," and so wrote only one more of the O'Halloran stories, "An Ambuscade." Private O'Halloran was an Irish sharpshooter on the Federal side, and his opponent in "The Comedy of War" was sharpshooter Jack Kilpatrick, of the Confederate forces, and the latter figures also in "The Ambuscade" and "The Baby's Fortune," all of which are included in "Tales of the Home Folks." Most of the stories deal with the Civil War, and of the four which are records of "peace," one is concerned with the mountaineer of North Georgia [1] and another [2] is an ingenious "take-off" on folk-lorists, in which the author proceeds to draw a humorous parallel between a supposedly Oriental folk-tale and a legend of middle Georgia. How he came in possession of the former, he explained as follows: —

On the 16th of February, 1892, I received a communication from Sir Waddy Wyndham, one of Her Majesty's officials at Jahore. Sir Waddy evidently had plenty of time at his command, for his letter contained fourteen sheets of note-paper, containing by actual count two hundred and eleven words to the page. The envelope had a weather-beaten appearance. It was literally covered with postmarks, save the address and one little spot in a corner, where some one, evidently a postal clerk in Georgia, had written, "All for Joe!" Sir Waddy's handwriting was trying, but I managed to make out that he had read with great pleasure the learned introduction to my plantation stories, and was proud to know that he and his coadjutors in India and other parts of the world had so worthy a co-worker in the fertile fields of *South America*.

[1] "The Cause of the Difficulty."
[2] "The Late Mr. Watkins of Georgia."

JOEL CHANDLER HARRIS

And then follows a most amusing satire in which the author cleverly pokes fun at himself, at the mythical Sir Waddy, and at folk-lorists in general.

In December of the previous year (1897) father had written Mr. Burlingame of "Scribners": —

ATLANTA, GA., 3 December, 1897

MY DEAR MR. BURLINGAME: —

I have just finished one of three stories that can be either published one after the other or two or three months after one another. I am aware how hampering the serial business is, and while the three stories are told by the same negro woman, and embody the same characters, they are independent. If you could find room for them month after month (three months) their general title would be, —

The Chronicles of Aunt Minervy Ann.

1.

How She Ran Away from Home and Ran Back Again.

2.

How She Involved Major Perdue[1] in a Difficulty.

3.

The Major's Bargain.

---

[1] This story appeared under another title when collected with the others in book form.

AUNT MINERVY ANN

They will make about 5000 words each, and the first one only awaits copying.

Yours faithfully

JOEL CHANDLER HARRIS

In February, 1898, he again refers to the "Minervy Ann" stories, with a request that Mr. A. B. Frost illustrate them: —

ATLANTA, GA.
10 February, 1898

DEAR MR. BURLINGAME: —

Say what you please, he is the only artist that understands American character sufficiently well to be able to represent it perfectly in black and white.

The three sketches are in negro dialect. That sort of stuff has seemed to be under the ban, but I have yet to hear of any reader or critic objecting to mine.

The difference between real dialect and lingo is that the first is preservative, while the latter is destructive, of language. Judged by this standard the negro dialect is as perfect as any the world ever saw.

Faithfully yours

JOEL CHANDLER HARRIS

"Aunt Minervy Ann" was one of his creations

which the author, himself, liked best, and, as he would have said in his youthful days, he "had some fun" in recording her stories of "old times." She is also one of his characters that the public has liked best: —

ATLANTA, GA.
31 October, 1898

MY DEAR MR. BURLINGAME: —

I have submitted the MS. to a number of old Southerners, and they say the character is hit off as completely as that of Uncle Remus. It has certainly been a pleasure to write the stuff. I am grateful to you for putting the other in Frost's hands — there is something about Frost's work in character that is beyond the grasp of all the rest. I find it even in his caricatures.

My regards to Mr. Bridges.

Faithfully yours

JOEL CHANDLER HARRIS

The stories had begun to appear serially in "Scribner's," and Mr. Burlingame's appreciative comment on them called forth the following response: —

AUNT MINERVY ANN

ATLANTA, GA.
14 November, 1898

DEAR MR. BURLINGAME: —

I thank you heartily for your kind letter. The main reason I send most of my stuff to "Scribner's" is due to the fact that your letters, now and again, seem to breathe a note of appreciation. And though I am old enough to know that such an expression belongs to the Art of Editing, and is prompted by a sense of sympathy with a poor provincial, who, having no time to do his best, is doing the best he can — though I am old enough to know this, I am not too old to feel the need of the encouragement that frequently takes shape even in your notes.

A date on the proof of "Miss Irene" misled me. It seemed to be marked for December, and I thought it would be out of the way. Otherwise I should have withheld the three additional "Minervy Anns." I have been intensely absorbed in the series, more so than in anything I have ever written. There have been moments when I could hear her voice as plainly as I now hear the youngsters talking in the sitting-room. Moreover, I am very fond of writing this dialect. It has a fluency all its own; it gives a new coloring to statement, and allows of a swift shading in narrative that can be

[403]

reached in literary English only in the most painful and roundabout way.

As, for instance, in Mr. James's "Turn of the Screw." Many will doubtless find that story somewhat horrifying without being able to account for it. I find it in the labored, panting diction, the painful effort to find the right word, the right phrase, the fitting paragraph. I have never before been able to hear the creaking of the cords and pulleys of the machinery of "preciousness." A man bursts in upon a company and stands with staring eyes, quivering lips and trembling limbs, to tell what he has seen in the dark. You know it was something dreadful, but after gasping and shaking, and talking wildly, kind friends take him away and put him to bed; and you go on with your whist and never know what the staring eyes have seen. The turn of the screw is that, in your devouring curiosity, you have forgotten the trump, and have lost the run of the cards. Some of these days "Aunt Minervy Ann" will preen her plumage and tell a ghost story, and I think . . .

But, really, I only intended to thank you and to say that when the time comes I'll whip "Miss Irene" into a "Minervy Ann" narrative.[1] Instead

---

[1] "Miss Irene" was never changed and did not appear in the "Minervy Ann" series, but in *Scribner's Magazine* some time during 1900.

of telling you these things quietly I've done gone
and given *you* a special turn of *my* screw.

Faithfully yours

JOEL CHANDLER HARRIS

"The Chronicles of Aunt Minervy Ann," as
published by Charles Scribner's Sons in 1899, comprised eight stories; the one referred to in the following letter, and entitled "The Case of Mary
Ellen," was the last in the book: —

312 GORDON AVENUE, ATLANTA, GA.
4 January, 1899

DEAR MR. SCRIBNER: —

I hope you'll like my Aunt Minervy Ann. She's
a more complicated character than Uncle Remus,
but that is because she's a woman. She told me
another story the other day, about how Colonel
Bolivar Blasengame turned his parlor over to an
octoroon girl so as to give her an opportunity to
receive a visit from a Northern young lady who
did n't know the girl had negro blood. But I dare
not send this story to Mr. Burlingame. I've imposed on his patience already; I've fairly crammed
his pigeon-holes with Aunt Minervy Ann's reminiscences.

You could not have sent me a more acceptable

present than Mr. Thompson's book. It is enjoyable from first to last. I was afraid to read it, owing to the fact that I am engaged on some animal autobiographies to be embodied in a successor to the Thimblefinger books,[1] but the pictures were so alluring in the first place, and the text in the second, that I could n't help myself — and now I'm afraid folks will find traces of Thompson in my stories. Well, if the traces are real, 'twill be all the better for me.

I enclosed an advertisement of a book[2] which I hope you will take over, reprint and put on your list of summer holiday books. It is really the most illuminating depiction of negro character ever printed in this country. Why do I want you to take it over? Because you can do it justice; you can make it a success. It is now in the hands of people who seem to be walking in the dark. The book in your hands would sell fifty thousand copies; in their hands it may sell a thousand; and I want the northern people to see what the southern people mean when they say we really loved the old plantation negroes. This book shows it by means of character portraits, and with an art that stands

---

[1] *Plantation Pageants*. Houghton, Mifflin & Company, 1899.
[2] Either *Shadows on the Wall* or *Bandanna Ballads*, by Howard Weeden. Father wrote the introduction to the latter book.

out almost alone. I was surprised and delighted, on turning its pages to find my Aunt Minervy Ann's portrait among the rest.

Well, I hope you and yours will have a happy and prosperous New Year!

Faithfully yours

JOEL CHANDLER HARRIS

The scene of the "Aunt Minervy Ann" stories is *Halcyondale* in middle Georgia, and of "Minervy Ann," herself, father wrote in the first story of the series: —

She was what is called a "character," and something more besides. The truth is, I should have missed a good deal if I had never known Aunt Minervy Ann Perdue, who as she described herself was "Affikin fum 'way back yander 'fo' de flood, an' fum de word go."

And he added that she was a descendant of the African prince, Qua, who died in Augusta, Georgia, at the age of one hundred years, which accounted in part for "Minervy Ann's" love of "kingin' it"! In the first story of the series is to be found a description of a printing office, which is said by Mr. W. T. Manry, who worked under father on the "Monroe Advertiser," to be an accurate representation of the office of that paper in Forsyth, Georgia; and Mr. Manry also recalls the roadside, bordered with Cherokee roses, on the way to Indian Spring, where the Gossett boys received their "frailin'" at the hands of "Minervy Ann."

Undoubtedly Chloe, the faithful general factotum of the Harris family for so many years, furnished hints for the character of "Aunt Minervy Ann." The old soul's unctuous humor, vivid speech, and downright ways are all reflected in her literary kinswoman. Mr. Manry is of the opinion that Mrs. Harrison's cook, Sallie, also suggested the character. He describes her as a "good-natured woman who could laugh louder than any one else, on the least provocation." When Sallie later followed the Harrisons to Atlanta, she frequently called on "Marse Joe," and entertained him with her gossip. There is no doubt that as a complete and vivid personality, "Aunt Minervy Ann" takes her place beside Uncle Remus, and if she were as widely known as the old man she would probably be as widely popular.

The year 1898 had been a peaceful and an uneventful one at Snap-Bean Farm, and the fall months passed happily, except for a slight illness which laid mother up for a short while. In the following letter to the girls at St. Joseph's, father makes reference to the forlorn atmosphere which prevailed about the house whenever its mistress

AUNT MINERVY ANN

was under the weather, and gives a little character sketch in the style of his old "Constitution" skits: —

6 November, 1898

Well! here comes the old man, a-writing to his gals and with nothing whatsoever for to write about. Mamma went to church to-day, and it seemed to do her good. She has been very cheerful and chipper all day, and I hope she has weathered her bad spell. Things are very bad about the house when mamma is ailing. It does no good for me to put on one of Chloe's frocks and try to keep things straight. They will go wrong. And I can't sit down and gossip with Mrs. Y——, and Mrs. A——, and the rest. I can listen — but that does n't satisfy them. When they tell something sweet about a neighbor or an acquaintance, they want to hear something sweet in return about somebody else. But how do I know that Mrs. So-and-so has taken off her mourning too soon, or that Mr. So-and-so is cutting his eye at Miss Prissy, and he old enough to be her father. No; everything goes wrong when mamma is ailing, and even the gossip gets stale. But as I told you, she is getting better now, and everything will brighten up — nothing more so than poor me.

Well, here comes the old man, a-writing to his

[409]

dear gals with nothing whatsoever for to write about. And it.'s a mighty bad fix for to be in, writing to somebody and with nothing whatsoever to write, but — ... As I was coming home from town yesterday, two negroes got on the car at High's corner — two negro men. One had a valise and was from the country. The other had met him at the train. They were probably related. The town negro asked about many people whom he had formerly known in the town or settlement where the country negro came from. Finally, after a pause, he asked: "An' how is ol' Tom Benson?" The country negro: "Humph! he dead; dat's how he is." Town negro: "Well, suh! Tooby sho', tooby sho'. Why, when did ol' Tom die?" Country negro: "Day 'fo' yistiddy; dat's when." Town N.: "Well, suh!—I thought he could n't 'a' been dead so mighty long. What de matter wid him?" Country N.: "Trouble wid his Mu-ky-ous Membrine. It sho' tuck an' tuck him off." Town N.: "De Mu-ky-ous Membrine! Well, suh!" Country N.: "Dat's what! An' I tell you right now, ef I has any trouble wid de Mu-ky-ous Membrine, I'm gwine ter sen' fer all de doctors in de town. I ain't sayin' dee 'l come, an' dee may not come; but dee ain't gwine ter sleep none dat night!" Town N.: "I believe you!" In spite of myself I had to drop a

laugh to the memory of poor Tom Benson (whoever he was) and his Mu-ky-ous Membrine —
which, I suppose, is another name for the Mucous
Membrane.

Your loving

DAD

And now come Christmas and the groggy fruit-
cake again! And to add to the bustle and flurry
of things, there's a riddle for the pupils of St.
Joseph's: —

Saturday evening
26 November, 1898

If my dear gals will collect their thoughts, and
put 'em in a bag, and shake 'em up, they'll see that
next Thursday is the first of December, with
Christmas only TWENTY-FOUR days off. Thus
does time fly when we're not looking; but the moment we begin to watch it, that moment it ceases
to gallop and seems to be almost too tired to walk.
I wrote you a little note about our Thanksgiving,
all of which you might have guessed, since it's
pretty much the same every year. We should have
been very happy to have had you with us, but that
fact will cause us to enjoy and relish Christmas the
more. And as for that Fruit-Cake! Well! I would

[411]

not advise a prohibitionist to take too big a bite if she does n't want to walk wobbly when she goes to bed. Mamma says it needs more stimulants right now, and if Christmas should happen to be put off this year by so much as an hour we 'll have to send it to the Keeley University for a post-graduate course.

I 'm glad Mrs. Glenn was on time with the turkey. I did n't order it because I thought you really needed it, for I knew better, but because I wanted to give you a little surprise, and make you both feel a little bit happier if that could be. But perhaps the whole truth about it can be best expressed when I say that 't was merely a little whim of mine, a sort of frolic for myself. I hope I 'll never be too old to have some kind of a frolic. You know how neglectful I am. I intended to send the book every day during the week, but here it is Saturday night, as cold as Flugeous, and the book not mailed yet. I have none of the original pictures, which were done in water color, but the reproductions in the book will give you an idea of their beauty. I 'll send it first thing next week — if I don't forget it.

I have received from some children in Virginia some copies of a little paper they are publishing. I read them all through, and I 'll send 'em to you. I judge, from the many items about Weewee's baby that Jean, the junior editor, is another Mildred. If she had a paper, half of the articles would be about Toody and Bumpus.[1] Those Virginia chaps seem to be very smart. I'm going to write to them and tell them the incident of the negro and his Mukyous Membrine.

No, on second thoughts, I'll send them a riddle that I wrote for my dear gals. Viz:

My Riddle lives in every zone,
In every land where the sun has shone,
(And where it has not, if the truth were known);
It has wings without feathers, and I freely own
I'd rather not meet it when I'm alone.
You may put it in closets, but when it is grown,
It fills half the earth, and, when shaped like a cone,
Flies as far as the moon: and when it has flown,
May be put in a thimble and will lie there prone.
  The wind may have blown on it,
  But the sun never shone on it,
And I hope that, in guessing, you won't have to groan on it.

    (From the pen of the Immortal Uncle Dremus, and
    respectfully dedicated to those who are not in it.)

The answer to this remarkable riddle will be printed in our next. At present it is only necessary to say that the Fruit-Cake has had another glass of grog.

The northwest wind came out yesterday without any overcoat on, and the result is, we have to sit

---

[1] The two grandsons.

on the stove to keep warm. Mamma is too heavy for the stove in her room, so she has to sit on the hall stove. She biled a right smart while to-day.

But why go on at this rate? There's nothing to write about, and why not admit it?

Your loving

DAD

And now for the answer to the holiday riddle: —

Saturday evening, December 3, 1898

DEAR BILLY AND TOMMY: —

As for that riddle —

> The simple riddle! So you could n't guess it?
> Dear Gals, I never would confess it!
> With all the wise heads St. Joseph's has in
> Its walls. Why, first there 's Father Bazin,
> Then Mother Clemence, and that bright Sister
> Sacred Heart, so keen, I wist, her
> Mind must have solved it; and Sister Bernard
> Who 's shy and gentle 'cause she 's learn-ard;
> And then there 's sister Mary Louis —
> I own to you that it 's mighty cu-is —
> (these rhymes are worse than any hammer
> To knock the stuffin' out'n grammar,
> And, while I 'm in the way of tellin',
> They knock it, also, out'n spellin') —
> > Now, where are you at night,
> > When some one "outs" the light?
> > In bed? Oh, Yes! but mark too —
> > In bed and in the DARK, too

Yours respectfully

RINKTUM RIDDLES

AUNT MINERVY ANN

Dear Gals, you ask so many questions in your letters that it quite takes my breath away, and by the time you get through asking them you are through with your letters. Now I don't think that's quite fair to a poor old man who expects to get letters every week and who goes solemnly to the post-office to get them. Suppose *he* were to do that way? Suppose he were to write seven lines on a page, saying, "How is Mildred? I hope she is well. How is Lillian? I hope she is better than she was week before last. And how is Mrs. Glenn, and Mrs. Kerr, and Mrs. and Mr. Wenn?" Well, you'd say I was cheating and you'd be correct — ahem! in your surmises. (I tell you, I'm right in the game when it comes to flinging big words at my esteemed correspondents!)

Things are beginning to smell like Christmas again, but the fruit cake will have to keep sober until the 15th, so mamma says. Fine weather or foul, mamma will be seen slipping off to town next week, and the only way I'll know she's not at Alleen's will be when the door-bell rings four or five times a day, and men and boys come delivering all sorts of mysterious packages and bundles, the messenger remarking, "De lady say p'intedly dat de bundle ain't to be open tell she git back — ef den." There's a good deal of whispering going on in the house, and various half-remarks and references that nobody is supposed to understand but those who are in the secret. As for me I sit and nod and write, and rouse up and write and nod just the same as ever.

Sunday, December 4

The weather is very cold to-day, thanks to a gale from the southwest. This morning we had snow, but the supply was shut off about ten and we have n't had any since. I hope we'll have no more. Snow is beautiful to think about, to remember, but it's not pleasant to deal with. I suppose you girls would enjoy it, but if you had to go back and forth to town and the cars were n't running, you'd soon say you had enough. I am willing you should have as much as you want in Wilkes if you'll keep it there. I'm sorry for the poor little guinea pigs to-night; they have good quarters, but there are so many of them, it's a problem to feed them when there's no grass.

Brother can stand alone and take a step or two. He's a very quiet baby — altogether different from Stewart in his ways. But Stewart is really smart. His memory is as long as a wire fence. He saw me shave a fortnight ago, and yesterday he got a toothbrush and said, "Alleen, Stewart goin' chave."

[416]

AUNT MINERVY ANN

Oh! the wind is howling up the chimney as if it had got caught in the flue and could n't get out, and I'm thinking now of the hundreds of poor little chilluns who have no fire to warm by and who are shivering with cold. There are many thousands of them in this broad land. Oh, what a pity that this should be so! I started out without having any news to write, and that's the way I'll have to end — no news, nothing.

My kindest regards to the sisters, and ask them to excuse the frivole — ivole — ousness of an old man.

Your loving

DAD

The year closes with a birthday letter, celebrating the writer's attainment of the half-century mark: —

10 December, 1898

No doubt my dear gals will be surprised to hear that I passed my fiftieth birthday yesterday — and it was not a pleasant day either. On the contrary, it was cloudy, and last night the sleet fell in such quantities that it seemed to be snow. To-night it is pretty much all melted, but the weather is cold — so cold, indeed, that I'm afraid to go out and shut the gate of the chicken pen. And the dogs

[417]

are quarreling over their boxes. Each has a box to sleep in, but each wants to sleep in the box with the other. This does n't suit the dog who is already in the box and has a warm place.

It usually happens that Ovid is the outside dog, and so, about every five minutes he manages to discover a nest of thieves in Richardson's lot, and he runs after them barking as loud as ever he can. The noise attacks the attention of Muldoon, who comes charging out of his warm place. Thereupon Ovid rushes to the box and gets in, and then Muldoon begins to see thieves by the hundreds. This sort of thing is kept up until late at night — in fact, until it gets too cold for either of the dogs to dispute about a warm place. Owing to the sleet on the ground, we thought we would n't have an early breakfast yesterday morning, but Lizzie managed to get here at half past six.

I'm very glad Mildred wants a pony. A "pony" is a small glass of beer, and I have n't the slightest objection to her taking that. Some of her friends and acquaintances had selected other things as presents for her, but they are happy to know that a pony — which costs 5 cents — is all she wants. Maybe she would like to have a pill with the pony. The little puzzle she sent in her letter is very cute — too cute for me, though mamma says *she* can do it;

in fact, she did it right before my eyes, but try as I will, I can't do as she did. This makes me feel giddy.

Sunday and Monday — Cuddled up in bed with a rag around my marble brow.

Tuesday — Able to be up and about — though the headache has dropped into the right eye-tooth. I discovered this morning that the tooth is a cold tooth. I opened my mouth getting on the street car, and could hardly shut it again owing to the terrible paroxysm of pain in tooth and jaw. It was quite an experience, being new to me, and made me feel like I resemble the man's bust of me.[1] He has made some small ones, and they all look as if they had had some sort of strange experience with their teeth. They are the queerest little weazened affairs you ever saw. Julia has purchased one, and I think Julian will grow more jealous of it as he grows older.

Alleen and Lucien ate their anniversary dinner, but, as for me, I was in bed and had nothing to eat but some nice medicine until this morning. Of course, under the circumstances, I had to hurry up and get well. The shopping is still going on. The streets to-day were a perfect jam, cold as it was. If everybody bought something, the stores did a

[1] Father had been sitting to Mr. Paul Okerburg for a bust.

rushing trade. To-night the weather is still colder and the weather man has promised us some more as soon as ever he can unpack it — and I have just returned from turning the water off though I found the stand-pipe in the front yard already friz. I hope it will thaw out in the morning without bursting. The exertion I had to undergo in turning off the water in the tank showed me that I am still surprisingly weak, and I am sure my dear gals will forgive me if this letter is neither as long nor as interesting as they might have had reason to hope.

I shall have to close this dull letter. A man who has been in bed with a rag around his marble brow has no news of interest to relate. Regards to the sisters and love to Burdeene.

Your loving

DAD

CHAPTER XXII

AWAY back in 1881 father had received a letter
from James Whitcomb Riley, then on the staff of
the "Indianapolis Journal," in which he spoke of
the pleasure "Uncle Remus" had given him and
added: "The touch of the master is in all you do —
in verse as in prose. Of your verse I would like to
see more." The next record of any correspondence
between them is in 1883, when Mr. Riley sent
father a volume of his poems and followed it up
with a letter referring to his friend's "gentle way
of accepting my book," and containing added
assurances of the "Hoosier poet's" appreciation of
the work of "Uncle Remus," which he calls "pure
poetry — the finest art — utterly forgetting self."

There seemed to be a bond of spiritual sympathy
between them almost from the beginning. Father
deeply appreciated the note of simplicity in Mr.
Riley's verse — its refreshing human quality and
its feeling for little children.[1] There was more

[1] Mr. Arthur Brisbane, now the editor and publisher of the
Washington Times, once telegraphed father for his opinion about
dialect poets, and the following reply was sent to that energetic and
enterprising journalist: "What under the flapping flag of freedom
ever put it into your busy head to ask me about dialect poets? I

correspondence and talk about a meeting, but the busy years flew by and not until 1900 did the two friends come together. In April of that year father wrote Mildred at Washington, Georgia: —

DEAR TOM: —

I did n't write to you last night because I did n't want to interrupt your conversation with mamma. I hope she arrived without any headache in her baggage. She always has the headache when she travels. If she starts from here without it, she manages to pick it up somewhere on the road. I know you enjoyed her visit. She's a mighty nice lady when she's not dusting and tearing up the house.

I had an Easter present myself in addition to the pretty cards you kids sent me. James Whitcomb Riley sent me a complete edition of his works in ten volumes, with something original on the flyleaf of each one. This was in the first volume: —

To Uncle Remus

The Lord who made the day and night,
He made the Black man and the White;
So, in like view,
I hold it true
That he hain't got no favor*ite* —
Onless it 's you.

---

know of only three that will be popular next year — Burns, Riley, and Stanton. Now, I'll give you a pointer: why not offer a prize for the man who can graft asparagus on the artichoke so as to make it eatable at both ends?"

Copyright by Moore & Stephenson

JOEL CHANDLER HARRIS AND JAMES WHITCOMB RILEY

UNCLE JEEMS

Now, I am mighty proud of that — mighty proud. The first thing you know I'll be awfully conceited. Mr. Riley will be in Atlanta to-morrow (Monday), and I'm to meet him at the train.

Your loving

DAD

Mr. Riley spent a fortnight at the Wren's Nest, and the two cronies had "lots of fun" together. It was the pleasantest time of the year on the "farm" — the roses and magnolias were blooming, the mocking-birds and thrushes singing, and the early vegetables coming in from the garden. It was father's custom to go every morning to the central post-office to get his mail, and Mr. Riley usually accompanied him. Then followed an hour's rest before the midday dinner, and afterwards long, lazy afternoons on the shaded porch or an excursion to Grant Park or a visit to a vaudeville show.

As Mr. Riley had come down just for a quiet time with his old friend, it was agreed that no formal invitations should be accepted, but the two, together with Frank L. Stanton, the poet, were prevailed upon to attend the annual "smoker" of a downtown club, under a pledge that they would not be asked to "show off." One of father's old friends, Mr. Sam Wilkes, gives the following account of this occasion: —

"Our guests had been presented to the members, and were seated discussing the relative merits of certain brands of chewing-tobacco, when the boys simply could not stand it longer, and the president forgot his promise and asked Mr. Riley to recite for us, 'That Old Sweetheart of Mine.' Of course, he refused, as did Mr. Stanton to recite 'The Bells of St. Michael.' Mr. Harris was spared a refusal. Members of the club made breezy little speeches, but in a remarkably short time none of our distinguished guests was with us — we had broken the compact with them, and they had quietly, almost imperceptibly, withdrawn. There had been no embarrassment, no confusion, in their going, but they had gone."

One of the reporters present wrote next day a humorous account of the affair which was printed in a local paper under the heading "Three Lions Who Would n't Roar."

Mr. Riley endeared himself to the entire family during his stay, for, as everybody knows, he was the most genial, kindly, and charming companion in the world. A letter written to Mildred about this time gives an idea of the gap which his departure left at the Wren's Nest: —

UNCLE JEEMS

Saturday, May 5, 1900.

DEAR BRIDGET: —

Your Unc. Jeems has done gone and went, and the house feels as if all the furniture had been taken out. (You see how my hand is trembling — I watered the violets for the first time this afternoon, and my arm is still shaking so I can hardly write.) Your Unc. Jeems was very gay while he was here.

Altogether, I have had a very enjoyable vacation. Bill has nearly laughed herself to death. Mr. Riley is a very fine actor and mimic. One minute he'd be taking the part of a six-year-old boy, declaring he was "the goodest boy in the world," and the next he'd be a very old man talking about another old man, and saying, "He's a-ag'in' — he's a-breakin'!" This sounds very silly on paper, but to hear your Unc. Jim say it, and see his actions and the movements of his face, was a spectacle as good as a show. He would have given you and the girls a good deal of enjoyment. However, he is gone, and the household will soon drop back to corn bread and dumplings, and return to its cold mutton and its warmed-over hash.

Julia took us to ride in the country, and we enjoyed it very much. We went to Westview, and then out the country road two or three miles. The

[425]

azaleas and rhododendrons were blooming in great style. Did you ever see the cyclorama here? I've been twice, and I'm ready to go again; but I believe I'll wait until you get home, and then we'll go out and shake hands (or snouts) with Clio. Mr. Riley said he dearly loved Clio, but thought a great deal more of her at a distance of a hundred yards than he did at close range.

Your loving

Dad

Shortly after Mr. Riley reached home a letter came to father from the poet's friend and business representative, Mr. J. M. Dickey, bearing a message which gave great pleasure to all the family. Mr. Dickey wrote of the many trips he and Mr. Riley had made together, to the Rockies, to the cities of the Mississippi, to the Great Lakes, and to New England, and added: "But never have I known him to bring home such riches as he brought this time from the South. To bring home money is one thing, but to bring home the memory of *love* and *laughter* is another thing — and vastly superior. And it is this dear memory of you and your home that Mr. Riley has now to enrich his daily life."

In 1902 father met Mr. Riley at Lithia Springs near Atlanta, and they spent another happy fortnight together. A fellow journalist who was much in their company, speaks of the "royal fellowship" which existed between them, and adds: —

James Whitcomb Riley came down from Indiana chuck full of stories, and "Uncle Joe" had one in reply for each the Hoosier poet would tell. For two weeks these rare characters loafed about the broad verandas of the hotel, rarely ever being separated, and only occasionally having with them a few select friends as guests of their story-telling bees.

Riley would tell one of his best ones and hold his sides in laughter as he watched the effect of the story on "Uncle Remus." Then "Uncle Joe," as we called him in those golden days when he was in his prime, would bat his eye a few times, the lips would curl in a suppressed laugh, and he would put over at Riley a story which would make a stoic laugh.

In all my experience I never saw such comradeship between two men. Each seemed absolutely happy in the company of the other.[1]

During 1900 father had been working on a series of stories relating to the activities of the secret service during the Civil War. The leading figures were Captain Lawrence McCarthy, head of the Confederate secret service, and John Omohundro, or "Texas Jack," the famous Southern scout. The first of these stories, "Why the Confederacy Failed," appeared in the "Saturday Evening Post" of December, 1899; the rest, of which there were

[1] From *The Singer and His Song*, by H. E. Harman.

four, appeared in the same publication at intervals until August of 1900. This series made a notable "hit," for certain "unrecorded incidents" of the Civil War were made to take on such a startling air of authenticity in these absorbing and skillfully told narratives that letters came to their author from all over the country asking for his "sources," and applauding him for having made certain "facts" known, or questioning the reliability of his information! One lady wrote from Mexico, where she was living in a settlement composed of American and English people, and described "spirited discussions" amongst the different factions as to the truth of the episodes. "One Philadelphian," she wrote, "who can give the statistics of every battle and a reasonable excuse for every failure of every Union general, says the stories are purely the fruits of imagination." The English disputants, on the other hand, were just as certain that the real facts of the case had been given by the author for the first time, and the writer of the letter begged that the author himself would settle the dispute!

Relatives of Omohundro came forward and wrote for more data about their dashing kinsman, and a gentleman from Palmyra, Virginia, "Texas Jack's" birthplace, protested that the scout's name should not have been used in such intimate connection with that of the slayer of Lincoln! In the story in question Omohundro is represented as being in the company of Booth just before the assassination, and the former's champion wrote: "On the day of Lincoln's assassination and all that week, Jack was at work on his farm, in sight of the window from which I write. . . . This fact can be vouched for by several persons here."

I mention these incidents as an indication of the singular ability which father had of investing his people with an air of reality and lending credibility to their actions; as Mr. Riley once said of him, "He makes his characters speak until there seems no artist anywhere."

"The Kidnapping of President Lincoln" was the most popular of these stories. On receipt of it Mr. Lorimer, editor of the "Saturday Evening Post," wrote the author: "This is the best story that has ever come to this office, and one of the best I have ever read. The picture of Mr. Lincoln and the old spy is simply perfect. . . . It is a rattling story and a splendid piece of work, and no editor has any business fooling with it or making changes." [1]

[1] During this year father also contributed to the *Saturday Evening Post* six editorials: "The Poor Man's Chance," "Cheap Criticisms of Dear Beliefs," "The Newspaper Habit," "The Tyranny of Tender-Hearted People," "Prophets of Ruin and the People," and "The Abolition of the Soul."

JOEL CHANDLER HARRIS

The series appeared in book form in 1900, issued by Doubleday, Page and Company, under the title "On the Wings of Occasion," and later under that of "The Kidnapping of President Lincoln." There was an English edition issued by John Murray.

That genial old Georgia countryman, Billy Sanders, made his first appearance in "The Kidnapping of President Lincoln," and he was very much liked. From this time until the author's death the "philosopher of Shady Dale" appears and reappears, and becomes the mouthpiece of father's opinions on a variety of things. He figures prominently in "Gabriel Tolliver" and in "The Bishop and the Boogerman," and in many essays.

He was supposed to be a grandson of Georgia's famous Revolutionary heroine, Nancy Hart; "he was old enough to be a good judge of human nature and the fact that he was born and bred in the country, and had little or no book education, had not interfered a particle with the growth and development of those elemental qualities which are the basis and not the result of book education. . . . One who knew Mr. Sanders well remarked of him: 'He looks like a busted bank, don't he? — all buildin' and no assets. Well, don't fool yourself. There

BILLY SANDERS

ain't a day in the year, nor an hour in the day, when he ain't on a specie basis.'"[1]

In August of 1900, Mr. Walter H. Page, then actively with the firm of Doubleday, Page and Company wrote father: —

DEAR UNCLE REMUS: —

We are going to have a magazine, and if I do say it myself, a bully good one. It is not going to publish fiction, but it will be rather a practical, man's magazine, handsomely illustrated and as well written as possible — a thing of serious purpose and broad scope. Of course, I cannot have a magazine without deviling you about it; and I cannot have a magazine such as I want without getting your help.

Since we cannot publish stories, my good partner, Lanier, has hit upon the suggestion which I now transmit to you, that seems to me a stroke of genius.

Take "Billy Sanders"; he is a genuine man, and he has his own point of view, and he has his own limited knowledge of things, and his absolutely unlimited imagination. Why not put into "Billy Sanders's" mouth an explanation once a month of some great thing that is going on in the world about which he knows nothing, but about which he would be willing to talk like a philosopher? I

[1] *The Kidnapping of President Lincoln.*

[431]

think that in this way you could find machinery for saying some of the best things that you or anybody else has said. Please write me how the idea strikes you. We all regard it as an inspiration.

Heartily yours

W. H. P.

This idea appealed to father mightily, and he wrote three "Billy Sanders" articles in accordance with it for the new magazine — "The World's Work" — during 1900–01: "Billy Sanders to a Boston Capitalist," "Billy Sanders on the Democrats," and "The Views of Billy Sanders." Mr. Page requested that a photograph be taken of a man of the Billy Sanders type and sent for use in "The World's Work"; and in reply to father's query, "What age man?" he replied: "It has never occurred to me that Mr. Billy Sanders had any particular age; I thought he was a perpetual youth. We want him to keep our magazine from being unnaturally solemn."

A passage in the contribution entitled "Billy Sanders to a Boston Capitalist" brought out an amusing protest from a reader who lived in the town of Harmony Grove, Georgia. He wrote: —

"In the December issue of 'The World's Work' the opening sentence of your article runs as follows:

[432]

BILLY SANDERS

'It should not be forgotten that the world's work goes on in Harmony Grove just as it does elsewhere, though it may be as well to pay the inhabitants of the village the compliment of saying that they are not trying as hard to get rich in a day as the people of some other communities.' From the above a casual reader would think Harmony Grove a regular 'Sleepy Hollow,' or a little crossroads town with no get-up-and-get about it, instead of being as it is to-day the best town of its size in Georgia."

The author was, of course, writing of the Harmony Grove· of his imagination; nevertheless, he was surprised that his comments should have been misunderstood, in any case. For progress, as commonly interpreted, was regarded by father as a doubtful blessing. Of it he wrote: "What is called progress is nothing more nor less than the multiplication of the resources of those who, by means of dicker and barter, are trying all the time to overreach the public and their fellows in one way or another." [1]

In this same year Doubleday, Page and Company proposed through Mr. Walter H. Page that father accept the editorship of "Everybody's Magazine," and also that he sign a contract with this firm put-

[1] *Gabriel Tolliver*. McClure Phillips Company, 1902.

ting all his work at their command for a stated period. It was a generous proposal and interested father, but even at this very time he was considering a similar proposition from the McClure Phillips Company, of which he wrote, in replying to Mr. Page: "I have not yet made up my mind in regard to it, but it gets very close to me. It would enable me to go right ahead with my work without regard to quenseconses, as Mr. Sanders would remark. . . . Anyhow, I'll be in the throbbing metropolis along about the 23d, when I hope to fetch some more remarks from the hot and heavin' bosom of our dear friend Sanders, and then I'll find out what my market price is and maybe get some stock issued on me, like the feller in a little tale I was readin' t'other day."

Father also touched on the proposal in a letter to Lillian, who was with mother in Canada for her annual visit: —

Sunday, 14 October, 1900

Dear Bill: —

I am writing this on Sunday, but it will not be posted until to-morrow afternoon, because I want to send poor mamma some money. I'll send it in the shape of a bill of exchange, and the captain can get it cashed at St. Hyacinthe. He should get gold for it, or American money. I don't know when mamma proposes to start back, but if she should chance to be in Troy about the 24th or 25th, I could run up there and see her.

I've just received a letter from the McClure Co., in which they say in the person of Mr. Phillips: "I am sending for transportation for you to New York and return, and also from New York to Troy and return; also transportation for Mrs. Harris back to Atlanta. We will send it along in a few days." I suppose mamma told you about the proposition they made. I have n't quite made up my mind about it, and won't be able to until I can have a heart-to-heart talk with the poor worried lady who imagines that I am still grieving because she did n't send a telegram. I've been able to do very little work, owing to various interruptions, propositions, and what-not; but before I come North I want to finish a short story, and write another Billy Sanders piece for "The World's Work," the first number of which will contain my purtygraph. I'm sorry I have n't got a patent medicine to offer to the public, for it is a pity to waste so much good advertising.

I'll not write a long letter this time, for I'm tired. Did you ever try to separate a young calf from its mother in a two-acre lot? No, you never did, and therefore you'll never fully appreciate my heroic qualities when I tell you that I have just succeeded in doing that very thing; and my whole nature is stirred and shaken, and the perspiration is gradually filling my shoes. I'll make this promise without compulsion — namely: that if there's forty calves with a cow I'll never try to separate them again unless I have a pack of hounds and a shot-gun. J. C. was with me, and it was as much as he could do to keep out of the calf's way. Phew! I'm tired!

My love to all.

Your loving

DAD

It was arranged that father should meet mother in Lansingburgh and make a brief visit to her relatives there before transacting his business in New York City. He gives a humorous account of his journey and "pop-call" in the following letter to Lillian's friend and schoolmate, Burdeene Biechele: —

Sunday, October 11, 1900

MY DEAR BURDEENE: —

You will think, of course, that I don't appreciate your kindness in sending me that nice letter; but if you only knew what an unusual experience

[436]

BILLY SANDERS

I have passed through, you would hold up both hands and say, "Poor man! I pity him." — Well, the day after I received your letter, I was drafted on the jury and had to serve one week. During that time I was out one night, and did n't sleep at all. They locked us up together in two rooms, and we had to try to sleep in beds not fit for a Chinaman. Some of us could n't sleep, and so we sat up and talked all night. You can imagine how I felt and looked after that experience.

All this time I had in hand a Christmas story for the "Saturday Evening Post," which should have been mailed on the 24th. On the 28th, while I was still nearly dead, I seized my typewriter and turned out 3000 words, and on the 29th the story was completed and forwarded. Meantime, a New York publishing firm had sent me railway tickets to their town, where I was to go and confer with them in regard to a permanent arrangement they wanted to make. So I went. I used to be able to sleep in a sleeping-car, but that time is past. All during the night I thought the coach was turning over every time we turned a curve, and once I squealed, just as a gal does when she sees a mouse. Squealing did n't do any good, and all I could do was grab the berth by the hair of the head and hold on for dear life.

Then, when I reached New York, I concluded to go right on to Lansingburgh, where Mrs. H. and Bill were holding receptions. At Albany, I was nearly lost, and if the folks had n't met me at Troy, it would have been a gone case with me. But they were on hand, and everything was forgiven. All the kinnery called to see me the Sunday I was there; they lined up at the back gate as the voters do at the polls, and passed through the house, each one pausing long enough to look into the pantry and to shake me solemnly by the hand. Well, we all returned safely, and I am beginning to be my old self.

Faithfully and affectionately yours

JOEL CHANDLER HARRIS

On the return to New York the proposed contract was discussed with the members of the firm of McClure Phillips Company, and there was signed an agreement by the terms of which the author was to have a fixed annual salary, and the firm was to make such disposition of his output as would be to the mutual advantage of both parties, and to have the privilege of putting the matter in book form on the basis of the usual royalties.

A logical outcome of this contract was father's retirement from the "Constitution," which took

EDITORIAL ROOMS OF THE "CONSTITUTION"

Seated: Clark Howell and Joel Chandler Harris

Standing (left to right): Wallace P. Reed, J. K. Ohl, Frank L. Stanton

place shortly afterward. Of this he said to a reporter, when approached for an interview: "Just say in a kindly way that an old family horse, growing tired of stopping before the same door every day, has kicked out from the harness and proposes to keep the flies off in his own fashion."

Father had been with the "Constitution" twenty-four years, and his editorials, especially those on nature and life, had found a host of readers in every quarter. Letters of regret poured in upon him from all those who had enjoyed his daily messages, so full of optimism, humor, common sense, and poetry. But those who were anxious that the leisure of his riper years should be employed in purely literary labors rejoiced in his liberty. Among the latter was his dear "Unc' Jeems," who sent the following characteristic letter early in 1901: —

INDIANAPOLIS, March 5, 1901

DEAR HARRIS: —

Wooh-ooh! Ole man Winter round here yit! Are you "settin' in de corner a-smokin' your" — cob-pipe? Well, God bless you, I'm wishin', every minute, I wuz right there with you, for I *know* that for about two hours anyhow I could *talk* to you engagin' enough to make us both forget the usual fascinations and allurements of *work*. How often I've thought of you since your retirement from the newspaper grind into the long-wished-for peace and respite of your own desires, inclinations, and *"gaits,"* as our dear Colonel Johnston would say! Even so I have been with you, at times, almost tangibly — and have felt, too, that you knew it, stayed the pen, in smiling pause, and, in a new chew, tasted *my* tobacco and ruminated right along the same whimsical, delicious lines. At such times I have peered up at your portrait above my desk and smiled, and said things, at it in a wholly silent yet vociferous way, high above the tumult of which I have heard your voiceless yet robustuous rejoinders. In such interviews, indeed, I have found many inspirations — in the far night especially, when the visionary material was a-workin' a little thick and "doughy." Then always the thought of you — and possibly your like vigils — has freshened the clay again and made it plastic and lovely as the squirrel dumplings to the palate of a joyous child. . . .

As always your affectionate old friend

JAMESY

CHAPTER XXIII

THE SECOND NOVEL

TOWARD the close of 1900 some of the Eatonton friends paid father a compliment which gave him the liveliest pleasure, and which Miss Frances Lee Leverette tells about in an issue of the "Teacher's Magazine": —

It was during a reading lesson, about a month before Thanksgiving, in 1900. The boys and girls of my grade in the Eatonton Public School had just finished reciting. They were very much interested in their new reader, Joel Chandler Harris's "Stories of Georgia," and particularly in that morning's lesson about Nancy Hart. . . . At this point, I told them the story of how Joel Chandler Harris, the author of their reader, had been born in the humblest sort of circumstances here in Eatonton, and how he had educated himself by reading good books to which he had access in the home of his employer.

"Miss Leverette, we ought to have a library and good books to read so we could educate ourselves, and maybe some of us will write books like Uncle Remus some day," said a bright-eyed girl of eleven, as we closed the reader. "We can and we will," I replied, "if you all really want one and will help me in the matter."

So the children and Miss Leverette went enthusiastically to work to collect money, and when a little nest-egg was in hand the first books were ordered and the library was named for Joel Chandler Harris. Margery Harris Leonard, the daughter of father's boyhood friend, Mr. C. D. Leonard, was appointed secrétary, and in due time she received the following letter from her father's old playmate in reply to the notification of the establishing of the library and in reference to a request for his photograph: —

AT-THE-SIGN-OF-THE-WREN'S-NEST
ATLANTA, GA., 26 November, 1900

DEAR MARGERY: —

Your letter, beautifully written and expressed, was a source of much pleasure in this house. Somehow or other, I always think of you as a little bit of a girl, but by this time you must be twelve years old, and of course, as beautiful as you are smart.

I received Miss Mary Allen's letter, telling me of your school library, but could not answer it sooner. I have just written her thanking the young people for the very high honor they have paid me in giving their school library my name. I was telling her that I had two pictures which the members of the library may choose from. One is a large photograph, the other is a print. They are large enough to frame, but that will be attended to here.

THE SECOND NOVEL

Give my best love to your father and the girls, and save out a large "hunk" for yourself.

Affectionately

JOEL CHANDLER HARRIS

Father wrote Miss Leverette also, expressing his keen appreciation of her part in the affair: —

ATLANTA, GA., 15 April, 1901

DEAR FANNIE LEE: —

Your letter of the 29th reminds me that I have not thanked you for the part you took in the library matter. I do so now, and most heartily. *It is likely to remain the most highly appreciated compliment that will ever be paid me.* The thought was yours, and but for you there would be no Joel Chandler Harris Library in Eatonton.

I thank you also for your letter. Your suggestion is a good one, and I wish I were able to carry it out. I have tried on several occasions to "write down" to what is supposed to be the understanding of children — that is to say, I have experimented on that line — but it is impossible. You are correct as to my intentions. The publishers asked me to write the stories[1] for supplementary reading in the more advanced grades, and if it is now used in the

[1] *Stories of Georgia.*

[443]

lower grades that is the fault of those who are authorized to name the books for the grades. In short, the stories are intended to supplement (let us say) the third or fourth reader.

Mrs. Harris sends her love, to which I add a slice. My love also to your folks and to Mrs. "Becky" Leonard and the gals, especially Margaret who seems to be an unusually bright youngster.

Faithfully your friend
JOEL CHANDLER HARRIS

The children continued to collect funds for books. "Uncle Remus" sent a number of volumes, and the library is now the largest "department" library in a Georgia school, containing nearly four hundred volumes.

The early part of 1901 found both mother and father in bed with grippe. Father had quite a serious time of it, and did not recover from the effects of his illness for a number of weeks. On February 22 he wrote Lillian, then visiting in Ohio: —

DEAR LILLIAN: —

I wrote to Mildred yesterday, thinking I would also write to you, but the effort was too much for me. I am up and about, but so weak I can hardly see myself in the glass — and I don't seem to gain in strength as I should. Grippe is a great thing; it is the most weakening disease that ever took hold of me. I was practically in bed for nearly three weeks.

Mamma was also in bed, and but for Evelyn and Essie, I don't know what we would have done. Essie is here to-day arranging for her club meeting, and mamma is flying around as if she had never been ill. This means that she will have to go to bed to-morrow, and she'll lie there and wonder what is the matter with her.

Everybody is well except the sick ones, and everybody is sick except those who are well. There is no news here — at any rate, I know of none, and I'm just writing this because I think it is about time for you to hear from me. I am using a pencil because I am too weak to tote a pen across the paper. Love to all.

Your loving

DAD

During February and March father continued too feeble to do much work or to be bothered with correspondence. Evelyn's intelligent and willing service at this time was invaluable to the invalid, for he would never tolerate the help of a secretary or professional typist, and since Lillian was in

Ohio, and mother still far from well, Evelyn had his hands full, in addition to his usual work on the "Constitution." That father appreciated his devotion is shown in the following letter of March 4 to Lillian: —

DEAR BILL: —

To-day I began for to commence for to start work again, and as I am feeling pretty well, I thank you, only a little shaky in the hands, the result of cough-drops and whisky sours, I thought I would dash off a page to you if only to say howdye.

I went to town last Sunday, the second time since the 27th of January. Evelyn has been very good; he has attended to all of my correspondence, and has put all my papers in shape. In various other ways he has demonstrated his tenderness. He is a son and a brother worth having — if I do say it myself.

Do you know that the last letter you wrote to me was the first genuine letter you ever sent me? There was something in it besides questions not intended to be answered. You are beginning to have thoughts of your own, and although one of the Rogers Brothers says it makes the eyebrows tired to think, I hope you will get in the habit of it. As you say, you are nineteen, with nothing to show for it but a beautiful disposition. Though this is not to be sneezed at, yet a good disposition does n't carry one very far. It is possible to have serious views and intentions without being sad: it is possible to be serious and yet have plenty of fun. If you could see your way clear to taking up some sort of a vocation, even if it is only a fad, you would be happier.

Don't think I'm preaching. I am perfectly sure that you will presently find a way of being all that I desire you to be, and therefore I'm giving myself no special concern about it. Our friends are certainly exerting themselves to make your visit one long to be remembered. I wish we could give dear Burdeene one half the pleasure that she and her family are giving you. We are going to do our best but will fall short. But I'm tired now and will close.

Love from all to all.

Your loving

DADDY

A brief letter, dated March 5, to Mildred, who was still at school in Washington, Georgia, displays more cheerfulness and indicates increasing strength:

MY DEAR LITTLE GAL: —
You don't know how glad I am to be able to write to you in the old way — with the same old

pen, and on the same old paper. I hope you missed my letters. I certainly wanted to write. Every Saturday and Sunday while I was held in bed by weakness that was stronger than I was, I said to myself — "What a pity I can't write to both of my dear gals! I wonder what they'll think?" Well, I'm feeling pretty well now. I'm a little weak, and somewhat shaky, as my handwriting will show, but I'm getting stronger every day.

Regards to the Sisters.

Your loving
DAD

A letter to Mr. Riley, the 1st of April, refers to the recent illness and explains the cause of the long silence between them: —

WES' EEN', ATLANTA, April 1, 1901

I would have written to you long ago, my dear friend, but for an attack of the grippe, which took me down and put me to bed on the 29th of January, and held me there steadily for three weary weeks. Even after I had recovered, I had to learn to walk again. It is only during the last few days, say a week, that I have been able to write a letter. I was so weak, I could n't see myself in the glass, and even now, I don't know whether I'm quite right in the mind; you'll have to judge that for yourself. It was a terrible experience, and I never realized it fully until I was nearly well. The affair developed into acute bronchitis, and I got $150 from one of these health insurance companies. It was a pick-up which will just about pay all the expenses of my illness, including the doctor's bill.

I was sorry to hear of the death of General Harrison. We need such men more than ever. I have about made up my mind that he was the best President the country has had since Lincoln. He was somewhat narrow when he first went into office, but he grew right along — and he's the only ex-President we have ever had who was capable of making an impression on public opinion.

I am trying to write a long story about the reconstruction period. It is about half-finished, and I'm afraid, — well, I'm afraid that long stories are not my best suit. I take so much interest in the episodes that the main thread is left hanging at loose ends.

You may rest assured that your name is often called in this house, and I have been wondering if it isn't about time for you to walk in whistling and ask if there's anybody at home.

The violets are simply beyond description. The walks and the borders are one mass of blooms. The neighbor-children pick and pick, but make no impression. But pretty soon the sun will get too hot and then the blooms will disappear. I have n't heard a mocking-bird so far, and I'm beginning to fear that some assassin has made way with the fine one that used to sing for you.

Lillian has been in Canton with the Biecheles for some time, and Burdeene will return with her in a few days. Mildred is having as much fun as ever, frequently asks if I hear from Uncle Jim — and that reminds me that I have never sent you a copy of my last book, a shameful piece of neglect it is, and not altogether without palliating features. You know how we keep open house here: well, I had fourteen of these books, and they have simply walked off with some of the visitors. Mrs. H. sent one to her mother, and another to Mildred. Well, when I started to send you one, there was none here. I laid off to get one uptown, and have been laying off ever since: you know how I am, weak-minded and forgetful, being the original Procrastinator.

I've been reading at Longfellow since you were here, and well, he's good enough for me. The reason I did n't like him has been discovered. He wrote "The Village Blacksmith," and I had to get it by heart and recite it to please a villain of a schoolmaster. I hated the poem, and the name under it in the book; but I find that it is a beautiful poem. I'm going to get all Longfellow's works.

When you feel lonely, or happy, or jest middlin' peart, write me a long letter and come and fetch it. Yours, as you know,

JOEL

The "long story about the reconstruction period," referred to in the preceding letter, had been in father's mind for some time. The first reference to it occurs in a letter to Mr. William Dean Howells, written in June of 1900, in reply to a request from him for a contribution to an enterprise which he had undertaken for his publishers. "One Mile to Shady Dale" was completed early in 1901, but the story of "Qua" was never written. Sketches of this interesting figure, as well as that of the Arcadian Saleth, had already been given by father in the "Stories of Georgia."

ATLANTA, June 1, 1900

DEAR MR. HOWELLS: —

The scheme set forth in the prospectus and advertising matter enclosed in your letter attracts me by its picturesqueness. There is an "Octopus" twang about it that charms and satisfies even a Southern socialist democrat. I have known all along that if I ever cross my legs in the seats of the mighty, I shall have to be lifted there by main strength: and Mr. Clark's derrick seems to be the thing I have been looking for.

But the question arises — comes in fact as the eclipse did, swiftly and darkly: Do you propose to edit this scheme in the interest of literature? If so, you can count me out. I am wondering all the time how it is that my name has been included in a list of Eminent Persons. I hope I know myself by this time, and a part of this knowledge clings mournfully about the fact that the stuff I turn out in my leisure moments is not literature and has no claim to distinction. I am literary in the meaning one gives to the word when we see the country correspondent of a weekly newspaper announce that Miss Nannie Goodwin Ketchum, of Greene County, Georgia, has a fine literary talent.

Still, if you think you can give a cornfield hand a showing, and you are not afraid to fish a cold dumpling out of the pot-liquor with your fingers, perhaps I can meet your wishes. I have two stories in prospect. One I have called (in my mind) "One Mile to Shady Dale." It is a story of Georgia folk about the time of the beginning of the Civil War. The other is "Qua: A Romance of the Revolution," Qua being the name of an African prince who was brought to this country about 1760. He died in Augusta less than fifty years ago. According to tradition, he cut quite a figure in that horrible cyclone of war, rapine, and murder which was centered in what is now Wilkes County. My great-grandmother and my grandmother were in the midst of this disturbance, and when a lad, I have heard them tell of their experiences by the hour. Both of them knew Qua, and Saleth, the son of an Arcadian mother, and Daniel McGirth, the cruelest and bloodiest Tory that ever lived.

You know, of course, that so far as literary art is concerned, I am poverty-stricken; and you know too, that my style and methods will cause you to pull your hair. You knew all about that before you invited me into the scheme.

Therefore, if I can send you something, which shall it be?

You will never know which is the worst until you have read both. It is a question whether I can send the manuscript by Christmas. I can't promise.

Yours faithfully
JOEL CHANDLER HARRIS

A later reference to the novel "One Mile to Shady Dale," rechristened by this time "Gabriel

Tolliver," occurs in a letter to Mrs. Georgia Starke, dated December 29, 1901: —

"I had a book already to be published this year — it was finished in June — but rather than forego the very comfortable sum to be made from serial publication, I concluded to wait another year. It was completed at a time when all the larger magazines had made their arrangements for next year, and so the serial rights were sold to the 'Era,' a Philadelphia magazine which is making a bid for popularity. The editor paid a good round sum for the serial rights, and I suppose he would have paid more, but I have not the heart to dicker and bargain."

"Gabriel Tolliver" appeared in the "Era" during 1901-02, and was published in book form in 1902 by the McClure Phillips Company. It was dedicated to James Whitcomb Riley. Of the nature of the book, the author said in a letter: —

"The book is not precisely autobiographical, but it is something more than reminiscent, for I have put myself into it in the most unreserved way. When I decided to quit newspaper work, I turned to this work, and, when I began it, I determined to write it in my own way, without regard to models, standards, or formalism of any kind. I determined to write something to please myself. The result

is what you have. It is mine; it is *me*. I do not say
this on account of any pride I have in the work;
it is, perhaps, faulty, but even the faults are mine.
I mean by this that I surrendered myself wholly
to the story and its characters, and the idea of art
simply never occurred to me until the thing was
complete."

In the prelude to the book, the author enlarged
somewhat on this absence of any "idea of art" in
the undertaking: —

Let those who can do so continue to import harmony
and unity into their fabrications and call it art. Whether
it be art or artificiality, the trick is beyond my powers.
I can only deal with things as they were; on many occasions they were far from what I would have had them
be; but as I was powerless to change them, so I am
powerless to twist individuals and events to suit the
demands or necessities of what is called art.

It was inevitable that certain critics should pitch
upon the statements in the foregoing paragraph,
and use them as a text for satirical comment: the
"Nation" regarded "Gabriel Tolliver" as a "very
poor work, rambling, shuffling . . . without form
or style"; and added, after quoting the author's
views, "Perhaps with such original notions of
what art is, it would be quite impossible to do anything even remotely artistic; therefore we should
perhaps congratulate Mr. Harris on not having

tried for art." The "Nation's" reviewer then added that the prelude includes, besides this "pearl of reflection," the legend of Dilly Bal, which is "beautifully told — we would say 'most artistically rendered,' if it were not for the fear of hurting Mr. Harris's feelings."

But any critic who attempts to analyze "Gabriel Tolliver," or any other work from the pen of its author, must have something at his command besides a "literary" equipment — he must add to that an "intelligence of the heart," and a sound appreciation of *character*, which lies at the foundation of true culture, else he will miss the viewpoint of the writer himself.

The whole question, perhaps, hinges on one's definition of "art"; it is true that father shied at certain terminology as a too sensitive horse shies at a piece of white paper. "Art," "unity," "harmony," and all the other literary catchwords were bugaboos to him. He had an amusing, and perhaps morbid, horror of waxing pedantic and getting away from simple things and plain ways. His work, however, was anything but "shuffling" and "rambling." He had unconsciously imbibed "style" in his youth, during hours of browsing in a library of classics, and up to the very last he was in the habit of carefully revising his work, and shaping it toward something as finished as his brain and hand could make. I have found eight different drafts of the opening chapter of one story, and the final draft was totally different from any of the other seven. But this is a digression!

The story of "Gabriel Tolliver" takes place in the vicinity in which father grew up, and it was partly for this reason that the task of writing the book was such a pleasant one. "My hobby was Shady Dale, and I was not ashamed of it," wrote the author; and, "The man or woman who cannot display as much of the homing instinct as a cat or a pigeon is a creature to be pitied."

As the story unfolded, "the past began to renew itself; the sun shone on the old days and gave them an illumination which they lacked when they were new. Time's perspective gave them a mellower tone, and they possessed, at least for me, that element of mystery which seems to attach to whatever is venerable."[1]

It was said of "Gabriel Tolliver" that it was "a remarkable story in many ways, remarkable for the material which the author omitted as well as for the material which he used. For instance, although the story opens in the days immediately preceding the Civil War, there is not a single battle

[1] *Gabriel Tolliver.* McClure Phillips Company, 1902.

described in the book, and although the Ku-Klux
Klan makes its appearance, it is not for any melo-
dramatic end. . . . And although the book is a
clear statement of conditions difficult for Northern-
ers to understand, and often entirely misunderstood
by them, there is about it no atmosphere of a novel
with a purpose."

A reviewer on a Western paper pointed out the
peculiar charm of the book — and, by inference,
its most noticeable weakness — when he said:
"Throughout one is held, not by a desire to know
how the problem of reconstruction was solved in
Georgia, or how the story ends, but by an anxiety
to miss no stray bit of humor or character sketching
which might be the reward of persistency."

Gabriel Tolliver, himself, has much in him that
is autobiographical, and Nan, the whimsical, mischievous, warm-hearted wild bird, was suggested
by Mildred. Billy Sanders plays a prominent part
in the story and makes his first appearance on the
scene as a warrior returning from the battle field.
As his wagon mounts the hilltop that looks down
on Shady Dale, he exclaims: "I'll tell you what's
the fact, boys, the purtiest place this side Paradise
lies right yander before our eyes. Ef I had some un
to give out the lines, I'd cut loose an' sing a hime.
Yes, sirs! you'd see me break out an' howl jest

like my old coon dog. Louder used to do when he struck a hot track."

In the fall of 1901 the people of Eatonton (Shady Dale) sent father, through Colonel Henry Capers, an invitation to make them a visit. He was touched and pleased by this evidence of their affection, but was compelled to decline, which he did in the following letter: —

ATLANTA, GA., November 12, 1901

DEAR COLONEL: —

I have delayed answering your letter hoping to see my way clear to accepting the invitation which you were kind enough to send me, and which I assure you is very highly appreciated. Though I have been away so many years, I still feel that Eatonton is my home and the people there my best friends. I love them all, so much so that I have never written anything to be published in book form that I did not ask myself if there could be anything in it which my friends there would not approve. Thus, in a way, they have been my most helpful critics. I thank you heartily for the invitation and regret that a pressure of work will prevent me from accepting.

Faithfully yours

JOEL CHANDLER HARRIS

COL. HENRY D. CAPERS
EATONTON, GA.

[459]

JOEL CHANDLER HARRIS

Another letter goes to Mr. Riley toward the close of the year, carrying a reference to "Gabriel Tolliver," and its defects, of which the author was fully conscious: —

WES' EEN', GA., 30 September, 1901

MY DEAR FRIEND: —

I've been reading "A Dream of Empire" with considerable interest. The author certainly makes his characters stand out before you with extreme vividness. I find in his work the very kind of weakness that is all through mine — the subordination of the story itself to the characters; but I have a sneaking notion that it is better to be able to draw a character than to construct a story. In the book I'm going to dedicate to J. W. R., you'll find the construction in a tangle, but I hope some of the characters will appeal to you.

Down here we're moseying along towards fall. The roses are fine, and occasionally I hear a young mocking-bird practicing his tunes in the bushes. I'm going to write a dozen or more plantation songs. McClure has promised to get Frost to illustrate them. Everybody here is well and all send love.

The passing of McKinley, to which you refer, is one of those events that I hate to think about. Sad as it was it has brought the sections still closer together. Down here in Atlanta a fund has already been raised to build a McKinley monument — a fact that will give you an idea of the feeling in the South.

Well, I hope you are well and happy. We must be happy and contented, you know, in spite of the mysterious ways of Providence.

Always faithfully yours

JOEL CHANDLER HARRIS

And it is "Uncle Jeems" who receives the first greeting of the New Year: —

ATLANTA, GA., 1 January, 1902

MY DEAR FRIEND: —

Your telegram of greeting was most highly appreciated, and now that the New Year has come upon us, I am just dropping you a line (this is not a sure-enough letter) to thank you for your thoughtfulness. As you know, we are constantly thinking of you and quoting you in this house, and wishing you all sorts of success and happiness. As for me, it makes me feel better to think that with the coming of the New Year summer is brought nearer — summer when you can afford to take a month or so off, and be with us again.

As I was saying, this is not a letter, but just a

[461]

note to thank you and to wish you many returns of the season. All join me in sending you love and good wishes.

Affectionately yours

JOEL CHANDLER HARRIS

During 1901 father had written several short stories for the magazines, and in 1902 the McClure Phillips Company gathered four of these tales into a volume under the title "The Making of a Statesman." The others were "A Child of Christmas,"[1] "Flingin' Jim and His Fool-Killer," and "Miss Puss's Parasol," the last-named being an "Aunt Minervy Ann" story. The English edition of this book was brought out by Isbister in London.

The spring of 1902 was an even harder period for father, as regards his health, than the previous one had been. A neglected tooth was the cause of a general septic condition which laid him low for weeks, and which seemed to sap his vitality to such an extent that his condition became a matter for grave concern. It was summer before he was able to be about and enjoy the flowers and birds as of yore. Mr. Riley was the recipient of one of the first letters he "tapped off" on his typewriter: —

---

[1] This episode was elaborated and later became a part of *Gabriel Tolliver*.

THE SECOND NOVEL

Atlanta, Ga., May 19, 1902

My dear Friend: —

Just a few taps on the typewriter to let you know that I am on the mend. I have tried twice now to write to you with a pen, for I detest the typewriter as a medium for private correspondence; but I am still too nervous and shaky to use the pen comfortably.

Therefore, I am hoping that you will excuse the medium, and overlook the circumstances that compel me to use it. I just want to thank you for all the kind messages you sent me, and for that last letter of yours, which contains news enough to make me proud for the rest of my life — but you are always doing things for to make a fellow feel good.

My ailment was septic fever, the result of an infected sore throat, the infection being due to bad teeth. Mr. Geiger was very kind; he has been to see me twice, and he has remembered me in other ways.

I have just read with delight your poem read at the dedication of the soldiers' monument, and it is very fine. You certainly rise to the occasion, for the poem is on a level with the very highest emotions and suggestions of the stupendous memorial that was dedicated the other day.

[463]

But, my dear friend, I must hush up and take a rest. I am living these days with old man Shakiness, and yet I am enjoying the fine weather, and the birds, and the flowers, and I'm not downhearted the least little bit. Now, what is to prevent you from coming down here and spending a few weeks with me? It will do you good, and I am sure it will help to make me strong again. Please consider the proposition seriously. Mr. Geiger will steer you straight here whenever you feel like taking the trip. And you will be happy, and make the rest of us happy.

Affectionately yours

JOEL CHANDLER HARRIS

Father was as pleased as a child when Mr. Riley's latest book of poems reached him in the fall and he found that it was dedicated to him. The tie between these good friends grew in warmth as the years passed, and father was always longing for "Uncle Jeems" to share the pleasures of the out-of-doors with him: —

AT HOME, 24 November, 1902

MY DEAR FRIEND: —

I hardly know how to describe my feelings with respect to your beautiful book. I have read it through from the first page to the last, and I am halfway through again. The idea of your saying that you are grateful to me! Why, I'm the one to be grateful, eternally so, and the obligations you have placed me under are a pleasure to me, and will remain so while I live. Your beautiful book will last as long as there are children and people who love them, and I could have no greater honor conferred on me than to have my name linked with it. The time will come when those who read it will forget, if they ever knew anything, about me; but they will see my name in it, and they will say: "We don't know who he is, but he must have been Somebody, Somewhere, Sometime or other, or his name would never have gone in this book."

I have been trying hard to make up for time lost during my long illness. I am making some headway, but not as much as I would like to make. I find I am growing more careful all the time, and that ain't a good sign. My health is better than it was when you were here, but that is partly due to the delicious weather we are having. Surely, nothing was ever seen like it in this old world of ours before. Crisp air early in the mornings, and then the glorious warmth of the sunshine the rest of the day. One day last week, I heard two mocking-birds singing at the same time in different parts of

[465]

the garden, and it made me feel just as if I had taken a big mint julep with plenty of sugar and only a small sprinkling of water in it — which I had n't had any at all; it was all on account of the beautiful birds. Nine tenths of the folks in this world don't know where to look for a good time, and don't know when they are having it; but you and I know that there is nothing better in the world than just to sit back and enjoy the little things — the little children, the little birds — and all the time a-chawin' of our little tobacco.

Your book, I see, is away up into the thirty thousands. Gabriel Tulliver, they say, is going well, and it is getting some tollable good notices. Some say it's dull, and some say it's all about nothin' in pertickler; and I speck it is. But there's two things I'd be glad of if not a copy was sold — it is dedicated to you and it is about old times. And if I keep my health, I'm going to write another, and another, and as many as I can, all about old times, and the old timey people. And if anybody does n't like it, why he can just go ahead speculating in futures, and I'll speculate on the past.

Mrs. Harris is naturally charmed with your book and its dedication, with the poems and with the fact that she's got a copy all to herself with your name in it. Mildred will be thanking you for hers. Lillian is in Canton, Ohio, and does n't know she has a copy. The poor child is running her tongue out going to frolics.

Are we never to have you here any more? Mr. Geiger reports that he is constantly urging you to come down. Well, whenever you "take a notion," as we say in Georgia, all you have to do is to come right home and see if everything is fixed up to suit you. Surely you'll come with the warm weather next year. Write when you can. All send love. Regards to Mr. Dickey.

Affectionately yours

JOEL CHANDLER HARRIS

CHAPTER XXIV

AFFAIRS AT THE WREN'S NEST — 1902-1903

Quite a little family community was growing up about the Wren's Nest in 1902; Lucien had enlarged his home for the accommodation of his three boys, and in 1901 Julian began the erection of a house on the beautiful lot which father had given us on the northwestern corner of the "farm." I had lost my own father the previous year, and the cares of the great old-fashioned home where I was born weighed heavily upon me. So it seemed best to leave it and go into a smaller and more modern house. Therefore, in the spring of 1902 my husband and I, together with our two little boys, my two young sisters, and one brother, moved to West End, just half a block down the street from the Wren's Nest.

Our eldest boy, Charles, was the only grandchild who had the red hair and bright blue eyes of his Grandfather Harris, and he resembled his grandfather, too, in disposition, being endowed with that combination of gentleness, mischievousness, and whimsicality so often found in red-haired boys. He and his grandfather were on very loving terms;

MRS. HARRIS AND A GROUP OF GRANDCHILDREN
Spring of 1908

from the time he was a little fellow in his old mammy's arms, he had held out his hands in friendly fashion and stretched his mouth in smiles at his "grandpa." Father often said, when the little grandson was a wee baby, "If I don't see Charles for a week or so, he always knows me."

One of my dearest recollections is of early summer mornings in the years 1902 and 1903, when, before breakfast, father was in the habit of strolling through the vegetable garden past the apple trees, into our back yard. There our great yellow cats would join him and escort him to the sand-pile under the willow tree where he would linger for a visit with our little boys and their Mammy Lucinda. After awhile he would continue his walk around the house into the front yard and stop on the porch for a little chat, sometimes bringing a bunch of roses or a bucket of berries from Snap-Bean Farm. He displayed as much interest in our place as in his own, and we rejoiced together over the bower of china-berry trees twined with honeysuckle, where the mocking-birds and catbirds nested, and where one summer we entertained a pair of golden orioles. He presented us with a beautiful little linden tree for our lawn and we gave him of our perennial phloxes and irises for his garden; and the first year of our residence in West End there was great rivalry between us in tomato-growing. One of my young sisters became his great chum, and together on summer afternoons they visited Grant Park and Ponce de Leon, and the weekly vaudeville matinée. Those were the happiest years of all — tranquil and secure — a golden interlude in life before sorrow took possession of us.

J. C., Jr., and my youngest brother were fast friends and schoolmates, and spent their vacations "roughing it" together in the Georgia mountains. When they were on one of these trips, father wrote to J. C.: —

ATLANTA, GA., August 5, 1902

My DEAR SON: —

I received your letter yesterday, and enjoyed your collection of fish tales immensely, as well as your very cute pretended misunderstanding of Mildred's bad spelling.

It is all the same here as it was before you left — that is, except the fact that you and mamma are not here. That makes a great difference, of course. I mean the days go by just as they do when nothing is happening. I have caught myself more than once getting up from my chair in the porch and coming to the back part of the house to see what mamma was doing, and a half-dozen times I have been on

[470]

the point of calling you, especially when Julian's cow would get out. Which reminds me that she is the worst cow I ever saw, and the greediest.

Forrest Adair's bull terrier has five puppies, four dogs and one female, and he says I can have my choice of the litter. They are sired by Woodcote Wonder, the fine dog that was on exhibition at the dog show. It seems to me that I heard you talk about him at the time you were going to the bench show. Well, anyhow, I told him I'd be glad to have one, and thanky, too, and then I asked him why he was so generous, and, being generous, why, why he had been good enough to think of me. He said that his wife had heard that one of our dogs was poisoned, and she told him that not one of the puppies was to go away until I had had my choice. I am sure she could n't have done anything that I would appreciate more.

Tell mamma that everything is getting along all right in every way. The new milker does his best, and gets as much milk as William. He milks the cows until their bags are no bigger than my two fists. No rain yet, and I am so tired of watering things that I don't know what to do. . . . I saw Georgia the other day — she was helping Alleen to get off . . . and I said to her that I had n't seen her before in a long time. She said she had been superseded down here. I don't know what she meant by that, but it reminded me of something Buck Adair told on old Ceily, who cooks for Mrs. G. A. Howell. She wanted old Mrs. Adair to hire one of her children named Lije. She said that Lije was one of the "hardes' workin' an' bes' exposed niggers" that could be found.

Well, this about exhausts my budget of news — if you can call it news. Nothing happens, not even rain. O'Donnelly's big dog got in the yard yesterday, and Muldoon rode him out. I never saw a worse frightened dog in my life. All here are well and have tremendous appetites. I am kinder one-legged in the mouth now. The doctor pulled the tooth that I did most of my chewing on. And now I have to limp when I chew. But I'll soon have plenty of teeth to chew on. My health is as good as it ever was. I haven't taken medicine of any kind in a long time, and I continue to get up early in the morning, and watch the birds catch worms.

All send love to all.

Your loving

DADDY

And again: —

"This trip will do you good in more ways than one. You will never forget it as long as you live. It brings you closer to Nature than you have ever been before, and it will give you a good idea of the power of the Creator, who made the mountains as well as the tiny grains of sand. A boy who is raised entirely in the city never has as broad a mind as one who is raised in the country, and who has time to think because he has little else to do for long hours. This is why the country boy comes to town so well-equipped for any business that may chance to be open to him."

One day, about this time, father amused himself by writing

The West End Gazette

We regret to learn of the illness of Mr. Evelyn Harris, the esteemed City Editor of our contemporary, "The Constitution." While we do not always endorse the policy of our contemporary, we feel that it has sustained a severe loss in the temporary absence of young Mr. Harris, whose fits of nervous prostration are received more seriously by his lady friends than by his family.

We also regret to chronicle the illness of Mrs. J. C. Harris, who will insist on eating cheese and dewberries. As Mr. Harris truly observes, we cannot be too careful about what we place in our several and various craws.

JOEL CHANDLER HARRIS

Complaints come from the telephone office that since Mr. Harris's son Evelyn has been laid up at home the young lady who has charge of the West End division is badly overworked. We imagine this is so, for we learn from private sources that the calls for Mr. Harris are continuous, and that there is always a young town lady at the other end of the line. The family of the young man have become convinced that he is by far the most popular beau of the season — and the season has hardly begun.

There was a spirited contest to-day (Saturday) between the Sluggers and the Hustlers, the favorite baseball teams of our fashionable suburb. The Sluggers won by a score of 20 to 4. In the language of Master J. C. Harris, Jr., it was the most crushing defeat of the season.

Some kind friend has sent to Mr. Evelyn Harris a bottle of apricot brandy. The gift was justified by his illness — and we may as well say here that we are not feeling very well ourselves.

Mr. John Collier has returned from New York for the long vacation. He is the same old John that he was when we first knew him; he has not been spoiled by his contact with the Chinese of the metropolis. If he eats with a chop-stick, he does it where no one can see him.

The drouth has been broken by a week's rain.

AFFAIRS AT THE WREN'S NEST

Those who like water in large volume will rejoice in the downpour, but as for us, give us a flood of Old Cabinet, manufactured on the Monongahely.

The "Journal" has just issued an extra stating that several cotton mills in the neighborhood of Spartanburg, S.C., have been destroyed by a cloudburst. Cotton factories cannot be too careful in rainy weather.

The sweet peas in the garden of Mr. J. C. Harris are more beautiful than ever this year. They are very large and fragrant. Thanks to Miss Lillian for a bunch.

Jamie Prince and Forrest Adair, Jr., have joined the Sluggers. They were formerly among the chief ornaments of the Hustlers.

The Hustlers and the Sluggers will play again this afternoon. Our Society Editress, Miss Lillian Harris, is reporting for the "Gazette."

It is said that one of the most fashionable dressmakers is creating a graduating gown for Miss Mildred Harris. It is to have a pointed yoke, and is to be cut bias in the neck. The whole design is based on the embonpointe now so fashionable in Paris.

Miss Lillian Harris has attended quite a number of functions recently. The most of them were in honor of the approaching nuptials of Miss Natalie

Heath. They were all marked by a superabundance of cold sandwiches and 'tater salad. Long life to the cold sandwich and the 'tater salad. Our housewives would be lost without them.

It is thought that the illness of Mr. Evelyn Harris is partially due to overwork at the telephone desk. Ladies, you should be more prudent in calling on Mr. Harris at the phone. He cannot stand everything.

Since the return of Miss Polly Vogner, Mr. Hook Spratling has a worried look. He is like a pig with two fresh roasting-ears — he does n't know which to bite first. Good luck to both of you, girls!

The club to which Miss Lillian Harris belongs is to attend the wedding of Miss Heath in a body. The members will enter the church together, preceding the bride and groom. This is due to the fact that they are all candidates for matrimonial honors.

This is probably the last issue of the "West End Gazette" for the summer. We return thanks to our numerous subscribers for their support and sympathy. We would continue to print it, but the truth is that the editor must have a vacation.

June 6, 1903

The young people of the neighborhood were on the friendliest terms with father and mother, and flocked with "Uncle Remus" to see the ball games between the Sluggers and the Hustlers; or sat on the front steps of the Wren's Nest on summer evenings, chatting with its master and mistress; or singing the old songs together; or discussing a scheme for buying a community telescope or plans for a minstrel show. None of their affairs was too trivial or too foolish to gain father's interest. In fact, as he grew older he gravitated more and more toward young people. In an editorial written for "Uncle Remus's Magazine" he said: —

The promoter of the Snap-Bean Farm has small success when he is dealing with those of his kind who are above forty. He is crusty, and his mind is full of deep and dark suspicions; but it is when old age comes tottering around that he is at his worst. It is then that he is bearish, churlish, and filled with a wild impatience. He admits that old age is or should be a venerable affair, but he can only tolerate it when it is serene and respectable. He knows very well that he will have to spend the day with it at some period in the near future, that he will have to take it to bed with him, and tolerate its various frailties and eccentricities the best he can; but he prays that he may not fall into the habits of those with whom it has already taken up its abode. For why should old age be gloomy and ill-tempered, rather than hale and hearty, wholesome and cheerful?

. . . But, after all, it is not old age I have been thinking of all this time, but youth — the youth that follows youth somewhat like a circus procession — the youth that is one of the whims of the Snap-Bean Farmer. He has many peculiarities, but this I call a whim in spite of the fact that it seems to be an outgrowth of his temperament. It may be a weakness, but it is politer to call it a whim. For instance, he is very fond of children, but this fondness does not show itself in the way common to most people. With him there is no "I'll chuck you under the chin, you sweet little thing!" He does n't tell them they are cute, nor does he show by his attitude that he looks upon them as little dolls that have in some strange way learned how to talk and walk. Consequently, he is more popular with them than those who make silly manifestations of an interest that has no existence.

Indeed, it was impossible for father to resist the claims of youth, and I believe he never intentionally overlooked a request from a child. As an instance of his genuine interest in young people I give a series of letters written to three brothers, the children of Mrs. E. D. Guinn, then living in Covington, Georgia, who wrote asking for autographs. Father replied to their mother as follows:—

DEAR MADAM: —

It has been two months, lacking a week, since I received your letter about the little boys, and no doubt they think it is a dreadful long time to wait. But I have two youngsters of my own, aged ten and thirteen, and they get to my table and knock my letters about hunting for stamps, and they get my papers terribly mixed. Your letter was slipped into a larger envelope, and so slipped out of my mind. But what they lost, they found. Don't you think it would be more satisfactory to the little boys to address them each by name, in a letter, than just to send them my name on slips? I never like to do things by halves when trying to please children; and, so, if you will take the trouble to send me the names of these little boys I'll write each a letter.

With my love to them in advance, I am

Yours faithfully

JOEL CHANDLER HARRIS

Mrs. Guinn replied, giving the names of the children and telling something of their characteristics, and in due time three letters arrived for the boys: —

DEAR DUVAL: —

You have a fine name to begin with. I used to know a Colonel Duval of Florida, and he was one of the finest gentlemen I ever met — perhaps the very finest. I lived in Savannah then, and he used to call and see me every time he came to town. I am going to put him in a book some day.

JOEL CHANDLER HARRIS

And so you are a fighter and a dandy, too? Well, it is a good combination, if the fighter is always on the right side, and the dandy does n't get to be a "Miss Nancy."

I hope you are kin to *my* old Colonel Duval. If you are, you 'll never go wrong in this world.

Your friend
JOEL CHANDLER HARRIS

DEAR MINOR: —

I know of an old toad who is almost too fat to hop. He lives under the top step of the terrace, and sometimes, just for fun, I tie a piece of cotton to a string and wave it before his front door. When he is not fast asleep, he 'll inch out little by little, and presently snap up the cotton so suddenly and swiftly that the eye can't follow his movements. He thinks it's a moth; but when he finds he is mistaken, he lifts up a forefoot and pulls the string out of his mouth.

J. C., Jr., has a pen full of guinea pigs. They are very pretty and hungry, and the young ones can hop about and eat the day they are born. And then there is Nelly, the donkey, and also Muldoon, the bull-terrier, and more bantams than you can shake a stick at.

Once a wren built a nest and raised a brood in

the letterbox on the front gate. That's why some folks call my place "At-the-Sign-of-the-Wren's-Nest." I hope you don't rob birds' nests. Confidentially, I don't think English sparrows are birds. Anyhow, they are not the kind of birds I like.

Your friend

JOEL CHANDLER HARRIS

DEAR DUDLEY: —

I have heard from your mother how you like books. It is good to like books, and I think a boy of thirteen should sometimes select his own books. If you like history, you should read it, but if you don't like it, let it alone. My folks used to try to make me read history when I was your age and older, and this turned me against it. Even now, I can hardly pick up a history without feeling uncomfortable. They tried to make me read in "courses," such as people have at their big dinners. You may be sure I never tried that with my boys. I simply place books and magazines where they can get at them. I hope you like fairy stories. I just dote on them. Did you ever read the "Slav Tales"? They are fine.[1]

[1] Father wrote once in an editorial on the uses of "light literature": "I take no stock in either the taste or the intentions of those who are continually warning people against what is called light literature. I venture to say that no family of young people ever

JOEL CHANDLER HARRIS

For the stamps you sent, my youngsters say,
"*Thanky! thanky!!*"

Your friend
JOEL CHANDLER HARRIS

In a letter to Mildred at the close of 1901, father
said: "You see what a dull letter I am writing?
Well, it is because I have some stories in my head.
One about Wally Wanderoon, who carries Buster
John and Sweetest Susan into his own country.
They have a very easy time going, but I don't
know how they'll get back."

These stories were under way all during 1902,
and were brought out by the McClure Phillips
Company, in 1903.

"Wally Wanderoon," explained Miss Elviry to
Sweetest Susan and Buster John, "says he came
from a foreign country not far from here. He comes
around occasionally and meanders around. We
think he is hunting for something he lost a long
time ago"; and Miss Elviry ended with a sigh, "I
reckon we've all lost something that we'd like
mighty well to find."

So one day the children came across the little

suffered from reading the weekly story papers. There ought to be
recreation in literature as in life: we are not all studying to be critics,
I hope."

old man, and he told them that he was looking for "the Good Old Times we used to have." He had hoped to find them in a lump, but he gave up that idea, and "now," said he, "I know that if I find them at all, I shall have to find them a piece at a time — an old song here and an old story yonder." [1] And finally Wally Wanderoon stumbles on a relic of the Good Old Times, an old-fashioned story-telling machine, and he sets the machine going for Sweetest Susan, Buster John, and Drusilla, and it grinds out some old-time stories about the Mouse Princess, the Flannel Night-Cap, the Crystal Bell, and others.

Father did not renew his contract with the McClure Phillips Company, in 1903, but the firm still retained the right to publish his books, and they made a very handsome one of "Wally Wanderoon." The relations between them and the author were of the friendliest, but father's health had been so uncertain during 1901–02 that it became burdensome to him to feel that he must deliver a certain amount of work each year, and a contract hampered him mentally and physically. Mr. Phillips was kind enough to write, "I want you to know that we are very proud and happy to have

[1] *Wally Wanderoon and his Story-Telling Machine.* McClure Phillips Co., 1903.

been your publishers, to have had the relationship with you that has existed within the past two years, but perhaps the arrangement has put too much of a burden upon you, and forced you to produce more than circumstances or your own desires would always justify." And father replied, "The personal interest you speak of has been very gratifying to me all the way through, and I hope you will not permit it to wane, even after the contract lapses; in other words, I hope that, like my regard for you, it is based on something that is better and more substantial than a mere business contract."

In the latter part of 1903 the "Saturday Evening Post" purchased the serial rights of a story of the Civil War in which General Forrest figured conspicuously, called "A Little Union Scout." This story was greatly liked and drew much attention from older readers on account of the vivid portrait which it contained of General Forrest. Brought out in book form by the McClure Phillips Company, in 1904, it had an excellent sale, and it was suggested by the publishers that it contained material appropriate for a play, but, as far as I know, father never entertained the idea of dramatizing it.

The following letter to Mr. Lorimer about one of father's stories purchased by the "Saturday

Evening Post" during this time throws an interesting sidelight upon the author's sensitiveness and proud conscientiousness where his work was concerned: —

Box 111, Atlanta, Ga., June 1

Dear Mr. Lorimer: —

I saw your portrait in the "Critic," and it has moved me to write to you in a somewhat free and familiar manner. The chin is large, but it has generous lines, and the face is Candor itself. Therefore I write this "heart-to-heart" talk.

The elisions in the first part of that story are all right; they will improve it immensely; but along toward the last there were some by Mr. Black Pencil which Mr. Blue Pencil had to protest against. Then there were changes which Mr. Blue Pencil thought doubtful, and so on.

Now, what I want to know is — and the question will strike you as somewhat peculiar — if you did n't hesitate about accepting a story which was not fit for a serial, but, instead of declining it outright, for fear of hurting an old duffer's feelings, you took this method of informing him as to the facts in the case? That is, indeed, a funny question; but I am so afraid of imposing on you that I do not hesitate to ask it.

JOEL CHANDLER HARRIS

The changes that can be made are all for the better, but even so, I am not so dead sure that the story will be what you want. You see I am almost out of the line of communication. If you knew me and could talk to me, you would soon perceive that what I write is not written primarily for the money it will fetch, and that my whole attitude toward what I write is entirely different from that of most authors.

If you will be perfectly frank with me in the matter, you will do me a greater favor than you can imagine. Mind, I am perfectly willing to make the possible changes, and to try to make the impossible ones, but I don't want to be under any delusion in the matter.

You have been so kind to me and so patient with me that I feel sure you will not misunderstand the motive of this letter.

Always faithfully yours
JOEL CHANDLER HARRIS

Father had been approached from a number of directions for "more Uncle Remus Stories," so quite contrary to his intentions and expectations he found himself during this year engaged upon more of the legends. They were told in this instance to the son of the original "little boy," who according to the introduction had been sent to the country, to be with his grandmother, "Miss Sally," until he could get some roses in his cheeks; and "Miss Sally" wisely turned him over to the old man who had made the childhood of his father so happy.

These stories appeared for the most part in the "Metropolitan Magazine" and in "Collier's," and were ultimately published by the McClure Phillips Company, in 1905, under the title "Told by Uncle Remus."

The following letter to Mr. Riley contains an interesting reference to these latest "Uncle Remus" tales: —

AT HOME, July 11, 1903

I have been trying for an hour, my dear friend, to think of some substantial reason why you are not here, but I can get hold of nothing that will satisfy me. I have no doubt there is a reason and a good one, but I can't think it out. I know that from my point of view you should be here, not only because it would be good for your wholesome, as we say in Georgia, but fine for mine.

As for myself, your letter came at a time when I am feeling better than I have felt since my illness of two years ago. In fact, I am beginning to feel as well as I ever felt, and the fact that I am growing old seems to be a mere rumor. I have n't been doing much this year besides the new Remus stuff — and I have a suspicion that it is n't quite up to the old mark. I had in my notebook a number of unverified outlines of stories, which I had thrown aside. But some one sent me a copy of Heli Chatelaine's book on Angola, and in that I have verified every outline that I had practically thrown away. The book lay about the house for months and months before I opened it, and then I found what a treasure I had discovered.

Mrs. H. has gone to Canada, and the house seems quite empty, in spite of the fact that the girls are here. I think if you were to stick your head in the door, or come whistling down the hall, I 'd fetch a yell of joy that could be heard a mile. Try it — do try it! Just to see whether I am lying about it. The mocking-birds, the catbirds, and the wrens all join me in the invitation; and we 'd fix it so that you 'd think you were at home — and we 'd try to make you stay for a longer time than ever. And the children of the neighborhood would come in to see us — the little children whose souls are white — and we 'd have a great time. Geiger says he 'll come after you any time you say so, and be glad to do so. Perhaps the " impossible " you refer to is one of the kind that will disappear with the thought treatment.

You'll have to excuse the typewriter, for I have become so accustomed to it that the pen seems awkward and slow beside it; and then my hand shakes when I hold the pen, so that however fine I feel, I know that age is a-creeping on. I am not disturbed by it, for I have as much fun now as I ever had — only it is in a different way.

I'll have a book of children's stories for the holidays.[1] The stuff is commonplace, but whimsical, and the McClures have secured an illustrator who enters fully into the spirit of the text, and he has made some very fetching pictures. I have no idea who he is, but he is a good one.

The girls and J. C. all send love; and Evelyn would jine in if he knew I were writing; but he's in town. I think he is fixin' up to get married, though he has n't admitted it yet.

I hope you can see your way clear to coming some time this summer; we'll be specktin' you any time, and, if you'll let me know when, I'll meet your train, and show you the way to the house where we live at.

Faithfully yours always
JOEL CHANDLER HARRIS

[1] *Wally Wanderoon.*

Evelyn was, indeed, "fixin' up to get married," and this happy event took place in October, 1903, his departure from the Wren's Nest leaving a void difficult to fill. J. C. was now the only son left at home.

CHAPTER XXV

THE tranquil happiness of the Wren's Nest and our nearby home was not to last, and 1904 opened tragically for us all. Mother had been summoned to Canada in December on account of the serious illness of Grandmother LaRose, and so the family circle was incomplete at Christmas-time. The day after Christmas our little Charles, now four years old, was taken suddenly ill and after three days of anguish he passed out of our lives. Grandmother LaRose died within a few days of this time, and mother's homecoming was fraught with the keenest suffering. The little boy whom she had left in perfect health was now no more. The winter months waned sadly, and with the coming of spring, just as the rugosa hedge surrounding our lawn showed its first rose and white blooms, our little Pierre, our only remaining child, gave up his life as suddenly as had his brother, — four months to the day having elapsed since Charles's body was placed in Oakland.

Even after the lapse of so many years, to recur to such losses is anguish, but they must take their place in the record of father's life. I have mentioned his fondness for Charles. After the latter's death father said to my husband: "I have felt that you would never bring him up; there was something ethereal about him; he was of too delicate a strain for this world." And indeed the little one's personality was strangely vivid for one of his years, and his mien was full of a sweet, old-fashioned dignity, unusual in a child so young. Of little Pierre, so-called after Grandfather LaRose, father was accustomed to say, "He is such a pink and white baby, as clean as a bowl of rice." In coloring he resembled little Rosebud, mother's first little girl who died at his age. The loss of these two dearly loved grandchildren affected father profoundly, and our common suffering created a new bond between us.

As father grew older, the beauty of the unseen world became more and more a part of his life, and his editorial writings, and his verses, in particular, reflected his mystical tendencies. After Charles's death he wrote one of the dialect poems later incorporated in "The Tar-Baby and Other Rhymes" which reveals his feeling of confidence before the mysteries of the Unknown and his sense of real contact with the spiritual world. It is called "It's Good to be Old if You Know How to Do," and is supposed to come from the mouth of "Uncle Remus." In part it reads: —

AFFAIRS AT THE WREN'S NEST

"Now I kin set right flat in my cheer,
  An' call back de days fum year to year —
  An' wid no need ter call, kaze, time I sets down,
Dey all comes a-flittin' an' a-flyin' 'roun',
An' all wid der Sunday doin's on,
An' all der troubles done clean gone.

"No shade fer me! I kin sit in de sun,
  An' hear dem chillun, an' see um run;
  An' over de hills when de day is long
I kin hear de plough-han's homin' song,
An' in de creek bottom — *go-bing! go-bang!*
I kin hear de racket er de new-groun' gang,
An' it seem mighty quare dat it come ter pass,
Kaze chillun an' niggers is under de grass —
Dey er dar, dey er here, an' one thing sho,
I never would 'a' b'lieved it fifty year ago!

"Little children die, an' you think dey er gone,
  An' you weep an' wail wid de mournin' on;

.   .   .   .

Dey all got ter answer ter de call er de roll;
Dey answer an' go. Does you speck dat 's all?
Is de oak tree sorry when de acorns fall?
Bless you, honey! I know what I know
Lots better dan I did some fifty year ago.

"Dey all come back, an' dey comes ter stay,
  An' you has um wid you bofe night an' day —
  An' dunner whar yo' eyes ef you can't see
Dem chillun a-stan'in' right at my knee,
Wid shinin' eyes an' ha'r fallin' free,
One little gal, an' little boys three;
An' mos' eve'y day when de light gits pale
I ketch myse'f a-tellin' um a tale,
An' I goes an' tells it — fer now I know
Lots better dan I know'd some fifty year ago."

And again he voices this feeling of unity with the source of all life: —

We are mysteriously bound, indeed, not only to the living, but to the dead, and to all who have ever lived; and no matter how we may conduct ourselves, no matter what whims we may display, and no matter what absurd antics we may cut up before high heaven, we know that we are merely reproducing what has been produced before; we are only living, on a little higher or a little lower scale, a life that has preceded us. Only the spirit is different; only the soul is original when we dare give it full play. That is why little children are so charming; this is the mystery that seems to hover over and about them, as vague and yet as palpable as twilight shadows. Their movements and their gestures are of the spirit. They have not been brought into the dull conformity with the habits and conventions of their elders; they behold life as it is and enjoy it to the utmost. Some one has characterized them as the Almighty's experiments with humanity — experiments in the direction of giving perfection to the spirit. They flit and flutter about us, and suddenly they disappear, some becoming the dull and hopeless people we see growing up about us, and some fleeing back into the hospitable courts of heaven, recalled because they are not fitted to deal competently with the troubles of the world. And others come to take their places, so we have a constant succession of fresh and untried spirits.[1]

Father once wrote of himself, "The Farmer feels that he must have been born with the knowledge

[1] "The Philosophy of Failure," *Uncle Remus's Magazine*, August, 1907.

that the overworld and the underworld and all the nooks and crannies of old Mother Earth, and all the myriad secret and hidden processes of Nature, fairly swarm with mysteries, the solution of which would carry us millions of years ahead of the stupid guesswork of those who call themselves scientists." And so when the passing years had robbed the family circle of many of its dearest members he felt more than ever that Snap-Bean Farm was peopled with "little children that he once knew and loved, with dear friends and familiars"; and he claimed that "All these and many more are neighbors, as they should be, and all that is necessary to their recognition and association is to achieve the distinction of unlearning all that is grossly material in our knowledge and experience, and clearing our minds of all that is binding and fettering to our souls; thus may we acquire something of the simple mysteries of the spirit and its infinite emanations." [1]

Of the ballads which went to make up the book of "Uncle Remus Rhymes" already mentioned, there were twenty-seven, mostly folk-tales in verse, but some were plantation and revival songs, and a few partook of the reflective nature of the one quoted. First drafts of some of the plantation songs had

[1] "On Knowing Your Neighbors," *Uncle Remus's Magazine,* June, 1907.

been submitted to the McClure Phillips Company, for criticism, — and of these, Mr. Phillips wrote: —

"I have put the ballads aside for a time because I want to take them up afresh and see if I cannot find something to say that would be worth while to you. . . . I like them both, yet I am not quite sure that I like them for 'McClure's,' I think possibly because there is a touch of the old Nick in both of them. I can see them placed properly along with others and giving one note of the varied presentation of the negro character. They amused me mightily, yet, when I come to the point of editorial responsibility, I hesitate. Yet there is in them a lot of that which you are after, the old primitive simplicity of human relationships and canny ways of the untutored."

In reply, father wrote in part: —

"With respect to the ballads, so-called, I understand your meaning in all its fullness, and I appreciate it, too. There is no editor with whom I have dealings who has been able to take all the sting out of a perfectly proper and just criticism. But the stuff was not offered for the magazine, but to draw out your own views with respect to a series of proposed ballads. Those I sent you were written without thought, merely to see if I had lost the knack. You may be sure that I would not print them in a book. In all of my writings you will find nothing that cannot be read and explained to a young girl. If I failed to tell you in sending the stuff that they were mere experiments, — rough notes on which something less crude and coarse might be based, — then I did myself an injustice. The primitive nature that is in them can be made to conform to the laws of decency — if I may so express myself."

Eventually, the McClure Phillips Company waived their right of publication under the existing contract in favor of D. Appleton & Co., which firm was anxious to bring out the ballads; and the book, a very beautiful holiday volume with illustrations by Frost and Kemble, appeared under the Appleton imprint late in 1904. It was appropriate that Appleton should bring out "The Tar-Baby and Other Rhymes," since they had published in 1880 the initial volume of "Uncle Remus" tales, which included the prose version of the famous Tar-Baby story.[1]

[1] When his firm obtained the publication rights of the "Rhymes," Mr. Appleton looked up the sales records of the first volume of "Uncle Remus" tales, and the result was the following reference in a letter to father, March 1, 1904: "On my return to New York I had the curiosity to see how 'Uncle Remus' had sold during the last few years, and I enclose you a statement of sales which perhaps you have already seen. Certainly, for a book twenty-four years old, a regular sale of four thousand copies yearly is most gratifying and unusual."

JOEL CHANDLER HARRIS

The following notice in the "New York Times Book Review" of October 15, 1904, inspired Mr. Riley to send father a poem on the new "Uncle Remus Book": —

The publishers of Joel Chandler Harris's new volume of verse, "The Tar-Baby and Other Rhymes of Uncle Remus," D. Appleton & Co., state that the advance orders for the book have been so large that three binding orders have been necessary in order to meet the requirements of the trade.

The poem: [1]

INDIANAPOLIS, INDIANA,
"LEVENTEEN HUNDERED-AN-
FULL-ER-FLEES."

Hit 's mighty good news er *new*-Ol' Uncle Remus Rhymes,
Which I done prophysyin' 'bout forty-leven times, —
All de whole kit-an'-bilin' er de jingles an' de chimes
   Ol' Uncle orter sing us ef he 'spectin' to redeem us —
   Remus —
      Ol' Uncle Remus an' his new-ol' rhymes.

O, it 's "Hi, my rinktum!" he 'low one day
When I tell him dat a ne'r batch er ol' rhymes pay —
En it 's "Ho, my Riley! youer leadin' me erstray. —
   I tas'e my last er singin' an' I gwine ter stay absteemus, —
   Remus —
      Ol' Uncle Remus tetchin' no mo' rhymes!"

---

[1] In a recent letter from Mr. Edmund Eitel, Mr. Riley's nephew, appears this reference: "My uncle used to keep a copy of the *Tar-Baby Rhymes* handy, and night after night in the last invalid years of his life he read and re-read and re-re-read these verses. I know that at the last of his life it was the favorite of all his books."

[498]

To James Whitcomb Riley.

It ho-my-Riley! Kaze all these my dreams
Tower allers a-skippin' dat Jim-along-Jeems
wid Jim-along-Joe, Twel 'it nachally seems
Yue er here sho' 'nough, whar you oughter bee, —
A-twixt a-wavin' an' a-loafin' wid me—
An' I wish you wuz—Yes-ser-see!

Well, dis's yer Book, it b'longs ter you,
Kaze you up'd an' tol' me what ter do,
An' when ter blow on my fil-a-ooa-loo:
An' I went an' done it, des ez you say,
Sometimes in de night, sometimes in de day,
An' when folks pestered, I had um sot away.

Now ol' Gabe Tolliver, he wuz a shame,
A little too long, an' a little too tame,
An' dish yer de book dat oughter have ya name!
Den its ho-my-Riley! I hope you pullin' fine,
But you'd feel lots better wid me an' mine,
A watchin' dat mocker in de honeysuckle vine!

Affectionately yours:
Joel Chandler Harris

Christmas, 190X.

INSCRIBED IN "THE TAR BABY, AND OTHER RHYMES"

AFFAIRS AT THE WREN'S NEST

But de stubbo'n devil in 'im one day git off his gyuard
An' he lef' ol' Remus snoozin' in de cornder er de yard
Whar de mockin'-birds dey wake him up a-singin' good-an'-
    hard,
    An' dey whistle, "Whirl in wid us des de same lak when
      yo' dream us —
  Remus —
    Ol' Uncle Remus an' yo' ripplin' rhymes!"

So, fo' he eveh know it — lak de dewdraps in de drouf
Dar' loosen' all de roses' lips dat 's bloomin' Norf and Souf,
De dewy songs des natchul come er-drippin' f'om his mouf,
    An' all dat honey-musicness he des divide between us —
  Remus —
    Ol' Uncle Remus an' his sweet'nin' rhymes.

Your ever grateful, faithful old Hoosier friend
               JAMES WHITCOMB RILEY

Three articles on the negro were contributed by
father to the "Saturday Evening Post" of January
2, January 30, and February 27, of 1904. These
were entitled "The Old-Time Darky," "The Negro
of To-day, His Prospects and Discouragements,"
and "The Negro Problem." I doubt if any contemporary man of letters was better posted on
these subjects than the author of "Uncle Remus,"
or could handle this theme with less of passion or
prejudice; therefore the series merits the attention of all who are interested in the prospects of
the colored race. It is inadvisable, in dealing with
a topic which has in the past stirred up so much

strife in our country and which is still the subject
of heated debate between partisan politicians, to
give scattered quotations from articles which should
be read consecutively and in entirety to be thoroughly understood. Therefore, since father's conclu-
sions on the so-called "race problem" must naturally
be a matter of interest to all who have followed
me thus far, the safest way to indicate them, in a
limited space, is to reproduce the major part of an
interview furnished by him to the "New York Journal" of November 3, 1901. It is simple enough for
those who are sufficiently interested to refer to the
files of the "Saturday Evening Post" for an elaboration of these views. Under the title of "How Education will Solve the So-called Negro Problem,"
father wrote: —

No doubt the historians who rise up in the future will
examine with amazement the records which contain the
discussions of the negro question during the past thirty
years. Was there ever, since the world began, such a
grievous misunderstanding of a simple matter, such
an unfortunate misinterpretation of perfectly natural
developments?

Every step taken by the negro race since its emanci-
pation has given rise to some new remedy proposed either
by those who knew nothing of the involved and complex
situation in the South, or by those who are all the time
afraid that the negro voters are simply awaiting an opportunity to repeat the wretched experiment that gave

rise to all the fears and troubles of the reconstruction period.

The result is that expectation persists in looking in the wrong direction, and such manifestations as chance to fall in the field of its oblique vision are misconstrued and misinterpreted.

Moreover, we constantly have with us the small but active group of sentimentalists, the various members of which persist in believing that the negro question, so-called, will never be settled under the sun until everybody and his brother insist on taking the negroes home to dinner with them. The idea is more singular when we bear in mind the fact that both negroes and white men would rather have a fair and free opportunity to earn their own dinners, than to receive casual and occasional invitations to partake of meals earned by other people; would rather have parlors of their own to sit in rather than to make a practice of sitting in the parlors of others. . . .

It has been said that the negro race is not yet in a position to be benefited by higher education. This is true, of course, but it by no means follows that all the work that has been done in that direction has been thrown away. In this, as in other things, much has been done in order that a little may avail.

It would be unjust to the negro race to make comparisons, but it is fair to say that a good deal of the higher education that is bestowed on the white race is worse than thrown away, if we are to view the matter from a purely practical and commercial point of view. You hear little or nothing at all from those who believe in education for its own sake. They have been crowded to the wall, and whatever their hopes and beliefs may be, they sing very small. Nevertheless, and in spite of the spirit of commercialism which is making our politics more hideous than ever, there will always be some people somewhere, white or black, to profit by what is called a liberal education, and the solace they will be able to receive therefrom, and the service they will be able to perform for their kind will more than repay the leakage and losses, to employ a familiar commercial expression. . . .

It is very likely true that higher education has not been beneficial to a majority of the blacks on whom it has been tried, but the excuse and plea of those who have made the experiment is that it has benefited some; and the excuse is sufficient.

Undoubtedly it is well that a new departure should be made under the auspices of Booker Washington and those who are acting with him, but it should be borne in mind that some of his most efficient workers are negroes who have received a liberal education. The trouble with the majority of the best-educated negroes, until Booker Washington came upon the scene, was the fact that they regarded politics as the chief end and aim of their ambitions. They could imagine no other field calculated to afford such a fair profit and so much notoriety. . . .

What is called the negro problem is simply the invention of men with theories. The spectacle spread out before us is not in the nature of a problem. It is made up of the actual efforts and movements of a race slowly and painfully feeling its way to a higher destiny.

The conditions and circumstances being without parallel or precedent in the history of the world, it was inevitable that serious mistakes should be made . . . that partisan politics should pour out its vials of wrath.

But what of it? The real progress of the race has not

been retarded a moment. Nothing has been lost, and now at last the whole conservative and intelligent element of the race is placing itself under the leadership of a man well qualified to lead it, and is making a new start.

Concerning the material progress of the negro, father later said: —

I have recently had a glance at figures authorized by the Comptroller-General of Georgia, and they show that during the year just closed (1903) the negro paid taxes on a property value of about $17,000,000, in round numbers; and this in view of the manifold difficulties under which he has labored — the chief difficulty being his ignorance — is something more than a good showing. The real value of the property assessed by the tax collectors must be somewhere in the neighborhood of $25,000,000.[1]

And again: —

I am bound to conclude from what I see all about me, and from what I know of the race elsewhere, that the negro, notwithstanding the late start he has made in civilization and enlightenment, is capable of making himself a useful member in the communities in which he lives and moves, and that he is becoming more and more desirous of conforming to all the laws that have been enacted for the benefit of society.

The "Saturday Evening Post" series attracted wide attention and brought many letters to its

[1] In 1916, the negroes of Georgia paid taxes on a property value of about $35,000,000.

author, from both whites and blacks. Of those from the latter, I give three as being indicative of the sentiment of representative negro citizens: —

TUSKEGEE NORMAL AND
INDUSTRIAL INSTITUTE
TUSKEGEE, ALA., February 1, 1904

MR. JOEL CHANDLER HARRIS,
Atlanta, Ga.

MY DEAR SIR: —

Will you allow me to thank you most sincerely and earnestly for your very liberal and helpful article published in last week's "Saturday Evening Post." It has been a long time since I have read anything from the pen of any man which has given me such encouragement as your article has. It has been read already by a large number of colored people, and it would surprise and delight you to hear the many pleasant things which they are saying about it. In a speech on Lincoln's Birthday which I am to deliver in New York, I am going to take the liberty to quote liberally from what you have said.

Yours very truly

BOOKER T. WASHINGTON

From the principal of the Branch Normal College at Pine Bluff, Arkansas, under date of February 1, 1904: —

AFFAIRS AT THE WREN'S NEST

Mr. Joel Chandler Harris,
      Atlanta, Ga.

Dear Sir: —

I have read with no little interest and pleasure your article on the Negro in the current number of the "Saturday Evening Post." I was a little surprised to find such candid and fair expressions relative to the colored people, and also to note your extreme optimism in the face of the many things which are being said with reference to the future of the Negro. Perhaps I ought not to have been surprised, for in our own little town of Pine Bluff we have a class of conservative white citizens who stand for justice and fairness to the colored people; and perhaps it should have been expected that a man whose knowledge of our people is so broad as yours is, judging from stories by "Uncle Remus," should be hopeful of our future. I am a product of *post-bellum* times, and I want to express my appreciation of the many kind things you said about the Negro in that article.

Believe me,

> Very truly yours
>
> Isaac Fisher, *Principal*

From the president of the Georgia State Industrial College, College, Georgia, February 1: —

JOEL CHANDLER HARRIS

MR. JOEL CHANDLER HARRIS,
      Atlanta, Ga.

DEAR SIR: —

I know you will be greatly surprised to get a letter from me, a person wholly unknown to you. The cause of this intrusion is an article which I have read in the "Saturday Evening Post" on "The Negro of To-day — His Prospects and Discouragements." I regard the article as one of the fairest and most sympathetic that I have read from the pen of any Southern man. I have read and admired much of your writings. I used to know you some twenty-eight years ago. At that time I was part student at the Atlanta University and part drayman around the streets of Atlanta. I have never seen you since, but I remember your auburn hair.

I wish it were possible for you to see some of the work we are striving to do here for the country boys who come to us five hundred strong.

          Very truly yours

                R. R. WRIGHT

Early in 1905, father received a notification from the University of Pennsylvania of the desire of that institution to honor him with a degree; but while he was appreciative of the distinction offered him, he could not bring himself to appear in person and claim it! Also in the spring of this year he was notified of his election to the American Academy of Arts and Letters.

Coincident with these honors came another which perhaps pleased the recipient even more than those just mentioned — a mark of the affectionate appreciation of his old Eatonton friends, to which a prominent Eatontonian refers in the following letter: —

EATONTON, GA., June 6, 1905

DEAR MR. HARRIS: —

Feeling that what you had put in permanent literature belongs as much to the reading world as to yourself, I obtained a copy of "Uncle Remus" and it is sealed up with other papers in a lead case and deposited under the corner-stone of the Putnam County Court-House. Outside of the United States you appear to be more identified with the tales of "Uncle Remus" than any other of your literary work, and "Uncle Remus" was my choice. I hope that you will excuse me if I have taken too much liberty with your name. When I go home to-day I will carry your letter and Mrs. Hunt will read it.

Cordially yours

B. W. HUNT

CHAPTER XXVI

"UNCLE REMUS" AND THE PRESIDENT

IN 1905 Mr. Clark Howell had received from the White House the following letter containing a reference and a request regarding "Uncle Remus": —

October 11, 1905

DEAR MR. HOWELL: —

Mrs. Roosevelt will only be a couple of hours in Atlanta. She will arrive with me at eleven o'clock, and will be obliged to leave on the one o'clock train. I wonder if Mrs. Howell would care to come to the train and take her for a drive to see the interesting points in Atlanta, and if she could bring Joel Chandler Harris with her, or arrange in some way for Mrs. Roosevelt to meet him. As you know, our entire household is devoted to Joel Chandler Harris. With regards,

Sincerely yours
THEODORE ROOSEVELT

Father had had letters from Colonel Roosevelt from time to time expressing the latter's appreciation of his writings and stating that the Roosevelt children were fond of the plantation tales. In a

UNCLE REMUS AND THE PRESIDENT

letter dated October 12, 1901, in which he thanked
father for a copy of "Uncle Remus: His Songs and
His Sayings," he had graciously written: "It is
worth while being President when one's small daughter receives that kind of an autograph gift. When
I was younger than she is, my aunt from Georgia
used to tell me some of the Brer Rabbit stories,
especially 'Brer Rabbit and the Tar-Baby.' But
fond though I am of the Brer Rabbit stories I think
I am even fonder of your other writings. I doubt if
there is a more genuinely pathetic tale in all literature than 'Free Joe.'" [1]

And again in June of 1902, after father's long
illness, the President wrote him: "Your letter was
a great relief to Kermit, who always becomes personally interested in his favorite writers and who
has been much worried by your sickness. He would
be more than delighted with a copy of 'Daddy
Jake.' Alice has it already, but Kermit eagerly
wishes it. Last night Mrs. Roosevelt and I were sitting out on the porch at the back of the White House
and were talking of you and wishing you could be
sitting there with us."

So the President's request for a meeting between

[1] About ten years later Colonel Roosevelt said to Julian: "In
my opinion, the two finest American short stories are 'Free Joe' and
'The Man Without a Country.'"

Mrs. Roosevelt and father suggested more the personal than the official note, and father gladly fell in with it, although he dreaded the publicity which the occasion would entail. Mrs. Roosevelt's simple kindliness and warmth robbed the meeting of any formality, and when she requested father to remain by her side on the balcony of the Executive Mansion in the face of the multitude, he could not but accede. "I read your stories to the little folks nearly every night of my life," she said, "and they never tire of their beloved 'Uncle Remus.'" Then father referred to the letters written him by Ethel, and the conversation turned upon the children of his family and of hers.

At the luncheon given the President the same day at the Piedmont Driving Club, father was seated next him; it was the only time that "Uncle Remus" was ever persuaded to appear at an official function, and on this occasion he was the recipient of a compliment that gave him deep pleasure in spite of the fact that it covered him with confusion. The President in the course of his address said: —

"Now, I am going to very ill repay the courtesy with which I have been greeted by causing for a minute or two acute discomfort to a man of whom I am very fond — 'Uncle Remus.' Presidents may come and presidents may go, but 'Uncle Remus'

UNCLE REMUS AND THE PRESIDENT

stays put! Georgia has done a great many things for
the Union, but has never done more than when she
gave Joel Chandler Harris to American literature."

And President Roosevelt proceeded to indicate
how much the author of "Mingo" and "Free Joe"
had done to bring together the different sections
of the country, "having written what exalts the
South in the mind of every man who reads it, and
yet what has not even a flavor of bitterness toward
any other part of the Union."

When "Uncle Remus's Magazine" was established in 1907, the President was one of its earliest
subscribers, and in the letter containing his subscription check was the following invitation: —

Now, can't you come up to Washington and give
me the very real pleasure of having you dine at the
White House? . . . Do try to do this.

Faithfully yours

THEODORE ROOSEVELT

The "New York Sun" of November 19 contained
a lengthy story of the visit, in which their Washington correspondent stated: —

The older Harris and the younger Harris left Atlanta
yesterday and got here to-day. It was a very reticent
"Uncle Remus" who sat around a local hotel and waited
for the time to come when he must depart for the White

House. He did n't care to discuss nature-faking or to say whether he thought that the President wanted to ask him if he really and truly believed that a rabbit and a fox could hold conversations in negro dialect. He denied, however, that the President had been urging him for some time to dine at the White House. The newspaper story to that effect was a human-nature fake, he said. There had been one invitation only, he explained, and that had been accepted promptly.

The article concluded with the following "bulletin": —

Midnight — Mr. Harris has not returned to his hotel. The White House is ablaze with light. It is said that Mr. Harris is telling the story of Brer Rabbit and the Tar-Baby.

On undertaking this biography, I wrote to Colonel Roosevelt, as I did to numerous other friends, asking for the use of any letters of father's in his possession. His reply was full of regret over the fact that father's letters to him had been misplaced, but he sent me a charming and generous testimonial of his affection for his old friend in the following letter, which I have his permission to reproduce: —

SAGAMORE HILL
June 28, 1917

MY DEAR MRS. HARRIS: —

From the moment when I first saw his writings, I was an ardent admirer of Joel Chandler Harris.

UNCLE REMUS AT THE WHITE HOUSE!

Cartoon in the ' Constitution," November 19, 1907

UNCLE REMUS AND THE PRESIDENT

There was a small ancestral element in this; my
mother and aunt, two Georgia girls, had brought
me up on all kinds of plantation tales, including the
B' Rabbit stories and play-rhymes like "Chickamy,
Chickamy, Craney Crow," so that I turned greed-
ily to the reproduction of these in print.

But my admiration very soon passed beyond this
stage. The writings of Joel Chandler Harris gave
to me, as they gave to so many thousands of others,
something that we got nowhere else. I am not a
literary critic; I am not competent to express
sweeping judgment on the "Art for Art's Sake"
theory. But I can speak of my own personal feelings! I certainly do not care for books that do not
have what I regard as literary worth, the quality
which entitles them to a place in literature proper.
But neither do I care for them greatly, as a rule,
unless they have in them something else also; unless one feels moved by something high and fine,
so that one feels braver and gentler, with keener
indignation against wrong, and more sensitive
sympathy for suffering, because of having read
them.

Joel Chandler Harris gave all of this to me, and
to my family — for his books were among those
to which the children listened most eagerly when
their mother read aloud. Aside from the immortal

B'Rabbit stories, and the children's stories, many of his sketches were among the most striking and powerful permanent contributions to literature that have been produced on this side of the ocean. And not one leaves a bad taste in the mouth! Not one teaches us to admire success unworthily achieved, nor triumphant evil, nor anything that is base or hard. There is plenty of sadness and wrong — Heaven knows there is enough of both in life, and the stories of Joel Chandler Harris are life. But our admiration is always for what is good in the girls or the men; and this whether the hero be lofty or lowly, white man or black.

When I became President, I set my heart on having Joel Chandler Harris a guest at the White House. But to get him there proved no easy task! He was a very shy, sensitive, retiring man, who shrank from all publicity, and to whom it was really an agony to be made much of in public. But I knew that he liked me; and I had the able assistance of Julian, who remarked to me: "I'll get father up to see you if I have to blindfold him and back him into the White House." Fortunately, such extreme measures were not necessary; but I shall never forget the smile of triumph with which Julian did actually deliver the somewhat deprecatory "father" inside the White House doors. But

[514]

UNCLE REMUS AND THE PRESIDENT

I think he soon felt at home. He loved the children, and at dinner that evening we had no outsider except Fitzhugh Lee, who was a close family friend, and with whom I knew he would get on well.

In a little while he was completely at ease; he was devoted to Mrs. Roosevelt, of course — he could n't help being; and after half an hour he was talking and laughing freely, and exchanging anecdotes and criticisms, and comparing reminiscences. When he left next morning all of our family agreed that we had never received at the White House a pleasanter friend or a man whom we more delighted to honor. We felt that our gentle-natured, sweet-tempered, almost humble-minded guest was also a really great man, a man utterly fearless in his flaming anger against wrong and oppression.

Always yours

THEODORE ROOSEVELT

Father's own account of his visit to the President was given in one of the Billy Sanders' articles: —

Thar's one thing about the White House that 'll astonish you ef ever you git thar while Teddy is on hand. It 's a home; it 'll come over you like a sweet dream the minnit you git in the door, an' you 'll wonder how they sweep out all the politics an' keep the place clean an' wholesome. . . .

[515]

Well, as I told you, that was the quintessence of home that reached from the front gate to — I dunner whar in that big house — an' to make it all more natchal, a little boy was in the peazzer waitin' to see me, an' what more could you ax than that a little boy should be waitin' for to see you before he was tucked in bed. It filled me full of the feelin' that a man likes to have when he's gittin' kinder lonesome. No sooner had I shuck the President's hand than the dinner bell rung — we call it the supper bell at my house — an' then a lovely lady come to'rds me, wi' the sweetest-lookin' young gal that you ever laid eyes on; an' right then an' thar I know'd whar the home-feelin' come from, the feelin' that makes you think that you been thar before, an' seen it all jest as it is, an' liked it all mighty well, so much so that you fergit how old you are, an' whar you live at.

It's a kind of a feelin' that you kin have in your own house, ef you've lived right, but it's the rarest thing in the world that you kin find it in anybody else's house; an' ef anybody had 'a' told me that I'd find it in full flower in the White House, a house that ten million politicians an' a good part of the public have tromped through, I never would have believed 'em.

We mostly talked of little children an' all the pranks they're up to from mornin' tell night, an' how they draw old folks into all sorts of traps, an' make 'em play tricks on themselves. That's the kinder talk I like, an' I could set up long past my bedtime an' listen at it. Jest at the right time, the President would chip in wi' some of his adventures wi' the childern. One time it was a red express wagon owned by one of the youngsters, an' then a red cheer, an' then a tunnel in the hay in the barn, an' a hole in the top whar the children fell in on him, much to his surprise; an' to cap it all off, one on 'em brung a kangaroo rat to the table for to show it to a visitor.

Well, I come away from the White House might'ly hope up, feelin' that Teddy is the President of the whole country, an' not of a party. I felt jest like I had been on a visit to some friend that I had n't seed in years. An' I went back to the hotel an' snored as loud as ef I'd 'a' been on my own shuck mattress, an' dreamed that the men in Wall Street had promised to be reasonably honest atter the fust of Jinawary.

CHAPTER XXVII

"UNCLE REMUS'S MAGAZINE"

FOLLOWING the loss of my children, I had a long
and severe illness which extended over a period of
months in 1905–1906, and during this time the
night work entailed by my husband's connection
with the "Constitution" became very irksome to
us both. It was in considering the kind of work
that would give him more freedom that the idea
occurred to him of founding a Southern magazine
with his father as editor. He and his father had
several times discussed the need for a Southern
publication, weekly or monthly, which would be
actually and absolutely independent. Father was
genuinely interested in such a possibility, and said
he would like to be connected with a magazine
the policy of which he could control. Mr. Roby
Robinson, at that time vice-president and business
manager of the "Constitution," and a very warm
friend of Julian's, was interested in the project
from the first. When my husband mentioned to
him that he and his father were thinking of starting
a magazine in a modest kind of way, Mr. Robinson
said, "Why not start in a big way?" The matter

Copyright, 1906, by Underwood & Underwood

JOEL CHANDLER HARRIS AT WORK

was discussed between them, and the idea began to take on definite form. I have prevailed upon my husband to take up the story of the magazine at this point, since all its details are familiar to him, and it was his project from the start: —

"Mr. Robinson was not only a fine organizer and an able executive, but a man of imagination. He said if he could not persuade me to remain with the 'Constitution,' he would get to work at once and see if he could interest sufficient capital to finance a monthly magazine. At that time the Constitution Publishing Company owned and published the 'Sunny South,' a weekly with a circulation of about one hundred thousand. At once he conceived the idea of using this as a basis of a monthly magazine, by naming the new company 'The Sunny South Publishing Company,' and changing the 'Sunny South' to a monthly publication under a new name, father to become the editor and I the business manager and secretary. With characteristic energy Mr. Robinson took the matter up and shortly announced that he saw the way clear to organize the 'Sunny South Publishing Company.' Father was consulted, and the plan appealed to him.

"Then arose the question of a name. Father made a number of suggestions. He liked 'The

Optimist,' 'The Spectator,' 'The New Republic,' 'The Observer,' 'The Onlooker,' 'The Home Magazine.' Of these he liked best 'The Optimist' and 'The Home Magazine.' We did not know it at the time, but there existed already 'The Home Magazine,' published by the Bobbs-Merrill Company in Indianapolis. (This was consolidated with 'Uncle Remus's Magazine' in the spring of 1907.) Mr. Robinson and I were not in favor of any of the names suggested by my father. In fact he and I agreed that the principal factor in making a Southern magazine a 'go' would be the ability of the publishers to link it up as closely as possible with a name that was already well known in many parts of the country. We also knew that the name we both had in mind — the suggestion was Mr. Robinson's — would not meet with father's approval.

"'You know,' said Mr. Robinson to father, 'this is to be *your* magazine and the public must identify you with it at once.'

"'Of course,' replied father, 'I know that my name as editor must be on it somewhere. I've no objection to it going on the table of contents.'

"'People should be able to see at a glance that it is "Uncle Remus's" magazine. And that's the name for it, "Uncle Remus's Magazine," edited by Joel Chandler Harris,' ventured Mr. Robinson.

"To this father absolutely objected. The discussion ended with his refusal to be connected with a magazine so named. In fact, he was very much annoyed and spoke to me without reserve after Mr. Robinson left. I explained that it would be impossible to make any headway in the matter — either to complete the stock subscriptions or afterwards to get quickly the attention of possible subscribers, except under such a title. His reply was that he did not care to be exploited in such a fashion.

"Nothing more was said about the matter for several days. But father was more interested in the idea of a Southern magazine than he had realized. He had, during the several months that Mr. Robinson was working to organize a stock company, thought a good deal about the magazine and its possibilities to be of genuine service to the South. Indeed, he regarded the proposed publication as an accomplished fact. So it was not surprising that, three or four days after the discussion at which Mr. Robinson was present, he said to me that he had been thinking over the proposal to call the publication 'Uncle Remus's Magazine,' and before he decided finally he wanted to consult with his old friends, Colonel Henry Watterson, Mr. Walter H. Page, and Mr. Thomas Nelson Page.

Whether he wrote to them I do not know, but about a week later he recurred to the subject, and I again went over the grounds of the belief of Mr. Robinson that in order to give the publication a chance for success father must be identified with it boldly. Still protesting, he agreed, but gave the warning that until the contents of the magazine spoke for themselves, many persons would regard it as a publication containing principally dialect stories. In this he proved correct, but the handicap in that direction was negligible when compared to the impetus obtained through the name of the magazine and that of its editor.

"Even the most sanguine of the stockholders in the company organized to establish a worth-while Southern magazine realized that, even with the strength of its editor, there was a chance that it might not prove the success that it was generally believed it would be. But the chance of failure seemed infinitesimal, provided the editor retained his health — for his enthusiasm was boundless.

"At 18–20 South Forsyth Street, just back of the present 'Constitution' office, a building was leased, and certain changes made to adapt it to the purposes of publication and printing. Roby Robinson was the president of the company, Robert F. Maddox, vice-president, W. G. Humphrey, treasurer, and, as before mentioned, I was business manager and secretary. Contracts were made for presses, linotype machines, an electrotyping plant, and all necessary paraphernalia. In order to obtain an additional income and keep the plant busy, a contract was made to print the 'Southern Ruralist,' a splendid farm periodical."

Preparations for the establishment of the magazine were well under way when father and I went to Florida in February of 1906, for a two months' stay, and he wrote to Julian from Clearwater about the matter of a prospectus: —

"A prospectus such as you speak of will have to be worked over many times before it embraces all the points necessary to set forth as the basis and purpose of our magazine; it will have to be the joint work of both of us, because you have ideas along new lines, such as would never occur to me. In fact, if the magazine is successful, that success will be due to the fertility of your ideas.

"We may come home earlier than I had intended. If we do, the matter can be arranged then. Meanwhile, I shall try to outline something. But it is a hard matter to work here, especially when the weather invites to the open air, as it has been doing lately."

JOEL CHANDLER HARRIS

The prospectus as eventually sent out embodied personal theories and convictions of the editor with which readers of this biography have already been familiarized, but in this shape he brought them together so clearly, forcibly, and characteristically that they should be offered again, as being something more than the advertising propaganda of a new publication. Indeed, this "prospectus," with its obviously personal note, might be called a sort of "credo" of the philosopher of Snap-Bean Farm:

PRINCIPLES AND SCOPE OF THE NEW MAGAZINE AS OUTLINED BY ITS EDITOR, JOEL CHANDLER HARRIS

For all practical purposes, the Monthly Magazine which is to be issued under the editorial supervision of the undersigned might well be called the Optimist: for it will preach a cheerful Philosophy and practice a seasonable toleration in all matters where opinions and beliefs are likely to clash. It will be a Southern Magazine by reason of its environment, as well as by reason of the fact that the South is a part — a very large and definite part — of this great Republic of ours, but all its purposes and intentions, its motives and its policies will be broader than any section and higher than partisanship of any sort. It is purposed to issue a magazine that will be broadly and patriotically American, and genuinely representative of the best thought of the whole country.

The note of provinciality is one of the chief charms of

all that is really great in English literature, but those who will be in charge of this Magazine will have nothing to do with the provinciality so prevalent in the North, the East, the South, and the West — the provinciality that stands for ignorance and blind prejudice, that represents narrow views and an unhappy congestion of ideas. Neighbor-knowledge is perhaps more important in some respects than most of the knowledge imparted in the school. There is a woeful lack of it in the North and East with respect to the South, and this lack the Magazine will endeavor in all seemly ways to remove. The new generation in the South has been largely educated in Northern and Eastern institutions, with the result that a high appreciation of all that is best and worthiest in those sections is spread farther and wider than ever before and is constantly growing in extent. On the other hand, at the North, neighbor-knowledge of the South is confined almost entirely to those who have made commercial explorations of this section, and who have touched Southern life at no really significant or important point.

It shall be the purpose of the Magazine to obliterate ignorance of this kind. It will deal with the high ideals toward which the best and ripest Southern thought is directed; it will endeavor to encourage the cultivation of the rich field of poetry and romance which, in the Southern States, offers a constant invitation to those who aspire to deal in fictive literature. Itself standing for the highest and best in life and literature, the Magazine will endeavor to nourish the hopes and beliefs that ripen under the influence of time, and that are constantly bearing fruit amongst the children of men. It will endeavor to represent all that is good and true, all that is sane and sensible, and all that is reasonable and just.

JOEL CHANDLER HARRIS

In all things it will be conservative, but its conservatism will represent energy instead of inertia, movement instead of rest. Its pages will be at all times open to new ideas and fresh thoughts, and it will be friendly to the hopes and aspirations of new writers who are earnest and sincere, and who have something to say. Literature will be dealt with in a large way. Such criticism as it will give place to will represent standards in literature rather than individual opinions.

Fiction is to be one of the main features of the Magazine, and yet no part of our industrial life and history is to be neglected. The needs of the South, its progress and development, the essentials of its growth, all are to play a large part in the programme that has been laid down. And so, likewise, of the whole Republic. Events that are of timely and satisfying interest will be presented graphically in paragraph and picture.

Moreover, as much care will be given to the editing of its advertising pages as to the rest of the Magazine, so that, from beginning to end, it may enter the homes of its friends clean, sweet, and wholesome.

In discussing and commenting on men and measures, or political propositions and policies, or matters affecting the social and economic welfare of the people, the Magazine will hold itself high above partisan politics and prejudices, and will refuse to mistake opinions for principles or to be blinded by the prolific and offensive suggestion of sectionalism. It shall be its purpose so faithfully to represent right and justice that every man in the land from the humblest to the highest, will stand on a plane of perfect equality in its pages.

Whenever anything interesting or important was in the wind, father thought of his dear friend,

Mr. Riley, and it was to be expected that when the establishment of the magazine was assured he should send him a message: —

Box 111, ATLANTA, October, 1906

MY DEAR FRIEND: —

I have been layin' off for the longest for to write; but I have my ups and downs, just as you have, only my downs are perhaps a little more frequent than yourn. And there's that good man Geiger, who invariably calls on me after he has been to your town. He tells me all about you, how you are getting along, how you are feeling, and everything of that kind; so that I feel as if I had heard from you. And there's that tremendous affair called Procrastination. It is my boss day in and day out. I have received several books from you from time to time, books that I appreciated and enjoyed, and I thanked the Lord that there was somebody to think of me.

I suppose Geiger told you that Evelyn has severed his connection with the Constitution; he is now the advertising man of the Bell Telephone Company in the South. The position seems to be a good one. Julian, the eldest, has also retired from the paper, and he is now busy arranging for the publication of a new magazine. He has interested

[527]

a number of men with money, and they have come down with the cash. He and they have bedeviled me until I have consented to become the Editor of the publication; but this consent was not obtained until I made the whole push sign a contract that I was to have absolute control of the contents, including the advertisements. The magazine will be able to pay for contributions, and the money in hand will carry the affair for two years if it does n't make a cent of profit.

But to the four winds with business! We are expecting something juicy from you, which may be sweet and sorrowful, or humorous and gay as the spirit moves you. Anyhow, I hope you 'll allow me to use your name as a possible contributor. A magazine edited by Joel Chandler Harris would n't look good to me unless the name of James Whitcomb Riley was somewhere close to it.

Don't you want to leave the cold North and spend from January 15 till April 15 in Florida? I 've found a delightful little town on the west coast where everything is quiet, and where the people are gentle, and good board comparatively cheap. There are flocks of mocking-birds there, and everything is charming. Why not come to your other home for Christmas and the holidays, and then go with me to Florida? This programme would delight all of us. This is a long letter, but don't throw it away until you have digested all the suggestions herein set forth. With unfading affection, I am

Faithfully your friend

JOEL CHANDLER HARRIS

And in a letter to the youngest son, J. C., then visiting in Canada (October 28, 1906), he comments on the formal announcement in the daily papers of the forthcoming magazine, deprecating, in his usual fashion, the flattering references to himself which the notices contained: —

"There is no news here except that the long-talked-of announcement of the new magazine appeared in the three Sunday papers to-day. Everybody seems to take some degree of interest in it. It is full of much about me (I mean the announcement), and I can hardly realize, after reading it, that I am such a 'dam' genius. Maybe that's what's the matter with my feet and legs when they feel wobbly. I hope to goodness that it won't strike in like the measles and take me off in the prime of senility — which is another name for a sick old age. . . . Julian is still hard at work on the affair, and I have written hundreds of letters to editors whom I used to know. All the responses have been more than kind, even cordial, and there seems to be no doubt that the magazine will receive more free advertising than any other publication ever received. This is due to the remembrance of my winning smile — you've seen it in action."

Early in 1907, father again wrote to Mr. Riley about the magazine and reminded him that he was to contribute something to its earliest numbers. From amongst the number of other letters which he sent out to writers, I have selected the following as characteristic, the first being addressed to his old friend, Thomas Nelson Page: —

"A number of gentlemen of this town have concluded to place themselves behind a monthly magazine, which will be somewhat out of the usual order of Southern products of the magazine variety. It will be a Southern magazine by being first of all an American magazine. It will not have to bid good-bye to sectionalism, or to prejudice, or to intolerance of any kind, for it will never know them. It will be built on lines as large and as healthy as the keenest kind of optimism can make them.

"In a venture of this kind that proposes to deal with both life and literature, one of the first thoughts of those who propose to be responsible for its editorial conduct is of you and the completeness with which you fill a most important part of our contemporary literature; and, as a matter of course, such a thought turns on possible contributions from you — short stories, essays, and discussions. May I hope to obtain something from you in the early days of the New Year, which is not so far away as the impatience of the children make it?

"And is it necessary to say that the proposed magazine is *not* based on the scheme so familiar to your experience with Southern publications, the formula being that the Vade Mecum is not as yet able to pay for contributions, but expects all the representative authors of our sweet, sunny Southland to take off their coats and aid the able editor in putting in his crops and harvesting them? Don't you remember the scheme with a sad, sad smile?

"I hope you are well, and that whenever you venture in this direction you will drop in at the Snap-Bean Farm and get a pitcher of buttermilk."

To F. Hopkinson Smith he wrote: —

"Greetings and remembrances! This is to say that a number of gentlemen in this town have concluded to issue a magazine, and to this end they have subscribed sufficient capital to justify a considerable literary splurge. It has fallen to my lot to shake the bushes so that shy contributors may be driven out into the open where they can be roped and dragged into the pages of the proposed venture. Hence these few lines. May I not hope to have something from your pen for the first number, and for as many numbers as may suit your convenience? The first issue will appear in the early spring, and it is proposed to make the publication somewhat different from any periodical that has heretofore been printed in the South."

To the late Mrs. Ruth McEnery Stuart, father wrote: —

"I have long desired an opportunity to tell you with what keen relish I have enjoyed your work, and that opportunity has come now, as the result of the fact that some of the substantial men of this town have undertaken to establish a magazine. They look to me to invite contributors, and to endeavor to interest them in the venture. Naturally, under such circumstances, my thoughts turn to you, one of the most representative of our Southern writers. I should be glad, indeed, to receive something characteristic from your pen — if not for the first issue, which will appear in an early spring month, why, then, for another number — and for a number of numbers."

To Sir Robert Barr, he wrote: —

"You don't remember me, of course, but I remember you when you were merely Luke Sharp, of the 'Detroit Free Press,' and I remember how you went to London to exploit the weekly issue of that paper on account of the popularity of M. Quad. (I have lost sight of that man.) I remember how you and Jerome started the 'Idler,' and what an extremely interesting little affair it was: I remember, too, that you once came through Atlanta, and made a genial examination of my shyness, and went your way, convinced that there are some very funny people in this world. I have kept up with you so well that when a number of men in our town concluded to put some easily-earned and easily-spent money in a magazine, and asked me to flush some contributors, I thought at once of you. Did n't your ears burn, or do you feel hot flushes between the shoulder-blades when trouble is pending? Well, I should like to get something from you for the early numbers of the magazine, which will be issued in one of the fresh spring months."

Again Julian takes up the story of the magazine at the point of the first issue: —

"It was planned to print the first issue of about two hundred thousand in March. As usual, unexpected delays arose. After the press was installed there was a long wait for adjustments. The electrotyping plant was new, the various employees had never worked together before, and the net result was that the first number to appear was dated June, 1907, and was not completely off the press until June 1st or thereabouts, instead of May 15th. And worse than all, the copies were uniformly bad in printing, the newness of the press lending calamitous assistance to a bad situation. A splendid list of contributors and a large spirit of tolerance for a publication edited by 'Uncle Remus' were the only things that saved the day.

"The whole appearance of the magazine was a severe shock to father. His training as a printer and pressman, combined with his keen artistic sensibilities, caused him to suffer something on the order of an outrage; and he also feared the result of the magazine's future. This was the first time he had exhibited any concern regarding financial matters, and he expressed regret that so disappointing a showing had been made for and to those who had invested in the company. His next worry was the fact that the cover design, which had been drawn at his request by my wife, had been 'botched' in the printing. Any criticism likely to fall upon him was not of interest to him.

"Despite the miserable appearance of the initial number the magazine was cordially received and the typographical deficiencies were excused, except among advertisers and the advertising representatives of the magazine in Chicago and New York. Little by little the printing situation was adjusted, until in December the magazine might have been said to be developing and growing. It seemed to be simply a question of patience and growth. The large advertisers noted the improvement in the magazine and spoke encouragingly; but a few notable exceptions — those who saw that such a magazine, if fostered, would develop into a splendid medium for them in the section that was so rapidly growing rich — waited for the magazine to 'age.'

"In the first months of 1908 'The Home Magazine' of Indianapolis was purchased and consolidated with 'Uncle Remus's Magazine.' This pleased father very much, and when the first issue of the magazine (now 'Uncle Remus's Home Magazine') was to go to old and new subscribers, he wrote an editorial in which he said in part: —

The Magazine has come to its first anniversary unharmed, and in great good humor with its readers, the world and itself. Of course, it is a mere toddler, so far as age is concerned, but it is able to get about very nimbly on its feet. It has never tried to take steps that were too long, and so it has escaped all the hard falls and bumps and bruises that belong to the period of childhood. It seems ridiculous to speak of the Magazine as

JOEL CHANDLER HARRIS

if it were endowed with a personality of its own — as if it were a real youngster.

Yet the editor does not find the idea at all strange. The Magazine has taken its place in his mind as a real person, as real to him as the person he sees in the looking-glass, the person who combs his hair with his left hand while the Editor is complacently combing his with his right; and he frequently has the queer sensation that, some day, when he is thinking of something else, this illusion in the glass will reach out and pluck him by the fore-top, or drag him bodily into the looking-glass country, where your right eye is your left. The illusion in the mirror is real after all, and in some such way the Magazine appeals to the Editor as a living personality, something more substantial than paper and print, with views and notions peculiar to itself — especially notions.

Well, whether the Magazine has a real personality, or whether it is merely another illusion, it is now twelve months old, for the Editor has counted it up twice on his fingers and thumbs. And it has been a very short twelvemonth, and a peculiarly pleasant one. The Magazine has flourished to such an extent, indeed, that it is celebrating its first anniversary by absorbing the "Home Magazine" of Indianapolis, a publication that had already scored a great success of its own. Its tremendous circulation, and its prestige have been transferred to "Uncle Remus's Magazine"; and the Editor can only hope that the readers and subscribers who embarked with the "Home Magazine" will endorse and enjoy the transfer that has been made. They will come, as it were, into a new climate and new surroundings, but the Editor thinks that their mental pleasures and comfort can be just as well provided for here as they were in the magazine that has been taken over by this lusty youngster whose anniversary he is trying to celebrate. To swallow, at one gulp, a popular Western magazine is a feat of considerable importance, and it is to be hoped that it will not at all interfere with the digestion of "Uncle Remus's Magazine." The Editor has no idea that it will. The import, as well as the details, of the transaction will be found fully set forth in the announcement of the publishers. That sort of thing comes so close to business that the Editor is inclined to avert his head when it is talked about, being rather shy of things that he knows nothing of.

Among the pleasant happenings of this first year of "Uncle Remus's Magazine" have been the kindly letters received from its subscribers, from young and old, some of them from the remotest parts of the earth, and some from neighborhoods near home. These letters have come in so constantly — some of them with such strange postmarks — that the Editor is inclined to rub his left ear (it would be the right ear in the looking-glass) and claim to be in some sense cosmopolitan. Yet, after all, provinciality is sweet and safe, and if he can sit in the little home-nest at the Snap-Bean Farm, and realize that he and his co-workers have been able to attract the attention of the reading public both at home and abroad, there is no reason why he should have any ambition to be a cosmopolitan.

The truth is, the Magazine has had a success far beyond the hopes of those engaged in producing it. It has had such high endorsement from the people and the press that the Editor feels sure that there is room for a periodical that is just a little different from the rest of its contemporaries. Everybody has been kind and helpful, and cordial and enthusiastic. This is all the more gratifying to the Editor when he remembers that he and his helpers have not been striving to produce anything wonderful or original. They have simply tried to make the Magazine just a little different from the rest. It has been their intention to uphold the old ideals of sentiment and affection, and to bring to bear on the flippant intellectuality of the day some sort of crude test of the truths it pretends to have discovered, and the wild and wobbling philosophies it is urging upon the popular mind.

The Editor has considerable respect for the good old times and for the people who made the times what they were, but he is just as deeply interested in the tremendous movements of the present, the onward rush of things, the pressure of events, the stimulating energy of modern progress and development; for all these things have their roots deep in the past, and the impulses that cause their growth are as old as they were new. Each generation, as it passes along, discovers something that it considers to be new, and gloats over its discovery with genuine enthusiasm, hugging it to its bosom or writing books about it. And then, presently, what was so new has become old and commonplace. The new times become the old times that are sure to be regretted and grieved over by old men in all the tongues with which this Babel world of ours has been gifted. So far as the Magazine is concerned, the Editor has tried to treat the old times as the new, and the new times as the old, for they are neither more nor less than this when the mind sets them against the background and perspective of the eternal sentiments and passions of the human race, and the ideals on which men and women hang their hopes and expectations.

UNCLE REMUS'S MAGAZINE

"Many leading advertisers who had been using the 'Home Magazine's' pages agreed to continue their contracts with the consolidated magazines, and 'Uncle Remus's Home Magazine' not only took on an air of prosperity, but began to show profits, much to father's gratification. It was about this time that I began to realize that he had been under a great strain, fearing for the success of the magazine, although he had said little or nothing about his feelings to any one."

Father contributed to each issue an editorial essay dealing with such subjects as "Progress in the Best and Highest Sense," "The Philosophy of Failure," "Houses and Homes," "The Old and the New South," etc., and a "Billy Sanders"[1] article, usually on political questions, or happenings in the world of business. The initial number (June, 1907) contained the first chapter of father's last long story, "The Bishop and the Boogerman," and he contributed from time to time new "Uncle Remus" stories, and conducted a department for children. All this work he thoroughly enjoyed, and he appreciated

[1] A three-part "Billy Sanders" story was contributed in 1907 to the *Saturday Evening Post*, "The Shadow Between His Shoulder Blades." (Published in book form by Small, Maynard & Co., Boston, 1908.)

the hundreds of delightful letters that came to him from both old and young readers who were interested in "Uncle Remus's Magazine." Of course, there were criticisms that were not always friendly, but the editor took them good-naturedly as a part of the day's work. Of one of these he wrote me while I was in the mountains of North Carolina in July, 1907: —

MY DEAR DAUGHTER: —

Your letter was very bright and cheerful, and gave me reason to believe that your trip would do you a great deal of good. You know how these things are: you have to recover from the effects of the trip, and then from the effects of the water! This is history; yes, it is truer than history — it is a fact. But now that you have Julian with you, you will be better than ever. I don't know what was the matter with Julian when he left; he seemed to have the blues — perhaps over the typographical appearance of the magazine. You can tell him for me that, so far as the magazine is concerned, the worst is yet to come. We shall have to drag through a very ragged and rusty period, and then after that, the sun will rise.

Only yesterday, I received an anonymous letter from some lady in West End, declaring that the magazine was a disappointment to all my friends. "Mr. Sanders is too coarse, and not a bit funny, and Don Marquis is flat and tame . . . and the time will come when all your subscribers will desert you." And much more to the same purpose. The letter was amusing to me, for I thought I could discover in it the chaste hand of Mrs. ——; but mother and the girls were inclined to take it rather seriously. Mr. Marquis was not amused by it as he should have been. It is curious what variegated results an anonymous letter can have! Some are amused by it, while others regard it as the culmination of public opinion. If it were signed, we should all know just whom it represents; but without signature it seems to possess a certain degree of authority. And that is very curious, too; it shows that what we call superstition has very simple and very natural beginnings. The mystery about an anonymous letter seems to be very impressive to some minds. They forget all the kind things that have been said about the magazine by people entirely competent to judge. This is the only sensation we have had lately.

It will interest you to know that the grass has been renewed on the spot where you fell, and we are nursing it as best we can. Last Sunday the mercury went up to ninety-eight, and everybody except Julian and myself were in a state of gasping helplessness. — Well, I know you are tired of all this foolishness. All send their best love, and all of us miss you very much.

Your affectionate

FATHER

CHAPTER XXVIII

THE DOROTHY LETTERS

In, the spring of 1906 father received a letter from a little girl in Baraboo, Wisconsin, and, as was his custom with childish correspondents, he replied to it promptly. This was the beginning of a correspondence which extended over two years. The Dorothy Loye of other days is now Mrs. Chauncey Holmes, of Milwaukee, Wisconsin, and though she is no longer the "lean, lanky girl" who wondered what Sweetest Susan and Buster John saw when they put their heads under the red cloth and looked into the mirror, she still *believes in fairies*. I have her permission to use a few of her letters, as well as those which were written her in reply.

Baraboo, Wis., March 21, 1906

Dear Joel Chandler Harris: —

I thought I would write to you and tell you how I like your books. We have a library here and that is where I read them. I have read "The Uncle Remus Stories," "The Story of Aaron," "Aaron in the Wild-Woods," "Little Mr. Thimblefinger," "Plantation Pageants," "Mr. Rabbit at Home," etc. Most of these I have read more than once.

[543]

I have often wondered what Sweetest Susan, Buster John, and Drusilla saw when they put their heads under the red cloth and looked into the mirror.

I liked "Aaron in the Wild-Woods," because it was about little Crotchet, but I cried when he died.

I like Brer Rabbit very much and I like to see him come out ahead of Brer Fox and I felt sorry for him when he stuck to the "Tar Baby."

I liked the story of the little Girl who went to Thunder's house and then to the Jumping Off Place where Sister Jane gave her a phial of sparkling water.

Yours truly

DOROTHY LOYE

Baraboo, Wisconsin

P.S. I am 13 years old and go in the 7th grade.

N.B. I will be terribly proud if I get an answer from you.

"AT THE SIGN OF THE WREN'S NEST"
ATLANTA, GA., 30 March, 1906

DEAR DOROTHY: —

You'll have to excuse the type-machine. I write on it with my own hands, and it is closer to me than pen and ink would be. Your charming little letter calls for a vote of thanks. I appreciate it very highly, because I think it is the prettiest letter I have ever received, and I know that the girl who wrote it is

DOROTHY LOYE

just as nice and sweet as she can be. I am just like you in regard to Buster John and Sweetest Susan; I wonder and wonder what they could have seen when they put their heads under the red cloth, and it has always been a great mystery to me. I think you would like "Wally Wanderoon," for I wrote it for just such a little girl as you seem to be, and therefore it must have been written for you.

Gratefully and Faithfully [1]

Baraboo, Wis., April 6, 1906

Dear Joel Chandler Harris: —

I thought I would write and thank you for the great pleasure your letter gave me. Now I long to read "Wally Wanderoon," but I suppose I can't because it is not in our library. The title sounds so tempting.

Did you ever go abroad? That is my highest ambition next to being a great author.

I suppose it is summer where you live now. I wish it was here. But still it is quite nice weather, only it snowed yesterday, but is all melted now.

It must be lovely to live down there where it is summer all the time.

I must stop now, always remaining,

Yours sincerely

Dorothy Loye

[1] The writer forgot to affix his signature to this letter.

[545]

P.S. You forgot to sign your name to your letter and I want your autograph *very* much.

ATLANTA, 12 April, 1906

DEAR DOROTHY: —

If I were in your place, I would n't write more than two or three dozen letters to a man who is silly enough to forget to sign his name when he is writing to a nice young lady. — The man we were talking about never went abroad because it is so far from home. It is spring here, but not summer. Atlanta has winters about as disagreeable as you have them in Wisconsin, and so this winter the man who forgot to sign his name (because he did n't have a pretty one like yours) went to Florida, and had a lovely time. So good-bye, Dorothy. (Oh, how he loves that pretty name! this man we were talking about.)

Faithfully your friend

JOEL CHANDLER HARRIS

BARABOO, WIS., April 18, 1906

DEAR JOEL CHANDLER HARRIS: —

I can't tell you how glad I was to get your letter. I must have gotten red in the face, I was so eager to open it.

I am glad you, mentioned Mr. Carnegie, for I

was just thinking of writing to him to tell him the realms of bliss his library gave me.

I wish I could have some one give me an invitation to go abroad, and I can tell you I would accept eagerly. I think England would be the most interesting.

I would like to return your compliment on my letter. I think your letter is the nicest I have ever received, because it is just like a story (and I love stories, especially yours).

I have sent a story of mine to a paper. I expect I will get a letter, which will decline (politely) with thanks. But my mother says that most of the best stories are declined a great many times before they are accepted. But if my story is accepted I will surely send you a copy.

Very truly

Dorothy Loye

Atlanta, 30 April, 1906

Dear Dorothy: —

(I declare, it makes my mouth water every time I write that pretty name!) I sincerely hope your story will be sent back to you. You'll firmly believe that I'm a mean old Boogerman, and that's just what I am. But listen: Could you make a chair or a piano? Could you paint a picture, or

[547]

do other things of that kind that required experience and training? Why, of course, you could n't! Then how could you, at your age, write a story that would be worth while? No, no! you will have to learn by observation and experience, and, when you do learn, as you are sure to do, you will write something fine. But if the editor prints your story, why, just feel humble, and promise yourself that you will write one twice as good the next time; and keep on promising to improve, and when I get to be seventy-five, I can sit in the corner and mumble to myself that I corresponded with Dorothy Loye before she became famous.

Faithfully yours

JOEL CHANDLER HARRIS

Nearly a year passed without a letter from Dorothy, and her friend writes again in April of 1907 to inquire what has become of the "lean, lanky girl" and Miss Gertrude: —

P.O. Box 111, 5 April, 1907

DEAR DOROTHY: —

As well as I can guess, you are now a little more than fourteen, and ploughing along in the eighth grade. I was just thinking the other day that I had n't heard from you in a mighty long time, and I wondered what you were doing, and what you

were thinking about all these many months. I had
a letter the other day from a little girl in Pennsylvania, whose name is Dorothy, and as soon as I
opened it and saw the name, I said to myself,
"What has become of my particular Dorothy?" —
and then I wondered why you never wrote any
more. Well, I am just writing this to find out how
you are getting along — you and Miss Gertrude,
the librarian. Some time, when you've nothing
else to do, write me a little letter, and tell me about
yourself.

Faithfully your friend

JOEL CHANDLER HARRIS

BARABOO, Wis., April 8, 1907

DEAR MR. HARRIS: —

Now I can never tell you how very, very glad I
was to get your letter. I thought that you had forgotten me for good. I was mighty glad to get it,
I can tell you. And so was "Miss Gertrude." I
am sure you would like to know what she is like.
Well, she is just like one of the Princesses in your
fairy tales. She is tall and very slender, with beautiful golden hair and big blue eyes. She is about
twenty-one years old. I wish I looked like her. She
makes me think of Lizzette or The Strawberry Girl
in your books. Or the little girl in the carriage in
Chickamy-crany-crow's story.

[549]

By the way, how are Chickamy-crany-crow and Tickle-my-toes? Or the looking-glass children? There was n't a thing about them in "Wally Wanderoon." I liked, I loved "Wally Wanderoon." I thought I would never get it, but I did, at last.

Perhaps you would like to hear about my pets. I have three cats, a horse, and a rooster for my pets. The cats are called Lily, who is white, Harlequin, who is gray, and Buster, who is black with white feet. The horse's name is Fly and sometimes (that is when I am on her back) I believe she is part of me. She is a little bay mare. The rooster's name is Benjamin Franklin. He is very tame. I think a great deal of him. Hoping you will write I am,

Your sincere friend

DOROTHY LOYE

About this time the magazine was very much on the mind of its editor and in the following letter he sends Dorothy a message about it and tells her she is to be a subscriber: —

27 April, 1907

DEAR DOROTHY: —

Your letter came just as I was on the point of sending you a prospectus of the magazine, which contains a fairly good picture of me. The picture in the prospectus shows me in a corner of the porch watchin' natur' cut her caper. It is a very good picture according to report. In this, as in other things, I have to depend on the word of others, for I have never really seen myself. That magazine will be published about the 15th of May. The press was lost on the railroads, and we were at some trouble to find it. I don't know how nice a magazine it is going to be, nor do I know whether you are going to like it or not. If you see anything in it that does n't seem to be just right, please let me know — and if you think I don't mean that, you will be very cruel and unkind. I am going to send you before long, or just as soon as I can remember not to forget it, a book called "The Tar-Baby Story, and other Rhymes of Uncle Remus," and in that book you will find something about Tippity-Toe and Flee-ter-my-Knee; and if you can look behind the rhymes you will find out all about me.

And so you are a tall, lean, lanky girl! Well, don't be too proud of that; I 've seen fourteen-year-old girls before, and many of them are very nice, especially those that forgot to be conceited. You have nearly all of life before you, and the kinder you are to people, the happier you will be. I have reached the point where I can look back on four fourteens, and I can see where I could have been much nicer than I have been — almost as nice as the lean, lanky girl. The only way that I can keep young is to believe in fairies — really and truly. That's the prescription I give you, so that you may always be young. When people tell you that there's no such thing as fairies, just ask them how the idea of fairies could have got in anybody's mind if there are no fairies? And if they answer that it is all imagination, just ask them how any one could think things that never had any existence. The only way they can answer that is to mumble and grumble, and when you hear grown people mumbling and grumbling, you may know they're at the end of their row.

The great thing is to believe in fairies even after you have grown old, and then you'll go through life with a satisfied expression on your face, as though you were just about to smile. (See the picture I'm sending you. It's ugly, but there is the satisfied expression that grown people can't understand. The lady took it when I had forgotten she was in the world.) Well, I've no business to be taking up the time of a tall, lanky girl. I'll have your name put on the subscription list, and I think the whole magazine will be the better for it.

Faithfully your friend

JOEL CHANDLER HARRIS

THE DOROTHY LETTERS

DEAR MR. HARRIS: —

I thank you over and over again for your lovely letter and your promise of a book. But I did n't get any picture; I suppose that will come later.

But I think you over-estimate me — I am only a lean, lanky, plain, common girl; not charming nor handsome. And I love fairy tales and fairies. When I tell some friends how much I like "Arabian Nights," why, they hold up their hands and say "Arabian Nights!" just as if to say, "Why, the idea of a great girl like you reading that!" It's just that way with "Alice in Wonderland," "Grimm's Fairy Tales," and all the rest. I shall always be fond of fairy tales; every time I see a new fairy tale in our library, I seize on it with a great gusto and hug it all the way home. (You see that's a habit I have; whenever I am especially delighted with a book, I hug it.) But this lanky girl must not tire you with a longer letter. But I must tell you that Miss Gertrude is as beautiful and kind as ever.

Sincerely your friend

DOROTHY LOYE

JOEL CHANDLER HARRIS

Box 111, 4 May, 1907

Dear Dorothy: —

I was just about to write to you about the book when your letter came. I had to send to New York for it, and it arrived yesterday. It will be forwarded as soon as I can have it wrapped up — and I am saying that because I am such a terrible old fellow for putting things off. I am a Professor of Procrastination. The picture I wrote about is contained in the prospectus of the magazine, and it's enough like me to be my twin brother. I enclosed the prospectus in a tube, and mailed it the same day I mailed the letter for which you think you are so thankful. Your reference to the "Arabian Nights" reminds me to tell you that the story of the forty thieves is one of the most perfect short stories ever written, and if you ever have the ambition to write stories you will find that a model to be studied. It is simple and direct. One of the best fairy stories I ever read is called "Grandmother's Wonderful Chair," or something like that.

I am glad that Miss Gertrude of the Golden Hair is still beautiful and kind. If she isn't proud or stuck up, you may give her my regards. I am fond of people who are good and kind — I mean young people. I can't say much in favor of old people like myself; I don't like to associate with them. They are always forgetting that they were once young, and they are constantly finding fault. I don't believe I could live in the same house with more than one of them, and that one, when he looked in the glass, would have to be myself. Would n't it be funny if you looked in the glass and found somebody else there? I am all the time expecting this to happen to me, and one morning I came as near as anything to finding some one else. I don't know who it was, nor how he or she got there, but I know I saw somebody dodge out of sight, just like a shadow. It may have been my other Me, but I don't see why it should have dodged, for I'm perfectly sure that I would have done it no harm.

I hear that you are still lean and lanky, not charming nor handsome. Well, so be it. It won't hurt you to think all these things. Sometimes we don't know ourselves. Any girl that is good and nice and that has ideals of the right kind — the high kind — is bound to be charming. And as to beauty — well, beauty does n't count for much in this world unless it stands for goodness. So you will have to allow me to have my own ideas about you. But I just intended to say that the book would be along presently, and here I am running along and writing as if I had known you for fourteen and a half years. If you are tired, you can put the letter down and read it when you get stronger.

Faithfully your friend

JOEL CHANDLER HARRIS

P.O. Box 111, 1 June, 1907

DEAR DOROTHY: —

I hope you have received the magazine by this time. Its appearance is not quite what we would have it, but that can be improved in a purely mechanical way.

You seem to have good and wise friends. What your teacher said is very true, truer even than she thought. We can do whatever we desire to do, and do it well. With patience and the constant desire that will spur you on, you can become a successful writer. But you will have to accustom your mind to the highest and best thoughts, the thoughts that really amount to something in this world. Matthew Arnold says that genius is only another name for energy, and I am sure that energy can only spring from a constant desire to *accomplish*.

In the beginning, you will have many disappointments, and there will be many obstacles to overcome; but these things should give you greater force. Water runs from the garden hose very weakly indeed, until it meets with an obstacle in the shape of a nozzle, and then it suddenly grows very powerful. You cannot play at literature; you have to work. Every result that is worthy must have work behind it, and to those who are going to be elected in the great campaign of ideas, work becomes a great joy. The difficulty with me is that I have never been much of a worker; I have been a shirker. This is a sign to me that I am capable of nothing great; but if I can give joy to children and to people who have not ceased to be children, that is enough for me — and a great deal more than I ever hoped for.

But, good gracious! Here I am on a high horse with no saddle and bridle, and I had better jump off before I fall off. I feel right dizzy. But don't get alarmed; these attacks don't come often — if they did I'd send for the doctor, and it would be a hurry call. Regards to gentle Gertrude with the golden hair. Write when you feel like it, for I am always glad to hear from you.

Faithfully your friend

JOEL CHANDLER HARRIS

Another considerable interval in the correspondence occurs here, and Dorothy's friend starts the affair off again by a request for her help in the children's department of the magazine: —

JOEL CHANDLER HARRIS

February 24, 1908

MY DEAR DOROTHY LOYE: —

I suppose you thought I had forgotten you, but no such ugly things happen with me; I leave them to the young people. I don't know whether the magazine is turning out to be much of a success or not. Anyhow, we are trying to improve it all the time. We are going to have a children's department that will be a little different from all the other children's departments that you ever saw, and I want you to write some letters for it. The only trouble is that you are getting to be a great big grown girl, and would scorn to write such nice simple letters as you used to write to me. In fact — and I shudder when I think of it — you may have left dear old Baraboo for a finishing school, and if you have, then I know you won't have time to bother with other things.

But if you have grown older, so have I. My red hair is beginning to turn gray, and that is a blessing, because I never did like red hair like mine — though I like other people's red hair fine. Well, we are going to have this children's department that I told you about, and we are going to try and make it so that even a great big grown girl like you will enjoy it. I have been thinking of writing to you for some time, and now I have the excuse — you have

to have excuses when you write to big girls. Give
my regards to that wise woman, your mother, and
tell her that I am always trying to light the home
light in the kitchen window.

Faithfully your friend

JOEL CHANDLER HARRIS

And give my regards to Miss Gertrude.

J. C. H.

Dorothy responded immediately to the editor's
request, and her good letter prompted him to make
another suggestion about a contribution to the
magazine: —

Box 111, Atlanta, Ga. [not dated]

DEAR DOROTHY: —

Please excuse copy paper, I just wanted to write
and thank you for your pretty letter. I think you
are the nicest girl in the country, and I don't believe
it will spoil you to be told so. You were so prompt
about that letter that it made my head swim; and
then, too, it was just the thing I wanted. You will
soon get the April number, and then you will see
whether this children's department is going to be
interesting. I am going to turn it over to the youngsters and Uncle Remus, and allow them to caper
about in it and do as they please and then if it turns
out to be uninteresting, I won't be so much to blame.

JOEL CHANDLER HARRIS

We have taken over the "Home Magazine" of Indianapolis, and this will add immensely to our circulation, at least for a while. I hope they will like the magazine as I get it up, but you never can tell about readers; they either know too much, or they don't know anything; and these "Home Magaziners" will be new people to me, and it takes me a long time to get used to strangers.

I have been thinking about writing a new American fairy story, and wondering if you would collaborate with me. For instance, I'd write the first chapter and you the second, and so on. You see I feel like I know you personally, and I am writing to you as familiarly as I would to one of my own brood. A fairy story, you know, does n't have to have a plot; you just let your pen run as your fancy dictates, and you can crowd it with the most curious and unheard-of adventures — little adventures that unthinking people are likely to have with live things that they know nothing about.

Well, I thank you again for your beautiful letter.

Faithfully your friend

JOEL CHANDLER HARRIS

P.S. The department in the April number is not a fair specimen. I was obliged to print what I could get. The two little letters are merely tributes to me,

Copyright by Frances B. Johnston

JOEL CHANDLER HARRIS

The photograph with the "twinkle"

and I am afraid people will think I am very vain because I used them, but I just had to have some children's letters, and the two I used were the mildest of several hundred.

J. C. H.

In the next letter father goes more into detail about the plan for a collaboration, the idea being to bring the "story-telling machine" of "Wally Wanderoon" into play again: —

ATLANTA, GA., Box 111,
March 26, 1908

DEAR DOROTHY: —

Did n't I say that your letter is a beautiful letter? Well, when anything is beautiful is it likely that I'd put it in the scrap-basket? I never saw such a doubting child! But I like it; it shows that you're not a bit stuck-up, and I hope you never will be. I can tell you one thing that I hope won't spoil you, and that is that you are going to make a successful writer. I hope that when you get grown and old somebody will pay you as nice a compliment as your mother paid me once on a time. I'll bet you a yard of ruching against a box of chocolate drops that you don't remember what it was. But I remember, and it won't be fair for you to ask your mother what it was; when you do that the bet's off.

[561]

JOEL CHANDLER HARRIS

No, I did n't know that you could squeeze any pleasure out of my letters; all that I knew was and is that it is a pleasure to me to write to such a bright child, and to receive letters from her. (Now, go and do up your hair and don't laugh!) There was a time, you know, when I did n't dare to write! — the time when you were swallowing those dreadful exams — when you were afraid to go to sleep for fear of forgetting everything you had learned after supper. And then there have been times when I could n't write; you know how wheezy and grippy old people get during the cold weather.

Don't forget that the South is far, very far from being a tropical country. Its winter climate is a great deal more disagreeable than that of Wisconsin — else why does n't Ringling's circus winter in Atlanta? Well, when I'm wheezin' and sneezin' I find it impossible to write letters to my friends — and I've had some awful scoldings from people who send stories to the magazine, and fail to hear from them in a reasonable time. But I just let them scold, and never say a word till I get so I can write, and then I make them feel awful cheap. "Dear Sir or Madam," I say, "how can you be so hard on an old man? Here I have been sitting close to the bed and next door to the doctor, hardly able to read your courteous abuse." And then they write and apologize, and I send 'em a note to say that pro-crastination is the chief plaything of an old man, who has nothing left but a little time. I don't know what all these people think of me, and I'm too pro-crastinatious to write and ax 'em.

Well, you see how I go on! All this was written just to have an excuse to ask you to get the char-acters in "Wally Wanderoon" well in your mind, and prepare to take them by the hand and lead them through the pleasant fog of an American fairy story.

My regards to your mother and Miss Gertrude. With much love, faithfully your friend

JOEL CHANDLER HARRIS

Was it a premonition that led Dorothy's friend to write of himself as "an old man who has nothing left but a little time"? The "story-telling machine" was not to be set in motion again. In less than four short months the lover of big and little children had become a dweller in that "country next door to the world."

CHAPTER XXIX
"ANNE MACFARLAND"

A SERIES of articles which aroused much interest
and speculation were the book reviews published
from time to time in "Uncle Remus's Magazine"
and signed by "Anne Macfarland." This lady was
supposed to be a Georgian who had been living
for a period of years in London. Her address was
"Terrace Road," and she wrote familiarly of London fogs and other peculiarities of English climate
as well as customs. Her heart was still in Wilkes
County, close to old Putnam, and she frequently
used the vernacular and referred affectionately
to old times and old friends. Her style and views
evoked the picture of a middle-aged woman of
downright opinions and home-loving tendencies; of
charitable disposition and unaffected manners; of
wide information and shrewd vision. She was a
"personality," a comfortable, companionable sort,
with an urbanity gained from a good-humored
contact with people, and possessed of none of the
"smart" flippancy of the fashionable critic. Her
reviews were much more than perfunctory notices
— they were leisurely essays, flavored with the

[564]

writer's common sense and humor. "Who is Anne Macfarland?" many readers asked. But her identity was not revealed for weeks after the reviews ceased to appear. "Anne Macfarland" (as the reader has already assumed) was Joel Chandler Harris himself, and she was the mouthpiece of his opinions on books and writers, old and new.

These critical essays now take on an added charm and significance when we consider them as the perfectly frank and unconstrained expression of father's ripened literary views. In fact, were it not for the genial mediumship of "Anne Macfarland," it would be difficult to record in any detail the literary prejudices and preferences of "Uncle Remus," for he was never "bookish," and had a horror of pedantic manifestoes.

On one occasion, when he was approached by a representative of the "Atlanta Journal" and asked for a contribution to a "Symposium on the Historical Novel," he was inclined to treat the matter as a joke, and it was only after being allowed his little fling at such serious affairs as "symposiums" that he proceeded to touch on the question under discussion: —

Now, if you had asked me something about the different brands of pot-liquor, whether that made from collards has a finer flavor than that made from cabbages, or whether the addition of dumplings is calculated to take away all degrees of comparison, you would have found me at home, as the saying is. Why, I can sit and discourse with you by the hour on such matters as pot-liquor and dumplings, and likewise fatty bread. And there are other important questions such as must occur to every liberal-minded and progressive person. For instance: Is the corn pone better form than the hoecake? To what extent has the frying-pan contributed to our civilization? If I were a Daughter of the Revolution, or even a Son of Temperance, I'd fire these questions broadside at the public and never rest until they were answered.

But you were speaking of the historical novel. Well, it seems to me that every successful novel is, in a sense, historical. It must deal with a certain period of time and must give us veracious reports of the character and habits of people who lived in that period. Looking at the matter from this side, it may be said that Mr. Howells's "Silas Lapham" is as historical as "Janice Meredith." War is not the only material that goes to the making of history. In this sense, "The Scarlet Letter" is our greatest historical novel, and next to it we must place "Huckleberry Finn," [1] though one is a romance and the other

[1] The following letter concerning father's estimate of *Huckleberry Finn* was received by him in November, 1885: —
DEAR UNCLE REMUS: —
I thank you cordially for the good word about Huck, that abused child of mine who has had so much unfair mud flung at him. Somehow I can't help believing in him, and it's a great refreshment to my faith to have a man back me up who has been where such boys live, and knows what he is talking about.
Sincerely yours
S. L. CLEMENS.

a report of character and manners. To-day is as much
a part of history as yesterday, and the writer who em-
bodies its atmosphere and action in a story of character
will produce a historical novel.

The technically historical novel has been much talked
about, but the truth is that a novelist who undertakes
to reproduce history is certain to have a fall, unless he
belongs to the class of Scott and Dumas — men who
were able to twist history about to suit their purposes.

Really, I should like to say something interesting on
a subject that seems to be interesting to the newspapers.
But you know how these things go. In a week from now
you and "The Journal" will have forgotten that the historical novel is a matter of any importance at all. But
it is as unimportant now as it will be then. I think I'll
have the advantage of you. You'll be worrying about
some other matter equally insignificant, and I'll be enjoying my pot-liquor and dumplings.

In a general way, those who were oftenest in
father's company knew that he enjoyed a good romance, detective story, or historical novel. He delighted in the novels of Dumas because of their
feeling for adventure and their rollicking love of life.
He loved Dickens for his humanity and his gift
of characterization. Cardinal Newman charmed
him because of the urbanity and crystalline beauty
of his style; he admired Stevenson for the same qualities, and Henry James, in his earlier period. Of
George Eliot he wrote in his young manhood,
"'Middlemarch' will become a monument to the

grandeur and greatness of a woman's intellect";
and of Walter Savage Landor, "Posterity will discover in him the genius of our own epoch." As
a creator of a literary era he placed Swinburne
along with Shakespeare, saying, "No writer in our
language has wrought such melodious effects and
discovered such marvelous fluency in the English
tongue." He disliked Zola and the French realists
intensely, never being able to appreciate Zola's
epic quality, because of the mass of sordid details
that obscure the basic grandeur of his social ideal.
The essays of Sir Thomas Browne were his constant
delight, and he also found much to admire in the
critical work of Matthew Arnold. Mark Twain he
enjoyed heartily and placed him first amongst contemporary writers and Kipling's "Kim" and the
"Jungle Books" he read with keen interest.[1] Of
the poetry of Walt Whitman he once wrote a short
criticism so eloquent and illuminating that Mr.
Burroughs thought fit to quote it in its entirety in
his essay "The Flight of the Eagle."

But these preferences (except the last mentioned

[1] In a letter to Julian, written when the latter was at school in
Canada, father said of Kipling's style: —

"About Rudyard Kipling: don't be impressed too much by his
style. It is vicious English, and he allows himself to be unnecessarily
vulgar. I wanted you to read his stories in order to give you an
idea of the '*go*' that a little enthusiasm will give a thing. The man
certainly has a genius for telling a tale in an off-hand way."

[568]

Joel Chandler Harris.

My favorite authors of prose . .	*Hawthorne, Thackeray, Lever*
My favorite poets . . .	*Shakespeare, Burns.*
My favorite painters . . .	*The Four Seasons*
My favorite composers . . .	*The People.*
My favorite book	*Vicar of Wakefield*
My favorite play	*Lear*
My favorite heroes in fiction .	*D'Artagnan, Jean Valjean*
My favorite heroines in fiction .	*They are all faded from my mind except Mrs. Touchett*
My favorite heroes in real life .	*Lincoln, Stonewall Jackson, Father Damien*
My favorite heroines in real life .	*Women who love their Homes*
What I enjoy most	*A Whirl at Kalamazoo Whist.*
What I detest most	*Applications for Autographs*
The historic event at which I should like most to have been present . .	*I give it up.*
The quality which I admire most in men	*Modesty*
The quality which I admire most in women	*Charity*
Where I should like to live . . .	*At Home*
My ideal state of happiness . .	*A cold night, a hot fire, and taters in the ashes.*
The occupation that I prefer . .	*That which I can never engage in*
What gift of nature I should like to have most	*The Gift of Gab.*
My motto	*Wait for the Wagon.*

Joel Chandler Harris

MR. HARRIS'S "FAVORITES" PRINTED IN "THE CRITIC"

one) were discovered by accident, for father was averse to any critical analysis of a book or writer in conversation, and never had occasion for the formal expression of his literary opinions in writing until "Anne Macfarland" gave him an opportunity. Undoubtedly he enjoyed the experience of masquerading in the comfortable, unconventional garb of the time-seasoned, cosmopolitan Anglo-American lady, and the piquancy of the situation added fresh humor and energy to his pen.

In an editorial he once said: "'The Farmer' is not a great reader; the things that are old in literature, the books on which several generations have left the stamp of their approval, are sufficient for him, though he is not averse to reading a rattling modern story, as full of the sensational as it can be packed." Though his style was fed and formed on the classic writers, toward the latter part of his life, when the stress of earning a living became lighter and he had more leisure, father enjoyed the recreation furnished by some modern novels, and he gave his impressions of them through the pen of the London lady.

It is not surprising to find the author of "Gabriel Tolliver" and "Sister Jane" laying more stress on lifelike characterization than skillful manipulation of plot, and I, for one, am in full sympathy with him when he says in reviewing the stories of Mrs. Deland, "What does a story matter, if we do not, somehow, find its characters close kin to us?" He had a great fondness for the good "Dr. Lavender," and asks: "Wouldn't you be glad to have the lovely old man and all his neighbors, even the worst, in Georgia?" In speaking of the gift of characterization, he continues: —

Can a writer properly portray the mental emotions, the aspirations as well as the inner habits of thought, of aliens and strangers of whom he has only a surface knowledge? . . . This is a question that goes to the very heart of successful fiction. A writer must not only have the knowledge of them, but he must know them to the very root of their being. Only in this way can character be created, and the creation of character is the chief end and aim of those who set themselves to produce masterpieces of fiction.

And again:—

Wherever, or whenever, you find in a book the apt and happy portrayal of *human nature*, its contests with its own emotions and temptations, its striving toward the highest ideals, its passions, its platitudes, its meanness, its native longing for what is true and wholesome, its struggles with circumstances, its surrenders and its victories, and, above all, its *humor*, there you will find the passport and credentials that will commend it to readers yet unborn.

Holding these convictions, father inevitably found much pleasure in Mr. Cable's studies of

ANNE MACFARLAND

Creole life in New Orleans, and through the pen of "Anne Macfarland" he rebuked the people of the South for "the hot criticism and social ostracism" which were handed out to the author of "The Grandissimes." He even dilated somewhat on the sensitiveness of the Southern temperament which cannot brook criticism, and said: —

Our romantic tendencies always threaten to run away with us; and we are dreadfully sentimental on the slightest provocation, permitting our local politics to interfere with what should be art. What great writers we should have in the Southern States if only we could make our traditions and our environments contributory to our fictive art! But it seems there are things we cannot deal with familiarly — things that we cannot touch with our finger-tips without drawing a blood-blister on the unseemly forehead of politics, and when our writers take their pens in hand, and begin to set forth in fiction the things with which they are familiar, and about which they have first-hand knowledge, they unconsciously feel that they are under some sort of pledge not to offend the abnormal sensitiveness of their neighbors. . . . This has been so and it is so, and we shall never have any great novel from the South until our writers shake off this Old Man of the Sea, and free themselves from the imaginary pressure under which they labor.

Owen Wister's delineation of life in Charleston as given in "Lady Baltimore" made a delightful impression on father. He said of it: —

This book is beautifully done, but there is something

about it besides its literary art, something quite as charming that cannot be adequately described, something that is akin to motherliness in the attitude of the author, something that is tender and gentle and delicate. . . . How easy it would be for this Northern-Western-Southern author to write the long-delayed American novel!

And there must always be something in a book "besides its literary art" to recommend it to the creator of "Sister Jane," "Aunt Minervy Ann," and "Billy Sanders." Its people must be "real folks" with sincere intentions. For instance: Through the medium of "Anne Macfarland" "The Farmer" expressed his wholesome contempt for the people of "The House of Mirth" and "A Fighting Chance." He quite relentlessly dubbed them "buzzards," and "buzzards" they certainly are. Always an admirer of Mrs. Wharton's technique, father wrote: —

I cannot but deplore the fact that an art so fine and so sure of itself should have been devoted to the exposition of the people whose characters are set forth in its pages. For who and what are they? And what part do they play in the general scheme of life? To answer is to laugh or weep, according to the measure of your humor or your sensibility. . . . I hear that the book has been a great success. This fact is owing as much to the attitude of Mrs. Wharton as to the consummate art she brings to the performance. She presides over the destinies of the Buzzards she has chosen to depict with the grim impartiality of fate itself. She is not moved by pity, nor scorn, nor contempt, nor does she smile when some particular Buzzard performs some specially amusing trick. The thing is finely done, beautifully done, but the question will arise in the mind of a person who has passed middle age, where was the necessity of doing it at all? We cannot become interested in the Buzzards; although we are very much interested by the fine and moving art which opens the pen and turns them loose upon the reading public.

He turns from "The House of Mirth" to Miss Wilkins's "By the Light of the Soul," and it is easy to perceive he does so with a sigh of relief. Here are "real folks" once more, and he says of Maria Edgham: —

She walks by the light of her soul, and suffers, and is happier for the suffering, as other people would be if their souls held any fire. I read some time ago, in one of your American magazines, a notice of this book that was as illuminating to me as the book itself. One of the many young women who make it their business to chatter in the magazines, declared that Maria Edgham, in leaving her beloved sister happy with the man who had been Maria's lover, and in going away, and changing her name, had lost her identity: and this seemed to be a terrible thing to the chatterer, who no more understood the purport of the book than she understands the Syriac tongue. Does a name constitute identity? If so, you have only to paint it on a dead wall, after the manner of Popham's Pills, and there you are! Identity is a much larger and more important thing than a name; it is character and conduct; it is the soul and its poor frame-work of flesh; and Maria Edgham never more completely identifies herself than when she makes her great renunciation and flings her name to the winds.

Critics have compared the uncompromising qualities of "Sister Jane" with some of Miss Wilkins's heroines, but I fancy that the grim reality of life in small, remote towns everywhere breeds this type, and it is no more indigenous to Maine than to Georgia. "Sister Jane's" creator intimates this when he says of E. W. Howe's book, "The Story of a Country Town": —

Those who are searching for American types will find them in Mr. Howe's book, where they are set forth with conscientious grimness. In the book there is no hesitation displayed when human nature is to be uncovered; consequently the impression the book makes as a whole is vivid and lasting. . . . No matter what phase of American life the novelist may choose to depict, he cannot fail to reproduce the American type if he but faithfully portray the human nature that underlies all types of life; the human nature that makes Mrs. Poyser as common to Georgia as to New England, to Maine as to Kansas.

Let not the reader think, however, that he who so insisted on the important part which character as well as characterization should play in fiction, was deaf to the subtle music of style. Of Laurence Sterne he wrote: —

ANNE MACFARLAND

"The Sentimental Journey" stands bravely by the works of the author of "Vanity Fair," and once a year, or oftener, the "Journey" is taken from its place and re-read for the fiftieth time — not for the matter in it, for that is slim enough, but for the nimbleness of the diction, and for the wonderful atmosphere that Sterne wraps about his writings; and for the skill with which he can write about nothing. So far as I have observed, Laurence Sterne is the only writer in our tongue who has shown that English can be handled with the extreme lightness and nimbleness which the best French writers bring to the use of their own flexible and fluent language.

Again, it is very interesting to read what father wrote of the style of Henry James. "Anne Macfarland" says regarding an attack upon the distinguished author of "The Golden Bowl": —

The American critics will finally have to take account of Mr. James, and they will be compelled to change their attitude. His diction is painful to me, but is that any reason why I should not enjoy his books? I say *diction*, where another would say *style*, for the reason that it does not represent Mr. James when he wrote that fine book "The Portrait of a Lady." One's style may improve, but it is almost impossible to change it; it stands for the person; but diction is quite another matter. The same writer may employ different kinds of diction, as in the case of Robert Louis Stevenson; but Mr. James has gradually changed his until now it is what we see it. He has become so habituated to its use that it is his style, in a sense. It suits his method of analysis, his descriptions of emotions, and his explorations of the mind, and it is impossible to deny that it is strangely subtle in the wonderful light it throws on the characters that Mr. James chooses to depict.

Of father's admiration for the writings of Cardinal Newman I have already spoken. In this case it was both the content and the form of the work which fascinated and moved him. Probably the most powerful single influence that swayed his later years was the subtle thought and the measured music of the great prelate's "Apologia."

CHAPTER XXX

THE "COUNTRY NEXT DOOR TO THE WORLD"

I HAVE mentioned the long and severe illness which kept father in bed for weeks during the spring of 1902 — a general septic condition resulting from an infected tooth. After this attack, he never seemed quite so robust as he had been before; not that he was invalided or that the routine of his daily life was seriously interrupted, but he seemed to have lost something of his physical resiliency and was more easily upset and fatigued than he had ever been before. At intervals during the year preceding his death he had periods of depression when he fancied that his best days were over and that his power as a writer was on the wane. This was so unlike him, so out of keeping with his outlook and his lifelong habit of optimism, that it puzzled and later distressed us. We could not know then that these moods were the reflexes of a physical condition which was slow to give more obvious symptoms. Had it been possible to look into the future, Julian would surely have hesitated to encourage his father to enter upon the magazine venture, for naturally it was an enterprise that

[577]

carried with it a large amount of responsibility and anxiety for all concerned. Father shrank from any responsibility connected with business affairs; he once said: "If the greatest position on the round earth were offered to me, I would n't take it. The responsibility would kill me in two weeks."

Julian was not aware of the full extent of the strain under which father had been laboring during the first year of the Magazine until after its consolidation with the "Home Magazine" in April, 1908. It seemed at that time that financial success was assured it, and so its editor allowed himself to relax, and for the first time it became apparent that the unwonted responsibility had not been good for him. Of course, all troublesome details of the business and the mechanical end of the affair had been kept from him as much as possible, for Julian was determined that his father's resistance should not be strained by any unnecessary demands upon it, but he had not calculated upon that intuitive and sensitive temperament which was so delicately balanced that it responded almost instantly to whatever was in the air.

Toward the last of May, 1908, mother began to notice that the "Farmer" was not as energetic as formerly in his old out-of-door interest. The vegetable garden and flower beds did not tempt him out into the open as often as usual, and he frequently sought the couch in the living-room for an hour's rest — something quite out of his ordinary habit, for he had never allowed himself anything more than a half-hour's nap in his chair after midday dinner. Mother felt anxious, and suggested that he see the doctor; but father could not bear to be "fussed over," and replied with a little irritability that when he felt the need of a doctor he would have him come.

About four weeks before his death his listlessness became very noticeable, and he discontinued his daily visits to the post-office. Then, in accordance with Julian's advice, mother called on the family physician and asked him to drop by the house in casual fashion and look father over. This would be a natural enough proceeding, since Dr. W. A. Crowe was an old friend and neighbor and frequently called on father as he was passing by. So late one afternoon Dr. Crowe stopped for a chat, asked father a few questions about himself, and ordered him to bed. Father unwillingly submitted to a thorough examination, and it was found that his trouble was cirrhosis of the liver, and already there was a sufficient accumulation of dropsical fluid in the tissues to make an operation advisable.

But father made light of the doctor's advice,

objected firmly to being kept in bed, and would not permit a consultation until two weeks later. Finally the pleas of the family, together with his own discomfort, led him to consent that two specialists be called in. The result was that an operation to relieve the dropsical condition was undertaken, and the outlook appeared more hopeful. At least, it was said that if conditions were favorable and there was no return of the fluid the patient might live six months or a year. The doctors, at mother's request, spoke quite frankly to father of his condition.

All this was a terrible shock to us; never had we thought of father in connection with death. He was not yet sixty years old; his spirit was so youthful, his interests so alert, his nature — except on the rarest occasions — so suggestive of the buoyancy and brightness of life's prime: it was as if a dark cloud had suddenly eclipsed the sunlight of a summer's day, shrouding the blue heaven in somber black.

Ten years previous to this time, father had sought and received instruction from Father James M. O'Brien, at that time in charge of the Catholic Church in Washington, Georgia, but Father O'Brien died before he had the happiness of receiving his old friend into the Church. In a letter to father from Sister Sacred Heart, of St. Joseph's Academy at Washington, this reference occurs: "Dear Father O'Brien! We miss him more and more. If he remembers his friends, which we believe he does more prayerfully than on earth, he is still interceding for you; 'the one thing necessary,' he thought was coming to you through him."

One day about two weeks before father's death, in passing from the patient's room to the sitting-room, mother saw her pastor, Father O. N. Jackson, coming up the front walk. She turned back to the sick-room and asked father if he felt equal to seeing Father Jackson, of whom he was very fond. He replied that he did, and suggested that he be left alone with the priest when he entered. After a short stay in father's room, Father Jackson joined mother on the porch and told her that he had been asked by father to baptize him. Mother, of course, was very happy, as she had long looked forward to the time when father would be willing to avow his acceptance of the Catholic faith.

When she returned to his room, he asked, "Did Father Jackson tell you of my request?"

"Yes," said she.

"And what did *you* say?" he continued.

"I told him how happy I was," she replied; and father seemed to feel well content in her happiness.

JOEL CHANDLER HARRIS

Of his baptism, Father Jackson says: —

"When Mr. Harris asked for baptism during the last interview I had with him about this matter, he said to me, 'I want all my family here, and want it to be known that I am doing this with my own free will, fully realizing that I have put it off too long already'; and as a matter of fact, when Mr. Harris was baptized he made his profession of faith in the presence of his family, and felt satisfied that he had done what God wanted him to do. Mr. Harris lingered some two weeks after his baptism, and I visited him daily; and always in some way he referred to his regret over not taking the step earlier, for fear, as he expressed it, that some might think that 'he did it because he was dying.'

"Previously, on many other occasions, we had talked on religious matters, and his mind was always in perfect accord with the teachings of the Catholic Church. Mr. Harris had never been baptized in any other church, hence he received this Sacrament absolutely, and would have made his first Holy Communion, had it not been for the nature of his sickness, which prevented him from receiving it.

"Shortly before his death, he said to me: 'I have put off this important matter too long, but procrastination has been the bugbear of my life; and

I feel that the Lord will make allowance for this weakness, for I have believed the teachings of the Catholic Church for many years. In fact, some years ago I had fully made up my mind to become a Catholic, but some event prevented my doing so.'

"Another time he said: 'The example of my wife and children has taught me more about the Church than anything else.' I asked him once whether fear of unintelligent comment had anything to do with his delay in coming into the Church. He replied, 'No; I should say shyness had more to do with it.'"

Of father's religious convictions, his friend Dr. J. W. Lee has written most truly and adequately:

"The religious lesson of Mr. Harris's life is difficult to formulate. His religion was expressed through every act and word of his life. It was like the sunlight, quiet, but managing to get itself embodied in every tree and flower and animal in the world. So Mr. Harris's religion found embodiment in all his writings, in all his relations in life. He would have been the last man to claim much for himself religiously, as he would have been the last man to claim much for himself artistically; but all who associated with him personally or through his writings knew that he was both an artist and a deeply religious man. He was a devoted follower of the Lord Jesus Christ. He told me not long ago that all the agnostics and materialists in creation could never shake his faith. But he would have felt about as awkward in proclaiming himself a pattern of piety as he would in proclaiming himself a pattern in literature.

"His religion pervaded his whole life, as health pervades a strong man's body. It was more of an atmosphere you felt than a distinct entity you could describe. His home was filled with it. You could never enter his door without a sense of a subtle, genial presence resting on everything about the home. Every child he had did seemingly as he pleased, but grew up to express, in orderly conduct and attention to duty, the sweet music of his father's house, to which he had adjusted himself almost unconsciously.

"Mr. Harris seemed to be regulated by no hard-and-fast rules, nor did he seem to bring those about him under the sway of hard-and-fast rules. His rules, whatever they were, were broken up, and diffused throughout his home; and this atmosphere he and his family breathed as the lungs take in the breath of the morning."

Of the matter of his belief in an overruling Providence, father himself wrote: "The Farmer knows that He who created life, which is the greatest mystery of all, is fully equal to the production of all other mysteries." And of the matter of his belief in humanity: "I believe in all good men and women. I would not want to live if I had no faith in my fellow men."

Touching on the belief in "things unseen," his last Christmas editorial contains the following: "The Farmer wishes for old and young the merriest Christmas and the happiest New Year the world has ever seen. He hopes the materialist may never be able to destroy in the minds of children the budding faith in things unseen, the kindling belief in things beyond their knowledge; he hopes that Santa Claus will come to them while they sleep, and that real fairies will dance in their innocent dreams."

During the last ten days of father's life countless messages were received from friends, conveying expressions of their affection and anxiety. By all of these he was sincerely touched, and seemed surprised that his condition should be a cause of so much regret and solicitude. His thoughts dwelt much on the fate of the Magazine in case of his death, and in regard to this feeling I give a portion of a letter written a few days before the end, by Julian, to father's warm friend, Colonel Roosevelt, then president: —

[585]

JOEL CHANDLER HARRIS

"Your letter, betraying the same generous interest you have always shown in everything which concerns my father, came yesterday. It is with the keenest sorrow that I write there is little hope that he will ever get well. In fact, it does not seem likely that he will live for many days; even when this reaches you he may be no more; or, as he once said: 'Do not say, when a man dies, that he is no more, but rather that *he is forever*.'

"It is in that spirit he has commented on his own illness. His first worry has been for the Magazine, and his only regret — save the breaking of home ties — is the possibility of the South losing what seems its first real opportunity to obtain recognition through a medium unbiased and broad enough to reflect a National sentiment, and to serve this section well by being honest enough to be severe when occasion requires, and interested enough to point out the way in a kindly fashion.

"'The Magazine must succeed,' he said a few weeks ago — just before he was confined to his bed. 'If this illness takes me off, and they try to start any monument business, don't let them do it. A statue will stand out in the rain and the cold, or, dust-covered, useless and disfiguring, will soon be forgotten except by the sparrows in nesting-time. If what little I have done is found worthy of commendation, tell the people of the South to let the Magazine succeed — to stand back of it with their subscriptions. And if it is not too much trouble to Mr. Pritchard' (foreman of the Magazine composing-room) 'run a little line somewhere — "Founded by Joel Chandler Harris."'

"Then he spoke at length about his ideas and ideals for the Magazine, and what it should stand for, and how it should be conducted; that it should be kept clean, wholesome, and unprejudiced, and filled with a spirit of friendliness toward all sections. Frequently he mentioned you, and how much your kindliness toward him had helped him and the Magazine. All this was some weeks ago, when we had no thought of a fatal outcome to his illness, but he seemed to possess a prescience that penetrated where we others were groping.

"Yesterday evening he seemed a little brighter, and I told him of your latest letter. 'Read it to me,' he said. It was necessary to read it twice. He did not open his eyes, but he smiled, if feebly, saying: 'Tell the President he has been very kind.'"

The complication which had been feared — uræmic poisoning — had set in, and nothing further could be done to improve the patient's condition. The family were prepared for the end which came peacefully and painlessly at sunset on Friday, July 3, 1908. Just before he sank into unconsciousness, he had been asked by Julian how he felt, and he had replied, with a glint of the old twinkle in his eye, "I am about the extent of a tenth of a gnat's eyebrow better." He had once said, "Humor is an excellent thing to live by, and all things being equal, an excellent thing to die by."

The funeral services were held on Sunday afternoon, the 5th of July, at the chapel of St. Anthony. It had been planned by the children of Atlanta that they would gather in the park in front of the old Howell mansion in West End and scatter flowers before the cortège as it passed this point on its way to Westview Cemetery, but a summer storm with heavy rain came up just before the hour appointed for the services, and the little ones could not pay their last tribute to their dear "Uncle Remus." All through the services the storm persisted, but just at the end, the clouds parted and a pale ray of sunshine crept in through the chapel windows and rested for a few moments on the bier.

On the green slopes of Westview, near his children and his mother, a grave was made for him, and there he lies, within sound of the sighing of the pine woods and of the songs of the little birds that

THE GRAVE OF JOEL CHANDLER HARRIS

Westview Cemetery, Atlanta

people it. A boulder of Georgia granite marks his grave and on it are recorded those lovely words from the dedication of the Frost edition of the "Uncle Remus" tales, a token of the affection offered years before by the writer to the artist who pictured "Brer Rabbit" and "Brer Fox": —

> I seem to see before me the smiling faces of thousands of children — some young and fresh and some wearing the friendly marks of age, but all children at heart — and not an unfriendly face among them. And while I am trying hard to speak the right word, I seem to hear a voice lifted above the rest, saying: "You have made some of us happy." And so I feel my heart fluttering and my lips trembling and I have to bow silently, and turn away and hurry into the obscurity that fits me best.

AFTERWORD

It would be neither practicable nor desirable to attempt to reproduce here the many beautiful tributes which father's death called forth from friends and fellow-workers in this country and in Europe. If I have in any measure succeeded in presenting a picture of the shyest and most genuinely humble of men, one who did so little to put himself and his doings before the critical eyes of this world, then my readers have divined already that he was very dearly loved and with abundant reason. Claiming nothing, he gained everything; believing himself unworthy, he unconsciously drew to himself a thousand subtle currents of tenderness and regard.

Most of the old friends are gone, — those colleagues of Savannah days, and early Atlanta days, — gifted, buoyant souls who worked and played together, and whose toil and jollity did much to render the name of Georgia honored and beloved. Of this circle of writers who were dear to father, two of the younger members are left; one of them, Mrs. Corra Harris, received from him her first encouragement in literary undertaking. When she

[590]

began to express herself he saw in her work both originality and energy, and he advised her to go on. From time to time they corresponded, and recalling this, I applied to her for letters, and asked her to tell me something of her friendship with father. In reply she wrote: —

DEAR MRS. HARRIS: —

I am so sorry not to be able to send you the letters which I received often from Mr. Joel Chandler Harris during the last years of his life. I kept them carefully among my dearest treasures. But during the year 1910, I was ill, in a hospital away from home. When I returned and was able to look after things, I discovered that Mr. Harris's letters and my father's sword had been taken from the old chest where I kept these and other dear things.

According to the wish expressed in your letter, I have set down some thoughts of your father. They are unworthy of his great fame, but I shall be honored if you find a place for them in the book you are preparing. If I ever had an idol in the literary world, it was Joel Chandler Harris. I have been able always to think of him as "present," very near and kin and kind to me and all grown-up children.

Joel Chandler Harris identified himself so perfectly with the illusive fancies of all children, and of the child in all men and women, that his spirit lives as if he were still with us in the flesh. He is not a memory, but a presence on the earth. It is not often that a man achieves so gentle and loving an immortality in this world even if he becomes a saint in the next one.

His fame was very great, surpassing in my humble opinion that of any other man of letters we have produced in this country. To him belongs the peculiar distinction, not merely of having recorded the folk-lore of the negro race, which is a shy and secret race, but he has interpreted this lore, made it a part of innocent, fanciful life of man, the child.

But from the standpoint of an author, one of the greatest and most wonderful things he ever did was to create the character of Miss Meadows and the gals. You cannot think of them as separate. You do not question their existence nor their natural relation to Brer Fox and Brer Rabbit, who used to ride up and hitch their horses when they went to see Miss Meadows and the gals. You cannot visualize them, yet you never doubt them. I think this is the subtlest, most whimsical creation ever accomplished out of the imagination. There is nothing like it anywhere else in the literature of the world.

AFTERWORD

Do you remember Charles Dickens's last words? "Keep my grave green!" Well, we have done that. We do not forget Dickens, but the grave of Joel Chandler Harris will keep itself green. There is a special dew box somewhere between the younger stars kept for just that narrow place where the lover of all little children sleeps. There are only a few such graves in this world, and I can think of them as green when the whole earth changes back to dead dust. The hearts which lie beneath these coverlids of the Lord never die, nor grow cold. They are chalices filled with starlight and stories that children love, and all the tenderness of life, buried deep that they may keep forever in the memories of men.

I am so grateful to you for allowing me the privilege of offering my poor wreath in honor of Mr. Harris. If words grew in gardens, I should have taken the fairest for him, little blossoming words that grow deep in the shade of his trees, in the meadows where his fancies spread like webs in the sun.

Faithfully yours

CORRA HARRIS

RYDAL, GEORGIA
"IN THE VALLEY"
July 1st, 1917

JOEL CHANDLER HARRIS

Frank L. Stanton, the poet, for so many years a colleague of father's on the "Atlanta Constitution," is the other friend whose tribute I wish to include here. It may be remembered that it was he, Burns, and Riley, whom father named as the three writers of dialect poetry who would be remembered "to-morrow."

Mr. Stanton's acquaintance with "Uncle Remus" extended back into the Savannah days, for at that time he was office boy to the rising young editor. During the long period when they met daily at the office of the "Constitution," and lived as neighbors in West End, Mr. Stanton grew to appreciate the sweetness of father's nature and the fineness of his gifts as only a man of poetic sensibilities could.

In the following poem, which appeared in the "Constitution" immediately after father's death, the sorrow of a loving friend is transmuted into sweet music: —

JOEL CHANDLER HARRIS

By Frank L. Stanton

Summer is in the world, sweet-singing,
And blossoms breathe in every clod;
The lowly vales with music ringing,
High-answered from the hills of God.

Yet hills, to dream-deep vales replying,
Sing not as if one flower could die:

[594]

AFTERWORD

He would not have the Summer sighing
  Who never gave the world a sigh!

Who heard the world's heart beat, and listened
  Where God spake in a drop of dew;
And if his eyes with tear-drops glistened
  The world he loved so never knew.

Its grief was his — each shadow falling,
  That on a blossom left its blight;
But when he heard the Darkness calling
  He knew that Darkness dreamed of Light.

And that God's love each life inspires —
  Love in the humblest breast impearled;
He made the lowly cabin-fires
  Light the far windows of the world!

He dreamed the dreams of Childhood, giving
  Joy to it to the wide world's end;
For in the Man the Child was living,
  And little children called him Friend.

  .   .   .   .
Wherever song is loved, and story
  Cheers the world's firesides, there he dwells —
A guest regardless of earth's glory,
  To whom Time waves no sad farewells.

From Life to Life he passed; God's pages
  Shine with his name, immortal-bright;
One with the starred and echoing ages,
  A brother to Eternal Light.

THE END

APPENDIX

THE WINNING OF THE WREN'S NEST

An account of the activities of the "Uncle Remus Memorial Association," as given in the memorial booklet prepared for the Association by Mrs. Myrta Lockett Avery

THE movement for a memorial to Joel Chandler Harris came as naturally as a flower might upspring from a grave, and while yet he lay at rest in his home, with the birds he loved singing unconscious requiem in his trees.

With the announcement, on July 4, of his passing away, the press voiced public feeling in calling for a monument to him. As is usual in the history of memorials, there was divergence of opinion as to the form the monument should take. A statue; an Uncle Remus park; a drinking-fountain; a bronze tablet; and the purchase and preservation of his home, were among suggestions as to its form.

At a meeting, called by the Mayor, July 10, in the City Council Chamber, the Uncle Remus Memorial Association was organized; a committee, appointed to decide on the form of memorial reported, at a memorial meeting in the Grand Opera House, July 19, in favor of the home; thirty thousand dollars, it was estimated, would cover purchase and equipment. A statue in a public place, the more conventional type, might have been chosen but for Mr. Harris's own protest as often expressed to wife and friends: "Don't erect any statue of marble or bronze to me to stand out in the rain and cold and dust." It was remembered how he had loved his home; how characteristic of him it was, the house built according to his own ideas; the grounds eloquent of his ramblings, and his tending. The committee's decision was generally approved, yet there lingered, as is usual, some division of opinion.

The gentlemen of the committee, who were burdened with

[597]

personal business responsibilities, presently found that they could not give the movement the attention it required, and welcomed the formation of the Ladies' Auxiliary in February, 1909; in October, they decided to retire as an organization, the ladies succeeding to the title and office of the Uncle Remus Memorial Association, and themselves appearing as Advisory Board. Colonel Frederic J. Paxon, chairman of this board, has been unfailing friend and counselor to the ladies; they feel that the successful issue of the movement is largely due to his readiness to give them his time, his advice, and his aid.

The official board of the Association, as existing, is nearly the same as of the Auxiliary when formed, with Mrs. A. McD. Wilson for president. The ladies, from the first, limited operations to what they could do themselves, without one paid officer on their board. They made no active canvass for funds. The idea was that as many loved "Uncle Remus," many might have a share in his memorial with special opportunity for small aids from children.

Assistance has been welcomed and utilized in whatever form it came. A gift of Greek coins from a friend in Illinois; five dollars from a woman's club with request for violet roots from the home; a tiny sum from a children's Sunshine Society in Florida; an offering from the Children of the Confederacy in Marietta; a modest check from Matthew Page Andrews, President of the Randall Literary Memorial Society; another from the Southern Club of Smith College — first Southern body in a Northern institution to remember their cause; one from Bessie Tift College in Forsyth where part of Mr. Harris's early struggles were made — these helped by the sympathy and interest thus evinced in the formative period of their undertaking.

Coöperation from schools and colleges has been, and is, highly valued. Miss Hanna's School, Atlanta, was first to render aid. Next came schools and kindergartens in Ohio, Illinois, Carolina, Alabama, and in Athens, Albany, and Covington, Georgia. Kentucky's children rank next to

APPENDIX

Georgia's in interest shown. Mrs. Frank L. Woodruff, the Association's Field Secretary in that State, has sent several contributions from "Uncle Remus's Circles" in Louisville and Lexington; once one hundred dollars given in pennies. Among Atlanta institutions, the Boys', and Girls' High Schools, Marist College, "Tech" Boys' High School, Miss Woodberry's School, and Washington Seminary have lent a ready hand.

The ladies gave several entertainments and essayed various feminine devices in the interest of the fund, all tending to social pleasure and good feeling. They felt that cheerfulness and sweetness of spirit must pervade all they did for a memorial to "Uncle Remus." The teas in the Governor's Mansion, by courtesy of the Governor's wife, Mrs. Joseph M. Brown, merit more than passing note. Much more than passing mention must be made of the May Festival at the Wren's Nest, inaugurated by Mrs. Brevard Montgomery, which has passed into an annual custom, having been observed every May since Mr. Harris died. Its growing beauty and popularity are a reward to the many ladies whose diligent labors go to making it the pretty pageant it is. Besides the chief reason — its memorial interest — for continuing the custom, there is another. Small admission fees and sales of simple refreshments and souvenirs supply revenue toward the support of the home.

"Uncle Remus Day" was inaugurated by the ladies in 1910, when through their efforts, seconded by Professor W. M. Slaton, Atlanta's Superintendent of Public Schools, the schools of the city held an "Uncle Remus" hour of song and story, December 9, Mr. Harris's birthday. Another year the interest was enlisted of the State Commissioner of Public Schools, Professor M. L. Brittain. In 1912, observance extended throughout Georgia and to other States; to colleges, women's and children's clubs, and public libraries.

The most important help the work ever received came in 1910 from Theodore Roosevelt. Mrs. Wilson, basing request on his known friendship for "Uncle Remus," asked him to

APPENDIX

lecture in Atlanta for the memorial fund. His acceptance and the lecture that followed, October 8, turned the balance of fate and public opinion in favor of the home's preservation, not only because of the money it brought, nearly five thousand dollars, but by this seal of approval from the "world's foremost citizen" as universally acclaimed. Andrew Carnegie duplicated the proceeds of this lecture. The largest single contribution has been five thousand dollars from the Harris family. Recital of these large gifts by no means minimizes smaller ones. The penny of a child he loved would be precious to "Uncle Remus." The smallest aid to the movement commands the respect of the Association; particularly when it comes from a measure which is, in itself, a memorial, as from "Uncle Remus Circles," "Uncle Remus Parties," and "Readings from Uncle Remus."

The formal transference of the Wren's Nest to the Association by deed occurred January 18, 1913, in "Uncle Remus's" favorite room. After this ceremony, Lucien Harris presented Mrs. Wilson with a loving-cup inscribed: "To Mrs. A. McD. Wilson in appreciation of her efforts in behalf of the Uncle Remus Memorial — Essie LaRose Harris, Julian Harris, Lucien Harris, Evelyn Harris, Mrs. Fritz Wagener, Mrs. Edwin Camp, Joel Chandler Harris," — a testimonial which the Association was happy to see bestowed upon its leader by those who loved "Uncle Remus" best.

"This has been my home for a long time," Mrs. Harris said of the transfer, "and I hate to give it up, but I feel that this is for the best. If it passed into private hands, it might suffer change. Now, I know that our home will be kept as he left it and as he loved it. I know that you will cherish every tree, flower, and shrub that he spoke of and loved, as I have cherished them. You will let the wild things feel at home here as he did and as I have done. It would please him, if he could know, that little children will always play about the place."

His bedroom and living-room are to be kept as he left them. His widow donates the furnishings, among which are his favorite chair, writing-table, inkstand, pen, and many relics

[600]

APPENDIX

besides. Other rooms will be used for a public library, a branch of the Carnegie, already established; a free kindergarten, it is hoped; and similar public utilities as they may be developed, all in keeping with the memorial sentiment. Mrs. Harris has given for the library a number of books which belonged to her husband. A valuable collection of author's autographed copies and of autographed photographs has been secured for it by Mrs. Lollie Bell Wylie. A feature of Mrs. Wylie's collection is the bronze medallion portrait of Mr. Harris by the sculptor, Roger Noble Burnham, a contribution from members of the Boston Folklore Society and Authors' Club. "Brer Rabbit," drawn by A. B. Frost, Mr. Harris's friend and illustrator, is a recent gift from the artist, made through Miss Katherine Wootten.

The grounds are to be equipped as playgrounds for children and as a resort for the innocent recreation and happiness of youth in general. The Association plans to add "Snap-Bean Farm" to present holdings, both because they regard it as an essential part of the memorial and because of its availability for playground purposes. The preservation of a great man's home, where he made wife and children happy for nearly thirty years, is an object lesson in the moralities and of very wholesome significance in many ways. It is a monument not to genius only, but to the domestic virtues, a guarantee of the world's respect for faithful married love and the hearthstones of the world.

BIBLIOGRAPHY OF
JOEL CHANDLER HARRIS

As compiled by Katherine H. Wootten
Atlanta, September, 1907
Revised and brought up to Date by Julia C. Harris

BIOGRAPHY

Adair, Forrest. Joel Chandler Harris. (See *American Illustrated Methodist Magazine*, 11: 124, Oct., 1899.)

Interesting article from a personal acquaintance.

Baker, R. S. Joel Chandler Harris, with portrait. (See *Outlook*, 78: 594, Nov. 5, 1904.)

Good biographical sketch.

Baskervill, W. M. Life of Uncle Remus. Nashville, Tenn.: Barbee Pub. Co.

Baskervill, W. M. Joel Chandler Harris. (See his *Southern Writers*, pp. 41–88. Nashville: Barbee & Smith, 1899.)

This article also appeared in *Southern Writers*, edited by Baskervill, July, 1896, pp. 1–48.

Brainerd, Erastus. Joel Chandler Harris at Home. (See Gilder, J. L., *Authors at Home*, pp. 111–24. New York: Wessels, 1902.)

Same article appeared in the *Critic*, 6: 229, 241.

Davidson, J. W. Joel Chandler Harris. (See his *Living Writers of the South*, p. 236. New York: Carleton.)

Derby, J. C. Joel Chandler Harris. (See his *Fifty Years Among Authors*, p. 433. New York: Dillingham, n. d.)

Garnsey, J. H. Joel Chandler Harris, a character sketch, with portrait. (See *Bookbuyer*, 13: 65.)

Halsey, F. W. Joel Chandler Harris. (See his *Authors of Our Day in their Homes*, p. 157. Pott, 1902.)

These papers were printed originally in the *New York Times Saturday Review*.

BIBLIOGRAPHY

Harris, Joel Chandler. Literary Autobiography of J. C. Harris. (See *Lippincott*, 37: 417.)

Holliday, Carl. Joel Chandler Harris. (See his *History of Southern Literature*, p. 380. Neale, 1906.)

Horton, Mrs. Thaddeus. The Most Modest Author in America. (See *Ladies' Home Journal*, May, 1907, p. 17.)

This article also appeared in the *Atlanta Constitution*, May 5, 1907.

Joel Chandler Harris. (See *National Cyclopædia of American Biography*, v. 1: 410. White, 1898.)

Knight, L. L. Uncle Remus. (See "Men and Women of the Craft," *Bohemian Magazine*, Easter, 1901. Fort Worth, Texas.)

Knight, L. L. Uncle Remus. (See his *Reminiscences of Famous Georgians*, p. 482. Atlanta: Franklin, 1907.)

Lee, Dr. James W., Memorial Volume, illustrated with photographs. Privately printed, and a limited number distributed by the author, Christmas, 1908.

Lewis, Fred. Some Incidents and Characteristics of Uncle Remus. (See *Atlanta Constitution*, Oct. 7, 1906, p. 3.)

A most interesting collection of anecdotes.

Reed, W. P. Joel Chandler Harris, Humorist and Novelist, with portrait. (See *Literature*, a weekly illustrated magazine, pub. by Alden, Oct. 27, 1888.)

Trent, W. P. Joel Chandler Harris. (See his *Southern Writers*, p. 423. New York: The Macmillan Co., 1905.)

Warner, C. D., ed. Joel Chandler Harris. (See *Library of the World's Best Literature*, 12: 6961.)

Watterson, Henry. Joel Chandler Harris. (See his *Oddities in Southern Life and Character*, p. 304. Boston: Houghton, Mifflin & Co., 1882.)

Books

Aaron in the Wildwoods. Illustrated by Oliver Herford. Boston: Houghton, Mifflin & Co., 1897.

Reviews. *Dial*, 23: 344; *Academy*, 52: 480; *Literary World*, 29: 62; *Athenæum*, 2: 252.

Balaam and his Master, and Other Sketches and Stories. Boston: Houghton, Mifflin & Co., 1891.

The Bishop and the Boogerman. Illustrated by Charlotte Harding. New York: Doubleday, Page & Co., 1909.

BIBLIOGRAPHY

Chronicles of Aunt Minerva Ann. Illustrated by A. B. Frost. New York: Charles Scribner's Sons, 1899.

Review. *Bookbuyer*, 19: 290.

Daddy Jake the Runaway, and Short Stories told after Dark. Illustrated by E. W. Kemble. New York: Century Company, 1889.

Free Joe, and Other Georgian Sketches. New York: Charles Scribner's Sons, 1887.

Gabriel Tolliver, a Story of Reconstruction. New York: McClure, Phillips & Co., 1902.

Reviews. *Dial*, 34: 243; *Nation*, 75: 467; *Bookbuyer*, 25: 623; *Critic*, n.s., 41: 581.

Little Mr. Thimblefinger and his Queer Country; What the Children saw and heard there. Illustrated by Oliver Herford. Boston: Houghton, Mifflin & Co., 1894.

For sequel see *Mr. Rabbit at Home*.

Little Union Scout. Illustrated by George Gibbs: a Tale of Tennessee during the Civil War. New York: McClure, Phillips & Co., 1904.

Making of a Statesman, and Other Stories. New York: McClure, Phillips & Co., 1902.

Reviews. *Dial*, 32: 389; *Nation*, 74: 471.

Mingo, and Other Sketches in Black and White. Boston: James R. Osgood & Co., 1884.

Review. *Nation*, 39: 115.

Mr. Rabbit at Home (a sequel to Little Mr. Thimblefinger). Illustrated by Oliver Herford. Boston: Houghton, Mifflin & Co., 1895.

Nights with Uncle Remus: Myths and Legends of the Old Plantation. Illustrated by F. S. Church. Boston: James R. Osgood & Co., 1883.

Review. *Nation*, 37: 422.

On the Plantation; a Story of a Georgia Boy's Adventures during the War. Illustrated by E. W. Kemble. New York: D. Appleton & Co., 1892.

Biographical of Mr. Harris.
Review. *Dial*, 13: 46.

On the Wing of Occasions; Being the Authorized Version of Certain Curious Episodes of the Late Civil War, including the Hitherto

BIBLIOGRAPHY

Suppressed Narrative of the Kidnapping of President Lincoln. New York: Doubleday, Page & Co., 1900.

Also published under the title of *The Kidnapping of President Lincoln.*

Plantation Pageants. Illustrated by E. Boyd Smith. Boston: Houghton, Mifflin & Co., 1899.

Reviews. *Nation,* 69: 451; *Bookbuyer,* 19: 34; *Literary World,* 31: 54.

Shadow Between His Shoulder Blades. Boston: Small, Maynard & Co., 1909.

Sister Jane, Her Friends and Acquaintances; A Narrative of Certain Events and Episodes transcribed from the Papers of the Late William Wornum. Boston: Houghton, Mifflin & Co., 1896.

Stories of Georgia. Illustrated by A. I. Keller, Guy Rose, B. W. Clinedinst, and others. New York: American Book Co., 1896.

Story of Aaron (so named), the Son of Ben Ali, told by his Friends and Acquaintances. Illustrated by Oliver Herford. Boston: Houghton, Mifflin & Co., 1896.

Tales of the Home Folks in Peace and War. Boston: Houghton, Mifflin & Co., 1898.

Reviews. *Public Opinion,* 24: 537; *Outlook,* 58: 1078; *Nation,* 66: 407; *Bookman,* 7: 353; *Independent,* 50: 729; *Bookbuyer,* 17: 62; *Critic,* n.s., 30: 204.

Tar-Baby, and Other Rhymes of Uncle Remus. Illustrated by A. B. Frost and E. W. Kemble. New York: D. Appleton & Co., 1904.

With the exception of the Tar-Baby story and one other all the folk-lore stories herein embodied are new, having come into my hands from various sources during the past ten years. The Tar-Baby story has been thrown into a rhymed form for the purpose of presenting and preserving what seems to be the genuine version. (Author's note.)

Told by Uncle Remus; New Stories of the Old Plantation. Illustrated by A. B. Frost, J. M. Condé, and Frank Verbeck. New York: McClure, Phillips & Co., 1905.

Reviews. *Critic,* 47: 576; *Independent,* 59: 1385; *Dial,* 39: 444; *Nation,* 81: 407; *New York Times,* 10: 864; *Review of Reviews,* 32: 753.

Uncle Remus and Brer Rabbit. New York: Frederick A. Stokes, 1906.

Uncle Remus and his Friends: Old Plantation Stories, Songs and Ballads, with Sketches of Negro Character. Illustrated by A. B. Frost. Boston: Houghton, Mifflin & Co., 1892.

BIBLIOGRAPHY

Uncle Remus and the Little Boy. Boston: Small, Maynard & Co., 1910.

A collection of stories and rhymes appearing in *Uncle Remus's Magazine* during 1907 and 1908.

Uncle Remus, his Songs and his Sayings. Illustrated by F. S. Church and J. H. Moser. New York: D. Appleton & Co., 1880. Edition of 1906 illustrated by A. B. Frost.

Reviews. *Nation*, 31: 398; *Spectator*, 445; *Current Literature*, 29: 708.

Uncle Remus Returns. Boston: Houghton Mifflin Co., 1918.

A collection of stories and sketches appearing in the *Metropolitan Magazine*, 1905 and 1906, and the *Atlanta Constitution*.

Wally Wanderoon and his Story-Telling Machine. Illustrated by Karl Moseley. New York: McClure, Phillips & Co., 1903.

TRANSLATION

Evening Tales. Translated from the French of Frédéric Ortoli. New York: Charles Scribner's Sons, 1893.

BOOKS EDITED BY MR. HARRIS

Life of Henry W. Grady. A memorial volume compiled by Mr. Grady's co-workers on the *Atlanta Constitution*. Edited by J. C. Harris. New York: Cassell & Co., 1890.

Merrymaker. Edited by J. C. Harris. Boston: Hall, Locke & Co. (*Young Folks' Library*, vol. 2, 3d ed.)

Issued in 1901 under title *The Book of Fun and Frolic*.

World's Wit and Humor. Edited by J. C. Harris. New York: Doubleday, Page & Co., 1904.

EDITORIALS AND ESSAYS

Abolition of the Soul. *Saturday Evening Post*, Dec. 29, 1900.

Cheap Criticisms of Dear Beliefs. *Saturday Evening Post*, July 21, 1900.

Hornet with Stimulating Sting. *Saturday Evening Post*, Oct. 13, 1900.

Haeckel's Unguessed Riddle. *Saturday Evening Post*, May 18, 1901.

Negro, the Old-Time. *Saturday Evening Post*, Jan. 2, 1904.

Negro of To-day. *Saturday Evening Post*, Jan. 30, 1904.

BIBLIOGRAPHY

Negro Problem. *Saturday Evening Post*, Feb. 27, 1904.

On the Newspaper Habit. *Saturday Evening Post*, Aug. 4, 1900.

Progress and the Performing Bear. *Saturday Evening Post*, March 11, 1905.

Poor Man's Chance. *Saturday Evening Post*, July 7, 1900.

Prophets of Ruin and the People. *Saturday Evening Post*, Dec. 15, 1900.

Safeguard Our Business Interests. *Saturday Evening Post*, Dec. 3, 1900.

Sanders, Billy: —

His Views. *World's Work*, 1:82.

To A Boston Capitalist. *World's Work*, 1:196.

On the Democrats. *World's Work*, 1:431.

He Discourses on True Love. *Uncle Remus's Magazine*, p. 16, April, 1907.

Some Suggestions. *Uncle Remus's Magazine*, p. 7, June, 1907.

He Discusses the Canal. *Uncle Remus's Magazine*, p. 7, July, 1907.

Some Political Reminiscences. *Uncle Remus's Magazine*, p. 22, Aug., 1907.

His Views of Problems and Remedies. *Uncle Remus's Magazine*, p. 22, Sept., 1907.

He Discusses a Few Belated Questions. *Uncle Remus's Magazine*, p. 22, Oct., 1907.

A Talk on Modern Business Methods. *Uncle Remus's Magazine*, p. 22, Oct., 1907.

He Organizes a New Legislature. *Uncle Remus's Magazine*, p. 22, Dec., 1907.

His Wishes, His Hopes, His Prophecies. *Uncle Remus's Magazine*, p. 20, Jan., 1908.

He Visits the White House. *Uncle Remus's Magazine*, p. 5, Feb., 1908.

He Discusses Lawson and the People. *Uncle Remus's Magazine*, p. 20, May, 1908.

He is Puzzled over the Political Situation. *Uncle Remus's Magazine*, p. 14, June, 1908.

Tyranny of Tender-Hearted Men. *Saturday Evening Post*, Oct. 13, 1900.

*

BIBLIOGRAPHY

Uncle Remus's Magazine:
Progress in the Best and Highest Sense, p. 7, Jan., 1907.
On Knowing Your Neighbors, p. 8, June, 1907.
The Old Letter Box, p. 8, July, 1907.
The Philosophy of Failure, p. 7, Aug., 1907.
Little Children of Snap-Bean Farm, p. 5, Sept., 1907.
Houses and Homes, p. 5, Oct., 1907.
Corn Bread and Dumplings, p. 5, Nov., 1907.
The Story of the Self-Educated Dog, p. 5, Jan., 1908.
Concerning Books and Critics, p. 15, Feb., 1908.
The Blue Jay in Vaudeville, p. 5, March, 1908.
Our Old Friend the Moon, p. 5, April, 1908.
In the Matter of Belief, p. 5, July, 1908.
Shakespeare of Modern Business, p. 5, Oct., 1908.
Santa Claus and the Fairies, p. 5, Dec., 1908.
A Melodious Mimic, p. 12, June, 1911.
The Old and the New South, p. 22, Jan., 1912.
Women of the South. *Southern Historical Society Papers*, 18: 277.

(N.B. It is obviously impossible to include in this list the editorials written for the *Atlanta Constitution* during a period of twenty-four years.)

INTRODUCTIONS

Field, Eugene. Complete Works. New York: Charles Scribner's Sons.
Frost, A. B. Drawings, with verses by Wallace Irwin. New York: Richard K. Fox, 1905.
Goulding, F. R. Young Marooners. New York: Dodd, Mead & Co.
Knight, L. L. Reminiscences of Famous Georgians. Atlanta: Franklin Co., 1907.
Russell, Irwin. Poems. New York: Century Co.
Stanton, F. L. Songs of a Day. Atlanta: Foot & Davies, 1893.
Stanton, F. L. Songs of The Soil. New York: D. Appleton & Co., 1894.
Weeden, Howard. Bandanna Ballads. New York: Doubleday, Page & Co., 1899.

POEMS

A Song In the Night. *Uncle Remus's Magazine*, June, 1912.
A Remembrance. *Uncle Remus's Magazine*, Aug., 1907.

BIBLIOGRAPHY

An Uncle Remus Song. *Uncle Remus's Magazine*, July, 1907.
Fashion of the Swamp. *Saturday Evening Post*, Jan. 7, 1905.
Juliette. *Saturday Evening Post*, April 21, 1900.
The East Wind. *Uncle Remus's Magazine*, Feb., 1912.

    (Collections of dialect verse will be found in *Uncle Remus, His Songs and Sayings, Uncle Remus and His Friends,* and *Uncle Remus and the Little Boy.*)

UNCOLLECTED STORIES

A Georgia Fox Hunt. *Uncle Remus's Magazine*, Oct., 1911.
Billy Boring and his Drum. *Saturday Evening Post*, Oct. 7, 1905.
Cousin Anne Crafton. *Ainslee's*, April, 1903.
Miss Irene. *Scribner's Magazine*, 27: 216.
Miss Little Sally. *Uncle Remus's Magazine*, Dec., 1907.
Mystery of the Red Fox. *Scribner's Magazine*, Sept., 1893.
Rosalie. *Century Magazine*, 62: 916.
Story of the Sea Islands Hurricane. *Scribner's Magazine*, Feb. and March, 1894.

INDEX

INDEX

Clemens, Samuel L. *See* Twain, Mark.

Comedy of War, The, 398, 399.

Commonplace, the, is the really great in literature, 183.

Conscript's Christmas, A, 270.

Countryman, The, first paper J. C. H. worked on, 23, 27–31, 38, 51, 52.

Crescent Monthly, the, New Orleans, 58, 59.

Crimm, Miss Matt, 181; letter to, 182.

Critic, the, J. C. H.'s work in, 167, 185, 208; biographical sketch in, 201 *n.,* 338.

Crowe, Dr. W. A., 579.

Culberson, Gus, 252.

Cuthbert, Aunt Betsy, 14, 15.

Daddy Jake, 230, 231.

Dana, Charles A., called *Uncle Remus* a great book, 153.

Daring Adventure, A, 328, 329.

Davidson, James Wood, 66; on the Uncle Remus dialect, 163.

Davidson, Kate, one of J. C. H.'s teachers, 15.

Davis, Edward S., killed in battle, 45.

Dennis, Harvey J., a famous fox-hunter, 15, 17–19; a letter from, 314, 315.

Depew, Chauncey, pays Julian a compliment, 256, 257.

Derby, J. C., representative of D. Appleton & Co., 146, 153.

Devereux, John, furnishes J. C. H. some up-country myths, 192.

Dickey, J. M., 426.

Diction, and style, 393–95.

Doubleday, Page & Co., publish *The Kidnapping of President Lincoln,* 430; invite J. C. H. to edit *Everybody's Magazine* and write exclusively for them, 433, 434.

Eatonton, Ga., 1–3, 9, 23; memorial library in, 441–44; people of, invite J. C. H. to visit the town, 459; honors J. C. H., 507.

Edwards, Harry Stilwell, letter from, 166.

Eitel, Edmund, 498 *n.*

End of Mr. Bear, The, 197, 198.

English sparrows, not birds, 481.

Estill, Col. J. H., proprietor Savannah *Morning News,* 93, 95, 108.

Evelyn, William, publisher of the *Crescent Monthly,* 59, 61.

Evening Tales, 315, 316.

Everybody's Magazine, J. C. H. invited to edit, 433.

Field, Eugene, plays a joke on J. C. H., 215, 216.

Fisher, Isaac, letter from, 505.

Flagler, Henry M., takes J. C. H. too literally, 255, 256.

Forrest, Gen. N. B., 484.

Forsyth, John, an editor with a purpose, 139.

Free Joe, and Other Georgian Sketches, 219–23, 228.

Free Silver campaign, 329–31.

Frères Maristes College, attended by Julian, 270.

Frost, A. B., illustrator of Uncle Remus, 152, 217, 218, 298, 331, 332; and of Aunt Minervy Ann, 401, 402.

Fruit cake, a confirmed toper, 376–78, 411, 412.

Fuller, Capt. W. A., anecdote of, 329.

Gabriel Tolliver, quoted, 433; published, 453–58, 466.

Garnsey, John Henderson, relations with J. C. H., 255 *n.,* 343–45.

Garrison, Wendell P., 315.

Gilder, Jeannette, 187.

Gilder, Richard Watson, editor of the *Century,* 190, 201, 218, 220, 223;

INDEX

131, 132; third son born, 133; leaves off drinking altogether, 137; death of youngest son, 137; fourth son born, 138; conducts "The Lounger" in the Sunday *Gazette*, 138; his view of the function of an editor, 139, 140; an accidental author, 142, 143, 145; origin of Uncle Remus, 142, 143, 146; the Tar-Baby, 145; his interest in folklore, 153–58, 161, 162, 268, 298, 399; never told Uncle Remus stories to his children, 159; method of gathering negro tales, 162, 163, 168, 193, 196, 197; appreciation of the tales, 163–67; meets Mark Twain and George W. Cable, 171, 172; his "immortal shyness," 172, 173; first daughter born, 173; buys the "Broomhead property," 173; the day's work, 175–77; described by Walter H. Page, 177, 178; exquisitely neat, 178; greatly interested in gardening, 179, 237, 240; considers writing a life of Thomas Jefferson, 186, 187; visits New York, 187–90; banqueted at the Tile Club, 189; steals away home, 190; visits Mark Twain, 192; second daughter born, 198; writes stories of Georgia life, 199–201; fifth son born, 205; enlarges the West End home, 206; goes to Lithia Springs for his health, 207; writes *Plantation Music and the Banjo*, 208, 209; plans a play with Richard Malcolm Johnston, 211, 212; declines money-making offers, 213, 214; victim of a joke by Eugene Field, 215, 216; takes a trip with A. B. Frost in search of "types," 217, 218; his interest in International Copyright, 231–34; the West End home, 235–54; another son and daughter born, 235; his opinion of house-cleaning, 242, 243, 389, 390; dodges one silver wedding and attends another, 243, 244; serves as "best man," 245 n.; enjoys the West End street car, 245–51; fond of practical jokes, 245–48, 354, 355; his conception of charity, 253, 254; takes a fishing trip to Florida, 255; relations with his sons, 255–91, 308; death of Linton, 273–79; death of his mother, 292, 293; writes account of Sea Island hurricanes, 309–13; his only book of translations, 315, 316; the Little Mr. Thimblefinger series, 318–27; espouses Free Silver on humanitarian grounds, 329; 330; on Kipling's peculiar gift, 332, 333; his first novel, 338–46; his conspicuous gifts, 339; the "other fellow" inside, 345, 346, 384–86; inclines toward Catholicism, 352; birth of first grandchild, 358; on the Spanish War, 391, 392; on style and diction, 393–95; on grammar, 395; appreciation of A. B. Frost as an artist, 401, 402; fond of writing dialect, 403; writes Introduction to *Bandanna Ballads*, 406 n.; writes a remarkable riddle, 413, 414; sits for a bust, 419; friendship with James Whitcomb Riley, 421–27; writes secret-service stories of the Civil War, 427–30; writes Billy Sanders articles, 432, 433, 515, 539; invited to edit *Everybody's Magazine*, 433; all his work sought by two publishing houses, 433, 434, 438; visits Lansingburgh, 436–38.

Retires from the *Constitution*, 438, 439; memorial library in Eatonton, 441–44; ill with grippe, 444, 445; writes a long story of the reconstruction period, 449, 451;

[614]

INDEX

enjoys Longfellow, 450, 451; ill with septic fever, 462, 463; fondness for his grandson Charles, 468, 469, 492; amuses himself writing the *West End Gazette*, 473–76; friendliness with young people, 476–81; his mystical tendencies, 492, 495; his views on the negro problem, 499–507; offered degree by University of Pennsylvania, 506; elected to American Academy of Arts and Letters, 507; again honored in Eatonton, 507; relations with President Roosevelt, 508–17; a guest at the White House, 511–17; editor of *Uncle Remus's Magazine*, 518–42; correspondence with Dorothy Loye, 543–63; writes book reviews as "Anne Macfarland," 564–76; on the historical novel, 565–67; some of his literary preferences, 567, 568, 570–76; failing physical energy, 577–79; last illness, 580–88; received into the Catholic Church, 581, 582; his religious convictions, 583–85; solicitude for the *Magazine*, in his last days, 586, 587; death and burial, 588, 589; tributes of Corra Harris and Frank L. Stanton, 591–95.

Books: Uncle Remus: his Songs and his Sayings, 147–58; Nights with Uncle Remus, 181–98; Uncle Remus and his Friends, 185, 298–301; Plantation Ballads, 185; Mingo, 203; Free Joe, 219; Daddy Jake, 230; Balaam and his Master, 270, 297; On the Plantation, 294; Evening Tales, 315, 316; Little Mr. Thimblefinger, 318–20; Mr. Rabbit at Home, 320, 321; The Story of Aaron, 322–24; Aaron in the Wildwoods, 324–26; Stories of Georgia, 327–29; Sister Jane and Her Neighbors, 340–46; Tales of the Home Folks, 397–400; Chronicles of Aunt Minervy Ann, 400–08; Plantation Pageants, 406; The Kidnapping of President Lincoln (On the Wings of Occasion), 430, 431; Gabriel Tolliver, 454–58; The Making of a Statesman, 462; Wally Wanderoon, 482; A Little Union Scout, 484; Told by Uncle Remus, 487; The Tar-Baby and Other Rhymes of Uncle Remus, 492–98; The Shadow between his Shoulder Blades, 539.

Poems: Nelly White, 42; The Sea Wind, 60; To Nora Belle, 73; A Remembrance, 74; Dolly Varden, 101; Juliette, 102; An Idyl of the Period, 111; In Memoriam (Addie E. Smith), 126; Revival Song, 144; An Ode on Weeps, 366; The Fruit-Cake, 378; A Riddle and its Answer, 413, 414.

Letters: to Henry M. Alden, 184; to Sir Robert Barr, 532; to Burdeene Biechele, 436; to E. L. Burlingame, 309, 316, 340, 400, 401, 402, 403; to Col. Henry D. Capers, 459; to Frederick S. Church, 148, 150; to Matt Crimm, 182; to Editor *Illustrated Mercury*, 48; to Editor *Youth's Companion*, 216; to Editors *Commonwealth*, 44; to Editors *Evening Post*, 147; to R. W. Gilder, 221, 223, 225, 227, 228, 232, 284, 286, 289, 347; to G. Laurence Gomme, 157; to Richard Green, 335; to R. W. Grubb, 192; to Dudley Guinn, 481; to Duval Guinn, 479; to Mrs. E. D. Guinn, 478; to Minor Guinn, 480; to Mrs. J. C. Harris, 255; to J. C. Harris, Jr., 470; to Julian Harris, 260, 263, 265, 267, 269, 271, 274, 276, 280, 282; to Mrs. Julian Harris, 540;

INDEX

to Lillian Harris, 348, 351, 352, 356, 358, 361, 370, 376, 386, 391, 393, 434, 444, 446; to Lucien Harris, 303, 305, 306; to Lillian and Mildred Harris, 409, 411, 414, 417; to Mildred Harris, 364, 367, 376, 379, 381, 384, 388, 422, 424, 447; to W. D. Howells, 451; to R. U. Johnson, 296; to Esther LaRose (Mrs. J. C. Harris), 113, 116, 119, 121, 122; to Esther LaRose (niece), 372, 374; to Margery Harris Leonard, 442; to Frances Leverette, 443; to G. H. Lorimer, 485; to Dorothy Loye, 544, 546, 547, 548, 550, 554, 556, 558, 559, 561; to Thomas Nelson Page, 530; to James Whitcomb Riley, 448, 460, 461, 463, 464, 487, 527; to Charles Scribner, 228, 405; to F. Hopkinson Smith, 531; to Mrs. Georgia Starke, 72, 76, 82, 87, 91, 454; to Ruth McEnery Stuart, 532; to Joe Syd Turner, 207; to Mark Twain, 168, 170, 191.

Harris, Joel Chandler, Jr., ninth child of J. C. H., born, 235; letter to, 470.

Harris, Julian LaRose, first child of J. C. H., born, 125; sent to Grandfather LaRose's farm, 257; eventful trip to Quebec, 258–63; first attempts at writing, 263–65; goes to the Frère Maristes College, 270; joins the *Constitution* staff, 291; interested in sparring, 302; goes to Chicago to study the newspaper game, 347; night editor of the *Constitution*, 373, 518; married, 373, 374; his home near the Wren's Nest, 468; tells the story of *Uncle Remus's Magazine*, 519–23, 533–39; letters to, 260, 263, 265, 267, 269, 271, 274, 276, 280, 282.

Harris, Lillian, sixth child of J. C. H.,

born, 198; at St. Joseph's Academy, 340, 347, 361; *Tales of the Home Folks* dedicated to, 397, 398; letters to, 348, 351, 352, 356, 358, 361, 370, 376, 386, 391, 393, 409, 411, 414, 417, 434, 444, 446.

Harris, Linton, seventh child of J. C. H., born, 205; dies of diphtheria, 273–76; his father's tribute, 277–79.

Harris, Lucien, second child of J. C. H., born, 125; shows that he can defend himself, 285, 286; sent to his grandfather's, 302; married, 337, 347; builds a home, 356, 468; letters to, 303, 305, 306.

Harris, Mary, mother of J. C. H., 3; marriage, 4, 6; reminiscences of, 5–8; gives J. C. H. her family name, 7; a great reader, 11; lives with J. C. H., in Atlanta, 133–37, 235; death of, 292, 293.

Harris, Mary Esther, fifth child of J. C. H., born, 173; death of, 198.

Harris, Mildred, eighth child of J. C. H., born, 235; confirmed, 353, 354; enters St. Joseph's Academy, 363; poem to, 366; letters to, 364, 367, 376, 379, 381, 384, 388, 409, 411, 414, 417, 422, 424, 447.

Harris, Pierre, grandson of J. C. H., 491, 492.

Harris, Stewart, first grandchild of J. C. H., 358, 364, 382, 416.

Harrison, President Benjamin, J. C. H.'s estimate of, 449.

Harrison, James P., of the *Monroe Advertiser*, 63; takes J. C. H. into his home, 69; their relations, 76–79; editor of the *Christian Index and Cultivator*, 129.

Harrison, Nora, sister of Mrs. Starke, 74, 85, 86.

Harrison, Z. D., brother of Mrs. Starke, 71, 74.

INDEX

INDEX

Longfellow, Henry Wadsworth, J. C. H.'s enjoyment of, 450, 451.

Longstreet, Judge A. B., *Georgia Scenes*, 317.

Lorimer, George Horace, on *The Kidnapping of President Lincoln*, 429; letter to, 485.

Loye, Dorothy, letters to J. C. H., 543, 545, 546, 549, 553; letters from J. C. H., 544, 546, 547, 548, 550, 554, 556, 558, 559, 561.

McClure Phillips Co., make proposition for exclusive control of J. C. H.'s work, 434, 435, 438; publish *Gabriel Tolliver*, 454; publish *The Making of a Statesman*, 462; publish *Wally Wanderoon*, 482, 483; publish *Told by Uncle Remus*, 487.

McClure, Samuel S., asks J. C. H. for stories, 214; syndicates *Joe Maxwell*, 294; asks for articles on Stonewall Jackson, 330; suggested O'Halloran stories, 398.

"Macfarland, Anne," pen name used by J. C. H. in literary criticism, 564–76.

McKinley, President William, death of, 460, 461.

Making of a Statesman, The, 462.

Manry, W. Turner, reminiscences of J. C. H., 64–68, 407, 408; on the name "Uncle Remus," 146 *n.*

Marquis, Don, 541.

Matthews, Brander, 155.

Maxwell, Joe, 13, 28, 50, 294.

Measles, male and female, 307.

Mingo, 200, 201; published, 203.

"Miss Meadows," meaning of, 149, 150, 195, 334.

Monroe Advertiser, the, 63, 64.

Morrow, James B., quoted, 93, 146.

Mr. Rabbit at Home, 320, 321.

Murphy, Anthony, anecdote of, 329.

Murray, John, publishes *The Kidnapping of President Lincoln*, in England, 430.

Mystery of the Red Fox, 314, 315.

Negro problem, J. C. H.'s views on, 499–507.

Neville, Harry J., city editor of the Macon *Telegraph*, 56, 58.

Newman, Cardinal, influence on J. C. H., 268 *n.*, 352, 394, 576.

Nights with Uncle Remus, 181–98; published, 185, 195.

O, Gimme de Gal, one of J. C. H.'s favorites, 185 *n.*

Ohl, J. K., gets J. C. H. for "best man," 245 *n.*

Okerburg, Paul, sculptor, 419.

Omohundro, John ("Texas Jack"), 427–29.

On the Plantation, quoted, 13, 23, 28, 50, 52; autobiographical, 294–96.

On the Wings of Occasion, 430.

One Mile to Shady Dale, 451–53; published as *Gabriel Tolliver*, 453, 454.

Ortoli, Frédéric, translation of his *Evening Tales*, 315, 316.

Osgood, James R., 170, 192, 199.

Osgood, McIlvaine & Co., publish *Balaam and his Master* in London, 297.

P. G. in G., the, 98, 99.

Page, Thomas Nelson, 164, 165; proposes to J. C. H. a joint tour of public readings, 213, 214; letter to, 530.

Page, Walter H., 164; describes his first call on J. C. H., 177, 178; opinion of *Sister Jane*, 342, 343; writes J. C. H. about Billy Sanders, 431.

Perdue, Aunt Minervy Ann, 400–08.

Phillips, John S., 435.

Piece of Land, A, 203.

INDEX

INDEX

[620]

INDEX

COLLEGE OF MARIN

3 2555 00105629 5

DATE DUE

Demco, Inc. 38-293